D0765285

WORKING WITH LESBIAN, GAY, BISEXUAL, AND TRANSGENDER COLLEGE STUDENTS

Recent Titles in
The Greenwood Educators' Reference Collection

Handbook of Academic Advising
Virginia N. Gordon

Handbook for the College and University Career Center
Edwin L. Herr, Jack R. Rayman, and Jeffrey W. Garis

Handbook of Cooperative Learning Methods
Shlomo Sharan, editor

Handbook of College Teaching: Theory and Applications
Keith W. Prichard and R. McLaran Sawyer, editors

The Training and Development of School Principals: A Handbook
Ward Sybouts and Frederick C. Wendel

Multiculturalism in the College Curriculum: A Handbook of Strategies
and Resources for Faculty
Marilyn Lutzker

Where in the World to Learn: A Guide to Library and Information Science for
International Education Advisers
Edward A. Riedinger

Planning and Managing Death Issues in the Schools: A Handbook
Robert L. Deaton and William A. Berkan

Handbook for the College Admissions Profession
Claire C. Swann and Stanley E. Henderson, editors

Student Records Management
M. Therese Ruzicka and Beth Lee Weckmueller, editors

Supportive Supervision in Schools
Raymond C. Garubo and Stanley William Rothstein

Substance Abuse on Campus: A Handbook for College and University Personnel
P. Clayton Rivers and Elsie R. Shore, editors

WORKING WITH LESBIAN, GAY, BISEXUAL, AND TRANSGENDER COLLEGE STUDENTS

A HANDBOOK FOR FACULTY AND ADMINISTRATORS

EDITED BY
RONNI L. SANLO

The Greenwood Educators' Reference Collection

GREENWOOD PRESS
Westport, Connecticut • London

Library of Congress Cataloging-in-Publication Data

Working with lesbian, gay, bisexual, and transgender college students :
  a handbook for faculty and administrators / edited by Ronni L.
  Sanlo.
      p.   cm.—(The Greenwood educators' reference collection,
  ISSN 1056–2192)
    Includes bibliographical references (p.) and index.
    ISBN 0–313–30227–8 (alk. paper)
    1. Homosexuality and education—United States—Handbooks, manuals,
  etc.   2. Gay college students—United States—Handbooks, manuals,
  etc.   3. Lesbian college students—United States—Handbooks,
  manuals, etc.   4. Bisexual college students—United States—
  Handbooks, manuals, etc.   5. Transsexualism—United States—
  Handbooks, manuals, etc.   I. Sanlo, Ronni L., 1947–   .
  II. Series.
  LC192.6.W67   1998
  378.1′98′0866—dc21   97–26182

British Library Cataloguing in Publication Data is available.

Library of Congress Catalog Card Number: 97–26182
ISBN: 0–313–30227–8
ISSN: 1056–2192

First published in 1998

Greenwood Press, 88 Post Road West, Westport, CT 06881
An imprint of Greenwood Publishing Group, Inc.

Printed in the United States of America

The paper used in this book complies with the
Permanent Paper Standard issued by the National
Information Standards Organization (Z39.48–1984).

10 9 8 7 6 5 4 3 2 1

To
E. Royster Harper
Associate Vice President of Student Affairs
and Dean of Students at the University of Michigan
who exemplifies the ideal of focusing on students

and to the Students

Contents

PART I
Lesbian, Gay, Bisexual, and Transgender Students: Who Are They and What Do They Need?

PART II
Special People/Special Places

PART III
Career Planning and Advising

PART VII
Administration and Policy

PART VIII
Lesbian, Gay, Bisexual, and Transgender Student Leadership and Organizations

PART IX
Programs and Possibilities

PART X
Unique Institutions

PART XI
Technology and the Lavender Web

Tables

Acknowledgments

The initiation of this book was filled with excitement and a vision of the finished product. Reality hit quickly, from the difficulty of selecting chapters to the enormity of the editing. At times it consumed my world, creating much frustration and concern. To add to the consternation, I moved from the University of Michigan to UCLA in mid-editing. Despite the obstacles, this project has been filled with the joy of meeting colleagues from around the country who care as deeply as I about providing services for Lesbian, Gay, Bisexual, and Transgender (LGBT) students, faculty, and staff.

I am grateful to the Greenwood Publishing Group for providing the opportunity to create this work. I offer my special thanks to editor Jane Garry, who was always available when I needed to do a cyber-scream. I deeply appreciate the editing skills and immense patience of production editor Norine Mudrick and copyeditor Susan Badger. I also thank Kathryn Lindblad for her initial editing assistance and attention to detail, and for the many gallons of coffee.

I am indebted to the people who submitted chapter possibilities. I remain in awe at the depth of the quality, passion, and work that went into each submission. Selection was the most difficult undertaking of this process. Each chapter was carefully considered for its quality of information that will assist faculty, staff, and administrators in making hard decisions about creative leadership at their institutions.

The students at both the University of Michigan and UCLA were and are my daily inspiration. They deserve recognition for their courage, their openness, and their hopeful spirits. My staff at both institutions never faltered for a moment to provide stellar service to our students and the community. I extend special thanks to Andrea Constancio and Ken Blochowski for their commitment to our work at Michigan which allowed me the time and support to do a major amount of work on this book.

Dear people who supported me throughout this project, cheered me on shamelessly, and occasionally offered delightful interludes were Judy Albin, Beth Harrison-Prado, JoAnn Kennedy Slater, Charles Outcalt, and Sue Rankin. Most significant was the love and unabashed carryings-on of my parents, Lois and Sanford Lebman, as well as my sisters and brothers, Sherry and Barry Horwitz, Barbra and Hal Miner, Len and Carole Lebman, and my 93-year-old grandmother, Mae Schonfield. Sarah, my demanding and otherwise annoying cat, refuses to go unmentioned. Rose Maly and the Corgi girls disrupted my life near the end of this project and I am grateful for their love and their spirit.

Finally, I offer my deepest thanks and appreciation to Royster Harper, both a mentor and a friend, who encouraged this project from start to finish and to whom this work is dedicated.

Introduction

It is no longer a matter of whether to provide services for lesbian, gay, bisexual, and transgender (LGBT) college students; it is a matter of when. The talent, energy, and hope with which LGBT students are arriving on our campuses must be acknowledged, honored, and encouraged. Some students are declaring their bisexual or homosexual orientations in high school, then knocking on our institutional doors with the expectation of being fully appreciated for who they are in their entirety—including their sexual orientations. Many more students come to us questioning their sexual identities: They're not yet ready to make pronouncements nor embrace labels, but they deserve our demonstrated and verbalized acceptance and attention.

As an undergraduate at the University of Florida in the 1960s, I struggled with my own lesbian identity. I experienced what Adrienne Rich calls "psychic disequilibrium"—knowing I was there but not seeing myself reflected in the classroom, in the curriculum, or in social gatherings of the institution. When I finally came out, my goal was to become an educator who cherished teaching and learning, who valued my own homosexual identity, and who understood that my sexual orientation was one of God's great gifts to me. I was honored to become the director of the University of Michigan Office of Lesbian Gay Bisexual Transgender (LGBT) Affairs in 1994, and then the director of the LGBT Campus Resource Center at the University of California, Los Angeles in 1997.

It is a great and precious opportunity to serve our extraordinary students. I have an intense belief in and love of these courageous young folks. They deserve to be treated with respect and with dignity for the talent they bring to our campuses and for the scholarship, research, and leadership in which they will engage.

Students do not live in a vacuum. To provide services for and about LGBT students on our campuses, we must be mindful that we also have LGBT people who serve as faculty, staff, administrators, maintenance support, residence staff, campus clergy, campus police—people in every area of our institutions, a small few of whom are willing to share their identities. However, on most campuses, the majority of LGBT faculty and staff are neither willing nor able to share. They watch from their windows, scratching their heads yet smiling with pride as they see our young LGBT students making the strides so many of us were and are still afraid to take.

This book brings together the varied viewpoints of experienced people who are deeply concerned with providing appropriate services to LGBT students on college campuses. It includes chapters that discuss topics of special interest for faculty and for administrative decision makers. I make the wishful assumption that most who read this handbook will be heterosexual administrators, faculty, and Student Affairs professionals who are exploring methods by which to make proactive changes. This book is also for campus stakeholders—some of whom themselves will still be undergoing a personal struggle with understanding non-heterosexual identities—who wish to create a welcoming and safe environment for their students. LGBT faculty and staff will also find this work useful as they discover themselves in the academic and educational literature and who are or wish to become role models not only for LGBT students but for all people in our campus communities. This book will be valuable as well as a text in the many Higher Education Administration, Educational Leadership, and College Student Personnel programs.

Primarily, though, this book is designed to assist with your decision-making processes and to provide guidelines and pathways for positive action. The contributors, whose sexual orientations are as varied as the readers', were invited to address topics within their areas of expertise related to LGBT issues on campus, then provide concrete recommendations for implementation. No two campuses or institutions are alike so faculty and administrators must modify these recommendations in unique ways to facilitate their use and their value in each particular setting. Readers are encouraged to contact contributors as questions arise or when consultation is required. The e-mail addresses for most of the contributors appear following their biographical sketches at the end of the book.

Each part of the book defines an area that has been the focus of much controversy and questioning. Chapters within the parts specifically address unique aspects of the issues within that broad area and offer practical recommendations or suggestions for change. For example, Part I describes LGBT students by addressing identity development theories—sexual identity, student identity, racial identity, and gender identity. It defines who our students are and broadly addresses their needs. These theories provide the foundation on which the subsequent chapters are built. Sexual identity development is an important concept that must be understood and interwoven with student development theories to be sure that services are appropriately provided to this population.

Part II focuses on concerns that arise because of the specific characteristics of differing populations and places on campus. Allies, both individual and institutional, are described. Residence hall concerns are explored in the context of the interdependent nature of college environments. The unique issues of Greek letter social organizations are addressed, as are the specific challenges relevant to LGBT students of color and to LGBT graduate students. Two librarians reveal the failure of libraries to recognize LGBT students and faculty and their research and their leisure reading requirements. The development of LGBT alumni organizations as well as insight into the creation of Indiana University's LGBT Campus Resource Center complete this section.

Like most students, LGBT students have career planning and placement needs. In addition to traditional career concerns, these students require realistic and compassionate assistance to prepare for a world that does not yet accept them in a matter-of-fact manner. Part III looks at career planning from two perspectives: the campus Career Planning Center and faculty or staff who individually offer career advising to LGBT students. These chapters address the career development needs of LGBT students and describe how these students will be best served in making and implementing career decisions.

Physical and mental health services centers can be places either of growth or of inadvertent or deliberate detriment for LGBT students. Part IV illustrates the multiple ways in which a variety of services are offered to LGBT students from health services centers and counseling centers to issues dealing with dating and domestic violence. The importance of HIV/AIDS (human Immunodeficiency virus/acquired Immunodeficiency syndrome) education and prevention for LGBT college students is detailed. This Part also explores the dimension of LGBT people with disabilities as well as describes the needs of transgender students who are transitioning, that is, moving from one gender to another.

Athletic departments have historically been recognized as bastions of anti-gay feelings and sentiment. Part V looks at collegiate athletics from three different perspectives. First, barriers to participation in sports by LGBT students and the components of safe athletic space are described. Following this generalized perspective, illustrations are presented that illuminate the concerns of both gay men and lesbians in college sports.

Part VI examines areas of importance for LGBT as well as non-LGBT faculty. Learning theory to understand LGBT students' experience in the classroom is discussed, as well as looking at how LGBT Studies can help young college students develop positive LGBT identities. Barriers for students as well as the needs of LGBT students and staff are examined. Part IV also outlines the responsibilities of faculty and staff as they assist LGBT students by providing positive educational services.

Campus climate and policies seem to drive one another interchangeably as Part VII demonstrates. At most institutions that acknowledge and validate LGBT students, faculty, and staff, extensive research and discovery of the campus climate preceded services for LGBT people. Campus climate reports are available for a number of institutions including Massachusetts at Amherst, Michigan, Minnesota, Pennsylvania State, Rutgers, and Wisconsin at White

Water. Campus climate reports are products of struggle and process as institutions grow. These chapters look at campus climate issues then define institutionalized heterosexism, the ways it is manifested, and how it may be eliminated. They discuss the importance of providing an atmosphere conducive to maximizing the creation of knowledge, review the current national climate for LGBT members of the academic community, and propose strategies for implementing change. In addition, they examine the extension of domestic partner benefits for employees and for students and how to do cost analyses of extending such benefits.

Leadership is a valued concept at each of our institutions, and leadership development experiences must be extended to LGBT students. Offering a specialized leadership program symbolically sends a message to the LGBT student population that they are valued by the institution. By providing professional staff support and financial resources, the institution affirms the experiences of LGBT students and implicitly communicates a message of care about LGBT student leadership development and success. Part VIII provides information about LGBT student leadership and the development of LGBT student organizations. It presents the justifications for LGBT leadership programming and offers an overview of LGBT student organizations on college campuses. The types of organizations, the multiple roles of LGBT student groups, and the legal issues faced by LGBT organizations are also examined, with public and private institutions addressed separately. Funding challenges are acknowledged as well. Models of leadership are defined, and suggestions are offered to enable student organization advisers to be more effective working with both LGBT and non-LGBT students.

Part IX offers ways in which individuals, organizations, or LGBT Campus Re-source Centers may provide LGBT-related programming on campuses. Specifically, speakers bureaus and the concept and operation of a safe zone are discussed in detail.

Educational institutions are almost as varied—by culture, economic influence, geography, and tradition—as the people who attend them. Part X describes the needs of specialized institutions, specifically commuter schools and church-related institutions. Commuter schools have both time and fiscal constraints to providing services for students who are rarely available on campus beyond class time. In church-related institutions, faculty and administrators who struggle with sexual orientation issues are concerned with questions of advocacy, perceived endorsement, and the college's role in espousing denominational sexual morality. At times, the answers to these issues are in conflict with the desire for a campus community where inclusion, concern for others, and the worth of each student are affirmed.

Part XI contains detailed information about the Internet and its usefulness for LGBT students, organizations, and programs. It includes a compilation of World Wide Web (WWW) sites, LGBT newsgroups, and information on significant mailing lists that relate to LGBT campus issues. The final chapter—The

Lavender Web—is written interactively with a host web site. The web site—whose URL is http://www.uic.edu/orgs/lgbt/internet_chapter.html—allows the web information in the chapter to be constantly updated and provides an immediate source through which this book may be ordered.

The glossary contains a list of words and their definitions that appear throughout this book. The definitions or abbreviations in the glossary are consistent throughout the book in an effort to eliminate confusion regarding meaning from one chapter to the next. The references have been compiled into one list at the end of the book rather than within each chapter because many authors cited the same works.

This is a handbook; it is meant to be used by all—in the office, in the classroom, in the boardroom of our colleges and universities. The use of this book is a gift not only to LGBT students who deserve our attention, but also to the faculty and administrators who struggle against great odds to do the right thing.

My grandfather taught me an old Jewish saying: *If not me, who? If not now, when?* Indeed, if we are focused on our students, as Royster Harper teaches, it then becomes a matter of *who but you?*—and not *if* but *when.*

Ronni L. Sanlo

Lesbian, Gay, Bisexual, and Transgender Students: Who Are They and What Do They Need?

CHAPTER 1

Sexual Identity Development: The Importance of Target or Dominant Group Membership

Patricia Sullivan

Within a campus climate that is often marked by homophobia, heterosexism, and marginalization of sexual minorities, most students of traditional undergraduate age, whether lesbian, gay, bisexual, transgender (LGBT), or heterosexual, are struggling with issues of sexual identity development (Levine & Evans, 1991). In their work on the racial identity development process of black and white Americans, Rita Hardiman and Bailey Jackson (1992) maintain that societal oppression influences the identity development of both target and dominant members of society. Consequently, they argue, the greatest progress in approaches to diversity on campus has been made through "a shift from asking *who* is on campus to understanding how each group views the world as a function of its experiences with social injustice and the influence of cultural orientation" (Hardiman & Jackson, 1992, 21). Similar attention should be paid to the effects of societal oppression and cultural identification on the identity development of both bi/homosexual and heterosexual students.

While LGBT students are grappling with their sexual and affectional orientation, they are also discovering their identity as sexual and cultural minorities— members of a targeted group within our society. Just as the identities of black Americans are shaped by both African-American culture and societal racism (Hardiman & Jackson, 1992), the identity development of LGBT Americans is influenced by their identification with gay culture and community and the climate of societal heterosexism (Wall & Evans, 1991). Just as important, the sexual identity of heterosexual students is shaped by an environment that is characterized by a fear of homosexuality, the denigration of gay persons and cultures, and either the invisibility or outright oppression of gay relationships.

Neither a heterosexual nor an integrated bi/homosexual identity can be formed in the context of acceptance and complicity with a heterosexist world view.

The following identity development model combines findings from the extensive research of Vivienne Cass (1979) and other experts on the sexual identity formation of gay and lesbian persons with the concept of target and dominant group identity development advanced by Hardiman and Jackson (1992) in their Racial Identity Development Model (RIDM). Each of the five stages—naïveté, acceptance, resistance, redefinition, and internalization—was identified and adapted to be relevant for work with heterosexual, lesbian, gay, and bisexual students. Possible manifestations of each stage are presented and appropriate faculty, staff, or administrative interventions are suggested.

STAGE ONE: NAÏVETÉ

According to Hardiman and Jackson (1992), the naiveté stage is characterized by "little or no social awareness of race per se" (24). At this stage, there is also very little, if any, social awareness of sexual orientation. Owing to the fact that sexual orientation is a less obvious difference than either race or gender, people might remain in the naive stage with regard to sexual/affection diversity much longer than they do with race or gender. During this stage, persons are beginning to be socialized to view heterosexuality as the only or correct form of human sexual/affectional expression, but they do not yet have an automatic fearful or hostile reaction to same sex displays of affection or familial structures that deviate from the norm. This is particularly evident in the tendency for young boys and girls to think nothing of expressing affection or holding hands with same sex friends up to a certain age (older for girls than for boys), at which point they are expected to have internalized the message that this is not appropriate behavior.

STAGE TWO: ACCEPTANCE

Upon moving into the acceptance stage, persons have internalized the dominant ideology. In a racist society "whiteness equals superiority or normality, beauty, importance, or power" (Hardiman & Jackson, 1992, 25). In a heterosexist society, everyone "is or should be heterosexual" (Friend, 1993, 211). According to Hardiman and Jackson's (1992) RIDM, people have begun to learn that there are acceptable and unacceptable roles and behaviors and that there will be negative repercussions for acting in a manner that is inappropriate. Children may begin to call each other homophobic names on the playground, same-sex affectional displays between boys are strongly discouraged, and children are expected to act according to the appropriate gender role. While the undesirable behaviors may not be explicitly identified as homosexual, the message is clear and sets the stage for later conscious and verbal acknowledgment that heterosexuality is "normal" and homosexuality is abnormal, disgusting, and wrong.

Acceptance Stage for Heterosexual Persons

In the passive manifestation of Stage Two, persons who are not LGBT tend to take their heterosexuality for granted and see it as normal. When they are confronted with the existence of homosexuality, persons in this stage are likely to maintain beliefs consistent with a heterosexist ideology. Some of the most pervasive assumptions of a heterosexist society, as adapted from Riddle and Morin (1977), are the following: Heterosexuality is more mature and is preferred; heterosexual relationships equal love and family, whereas homosexual relationships equal sex; homo/bisexual persons need counseling or religious guidance and should avoid the temptation to act on their feelings; there is a need to find the "cause" of homosexuality, and homosexuals are to be pitied if they are "born that way"; gay men are effeminate and weak, lesbians want to be men, and other false, negative stereotypes; and if people are gay, they shouldn't "flaunt" it. *Flaunting* is generally defined as a lesbian, gay, or bisexual person doing or saying anything that might make other people aware of her or his sexual orientation.

In the active acceptance stage, the opinions held are more overtly negative and aggressively upheld (Hardiman & Jackson, 1992). Persons may feel compelled to act on their beliefs. Common beliefs include: Homosexuality is a crime against nature and is repulsive; gay persons are mentally ill and/or immoral; and any action is justified to change them or to protect society from them (Riddle & Morin, 1977).

Researchers have found that homophobic prejudice, harassment, and violence are pervasive on college and university campuses (Berrill, 1990; D'Augelli & Rose, 1990, as cited in Croteau & Lark, 1995). In a survey conducted by the National Gay and Lesbian Task Force (NGLTF), 1,329 episodes of anti-gay verbal and physical violence were reported on 40 sample campuses (as cited in Liddell & Douvanis, 1994). Student behaviors indicative of this stage include excessive pride in being "straight," male machismo, hyper-heterosexuality, premature sexual involvement (Blumenfeld, 1992), and committing hate crimes, harassment, threats of violence, and acts of violence.

Lesbian, Gay, and Bisexual Persons in Acceptance

Persons beginning to question whether they are heterosexual may react to Stage Two differently as they begin the journey toward a homosexual identity formation, described by Cass (1979). During the first stage of homosexual identity formation, which Cass called identity confusion, an individual has a growing awareness of sexual/affectional feeling, thoughts, and/or behavior toward persons of the same sex and begins to personalize information about homosexuality. Owing to previous acceptance of the societal heterosexist ideology, the individual experiences considerable inner turmoil. Feelings are generally not shared with anyone.

Cass's second stage, identity comparison, can also be seen as taking place within the context of passive or active acceptance of heterosexist messages. In this stage, students may seek to rationalize their feelings and/or behaviors and, due to their continuing reluctance to discuss their feelings with others, may experience strong feelings of isolation. Even as a student begins to gather information about homosexuality and seek contacts with other gay people, he or she is likely to continue to see heterosexuality as "right" and "normal" (Cass, 1979; Levine & Evans, 1991).

Lesbian, gay, bisexual, and transgender students in the passive manifestation of the acceptance stage may attempt the following: act straight to gain approval, self worth, jobs, housing, and privileges; avoid interaction with other LGBT persons and issues including the confrontation of homophobic jokes; and repress feelings. The active manifestations of the acceptance stage, on the other hand, display a clear rejection and devaluation of everything "gay," just as for black persons in this stage there is a "rejection and devaluation of all that is black" (Hardiman & Jackson, 1992, 26). Student behaviors might include: attempts to choose to be heterosexual through dating and even marriage; hyper-hetero-sexuality; a search for a "cure"; and participating in gay bashing or becoming an anti-gay moral crusader.

Intervention

For both homo/bisexual and heterosexual students in the acceptance stage, it is most important that negative stereotypes of homo/bisexual persons and damaging myths about homosexuality are confronted and that the campus environment is made into as safe and affirming an environment for LGBT students as possible. Important administrative and curricular interventions at this stage include the creation of an LGBT Concerns Task Force and the development of a campus climate report; a campus-wide educational effort involving residence hall staff training and residence hall programming, campus-wide programming, speakers bureaus, and the inclusion of LGBT issues in the curriculum; formulation of a strong institutional non-discrimination policy that includes sexual orientation; authoritative and prompt response to incidents of hate speech, harassment, violence, and anti-gay bias on campus; and improved campus counseling and support services for LGBT students.

STAGE THREE: RESISTANCE

The transition from acceptance into resistance generally occurs for both target and dominant group members when there is a conflict between the views one has held and new experiences (Hardiman & Jackson, 1992). These experiences take the form of personal encounters with those who have a positive LGBT identity; with LGBT persons who do not fit the negative stereotypes previously held or who are in loving gay relationships; through community or political events such as anti-gay legislation, gays in the military, or National Coming Out Day; in the media such as gay characters on television or in the movies; in the classroom with gay literature and history, speaker's panels, or class discussions; or on campus through a strong administrative response to a gay-bashing incident on campus or a program in the residence hall.

In resistance, both target and dominant group students recognize societal oppression on many levels (Hardiman & Jackson, 1992). For homo/bisexual and heterosexual students, there is shift in focus from seeking approval and acceptance from the nongay society to seeking such approval from the LGBT community (Cass, 1979; Hardiman & Jackson, 1992). While dominant group members experience guilt at having accepted heterosexist messages, target group members hesitantly acknowledge their participation in their own oppression, and both generally feel some anger toward the institutions and people who indoctrinated them with heterosexist and homophobic messages (Hardiman & Jackson, 1992).

Resistance Stage for Heterosexual Persons

In passive resistance, dominant group members may recognize the problem of societal heterosexism, but feel powerless to effect change (Hardiman & Jackson, 1992). On the other hand, persons in active resistance generally recognize their own homophobia and are willing to work on their own attitudes as well as confront others. According to Hardiman and Jackson, "[S]ome Whites in active resistance become so distressed at being part of an oppressive dominant group that they distance themselves from other Whites and White culture by gravitating to communities of color and trying to adopt a new identity" (28). While little study has been conducted with women who define themselves as political or ideological lesbians (Levine & Evans, 1991), this may be a manifestation of a similar attempt to distance oneself from the oppressor and gain a new identity. Less extreme forms of this gravitation to "gay" culture can be seen in the adoption of cultural expressions of the gay community by straight allies. For all heterosexual students in resistance, there is at least a greater appreciation for gay cultures and LGBT persons as a valid part of a diverse society (Hardiman & Jackson, 1992; Riddle & Morin, 1977). Students in resistance may wear ally buttons and freedom rings, join political organizations advocating for gay rights, increase their social interaction with LGBT students, and put up safe zone or pink triangle stickers.

LGBT Students in Resistance

Lesbian, gay, bisexual, and transgender persons in the identity tolerance and identity acceptance stages of homo/bisexual identity formation (Cass, 1979) are similar in description to the target group members in the passive resistance stage of the Racial Identity Development Model (Hardiman & Jackson, 1992). Target group members in passive resistance are often concerned that more active resistance will result in a loss of "benefits" (30). LGBT students in identity tolerance and identity acceptance often present themselves as "straight" within the larger society. Even if individuals choose to disclose their identity selectively, care is taken not to create too many waves (Cass, 1979). LGBT persons in identity tolerance may seek out contacts with the LGBT communities. Nevertheless, while there is generally a high need for positive LGBT role models and positive experiences of LGBT culture and community in daily life, these students remain in the closet. Owing to the pressures of leading such a double life, LGBT students in the tolerance and acceptance stages of sexual identity formation—like target group members in the passive resistance stage of Racial Identity Development—may choose to have less contact with the gay world (Cass, 1979; Hardiman & Jackson, 1992). Throughout these stages, and particularly in identity acceptance, the conflict between self and heterosexual others is felt to be at an intense level by the homo/bisexual student (Cass, 1979).

As one moves into the identity pride stage of sexual identity formation, one also moves into a more active resistance (Cass, 1979). Hardiman and Jackson (1992) describe active resistance as the "antithesis of the acceptance stage of development" (29), which is characterized by anger and pride. For the LGBT student in active resistance, the world appears to be divided into gay (valued) and straight (devalued), and there is a rejection of the norms, values, and institutions of the heterosexual establishment (Cass, 1979; Hardiman & Jackson, 1992). In identity pride and active resistance, there is often more disclosure of identity in nongay environments, and energy is focused on being clear about who one is *not* as well as who one is (Cass, 1979; Hardiman & Jackson, 1992). LGBT students in active Resistance may find the fight against heterosexism to be all consuming and may have difficulty devoting time to class work that is seen as irrelevant (Hardiman & Jackson, 1992).

LGBT students in this stage may also be focused on "challenging and confronting" (Hardiman & Jackson, 1992, 30) the following: closeted professors, staff, and peers; persons who identify as bisexual or refuse to claim an identity; and non-angry members of the community. These students may be highly confrontational in addressing discrimination within the university. They also tend to denigrate all that is "straight" and glorify all that is "gay" (Cass, 1979; Hardiman & Jackson, 1992). Possible manifestations could include the adoption of new mannerisms, a radical shift away from societal expectations (i.e., gender or sexual norms), and the rejection of "traditional" and "family" values. Negative responses from heterosexual persons and/or society only serve to confirm their dichotomous perception (Cass, 1979).

Intervention

Heterosexual students in the redefinition stage can be particularly responsive to ally programs and training as well as safe zone campaigns. It is important that these students have opportunities to direct their energy and anger toward changing the campus climate. This may also be a time during which hetero-sexual students need the counseling and support services available on campus as they come to recognize their own homophobia and complicity with hetero-sexism.

Heterosexual and LGBT students in this stage will all benefit from and appreciate the discussion of heterosexism, homophobia, and discrimination in the classroom. Both faculty members and administrators can play a role in advocating for the inclusion of sexual identity issues and sexual minority history, literature, and perspectives in the classroom. This inclusion is particularly crucial in order to keep both homo/bisexual students in the resistance stage engaged in academic work. Visible allies and positive gay role models and mentors are also particularly important to lesbian, gay, and bisexual students during this period. LGBT student groups, campus LGBT program offices, resource libraries, and LGBT studies courses can all be particularly important to students struggling through the conflicts, anger, guilt, pride, and discovery of the resistance stage.

STAGE FOUR: REDEFINITION

For both dominant and target group members, redefinition begins to occur when individuals seek self definitions that are based less on reaction to and rejection of being defined by a heterosexist society (Hardiman & Jackson, 1992). Heterosexual persons coming out of the resistance stage are struggling to accept a positive heterosexual self-identity and dominant group identification after having devalued everything about heterosexuality. They must be able to redefine heterosexuality in a way that is not dependent on heterosexism (Hardiman & Jackson, 1992).

LGBT persons, on the other hand, withdraw their attention from a primary concern with their interaction with dominant group members and the rejection of dominant society. LGBT students in this stage may tend to "self segregate" in an attempt to limit their interactions to other LGBT students as much as possible (Hardiman & Jackson, 1992). In this stage, focus on LGBT culture is less a reaction to the dominant society and more an attempt to find a meaningful ident-ity in the history, traditions, language, customs, and values of their community (Hardiman & Jackson, 1992). Students may work toward the creation of programs, housing, LGBT centers, and safe zones where they can increase meaningful interaction with other gay, lesbian, and bisexual persons (Hardiman & Jackson, 1992).

No stage within the Cass (1979) sexual identity formation model exactly corresponds to the Hardiman and Jackson (1992) redefinition stage. While most of the anger of the pride stage has subsided, there is little desire for the cultivation of allies or the building of alliances with other oppressed groups (Hardiman & Jackson, 1992). According to Sophie (1986), lesbian identity has two possible end points: integration, in which a woman is open about her sexual identity in both lesbian and nonlesbian communities; and separation, in which she limits interaction to the lesbian community as much as possible (as cited in Levine & Evans, 1991, 16).

Similar choices are available to students. Integration as defined by Sophie (1986) is comparable to Hardiman and Jackson's Fifth Stage, internalization, but an LGBT student may remain in Hardiman and Jackson's redefinition stage indefinitely if he or she has consistently experienced negative reactions from heterosexual peers, faculty, and staff. Owing to their perception of dominant society as hostile and less valuable than the gay community, LGBT students may choose simply to limit interaction with heterosexual others as much as possible. Such students might reevaluate friendships, change their living arrangements, and/or drop co-curricular activities in which they are in the minority (Hardiman & Jackson, 1992). Because the focus in redefinition is on the LGBT community and LGBT students are discovering pride in their cultural identity, a student may also take it upon himself or herself to represent homo/bisexual perspectives in class (Hardiman & Jackson, 1992).

Intervention

Many of the programs and curricular changes appropriate in the resistance stage continue to be important to students in the redefinition. In addition, LGBT students in redefinition may find campus programs, events, courses, and opportunities specifically designed to address issues of importance to the LGBT community of particular appeal. Heterosexual students in this stage may be especially interested in campus programming that addresses male and female gender identity, responsible sexuality, women's and/or men's issues, gender communication, spirituality and sexuality, broad issues of discrimination and oppression, and other topics that support them as they redefine their identity as heterosexual individuals. In addition, the creation of opportunities for heterosexual and LGBT students on campus to dialogue with one another about issues of concern may help ease the transition to internalization.

STAGE FIVE: INTERNALIZATION

Movement into the internalization stage for both target and dominant group members is characterized by integration of some of the "newly defined values, beliefs, and behaviors into all aspects of life" (Hardiman & Jackson, 1992, 33).

Heterosexual Persons in Internalization

For heterosexual persons, a positive identity as a heterosexual individual, independent of heterosexist societal definitions of heterosexuality, has been accepted. Just as for white members of society internalization assumes a self interest as members of the white group in ending racism, heterosexual persons who have reached the internalization stage recognize what they can gain from dismantling heterosexism (Hardiman & Jackson, 1992). Dominant group members acknowledge that heterosexism inhibits fathers from showing affection to their sons, men from developing intimate relationships with other men, heterosexual women from accepting the romance and innocent attraction that is part of an emotionally intimate female friendship, and most children from having the time and space to develop for themselves their unique sexual identity (Blumenfeld, 1992).

Lesbian, Gay, and Bisexual Persons in Internalization

The movement from the redefinition to the internalization stage—identity synthesis in the Cass (1979) model—is in large part dependent upon an LGBT individual's experience of positive reactions and support from significant heterosexual others (Cass, 1979; Levine & Evans, 1991). There is a growing awareness that the world is not strictly divided along sexual orientation lines and an increase in interest in forming connections with straight allies and other targeted minorities. There is an "ability to consider other identity issues" (Hardiman & Jackson, 1992, 35) and a recognition that whereas their identity as a sexual minority is a critical aspect of themselves, it is not the only facet of their identity (Cass, 1979; Hardiman & Jackson, 1992). Exactly how large a part a person's identity as gay, lesbian, or bisexual plays in his or her total identity varies for every individual and may change over a lifetime. Unfortunately, the achievement of the internalization stage by LGBT students is made extremely difficult by the pervasive heterosexism of the campus environment.

CONCLUSION

For faculty and administrators, an awareness of the sexual and target/dominant group identity development process for both heterosexual and homo/bisexual students in the context of a heterosexist environment can be helpful on multiple levels. Persons working with LGBT students can have a better understanding of the challenges of each developmental stage and the particular supports that might be necessary whereas persons working with the dominant heterosexual population can realize the adverse effects of a heterosexist ideology on the sexual identity formation of all students.

The broader perspective offered by the combination of sexual identity development models and dominant/target group identity development models like Hardiman and Jackson's (1992) Racial Identity Development Model can also better enable faculty and staff to see the complexity of the identity formation process. LGBT students are not only in the process of forming a sexual and affectional identity; they are simultaneously becoming aware of their minority and targeted social status, becoming acquainted with a minority culture, and rejecting aspects of the culture into which they were born. With an understanding of the beliefs and behaviors students may make manifest in each of the stages of sexual identity development, administrators, faculty, and staff can better respond to the inevitable conflicts between target and dominant group members, as well as the in group conflict that can arise as students are at different stages in their identity development.

CHAPTER 2

Lesbian, Gay, and Bisexual Identity and Student Development Theory

Ruth E. Fassinger

Student Affairs professionals utilize a wide variety of developmental theories and models in their work (McEwen, 1996; Moore & Upcraft, 1990). There is a basic assumption that a campus environment that offers both challenge and support will help students to redefine themselves gradually in complex, distinct, and integrated ways across a variety of intellectual, affective, and behavioral domains (McEwen, 1996). Theoretical perspectives commonly used include models of intellectual development (Baxter Magolda, 1992), spiritual development (Fowler, 1981; Parks, 1986), moral development (Gilligan, 1982; Kohlberg, 1981), psycho-social development (Chickering, 1969; Chickering & Reisser, 1993), career development (Brown & Brooks, 1996), learning styles, and other identity development models, particularly racial/ethnic identity development (Atkinsons, Morten, & Sue, 1993; Helms, 1990; McEwen, 1996).

Identity models are thought to be particularly important in understanding student development because students' experiences of their own identities create a lens through which all cognitive, affective, and behavioral events are filtered (McEwen, 1996). Students also experience multiple aspects of identity simultaneously, and the environmental context appears to be a critical factor in determining which aspects of identity are most important to an individual at any given time (Evans & Levine, 1990). One might expect, then, in this context of pervasive heterosexism and homophobia characterizing many college campuses, that sexual orientation will be the most salient aspect of identity for many lesbian, gay, and bisexual (LGB) students. Moreover, on some college campuses, LGB individuals compose a significant minority group, and receive considerably less attention and limited services than do other groups (Wall &

Evans, 1991). To be helpful, Student Affairs professionals need to be aware of the models of LGB identity development and the "coming out" process, as well as the potential impact of LGB identity on other theories and models of student development (Fassinger, 1994; Washington & Evans, 1991). The purpose of this chapter is to address those two points by presenting a brief overview of existing models of LGB identity development and by presenting examples of the way LGB identity may impact the applicability of student development theories.

THEORIES OF LESBIAN, GAY, AND BISEXUAL IDENTITY FORMATION

Theories of lesbian and gay identity development, or "coming out" to self and others (Cass, 1979, 1984; Chapman & Brannock, 1987; Coleman, 1982; Fassinger & Miller, 1997; McCarn & Fassinger, 1996; Sophie, 1986; Troiden, 1989), are important theoretical growths of the past two decades. These models are grounded in the assumption that oppressive contextual influences exert impact on normative developmental processes and attempt to articulate a common sequence of recognizing, accepting, and affirming a stigmatized sexual identity that is unique to lesbians and gay men in this culture at this time (Fassinger, 1994; Gonsiorek & Rudolph, 1991; McCarn & Fassinger, 1996). These models are primarily concerned with the development and expression of same-sex attractions and behaviors; thus they focus on the homophilic aspects of one's sexual orientation. Although recent work has begun to address apparently unique aspects of bisexual identity (Pope & Reynolds, 1991), the focus of existing models is relevant to the same-sex attractions of bisexual orientation. Therefore, LGB terminology is used inclusively throughout this chapter.

Existing models focus on social versus psychological aspects of identity (Cox & Gallois, 1996) and generally assume a somewhat linear progression of discrete, discernible stages or phases. The number of stages varies from three to seven, but all articulate a similar sequence in identity formation. Each begins with a lack of awareness of same-sex inclinations and proceeds to dawning awareness of same-sex preferences and the LGB community. The individual then experiences a gradual firming of same-sex lifestyle and intimacy choices and increased immersion in the LGB community (often with deliberate withdrawal from heterosexuals). Finally, the developmental process culminates in identity affirmation and successful integration of sexual orientation into one's life. The final stages of these models explain that developmental maturity involves relatively permanent homophilic identification and at least some public disclosure of identity.

Cass's (1979, 1984) model of lesbian and gay identity development was one of the first to be published with an empirical measure (1984). It remains the most widely cited and used of the existing models and forms the foundation for subsequent work in this area. The six stages integrating lesbian and gay identity into the self-concept are useful in examining other LGB identity theories. The stages are: identity confusion involves questioning assumptions about one's sexual orientation; identity comparison involves feelings of isolation and alienation, both from prior assumptions as well as from nongay others; identity tolerance involves seeking out other gay people and merely tolerating a lesbian or gay identity; identity acceptance involves selective disclosure of identity to others; identity pride involves immersion in lesbian and gay culture and rejection of heterosexual values; and, identity synthesis takes place when lesbian or gay identity becomes one aspect of the self rather than an independent, overriding identity. Although there has been criticism of Cass's model (McCarn & Fassinger, 1996), its familiarity to many and the brevity of its assessment instrument suggest that it will remain widely used within Student Affairs as a model for understanding LGB students.

Although the Cass model and other identity models have wide appeal and appear intuitively to capture an important process, they have limitations. Most of the existing models were developed based on clinical and anecdotal data, and few have been tested adequately (Fassinger, 1994). Common problems in the limited research that has been conducted include small or biased samples (individuals who belong to gay social or political groups) and measures that are psychometrically undeveloped or unsound (using two or three brief sentences to depict a complex stage location). In addition, many of the models were developed based on the experiences of gay men and then generalized to include lesbians. The growing body of literature in LGB issues suggests that many of the important differences between the experiences of men and women in current United States culture are mirrored in the LGB community and therefore implies critical distinctions between lesbians and gay men that must be taken into account in identity development models (Fassinger, 1994; McCarn & Fassinger, 1996).

From the point of view of Student Affairs professionals who respect and value student diversity, the most serious limitation of the existing models is that they ignore demographic or cultural factors that influence the LGB identity formation process (Fassinger, 1991, 1994). The models do so by confusing two separate developmental paths: One is concerned with the internal clarification of same sex desire, and the other focuses on fostering identification with an oppressed group (Fassinger, 1991, 1994; Fassinger & Miller, 1997; McCarn & Fassinger, 1996). The melding of these two processes in existing models is not surprising, since they grew out of the models of the 1970s—the influences of the Stonewall riots, the subsequent gay rights movement, and the women's movement, all of which have contributed to an interest in the politics of identity pride (Fassinger, 1994).

LGB identity development exhibits a critical distinction from other kinds of minority identity development (based on race, ethnicity, gender, etc.) in that LGB identity usually is not visible to oneself or others (Wall & Evans, 1991).

For most minority groups, identity transformation involves changed attitudes toward the meaning of an identity already known, whereas according to McCarn and Fassinger (1996), LGB individuals must pursue two goals simultaneously: They must personally deal with a sexual identity that they previously considered reprehensible and/or irrelevant; and they must acknowledge their membership in, and change their attitudes toward, a largely invisible minority group that they also previously considered reprehensible and/or irrelevant (McCarn & Fassinger, 1996). Thus, identity development is a mixture of self-categorizations related to both personal and social identities (Cox & Gallois, 1996).

The confusion of these two separate (but related) processes in existing models results in highly politicized frameworks that tend to focus on the internal developmental tasks in the beginning stages but then shift to the more group-oriented tasks in the later stages. Developmental maturity thus becomes synonymous with public disclosure of identity, and less public ("closeted") behaviors are viewed as developmental arrest. Not only does the importance of homoerotic intimacy disappear altogether in the focus on accommodation to minority group membership, but the linking of public disclosure and involvement in the LGB community with integrated identity ignores the social realities of many LGB people who feel compelled to maintain the privacy of their sexual identity for pressing contextual reasons. For example, LGB individuals who are members of racial/ethnic, religious, or occupational groups in which homophobia is especially virulent are likely to experience strong pressure to hide their identities in order to maintain needed and valued ties to those groups. For these individuals, coming out publicly may not be a reasonable option, and developmental models must theorize maturation possibilities that are sensitive to diverse demographic realities (Fassinger, 1991, 1994; Fassinger & Miller, 1997; McCarn & Fassinger, 1996).

The work of Fassinger and colleagues (Fassinger & Miller, 1997; McCarn & Fassinger, 1996) represents an attempt to create a model of LGB development that is more inclusive of demographic and cultural influences and less reliant on identity disclosure as a marker of developmental maturity. This model (Table 1) espouses two separate but reciprocal processes of identity formation: One that involves an internal, individual process of awareness and identification with a homophilic intimacy orientation (Am I lesbian or gay?) and one that involves changed identification regarding group membership and group meaning (What does it mean, to me and to other LGB people, to be lesbian or gay in this society at this time?). A four-phase sequence (preceded by non-awareness) characterizes both the individual (I) and group (G) branches of the model. In Phase 1 there might be an *awareness* of feeling or being different as an individual (I) or of the existence of different sexual orientations in a group (G). Phase 2. denotes *exploration* of strong/erotic feelings for same sex people or a particular same sex person by an individual (I) or of one's position regarding lesbians or gays as a group (G), in terms of both attitudes and possible membership. Phase 3 is a *deepening commitment* to self-knowledge, self-fulfillment, and crystalization of

Table 1
Inclusive Model of Lesbian/Gay Identity Formation

Individual Sexual Identity (I)	Group Membership Identity (G)

1. Awareness

*of feeling or being different	* of existence of different sexual orientations in people

Self-Statement Examples (for women):
"I feel pulled toward women in ways I don't understand." (I)
"I had no idea there were lesbian/gay people out there." (G)

2. Exploration

*of strong/erotic feelings for same sex people or a particular same sex person	*of one's position re: gay people as a group (both attitudes and membership)

Self-Statement Examples (for men):
"I want to be closer to men or to a certain man." (I)
"I think a lot about fitting in as a gay man and developing my own gay style." (G)

3. Deepening/Commitment

*to self-knowledge, self-fulfillment, and crystallization of choices about sexuality	*to personal involvement with a reference group, with awareness of oppression and consequences of choices

Self-Statement Examples (for women):
"I clearly feel more intimate sexually and emotionally with women than with men." (I)
"Sometimes I have been mistreated because of my lesbianism." (G)

4. Internalization/Synthesis

*of love for same sex people, sexual choices into overall identity	*of identity as a member of a minority group, across contexts

Self-Statement Examples (for men):
"I feel a deep contentment about my love of other men." (I)
"I rely on my gay/lesbian friends for support, but I have some good heterosexual friends as well." (G)

Source: Fassinger & Miller, 1997; McCarn & Fassinger, 1996

choices about sexuality as an individual (I) or to personal involvement with the reference group, including awareness of oppression and consequences of choices (G). Phase 4 is *internalization/synthesis* of love for same sex people and sexual choices into overall identity as an individual (I) or of identity as a member of a minority group, across contexts (G).

The model assumes that because the branches are separate and not necessarily simultaneous, an individual could be located in a different phase in each branch—for example, a young woman actively involved in campus gay rights advocacy (G3) who is just coming to realize that she has strong erotic feelings for a female friend (I2). The branches of the model also are assumed to be mutually catalytic, in that addressing the developmental tasks in either branch is likely to produce some movement in the other branch. Moreover, a cyclical process is assumed, in which recycling through phases occurs as developmental pathways shift in response to the demands of external circumstances; an individual, for example, who has resolved conflicts about how "out" to be in college classes may be forced to revisit those decisions with a change of major. Finally, self-disclosure in this model is not viewed as an index of developmental advancement, allowing for diverse paths to an integrated LGB identity (Fassinger & Miller, 1997; McCarn, 1991; McCarn & Fassinger, 1996).

This model has been empirically validated on samples of diverse lesbians (N = 38) and gay men (N = 34) using a Q-sort methodology (Fassinger & Miller, 1997; McCarn, 1991; McCarn & Fassinger, 1996). In these studies, support for the two branches of the model was strong, and support also was found for the four-phase sequence, particularly the first and last phases. Self-report measures based on the model also have been developed (40 item Likert scales, available from the author) and currently are being tested. It is hoped that this model will provide an additional resource for those interested in culturally sensitive models of LGB identity formation. The implications of LGB identity development models for theories of student development are discussed in the following section.

LGB IDENTITY AND STUDENT DEVELOPMENT THEORIES

A comprehensive review of all theoretical frameworks used by Student Affairs professionals in terms of their applicability to LGB individuals is not possible in this limited space. The aim here is to present examples of ways in which LGB identity development models have important implications for the use of developmental theories in the daily work of Student Affairs professionals. The examples, discussed in the form of questions about the viability of theoretical assumptions, are presented for two broad classes of student development theories involving psychosocial and cognitive development.

Psychosocial Development

Chickering's theory of seven developmental vectors (Chickering, 1969; Chickering & Reisser, 1993) represents the most current, comprehensive, and widely used theory of student psychosocial development (McEwen, 1996a). The vectors include the developmental tasks of developing competence, managing emotions, moving through autonomy toward interdependence, developing mature interpersonal relationships, establishing identity, developing purpose, and developing integrity. A close examination of these vectors reveals theoretical assumptions that put LGB students at considerable disadvantage in terms of achieving successful resolution of developmental tasks.

Consider, for example, the first four tasks, which provide a foundation for later, more advanced tasks (Chickering & Reisser, 1993). These first tasks all center in some way around developing competency in handling interpersonal relationships and issues, including emotional expression, capacity for intimacy, and appreciation of differences among people. One might ask, How can a young gay man who is feeling alienated from his nongay peers but fearfully hiding his identity seek out other gay people and learn to become part of a community that is appropriate for him? In other words, how can this individual achieve interpersonal competence in a context of isolation, lack of an appropriate reference group, and unknown reference group norms? Similarly, how can a young lesbian deal with her dawning physical and emotional attraction to her roommate or teammate when to reveal those feelings would likely result in hysteria and ostracism? In other words, how can this individual learn to recognize and manage complex emotions in a context of homophobia and repression?

Similar questions can be raised regarding the development of autonomy and mature relationships. How does a young bisexual woman deal with the disapproval she is likely to experience in both the gay and nongay communities? In other words, how is this individual's development of autonomy and interdependence affected by lack of an appropriate community or marginalization in existing communities? Interpersonally, what lessons does a young gay man learn about tolerance of differences when he is physically assaulted by other students? How does he learn to trust others and develop intimacy in relationships when he is consistently regarded with fear and hatred? In other words, how can this individual possibly develop mature interpersonal relationships in an environmental context of oppression and prejudice?

Clearly, the difficulties encountered by LGB students in resolving these preliminary developmental tasks are, as Chickering's theory posits, likely to lead to difficulties in resolving more advanced tasks related to identity, purpose, and integrity (Chickering & Reisser, 1993). One might ask, for example, how an individual can possibly establish a secure identity in the face of marginalization, invisibility, and societal censure. Moreover, one might expect that developing purpose—clarifying vocational, avocational, and lifestyle plans and goals—is very likely to be ignored or stalled in the face of more pressing identity concerns related to safety, acceptance, and belonging (Fassinger, 1995, 1996a). Finally, one might ask how the process of developing a personally relevant set of beliefs and values by which to live—such as integrity—is influenced by invisibility and stigmatization of lifestyle.

The point, of course, is not that Chickering's theory is irrelevant or useless but simply that the unique needs of LGB students must be taken into account very consciously in implementing programs and interventions based on its assumptions. If, for example, we truly wish our students to develop awareness and tolerance of differences and we do not want any student ignored or mistreated based on his or her differences, then we must be sure that LGB issues are included in all of our campus programming, not just interventions targeted toward "gay awareness." Programs on dating that are oriented toward heterosexual couples should be noted as such and comparable programs offered for LGB students. Similarly, career workshops should include attention to the special problems of representing gay-related activities in resumes or job interviews or dealing with a two-career job search when the relationship is not public. Commitment to optimal psychosocial development for *all* students in Chickering's theoretical terms (Chickering, 1969; Chickering & Reisser, 1993) would suggest the need for vigorous efforts to address the unique and pressing emotional, interpersonal, and social needs of LGB students.

Cognitive Development

Cognitive student development theories focus on how students think and reason, with moral thinking included as a special kind of cognitive process (McEwen, 1996a). The cognitive theories most widely used by Student Affairs professionals are Perry's (1970, 1981) and Belenky et al.'s (1986) schemes of intellectual development, and the moral development theories of Kohlberg (1975) and Gilligan (1982). The assumptions in these theories raise critical questions about their applicability to LGB students, but in this case, LGB students may experience some advantages over their nongay peers.

Consider, for example, the intellectual progression posited in the theories of both Perry (1970, 1981) and Belenky et al. (1986). These theories assume early positions in which knowledge and discourse are largely molded by external others whose ultimate authority is to be accepted, gradually maturing to positions in which multiple realities and options are considered and evaluated by an increasingly self-referential thinker. It is a maxim in the LGB community that "coming out is a crash course in how relative everything is," a reference to the cognitive shifts that occur as one negotiates a new identity and lifestyle that often are at odds with the larger community in which one lives. The extensive reeducation and resocialization that occur during LGB identity formation often result in the recognition that authority figures—parents, teachers, and clergy as examples—can be wrong about issues fundamental to one's being, an increasing degree of reliance on oneself and one's own needs to guide experiences, and a live-and-let-live attitude of acceptance regarding others' lifestyles and beliefs.

These cognitive shifts clearly parallel those posited in theories of intellectual development.

Consider also the moral/ethical positions that are theorized by Kohlberg (1975) and Gilligan (1982). Kohlberg (1975) explained a sequence in which moral reasoning matures from positions focused on personal safety and approval from others to positions increasingly motivated by higher principles of social order, universality, and conscience. Gilligan (1982) noted a mode of moral reasoning focused on an ethic of care in which responsibility toward others increasingly becomes integrated with responsibility toward oneself. It is interesting to note that the maturation point in both theories involves balancing commitment to self with a responsibility toward others in society. This also is the inherent tension in the identity formation process for LGB people—to reconcile personal needs and desires with the (usually conflicting) demands of society.

Taking these theoretical assumptions into account, we might ask such questions as: How do the personal awareness and acceptance of a stigmatized identity affect an LGB student's cognitive shifts from dualistic through multiplistic to relativistic points of view (Perry, 1970, 1981)? How do LGB individuals committed to social justice manage to express and maintain that commitment in a context of personal and societal oppression (as in Perry, 1970, 1981)? In terms of moral/ethical development, we might ask: How is the development of an ethic of care influenced by same-sex commitments, and is it different for lesbians versus gay men (Gilligan, 1982)?

Scholars (Friend, 1987; Kimmel & Sang, 1995) have argued that LGB individuals are forced to learn an array of cognitive, interpersonal, and emotional coping skills during the process of coming out in a heterosexist and homophobic environment that provide them with uncommon resiliency and flexibility in managing other life stresses and developmental tasks. Services to LGB students might be targeted toward strengthening and building upon existing cognitive strengths, for example, support groups that focus on cognitive coping strategies. LGB students might be invited to assist in campus programming targeted toward prejudice reduction and awareness of differences, sharing their own experiences and coping strategies with others.

IMPLICATIONS AND CONCLUSION

It seems clear that the development of LGB identity has important implications for student development theory and practice. This author has argued elsewhere (Fassinger, 1996a) that assumptions regarding optimal development based on maturational markers attainable only by small segments of the population are not particularly helpful in guiding practice. Student development theories, like most mainstream developmental theories, have not given adequate attention to the unique ways in which LGB individuals traverse the maturational maps posited in those theories (Evans & Levine, 1990a; Fassinger, 1994; McEwen, 1996b; Wall & Evans, 1991). Clearly, scholars need to be actively addressing the paucity of research in this area (Wall & Evans, 1991) in order to provide more inclusive theories from which professionals can work. Student Affairs professionals can begin the important task of raising questions about the theories that guide their practice. They can examine the myriad ways in which those theories may be inadequate or inappropriate for use with LGB students, either because they ignore the difficulties in developing a healthy LGB identity and therefore inadvertently pathologize lengthy or deviating paths to psychosocial maturation, or because they fail to acknowledge and draw upon the cognitive and emotional strengths developed by LGB individuals during the identity formation process. We have much to learn from and about LGB students—their unique experiences can inform and sharpen our understanding of the development of *all* students with whom we work.

CHAPTER 3

Making Meaning: Providing Tools for an Integrated Identity

Laura C. Engelken

In the midst of a society embedded with heterosexism and homophobia, gay, lesbian, bisexual, and transgender (GLBT) students are forced to develop new meanings of self and world. Without the essential tools for constructing such an understanding, many students do not succeed. These feelings may contribute to high suicide rates among GLBT youth as they are overwhelmed by the challenge of making sense of their sexual and spiritual identities (Jennings, 1994).

Charged with promoting the academic and personal development of all students, both faculty and administrators play an important role in assisting GLBT students in their search for new meanings of self. As Parks (1986) states, the power and vulnerability of young adulthood lies in "the experience of the dissolution and recomposition of the meaning of self and world. Yet the quality of that recomposition depends upon the leadership of adult culture, as mediated through both individuals and institutions" (xii). By providing essential tools for making meaning, administrators and faculty can assist GLBT students in redefining themselves and their world.

TOOLS FOR MAKING MEANING

The meaning-making tools recommended in this chapter—resources, interpersonal opportunities, and role models—are derived from the analysis of two developmental theories: Vivienne Cass's (1979) model for homosexual identity formation and James Fowler's (1981) stages of faith. Both theories assume that the basis for both change and stability in individual behavior and understanding is found in interactions between self and society. According to Cass, individuals seek congruency between personal and societal perceptions of self, and development occurs when individuals work to rectify incongruencies arising between these two perceptions. Fowler characterizes incongruencies as "disruptions of normality" requiring explanation (96). Consequently, as individuals begin to make sense of their lives, they effectively redefine their conceptions of self and world.

Although all students must "formulate a personal strategy to address the most important question human beings face—the need for their lives to have enduring meaning" (Willimon & Naylor, 1995, 130), spiritual development has special implications for the GLBT student. Faith development requires community, language, ritual, and nurturance. Those who have been harshly excluded from society are hindered in constructing positive understandings of self and world (Fowler, 1981). When revealing their GLBT identity to self and others, GLBT students potentially lose the three essential pillars supporting both self and identity—family, friends, and faith (S. Fritz, personal communication, August 4, 1995). Consequently, the GLBT student must reach deeper within, to "spiritual roots," to develop meaning that will ground and support in the face of such rejection (J. McNeill, campus lecture, October 13, 1995). Informational resources, interpersonal opportunities, and role models are essential tools for the GLBT student's construction of supportive new meanings.

Resources

According to McNeill (1994), GLBT individuals have "a desperate need to understand [their] lives and experiences in a positive spiritual context" and "need to hear the story of others" who have journeyed toward new meanings (315). Students in the early stages of homosexual identity formation are searching to find what it means to be homosexual and whether such knowledge applies to them directly. Consequently, it is essential for faculty and administrators to ensure the availability of such information.

More than in a mere paragraph in a psychology text, GLBT students should find themselves reflected in materials throughout the campus—in library acquisitions, class texts, magazines on sale in the bookstore, and professionals' offices. "As institutions of learning, colleges and universities are obliged to present information by and about as full a range of knowledge, behaviors, and cultures as possible" (McNaron, 1991, 20). Failing to acknowledge GLBT life and culture on campus—from the art hanging on building walls to syllabi in the classrooms— communicates to the GLBT student that he or she is nonexistent. Through such omissions, it is easy to understand how GLBT students' attempts to make meaning are invalidated by the educational institutions and experiences that are designed to enrich their lives and deepen their understanding of the world (DeSurra & Church, 1994).

The invalidation and alienation of the GLBT student's life is often communicated by the deafening silence of the curriculum. According to

D'Augelli (as cited in DeSurra & Church, 1994), "When [GLBT students] pursue an understanding of themselves, they do not encounter a literature affirming their lives. More importantly, when they look to their undergraduate curricula for insight, they find themselves deleted from most courses. They are the 'invisible' minority, yet the 'hidden curriculum' that devalues the existence and contribution of lesbians and gay men is quite clear" (11).

Feeling unconnected to course material and class discussion causes many students to remove themselves from the educational process. For example, one student interviewed by DeSurra & Church (1994) noted:

My teacher was talking about relationships and that the only reason we date and court and stuff is to get married, that the only reason for relationships is to lead to marriage, and I'm thinking OK, where does that leave me? I'm never going to get married. I totally do not belong in that class, I just get depressed, nothing relates to me at all. (27)

Educators do all students, both gay and straight, a disservice when failing to seriously consider the lives and contributions of those whose efforts help build societies (Crumpacker & Vander Hagen, 1984).

One highly visible and effective way to ensure that GLBT resources and information are available to all students is through the creation of a GLBT Campus Resource Center as a safe, student -centered space to gather informally, hold meetings and lectures, and house educational materials and referral files of gay-friendly professionals in the area (doctors, lawyers, counselors, etc.). "Such physical locations would signal to students that their universities or colleges 'see' them and want them to have as positive an experience as possible" (McNaron, 1991, 21).

The creation of such a center must not be construed as sufficiently meeting all the needs of the university community, let alone GLBT students on campus. GLBT education, resources, and support cannot be the sole responsibility of only one office, department or program. There must be an "interrelation of campus resources" in order to serve students well (National Association of Student Personnel Administrators [NASPA], 1989, 39). There must be a concerted effort among all professionals on campus to fight heterosexism and homophobia and facilitate GLBT students' positive identity development.

It is important to charge a professionally trained individual with the responsibility for these educational efforts. According to McNaron (1991), most administrators act on behalf of GLBT issues and individuals only after repeated requests and/or increased pressure. Those few GLBT students who advocate for their constituency may be hindered due to limited time, resources, and experience. For example, Evans and Levine (1990) note that although the number of GLBT student organizations has increased, they often function without official administrative support. "Their persistence in visible activism often leads to physical exhaustion and demoralization" (130). Administrators and faculty must take primary responsibility in advocating for change and relieve open lesbian and gay students from the burden of solving the problems of their own victimization (D'Augelli, 1989a). It is unacceptable to expect these students to do the job of a higher education professional—they are at the institution to earn a degree. According to D'Emilio (1990), hiring an "omsbudsperson" for GLBT concerns makes "good institutional sense" (19) as they can think expansively about issues, provide departmental educational training (police services, financial aid, admissions), and intervene decisively in emergencies (hate crimes) to guide the campus forward.

Interpersonal Opportunities

Faculty and administrators can facilitate GLBT students' identity development by creating opportunities for meaningful relationships and quality interaction. Since individual development is conditioned by the quality of interpersonal and group relationships and the kind of society in which he or she lives, educators must create time and space for positive relationships to grow (NASPA, 1989). This is especially true for the GLBT faculty who—fearing harassment, discrimination, and violence—must continually monitor how "out" he or she will be in various situations and relationships. As a result, GLBT individuals experience a sense of loneliness, alienation, and detachment from the campus community unequaled by their heterosexual peers (D'Emilio, 1990).

In order to facilitate greater connection and inclusion in the campus community, faculty and administrators must support intentional programming both inclusive and celebratory of GLBT students and culture. For example, dances that are advertised and that welcome same-sex couples and campus films and art exhibits with GLBT themes—not only during National Coming Out Week each October but throughout the academic year—are important tools in "fostering toleration, understanding, and enthusiasm for differences in culture and identity," as well as in creating affirming and inclusive social opportunities for GLBT students (D'Emilio, 1990, 19).

As students engage one another and their professors in the classroom, faculty have responsibility and an opportunity to create a climate conducive for the growth of meaningful relationships and quality interactions. In their study of GLBT students' perceptions of alienation and inclusion in the classroom, DeSurra and Church (1994) discovered that instructors' responses to issues regarding sexual orientation greatly impacted GLBT students' experiences and learning. A gay student shares:

We were talking about Achilles and his love for Pericles, and the teacher elaborated on it, not like graphically, he just gave enough, then said if anyone was interested in this kind of stuff to go to the library and follow up with reading the Persian Boy or reading about Alexander the Great. I was always going over to the library and looking in the computer for these obscure titles; it was such an enhancement to my education. (28)

In contrast, when professors make negative comments or refuse to include information about GLBT life and culture relevant to course materials and discussion, they reinforce the concept that homosexuality and homosexuals are invisible and unwelcome in the classroom (DeSurra & Church, 1994). GLBT students are then forced to respond to this hostile climate by either confrontation or withdrawal—coping mechanisms hindering academic and personal development (DeSurra & Church, 1994).

In addition to creating a positive classroom environment and inclusive social programming, administrators and faculty must facilitate opportunities for relationships and communities to form that enable GLBT students to share intimately of themselves and learn from others. Alternative spring break programs are excellent examples of time and space carved out of the college experience to facilitate interaction among students, faculty, and staff. As one lesbian student reflects:

We had a thirty hour van ride to Missouri, and so of course we all got really close, really fast. So she [the student leader] brought it [sexuality] up with me over the week-long trip and it was such a peace—I mean I read my journals now and that's what I talked about and that's why my alternative spring break trip was so wonderful. When I came back, she was there for me, there with me, from a point at which I said I would never come out—if this is a part of my life, I would never come out—to her all of a sudden hearing me one day refer to myself as a lesbian. (Jess, personal communication, October 28, 1995)

Through organizing and involvement in such efforts, faculty and administrators responsibly share in the creation of community—"a partnership of people committed to the care and nurturing of each others' mind, body, heart and soul through participatory means" (Willimon & Naylor, 1995, 145).

Originally, institutions of higher education in America were created with the purpose of preparing young men for the clergy. As time has progressed, higher education has become increasingly removed from examining and facilitating students' development of faith and spirituality. Faculty members Willimon and Naylor (1995) lament the "abandonment by higher education of the moral, character-related aspects of education, the widespread erroneous assumption that it is possible to have a college or a university without having an opinion of what sort of people ought to be produced by that institution" (15). Far from trying to orchestrate specific answers to life's greatest questions, faculty and administrators must assist students' reflection upon their lives to discover those answers for themselves. As faith shapes the way we invest our passion and energy, it is essential to engage students in discussion that helps bring their meanings to light (Fowler, 1981). Thus, students must be given the opportunity to share their thoughts, concerns, and questions of faith in order to greater understand them.

Such opportunities for faith discussion can be facilitated by educators through interfaith dialogues in classrooms, residence halls, student centers, campus ministry offices, and campus newspapers. Professionals must encourage dialogue among students of all perspectives. This is especially crucial for GLBT students who "must learn a new level of spiritual maturity, basing their spiritual life on inner convictions and not on outside expectations" (McNeill, 1994, 317). Such encounters with the faith stances of others give words to those "inner convictions" (317) and illumine GLBT, as well as all, students' efforts to make sense of their own lives.

Role Models

Faculty and administrators must provide and serve as role models for students. Just as it is important for women and students of color to see themselves represented in faculty, staff, and administrative positions, so too is it important for GLBT students to see themselves reflected in campus life. These role models testify to the possibility of the positive integration of sexuality with the rest of one's life. For GLBT students struggling to make sense of self in a hostile environment, these examples are crucial.

Consequently, closeted professionals must "rethink their silence and invisibility." Research shows that when a heterosexual learns a family member, friend, or colleague is lesbian or gay, homophobia often decreases (Tierney, 1992, 46). Yet the same hostile environment existing for the student also exists for the GLBT professional. Without federal, state, or local protection, GLBT professionals can be fired for their orientation without any grounds for recourse (D'Augelli, 1989b). Administrative divisions and academic departments must actively encourage and support the professional in coming out and ensure his or her ability to do so. Minimally, this means formally enacting a non-discrimination policy regarding sexual orientation that is openly announced and in print wherever the institution proclaims its policy with regard to race, gender, and religion (D'Emilio, 1990). According to D'Emilio, such policies would apply to hiring, promotion, tenure, admissions, and financial aid. "Because of the history of discrimination in this country, it is not enough for an administration to claim that it subscribes to the principle of fairness for everyone" (18). It must explicitly acknowledge protection for GLBT community members.

Ensuring against employment discrimination on the basis of sexual orientation is a crucial action. Harassment and other hate crimes directed at staff members, as well as students, must be immediately and intentionally addressed. Administrative response to anti-gay harassment directed at GLBT live-in, residential life professionals must be clear and decisive, communicating that such behavior is not tolerated in either the residential or the greater campus community. Support for faculty members conducting research in GLBT -related topical areas is also important—honoring academic freedom and financial recognition—for special appointments and tenure decisions. Individuals are most efficient and effective when able to study and work in an organization where they feel appreciated and affirmed. If this support is absent, GLBT professionals will remain in the closet or go elsewhere, and wisely so.

Self-Reflection

Faculty and administrators must also exert moral courage in turning inward to the spiritual self, examining the faith by which they make sense of their world. As we encourage students to explore and clarify values, so must we review our own. Professionals must not perpetuate the false division between "home" and "office" (the spiritual and the professional). Fowler (1981) notes that failing to acknowledge our faith makes it no less influential in determining our initiatives and responses in life. Thus, as educators, we must be willing to respectfully share how we make meaning of life, listen attentively to the perspectives of others, and encourage students to do the same.

Given such an "objective" analysis, it is tempting to survey some strategies for institutional change. Those strategies can be helpful—but not until we have done some "inner work." For our tendency to blame institutions for our problems is itself a symptom of our objectivism. Institutions are projections of what goes on in the human heart. To ignore the inward sources of our educational dilemmas is only to objectify the problem—and thereby multiply it (Palmer, 1993, 107).

In order to facilitate individual, communal, and societal growth, faculty and administrators must "more than tolerate homosexuality. You must be active against GLBT oppression in order to combat and overcome society's message" of isolation and condemnation (A. Reynolds, personal communication, 1995). Such action first requires self-reflection.

Faculty and administrators, through the power vested in them as educators, have tremendous influence on the environment shaping students' lives and experiences. People in positions of power are able to create either healthy or unhealthy living conditions for others (Palmer, 1993). Possessing such influence, educators must examine their personal beliefs and attitudes toward homosexuality as these effectively shape "the manner in which they work with individuals and groups, the ways in which policies are made, and the content of programs and services" (NASPA, 1989, p. 15). As John McNeill (personal communication, October 13, 1995) maintains, a homophobic counselor cannot effectively advise a homosexual client; so also a homophobic administrator or faculty member cannot successfully serve the GLBT student.

Although many GLBT students, staff, and faculty remain in the closet for fear of discrimination, harassment, or violence, they are not alone in their silence. "The 'closet' is shared by heterosexual people on campus who know of the needs of lesbians and gay men but who do not speak on their behalf" (Tierney, 1992, p. 129). As a result, educators must develop "moral courage" (Tierney, 1992, 46) and speak out concerning issues of social justice.

CONCLUSION

Faculty and administrators must intentionally respond to the developmental issues of GLBT students by equipping them with the tools needed to make meanings. By providing resources, interpersonal opportunities, and role models—tools to dig and "drink from their own wells" (McNeill, 1994, 314)—educators assist the GLBT student's effort to create an integrated self and world.

CHAPTER 4

The People in Between: Understanding the Needs of Bisexual Students

Kirsten M. O'Brien

Like lesbian and gay people, bisexual people face a major obstacle: Our society assumes that heterosexuality is normal, natural, and preferable as a sexual orientation. Whether sexual orientation is biologically determined, socially learned, or a combination of these factors, it is a central part of the soul of an individual. The affirmation of one's sexual orientation is a necessary step in affirming her or his validity as a person. The heterosexual orientation of people in our culture is affirmed in many ways: by legal, publicly celebrated weddings; on television shows; and in the media through music, articles, and advertisements. The validity of heterosexuality is broadcast everywhere. Other sexual orientations are less affirmed: Gays and lesbians often depend on the "gay subculture" to affirm their orientation as opposed to mainstream culture. For bisexual people, there is no large-scale or widespread "bisexual subculture," no bisexual Mecca (as San Francisco is, for example, for gays). Bisexuals depend largely on individual support and understanding for their affirmation. Through interactions with bisexual students, administrators and faculty have the potential to affirm or deny their personal realities. By making a decision to affirm them, faculty and administrators are helping them to become secure and healthy individuals and, as such, better students.

This chapter consists of two sections. The first discusses and defines bisexuality, contrasting preconceptions with popular notions of what it is. The second section addresses the specific needs of bisexual students. This chapter is written primarily for heterosexual readers, and secondarily for readers who are gay or lesbian. The assumption is made that bisexual faculty and administrators understand the needs of bisexual students, although practical advice is given specifically for them near the end of the chapter. However, in general, this chapter targets people who have little familiarity with bisexuality and bisexual people.

BACKGROUND: "YOU'RE WHAT?"

Kinsey said, "There are not two discrete populations, heterosexual and homosexual. Only the human mind invents categories and tries to force fact into separated pigeon holes" (Hutchins & Kaahumanu, 1991, 7). Despite Kinsey's support of the idea of a valid bisexual identity, bisexuality has been denied to a large extent by our society. Sadly, even those working to recover gay and lesbian history often claim demonstrably bisexual historical figures as homosexual, rendering the genuine history of bisexuality even more invisible (F. Klein, 1993).

Bisexuals have either been rendered invisible or parodied so thoroughly that misconceptions are all that most people know as working definitions of bisexuality. Such misconceptions are prejudices based on the most marginal and confused understanding of bisexuality. Worse, they harm bisexuals by creating a largely hostile environment and encouraging a negative self-image. Some of the common stereotypes in connection with bisexuality are the following: All bisexuals are "swingers," sexually insatiable and/or indiscriminate, out for thrills, unfaithful to their partners; bisexuals are really in transition to becoming gay or lesbian; they don't want to give up heterosexual privilege; there are no real bisexuals; bisexuals spread AIDS (acquired immunodeficiency syndrome) to lesbians and "straight" people; sex is the most important thing in life for bisexuals; bisexuals can't make up their minds; bisexuals cannot have a committed relationship; they will dump same-sex lovers for heterosexual relationships; they can't be monogamous. The list could go on much further. The point, though, is that these stereotypes are just that: stereotypes—false presumptions about a population based on behaviors and characteristics of a minority of it members. An essential thing to remember—as with gay or lesbian people, black or Native American people, or tall or short people—is that no blanket statement about a group of people who share one trait will be true of all of them.

What is known about bisexuals? According to Klein (1993), studies have shown that there are between 2 and 11 times more bisexuals than homosexuals; Klein favors a figure between 5 and 10 times the number. Bisexual people are single or married or divorced, have same-sex or other-sex partners, are monogamous or not, right-handed or left-handed—maybe just like you or very different. The full range of human variation is present in the bisexual population, with only one exception: Bisexuals are neither heterosexual nor homosexual but some of both. On both Kinsey's (in Hutchins & Kaahumanu, 1991) and Klein's (1993) scales of human sexuality, bisexual people are the people in between the extremes of heterosexuality and homosexuality. We may have equal attraction for men and women or favor one gender over the other, but we do not exclude potential partners based only on gender. Being in between causes some confusion in our culture with its black-and-white dichotomous world view, but it is the reality for bisexual people.

If it is hard to imagine such a reality, this example may help: There are people who prefer men with beards as partners, or women with red hair. This does not mean that the beard or hair is necessary, though, if another specialness is found in a person. For bisexuals, gender is similar: A bisexual woman may prefer women, for example, but a special man would be an acceptable partner. But gender might not necessarily be a factor: It may be—like blue eyes, the ability to knit or drive a stick-shift car—immaterial to making a choice of partners. It all depends on the individual.

The reasons that this may be difficult to understand are entirely social and cultural. We are taught in early childhood that members of each gender will naturally be sexually interested in the other gender. Our education is occasionally widened to make an exception for gays and lesbians, but they can be mapped into the other gender's role, which is where we get the effeminate gay man/ butch lesbian stereotypes. Our education is rarely widened further to recognize the possibility of attraction to both genders. This lack of recognition has often led bisexual people to feel a need to choose one gender only and accept the identity that comes with that choice: Either gay or straight. Bisexual people are urged to deny a part of self and "pass" as a member of an accepted category.

Such pressure comes from both sides. The heterosexual assumption tells us to choose the straight option, since it is easier and certainly seen as better. When we come into contact with gay people and gay culture, we are often told that we are just in transition, that we are clinging to privilege, that we have to make a choice. We are told on both sides "You are not welcome here unless you are one of us. Make up your mind. What is it going to be?" The answer, "I am going to be myself," is rarely an option, at least not without a struggle.

You can help to ease that struggle for your students.

HOW YOU CAN HELP

As I researched information for this chapter, I asked my bisexual students for their input. What were their needs as bisexual students? They were surprised by the question; no one had asked them before. One answer was overwhelmingly common: They wanted unbiased and considerate treatment. Why are they not being treated appropriately, and what can we do to change our approach in providing inclusion?

To answer these questions, we first need to look at the way normality is constructed in the college environment. Normality is depicted in the college newspapers, flyers, and other forms of publicity; it is also taught in classrooms and counselors' offices. Who and what are normal? In colleges around the United States, normality is rooted in some fairly standard ideals: Heterosexuality is assumed, and everyone is monosexual—the idea that one gender, and only one, can be attractive to any one person.

To look at how bisexuality is often marginalized, think of a classroom situation in which a professor, lecturing on some famous figure in history, mentions the hero's same-sex lover. When a student asks, "Was so-and-so gay?" a common answer might be "Yes" or "Perhaps." But how often is the possibility mentioned that they might have been bisexual? It happens so rarely that some students will graduate from college not knowing that bisexuality exists. If a student, in speaking with her counselor, mentions her recent breakup with a female lover, the counselor is likely to make a quick assumption that this student is a lesbian. Later the counselor sees her arm in arm with a man: What adjustment is made in the counselor's mind?

A slogan that is currently to be found on pins, bumper stickers, and t-shirts says "Assume Nothing." This is a good standard from which to work. Although the majority of students with whom you work may be heterosexual, gay, or lesbian, a conscious effort to avoid assumptions will make bisexual students more at ease. You will also teach by modeling that no one sexual orientation is more or less important than another. In much the same way that you avoid using masculine pronouns to affirm the equal value of women, so does the inclusive recognition of all sexual orientations affirm the equal value of all people. As such, recognition becomes more widespread, and homophobia and biphobia will diminish.

Professors of the arts and history, for instance, can make a conscious effort to be aware of the sexual orientations of artists, authors, musicians, and public figures and, when appropriate, make mention of them without assuming that a same-sex lover necessarily implies homosexuality. Classes on gay and lesbian authors, history, sociology, and sexuality are being offered at many universities; a similar class with a bisexual focus could easily be arranged. It might be surprising to review, for example, lists of historical figures who are "claimed" as gay or lesbian in spite of known heterosexual involvement. Other suggestions are more widely applicable: When sexual orientations are being listed for some reason, as in written materials for distribution or in a lecture, include the word *bisexual* as well. Giving support to student groups that include openly bisexual students is another way to foster inclusion.

College years are a common time when people begin to come out, whether as bisexual or as gay or lesbian. In a survey of bisexuals, Klein (1993) found that the average age at which respondents first identified as bisexual was 24 years. The coming out experience is often very stressful for people; it can be doubly so for bisexuals, who often meet with resistance from both the straight and gay worlds, as well as with their own internalized cultural values, which rarely see bisexuality as a valid option. If a student confides in you that she or he may be bisexual (whether they use that term or not), your best response would be to assure them that their feelings are healthy and that their concerns will be held in confidence.

Keep an updated list of local contacts and organizations for bisexual people to give to students. Be aware of available counseling services on your campus that might be of assistance to students in crisis and offer this information as gently and empathically as you can. If possible, interview counselors and/or groups to which you will be referring students to prevent a traumatic negative experience. Additionally, attitudes such as "I was bisexual once, too" are not at all helpful; they only deny the possibility of bisexuality as a genuinely valid orientation. It may take some effort, but by interviewing and making referrals to supportive service providers, you will save students much pain.

Bisexual faculty and administrators are in positions to be helpful. Although it may be difficult, the best thing you can do is be out on campus. Making appearances at meetings of student lesbian, gay, bisexual, and transgender groups and offering your services as a mentor or speaker on bisexuality are some of the most helpful things you can do. It is encouraging to bisexual students to see that there are people available with whom they may talk. Even if they never actually speak with you, you will have given courage to many students who might not have had any positive bisexual role models before.

You may never have had a bisexual student disclose his or her orientation to you. As you become more aware of differing sexual orientations, and implement some of the suggestions in this book, students may come to see you as a person they can trust.

CHAPTER 5

Transgender Students on Our Campuses

Lisa J. Lees

This chapter comes largely from my own experience of being a transsexual person and of helping transgender students and staff at Michigan State University (MSU). I did my "sex change" while employed at MSU and have been "out" on campus about the process and about the reality of being transsexual (and lesbian identified). Many students undertake a quest for their true identity during their college years. For the transgender student the time away at college is often the first chance to challenge the gender role assigned at birth and to decide how to integrate transgenderness into life as an adult. This can become a consuming concern, interfering to a disastrous extent with their education. These students need understanding and assistance during this period.

Transgender persons are those who are not comfortable living within the confines of the social stereotypes of gender as applied to themselves. Labels used include cross-dresser, drag king, drag queen, intersexed, transsexual, butch, femme, ungendered, androgynous, and more. The labels are many and changing, and they are not always accepted by the people to whom they are applied. It is important to allow transgender people the freedom to define who they are.

WHAT IS TRANSGENDER?

The slogan that captures most eloquently the transgender spirit is "Genitals do not determine identity." Some women are born with a penis, some men are born with a vagina, some people have neither or both or are in between. What a person has "down there" does not always predict how they will think, feel, or behave. The two categories "men" and "women" are much too narrow and well-defined to contain all the feelings people have about their gender roles and their place in society.

Some people seem to be born with transgender feelings. Often expression is given to these feelings at a very early age, before a person learns she or he is different. I was always aware of being transsexual, though it was a long time before I understood what that meant and could give my feelings a name. The reaction to one's initial attempts to give voice to feelings is often not positive. As a result, it is not unusual for transgender feelings to be hidden or suppressed until adulthood. When I tried as a child to act on my feeling that I was a girl, I was teased, tricked into making mistakes, and humiliated. I soon learned what lies to tell. The early experience that teaches that deception is the key to life leaves lasting scars.

Transgender feelings are intensely personal, yet they are also a subtext to the societal debate on the meaning of gender. Industrialized countries have a society in which, supposedly, each person has equal economic and political opportunity, yet we still have sex-labeled rest rooms, prohibitions on same-sex marriage, and other taboos on gendered behaviors. Transgender people are very much aware that our society is anything but gender neutral. Transgender feelings are not a whim, any more than are homosexual feelings. Giving expression to transgender feelings involves choices, as does engaging in homosexual behavior. Suppressing transgender feelings can be just as destructive as suppressing homosexual feelings. Transgender people tend to go through "purge cycles" in which they alternately deny and embrace their feelings, disposing of and then reacquiring information, clothing, and so on. The feelings are too strong to remain buried, yet too dangerous to risk discovery. These cycles can be emotionally exhausting, interfering with everything else in one's life. The strong cultural message that gender is bipolar has its effect on transgender people. If you are not female, our culture offers but one option: male, with a set of images and stereotypes ready made. But a transgender person is neither male nor female in the rigid sense advertised by our culture. The path of self-discovery often involves going from one gender extreme to the other, then settling down somewhere in between (though for some transsexual people, the opposite extreme is where they are comfortable and so is where they belong).

Transgender behavior has been sensationalized and stereotyped in movies and on talk shows to the point where it is difficult to hold a rational conversation on the topic with a member of the general public. Too little information is available, and few therapists and doctors know about the various forms of transgender behavior.

THE TRANSGENDER CLOSET

In many parts of the country there exists a separate homosexual culture of bars, bookstores, theaters, and so forth. One can be actively homosexual and remain largely closeted from the "straight" community. Expression of transgender behavior, on the other hand, involves being seen. One can drive to a gay bar and not be identifiably gay on the way to and from the bar; this is not the case if one is cross-dressed or has made a gender transition and does not have the correct identification or paperwork. In any community there is an invisible population who have transgender feelings. Most of these people keep their feelings in the closet. They do not know other transgender people nor how to find them safely. The Internet is to some extent changing this, although much of the activity there is anonymous.

Reaching an Invisible Population

Transgender awareness at Michigan State University began in the lesbian, gay, and bisexual (LGB) community. The first two people to go public as transgender (an undergraduate student and myself) are LGB identified. We received the support of many people in the LGB community. Indeed, it is unlikely that either of us could have come out if we had felt we were alone. The transgender population on a campus is not at all homogenous: Some transgender students pass as LGB, but most will be hiding their transgender concerns, passing as straight. These latter students probably have not had the opportunity to explore their transgender feelings. Very few transsexual students may have changed their names and made transitions to a new gender role or may be planning to do so while in college.

These different categories of transgender students have different needs and must be reached in different ways. Closeted transgender people in the student population are the largest set of transgender people on campus and the most difficult to contact. Although they may have a high need for information and a desire to be able to discuss transgender issues, they are likely to be afraid of taking any action that would mark them as transgender. You must reach this population in a way that makes information available and gives them reason to believe they can safely ask for help. The best way to do this is to increase the general awareness of transgender issues on campus.

Tactics to Increase Awareness

You cannot target only the transgender population on a campus. Your efforts must be aimed at increasing the awareness of what it means to be transgender. Such efforts will reach and help everyone and will improve the reception transgender students receive when they come out or are outed without their permission. These tactics include using the campus newspaper, increasing official awareness, adding "T" to the "LGB" events, and encouraging mentors and role models.

Use the College Newspaper. A surprising number of stories appear each year in the popular press that mention some manner of transgender behavior. These stories provide opportunities to educate about the realities of being transgender.

Use letters to the editor and opinion pieces to counter incorrect public perceptions of transgender people; I gave an interview (with photograph) shortly before Pride Week. A transsexual person on staff who is willing to do this sends a powerful signal to students that transgender people exist.

It is important for people who are out to work at being out. One particular point on which the press does not do well is the use of pronouns and names with transsexual people. Many publications follow the lead of the *Associated Press Stylebook and Libel Manual*, using the so-called sex change operation as the criterion for changing the pronoun used in speaking of a transsexual person. This is not right. A person who has undergone a name change and is living full-time in one gender deserves to be called by the pronoun appropriate to that gender, whether or not she or he has undergone surgery.

Increase Official Awareness. At MSU the option to check "transgender" instead of "male" or "female" has been added to a residence life opinion survey. The option resulted in a somewhat spirited exchange of letters in the campus newspaper. Discussions also ensued among residence hall staff and students. The director of residence life acknowledged that the option and the response have been a "positive, thoughtful experience."

Add the "T" to LGB Events. Explicitly include transgender people in Pride Week and National Coming Out Day activities. While it is true that not all transgender people consider themselves to be LGB—indeed, some transgender people would be happier without this tie being made in the public mind—this is currently the only place in which to provide public recognition to transgender people.

Encourage Mentors and Role Models. Transgender people are not freaks or weirdoes; we have families, jobs, and we are active in our communities. The students, staff, and faculty in my department see me performing my job, see me with my partner and our children, worshipping at church, volunteering in the community, and in many ways as a participant on campus and in the local community; that I happen to be transsexual is generally irrelevant, although I am out as a transgender person. Being out as such is not quite the same as being out as an LGB person. In particular, for a transsexual person to be out is to acknowledge publicly a past that may have been very painful. I do not mind being out if I am accepted for what I truly am, but I am painfully aware that to some people my past is seen to be more important than my present.

SUPPORTING TRANSGENDER STUDENTS

Once you have been contacted by transgender students, you must offer support; they need a place in the scheme of things. They need a chance to help themselves and to help others who are like them.

Make a Place in Existing Organizations

There are not likely to be enough out transgender students on most campuses to form their own organization. One must make use of existing organizations, most likely the LGB organizations. Again, not all transgender people want to be associated with these organizations, but there is usually nowhere else to hang that "T." MSU has a student organization—the Alliance of Lesbian, Bisexual, Gay, and Transgender Students (ALGBTS)—and a non-student organization— the Gay and Lesbian, Faculty and Staff Association (GLFSA). Both are transgender inclusive. The student organization was ALGBS until last year, then visibly added the "T."

Use Electronic Media

Make use of e-mail lists, newsgroups, and web pages to distribute information. These technologies are fast becoming commonplace. Electronic media provide a way for anonymous "lurkers" to acquire information they cannot otherwise obtain safely. I receive 5 to 10 e-mail messages weekly from people who have seen my web pages and decided it is safe to make contact with me. Although the nature of electronic media is such that people can have anonymous access to information, on most campuses people cannot interact anonymously.

One way to create anonymous interaction is by the use of an e-mail analog of an anonymous telephone hot line. This would be set up as a specific address to which e-mail is sent and from which replies are generated. Internally, the sender's identity would be masked from the staff people responding to the e-mail. A limit could be placed on how much anonymous interaction is allowed before face-to-face contact is required. Another possibility is the use of electronic role-playing situations in which the "true" identity of the players is hidden. This could be done in a structured manner as part of a class.

Establish a Support Group

Our transgender support group first met in November 1995. This group has been a great success, reaching out into the surrounding community (and in fact to this entire corner of the state). Our support group has no set agenda or program. The group is simply a safe place to say or discuss whatever is on one's mind. We have a small core of regulars and two facilitators (a student and myself). Most meetings have between 5 and 15 people in attendance. About 30 people have attended at least once, and another 20 or so have asked for information. It is difficult to advertise such a group in ways that reach beyond the LGB community: Word of mouth, area therapists, and area telephone help lines account for most of our referrals. A personal contact with one of the facilitators is a necessary first step for one wanting to attend a meeting. Resources must be found for people whose needs cannot be met by an informal support group: The campus counseling and residence life staffs are likely to know too little about the reality of being transgender. Information about this area has changed significantly in the past ten years, so staff should be encouraged and assisted to become fully informed.

Provide Guest Speakers

At MSU I have given guest lectures both alone and with a person from an area transgender organization. Students responded well and asked thoughtful questions. Several students have contacted me following such presentations, either to seek further information or simply to thank me for speaking.

Conduct Public Discussions

During Pride Week 1996, we held a two-hour open panel discussion in the MSU Union Building. Widely advertised, about 70 people attended including students, staff, faculty, and people from the local community. We conducted a similar panel discussion as part of National Coming Out Day activities in the fall. Some closeted transgender students deliberately avoided these events for fear they would somehow be identified, a phenomenon not unusual in the LGB communities as well. On the other hand, several transgender people from the local community learned of our support group because they attended these panel discussions or saw them advertised.

TRANSGENDERS WHO ARE NOT LGB

There is a great deal of confusion, even within the LGBT community, as to whether there is any necessary connection between sexual orientation and being transgender. The short answer is no. What do the terms *homosexual* and *heterosexual* mean when applied to someone who presents in more than one sex/gender or who has changed sex/gender? The general public tends to lump together all LGB and T people regardless of the sexual orientation of the latter. A female-to-male transsexual is accused of being a butch lesbian if he is attracted to women in his newly presented gender, and he is accused of being gay if he is attracted to men. We're assumed to be lesbian or gay, one way or another.

TRANSSEXUAL STUDENTS

Transsexual students may be at any stage of their journey—thinking about transition, going through transition, or moving beyond transition. At each stage they have unique needs and problems. Helping them meet their needs is critical to their being able to get the most from their educational opportunities and begin their adult lives on the right footing. A support group or contact with other transsexual people is invaluable for the student who is wrestling with questions concerning her or his transsexuality. Campus or area therapists with experience in this area should be identified. Professional help is an essential part of the journey to and through a gender transition. A poorly timed or ill-considered transition can be very damaging to the student, family, and friends.

Should a person consider "changing sex" while in college? The answer has to be yes. This is a step best taken while young, both for medical reasons and for social reasons, not to mention a simpler paper trail. If managed properly, a college community can be one of the best places to carry out such a transition. Transsexual students who transition while they are students need an understanding contact for changing their name and gender in college records and perhaps in the local community (voter registration, leases, and so on). Additionally, transsexual students may need help with college housing problems. Their needs for regular counseling or therapy, hormone prescriptions and blood tests, and so on, may be met by providers in their home community or may need to be met by campus or campus community resources.

Resources must be available if a transsexual student runs into serious problems with their peers. How will the campus react if the student is "outed"? The transgender community is itself very divided on how one should go about transition and with what goals in mind. If there is such a thing as a "traditional" transition, it is to be as secretive as possible, cut all ties with the past, and emerge in the "new" gender with no one the wiser. The reality is that this scenario is not possible for many people, does not always work when attempted, and when it does not work, fails badly exactly because the transsexual person has not developed a support network as transition has proceeded. The process of educating the wider community about transgender issues can be difficult: Most transsexual people choose to live a quiet life not identified as having "changed sex," yet there is increasing transgender awareness in the general community. There is considerable debate within the transgender community about the number of transsexual people who succeed in living quietly—"going stealth"— and what effect this has on their quality of life.

CONCLUSION

Helping transgender students is a complex task, but information and resources are becoming more readily available. There are transgender students at your institution. Listen to them and let them tell you who they are.

NOTE

Thanks to Anita, Brent, Madeleine, and Susan for reading and commenting on a draft of this chapter, to Deirdre and Keiran for help with the support group, and to Maggi for adding the "T" in many places.

PART II

Special People/Special Places

CHAPTER 6

A Far Better Place: Institutions as Allies

Elisa A. Lucozzi

It was my senior year at college, and I decided to give campus living a final chance after a difficult first year of being "out" at school. I chose to live alone because I didn't want to risk living with a homophobic roommate. Most of my dorm mates were new transfer students. I was hoping they'd get to know and like me before they found out I was a lesbian. There was only one other openly gay student besides myself on campus; she happened to live on the same floor. I felt relieved to have found a friend, but my dorm mates began to act nervous and uncomfortable around us. One night we walked into the lounge together to join the laughter and conversation, but as we entered the room all talk suddenly stopped. The other girls snickered and exchanged nervous glances. It was evident that we were not welcome. Several days later, harassing notes began to appear on the door of my room. It was going to be another difficult year, and the thought of leaving school was constantly on my mind.

I probably would have left school if it wasn't for Mary. Mary was my straight resident assistant who had been keeping a watchful eye over everything that had been happening. Mary came to my room to lend some support and asked how she could help. She arranged for a house meeting and invited a staff person who was an out lesbian to talk. Mary talked with my dorm mates and helped them to look at their own homophobia. At the end of the year, everyone received "awards" created by their fellow dorm mates. They presented me with the "what happened to your closet award" for having the courage to be out on campus.

I still have that award. It is one of the most significant awards I ever received, and Mary's vigilance was one of the most important gifts I received in my coming out process. It is people like Mary who remind me how important an ally can be to gay, lesbian, bisexual and transgender (GLBT) students whether they are struggling with their identity or with others' homophobic responses.

WHAT IS AN ALLY?

An *ally* is defined as one in helpful association with another; to unite or join for a specific purpose (*American Heritage Dictionary*, 1991, *Webster's New World Compact School and Office Dictionary*, 1982). When I hear the word *ally* the first thing that comes to mind is an allied country as in a war. Indeed, many of us view homophobia as something against which to wage war. Being an ally means taking the political and making it personal. An ally is someone who is willing to confront and challenge the institutional and cultural structures that support injustice. At times an ally risks personal loss to challenge those injustices. Mary was an ally. She had obviously educated herself enough to recognize homophobia. She took the initiative by coming to me to lend support and set up a dorm meeting. She provided me with a role model by asking a lesbian staff member to attend our meeting.

While it is clear that Mary, acting as an individual, made an intervention that was critical to the outcome of my college education, she obviously felt supported by the institution for which she worked. In that way, the institution itself was acting as an ally to both Mary and to any GLBT student she supported. In a college environment it is important to examine the role of the institution as an ally. For students, particularly resident students, the college they choose becomes not only their learning environment; it becomes their home.

WHY BE AN INSTITUTIONAL ALLY?

Recruitment

When developing an ally recruitment plan, it is extremely important to understand the population to which you are marketing. Due to the hard work of many public and private high schools across the country, it is becoming safer for high school students to come out. Initiatives like Project 10 in California and the Harvey Milk High School in New York[1] are creating positive and supportive environments for our future GLBT college students. In Massachusetts, the creation of the Governor's Commission for GLBT Youth sent a clear message of support to the state's schools that boast almost 100 high school gay/straight alliances (GSAs) since the commission was formed in 1993 (Massachusetts Governor's Commission on Gay and Lesbian Youth, 1993). This means more students will be entering the college selection process already established in their gay identities.

Sherrill and Hardesty (1994) reported the results of a survey they sent to GLBT students asking them to evaluate their colleges' attitudes and actions concerning homophobia.[2] They collected over 1,400 completed evaluations from approximately 189 colleges and universities such as Harvard, Brown, and Barnard. The data showed that over half of the respondents were self-acknowledged in their identity before entering. Therefore, students' criteria for college selection will most likely include an institution that has well-established acceptance and proactive support of its GLBT students.

Most high school students, however, do not have the support or safety of a high school GSA. Finding a gay-friendly college environment could represent a student's first opportunity to experience an accepting and supportive community. Regardless of the level of support a student received in high school, colleges and universities need to be cognizant that more GLBT students are aware that support does exist for them. Understanding this will open college recruitment efforts to a largely untapped market.

Retention

Blumenfeld (1992) outlines ten ways in which homophobia hurts not only the oppressed group but heterosexuals as well. He describes the harmful effects of homophobia and likens it to acid rain. He makes the point that regardless of the impact homophobia may have, all are nonetheless affected; the same is true of our college communities. While it is obvious that our GLBT students will suffer the greatest consequences of an intolerant environment, it is also true that institutions will also suffer some consequences in the form of declining retention.

According to Blumenfeld, homophobia is energy draining; it diverts energy from constructive endeavors. As faculty, staff, and administrators we are aware of the barriers that get in the way of a student obtaining and completing a college education; in fact, many of our jobs are structured around limiting some of these barriers. A GLBT student who worries about harassment or an unsupportive environment is not going to focus on academic or co-curricular learning. Data show that "31 percent of GLBT students left school for one semester or longer and 33 percent dropped out or transferred because of coming out or harassment issues prior to coming out" (Sherrill & Hardesty, 1994, 269). Supporting our GLBT students is a vital matter of retention.

Diversity

Blumenfeld (1992) notes that homophobia prevents an appreciation for unique traits not considered mainstream or dominant, thereby making a culture unsafe for everyone. Allowing your college environment to remain predominantly or covertly homophobic is sending a clear message of intolerance to other diverse populations on your campus. Likewise, if your institution is lacking support for other minority groups. This will send a clear message to prospective GLBT students. If colleges profess to prepare students for life as well as careers, then we are doing students a great disservice by not giving them the tools to cope with and embrace the diversity they will encounter in the real world. Providing students with an opportunity to experience diversity will better equip them to interact with people with whom they will work in their careers.

HOW INSTITUTIONS CAN BE ALLIES

While examining my own thoughts about ways to be an ally, I reflected upon individuals like Mary, who assisted me through college. I also drew on my own experience working in student services. The works of DeVito (1979) and Schoenberg (1989) verify my own personal and professional experiences. It is consistent throughout the research that GLBT students need clear and visible indicators that they will be embraced and supported in order to flourish in their college careers. The following suggestions reflect the recommendations made by DeVito (1979) and Schoenberg (1989):

1. *Go to the source.* The best way to find out what your GLBT students need or want is to ask them. For some institutions, the hardest part may be "finding" GLBT students. Each institution has its own methods of communicating with students. Form an advisory committee for GLBT concerns on campus. Set-up a series of meetings with the GLBT student group on campus. Do an anonymous survey about GLBT student needs. Initiate conversations with individual GLBT students.

2. *Be pro-active.* While it is important to find out from students what they need, it may not always be possible to do so. Moving forward with policies or programming that validate GLBT students can be a sign of an institution's commitment to being an ally. Some examples include celebrating Gay and Lesbian History Month (October), conducting a sensitivity training before rush for Greek organizations, or reexamining the language used in the student handbook for inclusiveness.

3. *Recognize and confront institutional homophobia.* Homophobia can often be difficult to recognize and acknowledge, especially if it is convert. GLBT students rarely report their victimization. Thus, a campus that assumes the nonexistence of anti-gay violence or harassment needs to examine whether the college has created a safe enough environment in which to report such incidents. Be sure to include sexual and gender orientation in non-discrimination policies. Examine harassment and hazing for sensitivity toward GLBT issues. Teach campus police to handle incidents of victimization respectfully and concisely.

4. *Educate about the connections between other oppressions and homophobia.* Blumenfeld (1992) talks about the importance of appreciating diversity. Educating about the commonalties in all oppressions will empower all oppressed groups on a campus and encourage alliances. Create alliances between your college GLBT group and other minority groups on campus such as the Black Student Union or ALANA groups (Asian, Latino, African, Native American), the Women's Group, Hillel, or other culturally diverse groups by cosponsoring events. Invite a speaker that crosses several groups. Be sure to include GLBT issues in any multicultural or diversity initiatives your school is involved in. If you don't have a formal group on campus, then form an advisory group for students concerned about diversity issues. Be clear about wanting input on the

committee from GLBT students.

5. *Become familiar with developmental issues of GLBT students and integrate them into your curriculum and services.* Understanding students' developmental issues is key to developing programs and curriculums that are both psychological and cognitively attainable as well as challenging. Understanding the nuances that are particular to identity development for GLBT youth is critical in retaining your students. Imagine that a student who is struggling with sexual identity issues is taking a class that requires self-disclosure as part of his or her class participation. That student clearly has a handicap in his or her ability to succeed in the class. Likewise, a GLBT student with a health issue may be too concerned with having to come out to seek the assistance he or she may need.

6. *Support GLBT employees.* Over 80 colleges and universities across the country are now offering some kind of benefits for domestic partners (Partner Task Force, 1995). Having domestic partner benefits will not only attract and retain GLBT faculty, staff, and administration at a college; it will offer a positive example for students in the treatment of GLBT staff and faculty. Another area to examine is employee policies. Be sure the policies are sensitive to GLBT employees, especially as they relate to maternity/parental leave, tuition, or bereavement. Encourage your GLBT faculty and staff to start a task force or advisory group. Be supportive of individual GLBT faculty, staff, and administrators who are out on campus.

7. *Provide positive role models for GLBT students.* Over 100 articles were written in the last ten years about the importance of role models in the retention of groups that are underrepresented. Articles about women in science, men in nontraditional jobs such as nursing, and minorities at college all emphasize the importance of role models in retention, achievement, and the successful completion of their endeavors. Sherrill and Hardesty (1994) revealed that 67 percent of the GLBT students surveyed indicated that the lack of role models was the largest problem these students faced on campus. Obviously the best way to provide role models is to create an atmosphere that will attract GLBT faculty, staff, and administrators to your campus. Some schools may not be ready to be proactive about attracting GLBT employees. In this case, integrating books and films with gay themes, famous GLBT historical figures and current news figures into the curriculum will be extremely important. Invite GLBT and straight allies onto campus to speak.

8. *Be sure all levels of your institution are involved.* Traditionally, Student Affairs is the first to address GLBT issues on college campuses. Often they have the most consistent and personal contact with students. Excellent programming and services have been developed in this area. However, without the support of deans and senior managers it will be difficult to create or expand services to GLBT students. Leadership is responsible for establishing the expectations for every member of the college community by setting forth clear goals, visions, and tone. A letter from a dean or the president denouncing a homophobic incident on campus can send a clear message about expectations to the community. Having a vision that includes support of GLBT students gives individuals within the institution the basis from which to act.

These suggestions are expressly offered for institutions; however, individuals make up an institution. As my opening story suggests, an individual can play a vital role in making the environment on campus a supportive one. The most important thing an individual can do is let GLBT students know that they are allies. Fahy (1995) outlines 50 ways to be an ally. Several of her suggestions include: display GLBT-friendly materials in your office such as a gay newspaper, books, or ally buttons like "straight but not narrow"; attend GLBT meetings or events on your campus; use inclusive language (e.g., "partner" instead of boyfriend/girlfriend); be open about your connections and experiences with GLBT people in your life; and confront homophobic jokes or remarks.

Although challenges manifest themselves in different ways at each institution, homophobia will always be at the core. The multitude of variables that give each campus its own unique culture would make it impossible to speculate how homophobia may reveal itself. The greatest challenge an institution will face is recognizing, admitting, and challenging heterosexism. Colleges and universities must reevaluate their institutions' written and unwritten policies that perpetuate cultural and institutional homophobia and heterosexism.

A FAR BETTER PLACE

Institutions or individuals may be at the beginning stages of reflecting upon these issues. Amending the values of higher education to include GLBT students is essential in the sound recruitment and retention efforts of a college or university. GLBT students are more confident and self-assured than ever before, which makes them more savvy consumers of their own education. Sherrill and Hardesty (1994) found that 40 percent of the students they surveyed stated that if they had had information concerning GLBT issues on their prospective campuses, their choices of where to attend college would have been different. Colleges and universities are microcosms of society; supporting GLBT students is one way to model inclusion and diversity. Most of the changes needed to create a safe and supportive environment for GLBT students do not require a large expenditure. What they do require is initiative, understanding, and courage.

NOTES

1. Project 10 was a pioneering program in Los Angeles created to support GLBT and straight allies in high school. The Harvey Milk School is an alternative high school whose primary focus is the support of GLBT students.

2. When the term *homophobia* is used in this piece, it is meant to also include biphobia (fear of bisexuals) and transphobia (fear of transsexuals).

CHAPTER 7

The Residence Hall: A Home Away from Home

Matthew W. Robison

Lesbian, gay, bisexual, and transgender (LGBT) college students face discrimination and hostility in the very environments designed to support them and assist their transition to the university community: residence halls. This chapter is divided into two parts: The first part defines and explores the issues that LGBT students face in residence halls. The second part focuses on eradicating homophobia in residence halls by exploring issues of preparation and practical solutions, including policy statements, staff development, and resident issues. The chapter concludes with notes regarding the interdependent nature of college environments; the context of housing must be seen in terms of the greater picture of creating educational environments where individuals are not disparaged for their sexual orientations.

INTRODUCTION

Despite minor differences in theoretical perspectives and approaches, one can say that the ideal of the residence hall is to facilitate and encourage the psychological, social, intellectual, and physical development and well-being of students (Blimling & Miltenberger, 1990). Residence halls constitute one way in which students round out their education, learning social values and norms of interaction while enhancing their academic achievement. Within this context, resident staff play numerous roles, including administrator, informant for the hall supervisor as well as the residents; disciplinarian, maintaining order and control; community builder, encouraging resident interaction and mutual interdependence; counselor, responding to student needs through crisis intervention and educational programming; and facilitator, encouraging residents to mold their community intentionally through hall governance and student-initiated programming. Essentially, a resident adviser (RA) is a role model, counselor, teacher, and student affecting the development of the residents under her or his control (Zirkle & Hudson, 1975).

Despite institutional variation, first-year students generally constitute the largest and most stable population of residents in university-owned housing. An entire body of literature has developed outlining various theories and conceptual models in an attempt to explain the difficulty adjusting to college from high school (Noel & Levitz, 1982; Upcraft, 1984; Upcraft & Gardner, 1989). Zeller and Mosier (1993) have argued that this transition is akin to entering a different culture, with student responses best understood in terms of culture shock. The stresses faced by the traditional first-year students can overwhelm even the most resilient: Sharing space with a "stranger" strips one of the privacy and control of one's own room; adapting to a culturally diverse environment; being unfamiliar with the campus, student services, academic issues, and the surrounding area; and perhaps most significantly, developmental identity issues, with students moving away from parents and becoming more autonomous and interdependent (Chickering, 1969). These factors often coalesce in a culture shock to create "a period of more intense personal conflict and anxiety" (p. 21). Resident staff are an invaluable resource in easing this transition.

Unfortunately, one subpopulation with unique needs and experiences has not been adequately addressed by the literature: lesbian, gay, bisexual and transgender (LGBT) residents. These students face all the same challenges of their heterosexual peers while simultaneously articulating a socially condemned sexual identity. LGBT students may face a profound culture shock as they are faced with new experiences of homophobia without familiar structures and coping mechanisms. They may experience retarded periods of initial adjustment from experiencing homophobia; enhanced mental isolation; and limited acceptance and integration into the university community.

Student development theorists identify the college years as intense periods of psychosocial maturation. Chickering's and Reisser's (1993) seven vectors of human development locate sexual identity development as a milestone in the process of defining an autonomous self. Though all students develop a sexual identity, LGBT students must grapple with social disapproval; their experiences violate acceptable norms. They must wrestle with self-acceptance, personal understandings of integrity, and the potential for social exclusion and rejection by their heterosexual peers. Additionally, the college environment may be the first time an individual is exposed to alternate constructs of sexuality and struggle to redefine their sexual identity amidst such changes. Thus, LGBT students may experience a profoundly different transition to college in comparison to similarly situated heterosexual students.

For most LGBT college students, struggling with issues of sexual orientation is nothing new; a majority of LGBT students were aware of their nonheterosexual identities before they came to college (Sherrill & Hardesty, 1994). Of the 7.2 million Americans under age 20 who are estimated to be lesbian or gay (Singer & Deschamps, 1994), many struggle with social disapprobation, isolation, higher than average instances of suicide, substance abuse, risk of dropping out of school, homelessness, parental rejection, emotional isolation, low self-esteem, physical and verbal abuse, and sexually transmitted diseases (Uribe & Harbeck, 1992). Moreover, according to Hetrick and Martin (1987) one in four out gay and lesbian youths are forced to leave home because of conflicts over sexual orientation, and many become homeless, often economically surviving as sex workers.

Against these odds, the number of LGBT youth who make it to college and are open about their sexuality has increased in recent years (Evans & Wall, 1991). The American Psychological Association estimates that one in six college students are LGBT, with one third of all LGBT college students living in residence halls (Sherrill & Hardesty, 1994). Many of these LGBT students are sharing their nonheterosexual identities. They are socially active and date other students on campus (Sherrill & Hardesty, 1994). In the past the invisibility of homosexuality would have avoided conflicts over sexual orientation; today such strife stems from self-actualized lives.

As colleges and universities are microcosms of society, they reflect the biases and prejudices of the broader social context. Indeed, college students bring to the residence halls the social scripts they have learned about LGBT people. Unfortunately, most first-year students have negative attitudes toward LGBT students (Herek, 1989). Studies indicate that 51 percent of first-year college students think lesbians and gay men should try to be heterosexual and 54 percent described themselves as "disapproving" or "very disapproving" of homosexuality (Comstock, 1991). In a 1988 survey of males ages 15 to 19, 89 percent said they found the idea of sex between two men "disgusting." Only 12 percent were confident they could befriend a gay person (Marsiglio, 1993).

College students, particularly first-year students, openly share their revulsion, disgust, and hatred for sexual minorities (Thorson, et al., 1991). Comstock (1991) found that 22 percent of first-year students had verbally harassed gay men. Despite such widespread victimization, LGBT students rarely report harassment or other hate crimes, because these students feel the incidents would not be taken seriously, the administration is not concerned with their welfare, and nothing would be done (Norris, 1992; Sherrill & Hardesty, 1994). Moreover, reporting victimization on the basis of sexual orientation raises coming out issues, deterring questioning and closeted LGBT students from reporting hate crimes (The Study Committee on the Status of Lesbians and Gay Men, 1991). This "victimization goes on within their dorms and workplaces" (Norris, 1992, 82).

LGBT students face this persecution without traditional support networks of family and friends. Remafedi (1987a) reported that half of lesbian and gay youths indicated their parents rejected them for being gay. In another study, 80 percent of LGBT youths reported severe isolation in multiple contexts: socially, having no one to talk to; emotionally, feeling distanced from family and peers because of sexual identity; and cognitively, unable to access good information about sexual orientation (Hetrick & Martin, 1987).

SOLUTIONS

Needs assessments, resources assessment, and action plans need to be developed and implemented in order to provide students with safe and inclusive residence halls.

Needs Assessment

As agents and proponents of more inclusive residential living environments for LGBT students, staff must formulate goals and objectives based on the actual needs of LGBT students. One simple method of conducting a needs assessment is an anonymous survey addressing students' comfort with issues of sexual orientation, interest in specific programming, informational flyers, library holdings, and other issues. Resident staff could distribute the survey at a hall meeting and collect it at another location (front desk, another RA); or it could be returned to the RA in an envelope. Electronic means of information gathering, via e-mail or the web, are other options and could potentially reduce expenses while maintaining anonymity (using an anonymous e-mail server). The result could be a more representative sample, potentially higher return rates, and the opportunity to access closeted and heterosexual populations anonymously. Alternatively, survey dissemination could follow networks of the LGBT community: campus organizations, social events, community centers, LGBT-related courses, and any non-university organizations. This approach would not be a representative sample of the university community as a whole and could underrepresented the needs of closeted and those LGBT individuals who are not active members of the LGBT community. Essentially, a needs assessment should ground one's objectives in the targeted community's concerns.

Resource Assessment

The goal of a resource assessment is to determine one's assets and one's necessities: What do we have; what do we need? First consider human resources. Who supports you and who is willing to say so? Who can help and what are they able to commit? How much time will this project take? Is this project feasible?

Second are institutional resources. What organizations, offices, programs, academic departments, or other arrangements are potential sources of support? Think expansively: Can I hang a flyer in this office? Will they permit me to use their Xerox machine? Will they agree to be cosponsors of this proposed change? Women's Studies Programs, English Departments (particularly those working in literary criticism and cultural studies), and Sociology Departments tend to be supportive of LGBT concerns.

Third, look beyond the university community and explore the resources of one's local, state, and national communities. Local community resources may include religious institutions, LGBT-positive groups within religious institutions, local activist groups, bookstores that sell LGBT-themed material, and nationally affiliated grassroots organizations, such as Parents and Friends of Lesbians and Gays (PFLAG). On a statewide and national level, look for LGBT activist and support groups and foundations such as the Human Rights Campaign (HRC), the National Gay and Lesbian Task Force (NGLTF), and the Latino/a Lesbian and Gay Organization. Use all available media—print, phone, fax, the Internet, e-mail, and personal connections.

Fourth, determine what type of information will be required. What will you have to prove? How will you prove it? What level of documentation or verification is necessary? If the administration demands formal scholarship or an in-depth study, seek a university-sponsored research project—task force, study group, or select committee. The goal is to eliminate surprise. Know the questions you will be asked; know your responses.

Finally, and perhaps most important, in conducting a resource assessment, work to build coalitions with other organizations with similar visions of social change.

Action Plan Development

Although people have personal planning styles, I have found operationalizing and systematizing plans to be an effective strategy. Treat each goal as an end in itself; identify the objectives of the goals; list required resources (human, informational, institutional); then create a plan to achieve the goal. The plan should identify who is responsible for what part of the project and include time lines and review at regular intervals.

This approach has a few advantages. First, committing everything to writing makes the project more real to you and others. If things do not proceed as anticipated, then the action plan may be revised according to the new circumstances. Breaking up a large task into numerous, manageable subtasks allows the project manager to maximize an individual's particular strengths.

This process of needs assessment, resource assessment, and action plan development is most effective when used in a group context. By the end of this process of preparation, one understands the needs of the target population and has formulated objectives to fulfill them, knows what resources are available, and has developed action plans to assess one's progress and maintain perspective.

CREATING SAFE SPACES

Institutional Issues

Institutional issues deal primarily with policy statements and official protocols. Policy statements of non-discrimination on the basis of sexual orientation are essential in creating an institutional stamp of disapproval on homophobic and heterosexist acts (Thorson, 1991). Non-discrimination policies, if enforced and implemented, provide substantial protections for LGBT students and symbolically express that LGBT participation and contribution to the campus community are valued and affirmed. Simultaneously, they demarcate acceptable from unacceptable conduct to the entire educational community as a whole: Language or behavior that disparages LGBT people will not be tolerated. As such, they facilitate a supportive and affirming campus climate by creating a floor of respect for LGBT people. These statements of non-discrimination may be within the housing division or university-wide.

Policy statements of non-discrimination empower LGBT students by recognizing them as valued members of the university community. Once students have a stake in the campus community, their generally held view of an uncaring, even hostile, institution, may give way to one in which students begin articulating demands for change with the expectation of some receptivity. As LGBT students are recognized as valued members of a residential community, homophobic acts are experienced as unjust harm capable of redress, rather than an old reality to which one must resign oneself. Once students know their concerns will be taken seriously, their experiences may be the impetus for further change. However, the effectiveness of these statements is dependent on their dissemination. Only if residents understand that homophobic acts violate community norms will policies of non-discrimination have any effect. At the University of Michigan, for example, the Housing Division produces a Living at Michigan Credo that explicitly values sexuality-based difference. This credo is given to every resident when she or he moves into the residence hall, is stressed at the first hall meeting by resident advisers and begins many disciplinary discussions. Thus, from the first day in university-owned housing, students know the residential community they have joined prohibits discrimination on the basis of race, gender, ability, and sexual orientation.

Protocol development is a mechanism to quicken and systematize institutional responses to foreseeable problematic circumstances. Given students' perceptions of institutional indifference to LGBT concerns, the timing of administrative responses becomes especially important. Even well-intentioned delays may be interpreted as disorganization and apathy or even tacit approval for the perpetrator's homophobic or heterosexist act. Official protocols enable multiple constituencies to participate in formulating official responses to sensitive situations, permitting swift, thoughtful resolution when they do arise. Protocols also increase the predictability and uniformity of institutional responses. Although circumstantially flexible, protocols define the guiding values and the procedures to follow in responding to certain issues, preventing inconsistent results regarding similar problems.

They may be as general or as specific as may suit the particular administrator. Most important, however, is the clarification of institutional values guiding the response. Some typical situations that should be solved following protocol guidelines include: roommate conflicts stemming from sexual orientation (dealing with the complexities of a homophobic roommate who wants the LGBT person to move or an LGBT person who wants to move to escape a homophobic roommate), continuing harassment, verbal harassment, random derogatory remarks, property destruction, physical assault, same-sex violence issues, and stalking. A final advantage of protocols is that they provide a mechanism to document homophobia in residence halls. If resident staff were required to document all discrimination issues, then this information could be used to monitor the situation of LGBT discrimination in residence halls continually.

Staff Issues

As information providers, community builders, and role models, resident staff members are empowered to set the tone of a residential community through peer and institutional influences. Through the implicit and explicit hierarchy of their position, a staff member may lead by proactively establishing a diverse community or solidifying preexisting stereotypes. Thus, staff development is an effective means to counteract homophobia and heterosexism in residence halls.

Resident staff members are also optimally situated to integrate intervention with information. Familiar with the campus and its resources, resident staff are customarily regarded as sources of accurate information. Myths about LGBT people are often dismissed through scholarship but not necessarily in popular culture. A resident adviser can challenge pejorative remarks, then offer the resident a fact sheet on LGBT people or other general information resources.

The second reason to pursue staff development is to meet the needs of LGBT residents. If resident staff members are unprepared to deal with coming out issues or crises stemming from issues of sexual orientation, then they will be less effective. Resident staff members must have the opportunity to explore their own feelings and become comfortable with their potential role as a counselor to an LGBT student. Moreover, as LGBT students are often indistinguishable from their heterosexual counterparts, resident staff members cannot be situationally "politically correct." Staff members will probably be unaware that a resident is observing their behavior and comments, searching for cues that the staff member is supportive or hostile to LGBT issues. If staff members are not committed to eradicating homophobia, then the needs of LGBT students will be unmet and they will continue to suffer. For example, if a lesbian resident is depressed because her family rejects her sexuality, she will not risk sharing this information unless it is clear the staff member is supportive. Even an otherwise stellar resident adviser is limited by her or his heterosexism when it precludes developing the mutual trust and understanding necessary for effective intervention.

Another reason to focus on staff development in recreating residence halls as safe spaces for LGBT students is to support existing staff members who may be wrestling with issues of sexual orientation themselves or learning more about LGBT people in general. Educating residence staff on issues of sexual orientation facilitates a more inclusive and tolerant resident staff community, encouraging existing closeted staff members to come out and challenging heterosexual staff members to explore the dynamics of heterosexism within their own lives.

Mechanisms for Staff Development

The first step for resident staff development regarding LGBT people is to educate existing staff members regarding issues of sexual orientation. The challenge is threefold: to expose individuals formally to accurate information, thereby debunking stereotypes; to create safe spaces where individuals may explore their feelings and identify sources of homophobia and heterosexism in the own belief systems; and to encourage continuing public dialogue on issues of sexual orientation. Emphasizing all three components—intellectual (exploring the other), emotional (exploring the self), and continuing public dialogue—in workshops leads to the greatest attitudinal change.

Research indicates that structured sessions intended to stimulate reflection and self-awareness are particularly valuable because they address the emotional underpinnings of cognitive structures. Becoming aware of one's feelings is a critical step in prejudice reduction, enabling further conscious efforts to alter one's behavior and belief systems (Sedlacek & Brooks, 1976).

One often hears that sexuality is a private matter best discussed behind closed doors among friends. However, this denies the existence of homosexuality while heterosexuality is freely expressed and affirmed in the most public ways: the media, television, and entertainment. Relegating sexuality issues to a private sphere is asymmetrical and stultifies the public discussion of sexuality (Norris, 1992) and equal rights for LGBT people in general (Caserio, 1989). Open and honest dialogue about one's prejudices is particularly important with regard to male homophobia, which research indicates is consistently more pronounced in comparison to female homophobia (Sanford & Engstrom, 1995). The idea is not to stigmatize those confronting their homophobia as bad people but to challenge them to explore their beliefs and emotions to eliminate prejudicial and discriminatory behaviors and stereotypes.

Staff education may be pursued in a number of ways. Antihomophobia workshops addressing the intellectual, emotional, and continuing needs may take many forms. The intellectual needs of workshop participants may be fulfilled by providing information packets with a variety of information obtained from such sources as the Queer Resource Directory whose website address is: http://qrd.tcp.com/qrd/youth/gay.fact.sheet.for.youth

A more costly and comprehensive approach would be to Xerox articles for participants to read before the workshop. Oral presentations of this material, plus defining basic terminology of LGBT people, is another option.

A strategy for staff development is to prepare staff to deal with resident issues: coming out, suicide and depression, substance abuse, verbal and physical harassment, and the destruction of property. Residence staff must be given accurate information and be fully prepared to deal with these crises should they occur. This means that open and honest dialogue needs to be initiated. For example, if a particular staff member realizes that he is unable to deal objectively and in a nonjudgmental manner with any issues dealing with sexual orientation, then this should be vocalized. The aim is not to ostracize this individual but to recognize a growth area. The group should determine how the situation will be handled if this is the case.

The emotional connection of participants may be stimulated through guided visualization exercises, facilitated discussion of controversial phrases, and coming out stories. Guided visualization exercises seek to create a world in which workshop participants place themselves in situations similar to those that LGBT people encounter and have them emotionally connect with that experience. Facilitated discussions seek to pose controversial questions, giving participants the opportunity to think about issues they may not have resolved and listen to opposing points of view. Coming out stories are short vignettes (three to five minutes) of an individual's experience recognizing, accepting, and sharing her or his non-heterosexual identity. These are often the most powerful parts of workshops, and participants integrate the emotional and intellectual aspects of a coming out story. Sanford and Engstrom (1995), in researching RAs opinions of LGBT students, concluded that "personalizing the experience of gays and lesbians is a powerful tool for challenging the validity of one's current operating assumptions" (29–30). Such workshops should be integrated into the training program of resident members, with continual training for resident staff members of all levels of experience (Sanford & Engstrom, 1995). A trained facilitator is advised for these sessions. Otherwise, discussions can become personal or heated and lead to polarization rather than mutual understanding and the initiation of continuing dialogues.

Beyond workshops, the resident staff should integrate issues of sexual orientation into the broader context of social justice and discrimination on the basis of race, ethnicity, gender, and ability status. Commemorating significant days of the LGBT community offers forum opportunities in which to address issues of sexual orientation and to educate staff. Such days include the anniversary of the Stonewall rebellion (June 28), National Coming Out Day (October 10), the anniversary of the assassination of Harvey Milk (November

27), the anniversary of the 1993 March on Washington (April), and October as LGBT History Month. Residence assistants could sponsor programs, put together bulletin boards, and bring in speakers to talk about the social, political and/or historical significance of these experiences in the context of LGBT people's struggle to gain acceptance and equality.

Another strategy for staff development is to include issues of sexual orientation as criteria for staff selection and staff evaluation. Rather than a separate category, sexual orientation should be integrated into a comprehensive vision of a diverse community, where difference is affirmed and validated, not ostracized and ridiculed. Research indicates that students who discriminate against LGBT people are more likely to discriminate against all minority groups (Ficarrotto, 1990). Thus, a potential staff member should be asked about his or her ability to meet the needs of LGBT students effectively if the need arose. At the University of Michigan, selection processes include questions regarding LGBT people as members of a residential community and possible responses to homophobic violence. Likewise, extant staff members should be evaluated according to their ability to facilitate a diverse community with individuals who are very different from themselves.

A concerted effort should be made to diversify resident staff. A staff that reflects the population it serves is an intentional community of diversity. LGBT students should be encouraged to apply for resident staff positions; their experience as LGBT people on campus bring a unique perspective to the resident staff community. Moreover, out LGBT staff members are the best people to facilitate continuing interaction between heterosexual and LGBT people. Although sensitivity training provides a starting point to address homophobia and heterosexism, continual interaction is critical in breaking down prejudice (Rutgers President's Select Committee, 1989). Herek (1989) described an ex- posure effect to LGBT people: The frequency of contact a heterosexual person has with a LGBT person is highly correlated with levels of tolerance. Thus, out LGBT staff members provide a means for ongoing, direct staff contact, leading to prejudice reduction on behalf of staff members (Sanford & Engstrom, 1995).

Establishing a full-time resident staff position, hired and trained to deal primarily with issues of sexual orientation, is an excellent mechanism for staff development. Dubbed a sexual orientation peer adviser (SOPA), this individual would be responsible for staff development on issues of sexual orientation and would work with resident staff members to deal efficiently with issues of sexual orientation as they developed throughout the year. This has many advantages: a proactive stance against homophobia and heterosexism in residence halls; an identifiable person on staff to whom LGBT students may turn for help; an ultimate extension of institutional legitimacy to the equality of LGBT people; and the assurance of continuous interaction with LGBT persons. The SOPA could facilitate a coming out support group in the residence hall, work with residence staff to integrate issues of sexual orientation into their social and educational programming, and document homophobia. The SOPA position would be equal to an RA with the same remuneration and benefits.

RESIDENT ISSUES

Norm Generation: Creating a Supportive Community

Proactively establishing residence halls as places where LGBT people are welcome, valued, and affirmed is the most important way in which homophobia can be minimized. Staff members cannot expect incoming first-year students to change significantly from year to year, but they can define the norms and values of the community that the first-year students are entering. Characterizing the residential community as an inclusive space where difference is affirmed and explored can be established during move-in through the selection of a floor or residence hall theme, hall meetings, personal interactions, and written statements. Social and educational programs are options—workshops on human differences that include sexual orientation, antihomophobia workshops, movies with LGBT issues. Different types of visual stimuli can also be effective, including: bulletin boards celebrating significant days in LGBT history, and creation of information packets on homosexuality, bisexuality, and gender identification.

Coming Out Issues

Although many LGBT youth come out to themselves before arriving on campus, the process in which they share this aspect of their identity with those around them, including their family, friends, and peers, may be both liberating and traumatic. The most important aspect of students coming out for residence staff is preparation. Resident staff need information regarding coming out, patterns of sharing one's sexual identity, and the potential problems that develop if the coming out process is particularly difficult for an individual. To this end, resident staff must have the skills of crisis counseling: active listening, being nonjudgmental, the use of empathy, effective referrals, and reflective communication.

Support networks must also be in place for the resident and the resident staff member. For the resident, the residence halls should have formalized networks with psychological counseling on campus. If these mental health professionals are not prepared to deal with issues of sexual orientation in a client-centered, life- affirming manner, the Housing division must seek to change those programs and to make outside referrals for those residents who require and are able to afford private mental health services. Beyond professional support networks the LGBT or questioning resident should be given ways to develop social support. Thus, the staff should have updated information regarding student organizations, coming out support groups, and the resources on campus or in the general community regarding LGBT issues. For example, although the school may not have a coming out support group, the local PFLAG chapter may sponsor meetings where individuals who are just coming out can meet similarly situated individuals and connect in a safe space. In such situations, the resident staff member must also be supported. The staff member should be supported by other staff members and by her or his supervisor.

When one member of a residential community shares his or her nonheterosexual sexual identity, then the entire community is potentially affected. In such situations, it is essential that the resident staff member is engaged and in tune with "the vibes" of the resident community. The ways in which this changes the education and social development of the residents are dependent on the response of the resident staff member and the LGBT person coming out. Coming out offers a potential educational intervention, where residents may learn more about issues of sexual orientation and collaboratively build an inclusive community. However, before sponsoring educational programs, talk with the resident who has come out. The individual may feel targeted by programs and resent the extra attention: Perhaps she or he only told a few people and was not comfortable telling others. Being overly ambitious without identifying the student's comfort zone may further alienate her or him by outing the individual.

Harassment

An important procedure to establish in residence halls is documentation of homophobia and heterosexism. Most victimization goes unreported, so the needs of LGBT students are never recognized nor addressed. Thus, a step in preventing harassment is to make it an issue. Educational campaigns could include flyers, bulletin boards, speakers, posters, notes in mailboxes—any way to get the word out that harassment of any kind, whether on the basis of race, gender, or sexual orientation, is not acceptable and should be reported. Such a concerted effort will work to overcome student perception of institutional apathy and disinterest. In creating a harassment documentation project, it is important to have uniform standards of reporting, one center of information and clear lines of communication so reports are not lost. Moreover, protocols should be developed to determine appropriate responses to specific types of harassment.

The most common type of verbal harassment is the generalized derogatory comment about LGBT people. Such comments are ubiquitous. In a survey at Oberlin College, a small liberal arts college known for its supportive atmosphere for LGBT people, 87 percent of the campus had overheard negative comments about LGBT people (Norris, 1992). Only 25 percent of those who opposed such comments actually verbalized their objections. Whether or not there is a direct target of the offensive comment, it is imperative to confront such comments. Otherwise, the resident staff member implicitly approves of the comment, subverting the norms of an inclusive community. Others—both heterosexual allies and LGBT people in the closet—may oppose the comment but not feel comfortable confronting the individual (Norris, 1992).

If a staff member overhears a derogatory comment about LGBT people, she or he should talk to the individual. Although this may be done either in public or in private, a balance of the two is often the optimal solution. For example, while watching TV, a resident says that "fags and dykes" are disgusting. In public, the staff member could defuse the peer influence of the comment by confronting the individual and asking why her or she made the comment, what was meant by the comment, if he or she understood its implications, how it could affect others in the hall who may be LGBT or have relatives or friends that are LGBT. Publicly addressing the issue has the advantage of addressing the group dynamics and influence of homophobic or heterosexist remarks, but is limited by the potential to cast one person as "right" and another as "wrong." To prevent this dynamic, the resident staff member should address the comment publicly, then later follow up with the individual and talk about the situation in depth. The difference between intent and impact of words is an important concept for residents to master and comprehend. Although the person may have only meant *fag* as a general synonym of disapproval, explaining that its impact could be to target a specific group of people who have been the subject of historical oppression could alter the individual's perspective on using that word.

If verbal harassment is targeted to a specific individual and continuing or systematic, immediately assess escalation potential. First talk with the LGBT individual (or the person harassed because she or he is perceived a LGBT), assess their emotional state, and connect them with a support network (either professionally or socially). Next, discuss the situation with the perpetrator. Ask why she or /he did this, listen, and constructively challenge her or his rationale for targeting LGBT people. Affirm the notion of a supportive, educational, diverse community and provide information on sexual orientation. The crux of the issue is the fact that one member of the residential community took it upon himself or herself to disrespect another member of the community, that such an act constitutes a violation of community norms, and that such violations cannot be tolerated if all members are to be treated equally and have equal opportunity to flourish in the residential community. If appropriate, sanction the individual in an educational manner; they could maintain a bulletin board on LGBT issues; attend a workshop on LGBT awareness and write a report reflecting on the experience; meet with or volunteer for an LGBT organization; or participate in various community service opportunities.

Physical harassment should be treated the same ways in which physical assaults are handled: with severity and immediacy. The victim's physical and psychological welfare should be assessed, along with feelings of safety and security. If the perpetrator is known, the residence hall administrator should meet with both the victim and the perpetrator, review the standard of residential life (mutual respect, community living), outline the violations, and determine what solutions should be pursued. Although the specifics will change from circumstance to circumstance, it is essential that the administration act quickly and that there not be a presumption against the LGBT person.

BEYOND THE RESIDENCE HALLS

Ultimately, the psychosocial flourishing of LGBT, students requires a transformation of the entire university culture. Although this chapter has focused on residence halls, residential life does not exist in a vacuum, but is influenced by the students, staff, faculty, and administrators of the entire university, surrounding community, and geographic region as a whole. Hence, any comprehensive strategy for eliminating homophobia and heterosexism must broaden its focus to include curricular issues, social and community building interactions, police, health care, AIDS and HIV, and victimization issues. One cannot create an insular residential community impermeable to homophobic influences. New students, staff, and administrators constantly shape the fluid and transient populations of colleges and universities. Thus, the challenge is to create a solid foundation of core values and principles of equality and inclusiveness that guide the actions of the institution. With the ultimate goal to create an educational institution where each person is able to flourish and be free from systematic and unjust discrimination, beginning with residence halls seems a fitting place to commence building a place called home.

CHAPTER 8

Lesbian, Gay, and Bisexual Issues within the Greek Community

Douglas N. Case

Two segments of the college or university campus have reputations for being bastions of sexism, heterosexism and homophobia—male athletic teams and fraternities. Common characteristics of both are that they are exclusively male groups, are relatively heterogeneous, are composed of young adults who are still developing and exploring their sexual identity, and are groups where male bonding is central to the achievement of the group's purpose. In the process of male bonding, men frequently feel compelled to demonstrate their virility to the others in the group. Unless taught otherwise, young men have a tendency to equate masculinity with heterosexuality, male dominance, and the sexual objectification and conquest of women. Thus young men in their role as group members are likely to exhibit behavior that is much more sexist and homophobic than their individual personal attitudes. Such groups often falsely presume that all members are heterosexual, and homosexual or bisexual members of the group feel compelled to either remain silent or even express homophobic attitudes in order to hide their true identity.

This chapter will examine the experience of being a gay, lesbian, bisexual, or transgender (GLBT) member of a traditional Greek letter social organization and will also provide information about the emergence of fraternal organizations specifically for GLBT students and their allies. Strategies will be presented for developing educational programming to foster more tolerant attitudes within the Greek community toward members of the GLBT community.

GAY, LESBIAN, AND BISEXUAL MEMBERS OF TRADITIONAL FRATERNITIES AND SORORITIES

Virtually no published research exists on GLBT members of social fraternities and sororities. In an attempt to learn more about such students, the author developed a survey consisting of 32 multiple-choice and open-ended questions that was distributed to both alumni and current undergraduate members of social sororities and fraternities. The availability of the survey was publicized by announcements in various gay and lesbian publications, postings on GLBT and fraternity/sorority electronic mail discussion groups and newsgroups on the Internet, and referrals from other respondents. Over a period of 30 months during 1992 to 1995, slightly over 500 surveys were completed and returned, with a wide representation from various age groups and regions of the country. Because the respondents were self-selected, the survey results cannot be considered a true random sample; however, several conclusions seem clear from the data collected.

First, GLBT students join fraternities and sororities for similar reasons as heterosexual members, namely, to find friendship and camaraderie, as a social outlet, and to have a support group and sense of belonging. With few exceptions, sexual attraction was not a motivation for joining.

Second, in all likelihood the percentage of gay men who are in fraternities is similar to the percentage of male students on campus who are gay or bisexual. On average, the male respondents were able to confirm (from knowledge received either during or after college), that 5 to 6 percent of the membership of their chapters were gay or bisexual. Many speculated that 10 to 20 percent of their chapters were actually gay or bisexual, but it's impossible to determine the accuracy of such speculation.

Only about 10 percent of all of the total number of survey responses came from women. Some sampling considerations partially account for the low response from women. For example, some of the publications that announced the survey cater primarily to gay men. It's also quite possible that the difficulty in securing surveys from women is an indication that lesbian and bisexual women are less inclined to join social sororities than gay and bisexual men are to join fraternities. The women who did respond reported that they were able to confirm that 3 to 4 percent of their chapters' membership were lesbian and bisexual.

Third, the sexual identity of GLBT students is commonly still evolving during their college years, and a homosexual or bisexual identify often emerges later for women than men. Less than half of the men and only one out of eight women in the survey had a postpubescent sexual experience with a member of the same gender prior to entering college. About 60 percent of the men and less than 25 percent of the women self-identified as homosexual or bisexual at the time they joined their fraternity or sorority. By graduation, the homosexual or bisexual self-identification had increased to over 80 percent for the men and almost 50 percent for the women. Substantial numbers of both men and women went through a period of identifying as bisexual before identifying as gay or lesbian.

Fourth, GLBT Greek members tend to be high achievers within their organizations. Over 80 percent of the men and 60 percent of the women held an elected office or a major executive office in their chapters. (There was a gender difference in the percentage of respondents who had served as president of their chapters—22 percent of the men and 6 percent of the women.) The tendency toward "overachievement" may reflect a need of GLBT students for both self-validation and acceptance from the group.

Fifth, fraternities and sororities tend to discriminate against prospective members whom they perceive to be gay or lesbian. Although the membership selection procedures vary widely among organizations, a negative vote or rank-ing by a small number of members, or even a single member, can prevent a rushee (prospective member) from being extended a bid (invitation to join). Many of the surveys included stories of rushees being rejected because of mannerisms that caused members to question their sexuality. Likewise, if the chapter discovers that a pledge (pre-initiate) may be homosexual or bisexual, the member is likely to be summarily "blackballed" (dismissed as a probationary member) without an opportunity to respond to the suspicion. Sadly, more often than not, GLBT members did not object to such discrimination for fear that to do so would have raised questions about their own sexual orientation.

Sixth, a majority of GLBT members remained in the closet while they were in college, never revealing their sexual orientation to even a single member of their chapter. Only about 40 percent of the respondents voluntarily came out, that is, admitted their sexual orientation to one or more nongay members, and less than 10 percent voluntarily came out to the entire chapter. There is a pronounced generational trend in the data. Of those who graduated prior to 1980, only 12 percent ever revealed their sexual orientation to even a single member of their chapter.

Seventh, despite fears to the contrary, most GLBT fraternity and sorority *initiated* members receive a relatively supportive response from the majority of their members when they voluntarily reveal their sexual orientation. Coming out to fraternity/sorority brothers/sisters is not unlike coming out to one's own siblings. Although many will be initially uncomfortable with the revelation, they strive to become accepting. Acceptance by all is seldom universal, however, and a few members may avoid interaction with the GLBT member or express overtly homophobic attitudes. Likewise, just as some families disown a GLBT family member, some Greeks face ostracism, harassment, or expulsion when their homosexual or bisexual orientation is revealed. The probability of a nega-tive response is much greater if the member is involuntarily outed—whose sex-ual orientation is made known by rumor or discovery—than in those situations where the member personally shares the information with others on his or her own terms.

Eighth, chapters with openly gay/lesbian members risk being victims of homophobic reactions from other chapters. Even when chapters want to be supportive of members who are bisexual, lesbian, or gay, they are concerned about their reputation among other fraternities and sororities. In the competitive Greek community, rumors spread rapidly, and a chapter with a member who is known to be GLBT may find itself branded as the "gay fraternity" or "lesbian sorority." Such a reputation can have a harmful effect on membership recruitment. Hence, GLBT members may feel pressure to keep their sexual orientation hidden. The member must then make the decision of whether to comply with the desires of the group or to withdraw ("go inactive") in order to be free to have a more open lifestyle.

Finally, there are indications that fraternities and sororities are becoming more tolerant of people with different sexual orientations. Change is occurring slowly, but the surveys completed by undergraduates are peppered with encouraging stories. There appear to be significant regional differences, with the most tolerant attitudes being expressed by Greek students in the West and the least tolerant attitudes demonstrated by the chapters in the South. Although not yet a common occurrence, accounts of chapters pledging GLBT members who are open about their sexual orientation, of members taking dates of the same gender to chapter dances, of Greek students becoming involved in campus GLBT organizations, and of students who have come out being elected as presidents of their chapters bring hope for the future. The changing times also make it even more critical that Student Affairs professionals implement educational programming to prepare students for new realities.

FRATERNITIES AND SORORITIES FOR GLBT STUDENTS

In recent years, fraternities and sororities oriented toward gay, lesbian, and bisexual students have formed on college and university campuses. Their formation is similar to the emergence of new fraternities and sororities for Latino/a and Asian students. Much like the predominantly African-American fraternities and sororities, founded in the early 1900s, these organizations provide students the benefits of a fraternal membership in a culturally sensitive environment.

Delta Lambda Phi Fraternity was established in 1986 by Vernon L. Strickland III in Washington, D. C. The organization was formed to provide the opportunity for a fraternal experience for openly gay and bisexual men who might feel unwelcome in a traditional fraternity. The mission statement of the organization states:

Delta Lambda Phi is a National Social Fraternity for Gay, Bisexual, and all other men who wish to participate in an inclusive, mutually supportive Brotherhood. Through the experience of our traditions and through community service, we work together to enhance the quality of life of those who join with us by providing dignified and purposeful social and recreational activities. (Delta Lambda Phi, 1995)

The fraternity has an open membership policy and does not discriminate on the basis of race, color, creed, national origin or sexual orientation. Most of the members identify as gay or bisexual, although some chapters have initiated men who identify as heterosexual.

The operations and activities of Delta Lambda Phi are very similar to those of other fraternities except that most social activities are gay oriented, and many of the community service projects benefit the GLBT community or AIDS-related agencies. Chapters stress that the fraternity is not a sex club. Dating fellow initiates is discouraged, and national fraternity policy prohibits sexual intimacy between an initiate and a pledge.

By the fall of 1996, there were 21 active chapters of Delta Lambda Phi. Five chapters, including the Alpha Chapter in the District of Columbia, are city-based chapters; the remainder are chartered at a specific college or university campus. Only two have official chapter houses. Eleven of the 21 chapters are located in the western region of the United States.

The relationship between Delta Lambda Phi and the other fraternities on campus varies widely. On some campuses the organization is a full member of the Interfraternity Council (IFC), whereas on others there is no affiliation with the IFC. The degree of interaction with other fraternities and sororities depends on the Greek governance structure of the specific campus, the campus climate for GLBT students, and the desires of the chapter membership. Some chapters maintain a high campus visibility; others, particularly where members are not out or where there is a less tolerant campus climate, keep a lower profile. Although the involvement by Delta Lambda Phi in activities with traditional fraternities tends to be somewhat limited, the chapters generally maintain cordial relationships with the campus Greek community. It is not uncommon, however, for the groups to experience some degree of harassment by members of traditional fraternities, such as tearing down rush posters or calling the chapter's telephone number and leaving homophobic messages. Student Affairs professionals can be instrumental in enhancing the relationship between traditional fraternities and nontraditional fraternities—including Delta Lambda Phi and ethnic-based fraternities—by serving as a liaison and recommending opportunities for inclusion.

On some campuses the fraternity has encountered opposition from other GLBT campus organizations because of the perception that the group is modeled after a heterosexist institution or because fraternity members devote their time and effort to the fraternity instead of to the other GLBT organizations. Here, too, a Student Affairs professional can be helpful in helping the groups to understand their respective roles on campus and encouraging the organizations to embark on collaborative activities.

For more information about Delta Lambda Phi National Social Fraternity, contact the Delta Lambda Phi National Office, 1008 Tenth Street, Suite 374, Sacramento, CA 95814. Their telephone number is 1-800-587-FRAT, and their e-mail address is camerala@csus.edu. The executive director is Louis Camera.

Lambda Delta Lambda, an alternative sorority where women of all sexual orientations are welcome, was founded at the University of California at Los Angeles in 1988. Although there was a flurry of nationwide media attention when the organization was founded, the organization has not generated as much interest as Delta Lambda Phi. There are only a couple of active chapters and no national structure. The most active chapter currently appears to be the Beta Chapter at San Francisco State University. The organization's philosophies are:

to share experiences with others and create a network of women who are bound together by similar ideals. Goals include [providing] a safe, alternative, social environment, [eliminating] minority oppression, and [creating] lesbian and gay issue awareness on campus and in the community. (Lambda Delta Lambda bylaws)

For more information about Lambda Delta Lambda, contact Lambda Delta Lambda Sorority, Beta Chapter, Student Activities Office, San Francisco State University, 1600 Holloway Avenue, Room BUS 114, San Francisco, CA 94132.

EDUCATIONAL PROGRAMMING ON LESBIAN, GAY, AND BISEXUAL ISSUES FOR THE GREEK COMMUNITY

Programming on sexual orientation issues within the Greek community involves both challenges and opportunities. In 1990, the Association of Fraternity Advisors, recognizing the need to address the issue, adopted a "Resolution on Heterosexism within the Greek Community" (Association of Fraternity Advisors, 1990). The resolution encourages colleges and universities, as well as national/international fraternities and sororities, "to implement sexual orientation awareness, education, and sensitivity programs for the Greek community" and "to challenge Greek chapter or member behaviors or attitudes that are heterosexist in nature." The association has regularly sponsored workshops and published articles in its publications on sexual orientation issues to assist its members in acquiring skills to develop such educational programs. Unfortunately, as of this writing, only a handful of (inter)national fraternity and sorority organizations have addressed the issue by adopting membership policies explicitly prohibiting discrimination on the basis of sexual orientation, by conducting training workshops for staff, volunteer alumni and undergraduate members, or by publishing articles dealing with directly lesbian, gay, and bisexual issues in their (inter)national fraternity/sorority magazines.

A major challenge faced by educational programmers is resistance by students within the Greek community to even discuss homosexuality or bisexuality, because they think it is too sensitive or not applicable to them. Many Greek students would be reluctant to attend an optional educational program on sexual orientation issues because they are uncomfortable with the topic, are afraid that their attendance might fuel speculation about their own sexual orientation, or believe that they are not homophobic and therefore don't need to attend a "sensitivity training" session. This resistance is not unique to issues of sexual orientation. Student Affairs professionals and faculty who organize and facilitate programming on topics such as acquaintance rape and alcohol and drug abuse face similar challenges in sparking interest and getting students to attend educational programs. These obstacles can be overcome by strategic programming.

One advantage in developing programming for Greek students is that they are an accessible population. Every chapter has weekly chapter meetings where it is common to have programs presented, and the Greek governing and coordinating councils often plan a multitude of leadership conferences, retreats, and workshops. There are also a variety of regional leadership conferences where Greek leaders from participating campuses gather.

Until recently the programming specifically for Greek students on the topic of sexual orientation has been very limited. Most of the Greek educational programs fall into one of two categories—operational or current issues. Examples of operational topics are financial management, academic achievement, alumni relations, leadership development, goal setting, new member education, and development. Some of the current "hot topics" are hazing, risk management, alcohol and drug use and abuse, date and acquaintance rape, AIDS and other sexually transmitted diseases, eating disorders, and diversity issues. Note that most of the current issue programs deal with the reduction or prevention of behavioral problems. Often the timing of these programs is reactive. A tragedy, crisis, or controversy sparks interest. A student killed in an alcohol-related driving accident, a rape in a fraternity house, a hazing incident, a party theme with racist connotations can all become "teachable moments." A homophobic incident within the Greek community can likewise create an opportunity for educational programming. For instance, at the University of Akron, in the spring of 1996, a letter to the campus and city newspapers alleging that a gay student experienced discrimination by certain fraternities during the rush period resulted in an emergency meeting of fraternity and sorority presidents. The outcome of the meeting was the affirmation of the Greek community's policy of non-discrimination and the establishment of a task force (composed of Greek leaders, Student Affairs staff, faculty, and GLBT Student Union representatives) that developed a comprehensive year long series of educational programs for the Greek community on GLBT issues.

Three strategies can be employed to build attendance at sexual orientation educational programs: taking advantage of captive audiences, providing incentives for attendance, and incorporating the topic into more broad-based diversity programming. Greek organizations frequently sponsor meetings and programs where there are captive audiences, that is, where members are expected or required to attend. For example, Greek councils often sponsor Greek convocations, leadership retreats, and new member conferences. In 1994, the Western Regional Greek Conference took advantage of a captive audience by having Brian McNaught, a renowned speaker on GLBT issues, as a keynote general session speaker—inspiring many of the student leaders in attendance to sponsor similar programs on their own campuses.

Educational programmers for the Greek community have long successfully used competitions and awards as incentives for participation. Giving points toward significant Greek awards—such as an annual President's Cup for the most outstanding chapter—can be one way of increasing attendance at programs. Although programmers may encounter reticence to establishing programs specifically on sexual orientation issues, many Greek communities have come to recognize the importance of addressing diversity issues. Incorporating programs on GLBT issues, along with segments on racial, ethnic, religious, and disability issues, is one way of "getting your foot in the door" in a way more receptive to students. At the University of Southern California, the Greek community has formed a Diversity Encouragement Council (DEC), a peer organization that assists chapters in planning panels, speakers, films, and other programs dealing with a variety of diversity issues, including sexual orientation. One popular activity the DEC has facilitated has been "diversity exchanges," evening social and educational events typically between a fraternity and a sorority.

Panels, role-playing, and case studies are effective programming techniques for use with fraternity and sorority audiences. These educational tools provide opportunities for interaction and analysis. Particularly in programs for individual chapters, it is recommended that students be trained as peer facilitators, since some students may feel inhibited in openly discussing their own feelings attitudes if they feel that an administrator might be making judgments about their chapter based on their statements. Careful training of the peer facilitators is critical so that the facilitators are able to sensitively handle, in a non-confrontational way, hostile or controversial situations that may arise during the presentation.

Many colleges and universities have GLBT student speaker panels (usually coordinated under the auspices of the LGBT Campus Resource Center, GLBT student organization, the counseling center, or other Student Affairs offices) that are willing to make presentations to classes, residence halls, and student organizations. Because students can relate to their fellow students, these panels are a tremendous resource. The educational impact of the panels can even be especially powerful when it is possible to find a GLBT student who is a current or former fraternity or sorority member willing to serve as one of the panelists.

Role reversal exercises, where participants are asked to imagine what it is like to be gay, lesbian, or bisexual, are another effective educational technique. Included in Table 2 is the facilitator's guide to one such exercise that has been used effectively with residence hall, fraternity, and sorority audiences. This particular program combines both a GLBT student panel and a role reversal exercise. Users should feel free to change the order or vary the question format.

At leadership conferences and retreats, case studies can be a useful analytical tool to prepare students to deal with actual situations that might arise within the

Table 2
Gay/Lesbian Role Reversal Exercise

This is a summary of a program similar to one originally developed by the Coalition for Learning About and Understanding Homophobia and Biphobia at the University of California, Santa Cruz.

Stage One: The Role Play (30 to 40 minutes)

1. Participants wear name-tags with first names written in large bold letters so they can be read across the room, and they sit in a large circle so everyone can see one another. Facilitator(s) introduce themselves and explain the process. Tell the participants that for the next 30 to 40 minutes they will be gay or lesbian. Have them close their eyes for about 1 to 2 minutes and image what it is like to be GLBT. (Optional: Read a narration of what is like to be gay or lesbian in a "straight" world.)

2. Go around the circle with each participant introducing him/herself by saying, "Hi, I'm [name] and I'm [gay]," if the participant is a man, or "Hi, I'm [name] and I'm a [lesbian]," if the participant is a woman. If a participant feels too uncomfortable to do this, he or she can be excused or assigned to observe the exercise. Mention that the role-play does not specifically deal with bisexuality, although that topic can be discussed in Stage Two. The facilitators act as though they know the participants well and ask each participant one question in a conversational tone to have them respond to various situations. The situations should be made to seem as real as possible, so if the facilitator is familiar with a particular participant, he/she may wish to give the role-player a situation to which the person can relate.

Examples of questions/situations: How long have you been gay/lesbian? How did you know you were gay/lesbian? I understand that you decided to come out to your parents over Thanksgiving. How did that go? How do you meet other gay men and lesbians? You served in the navy. Obviously, you had to hide your sexual orientation to stay in. How did you feel about that? I know you're from a very religious background. How do you deal with your religion and who you are? Do you plan on adopting children or having children of your own? What is your experience as a lesbian/gay man of color? Your partner went home with you for the holidays. Did your family know that he/she was your lover or did you just pretend to be friends? I understand that you once attempted suicide as a teenager because you were ashamed of being gay/lesbian. Tell me about that. I've seen you and your partner walk across campus holding your lover's hand. Has anyone ever harassed you? You're in Alpha Beta Gamma. What is it like being gay/lesbian and being a member of a fraternity/sorority? Do any of your members know about your sexual orientation? If so, how did they react?

Processing: The facilitator may choose to pair up members of the audience and give them scenarios that involve them as partners. Try to ask follow-up questions. A common one is, "How did that make you feel?" The facilitator should make a note of any heterosexist responses so that myths can be dispelled during the discussion in Stage Two. Conclude by giving participants a chance to answer these questions: What is the best thing about being gay/lesbian? What is the worst thing about being gay/lesbian? After you've completed the role-play, tell the participants that they can now go back to being whoever they really are—gay, lesbian, heterosexual, or bisexual.

Table 2 (Cont'd)

Stage Two: Debriefing (15 to 20 minutes)

Ask participants for their reactions to the role-play. Discuss any situations of misinformation or examples of heterosexism that occurred in the role-playing. Include a brief discussion of bisexuality.

Stage Three: Questions and Answers (30 to 40 minutes)

In this segment, a panel of GLBT students answers questions from the participants. It is best if the panel is as diverse as possible including at least one gay man, lesbian, bisexual, transgender person, and person of color. Students tend to relate best with panelists who are fellow students. The facilitator may want to offer the option of submitting questions on note cards so that participants can have questions answered that they may be embarrassed to ask.

Stage Four: Wrap-up (10 to 15 minutes)

Give participants a chance to tell what they learned from the workshop. A "pass the gavel" format works well. Conclude with comments on the importance of the role of allies of GLBT people and how everyone can help to combat heterosexism.

Greek community involving matters of sexual orientation. The cases studies can be used in a workshop that deals specifically with GLBT issues or as part of a workshop that deals with broader issues such as diversity awareness or handling controversy within the chapter. A series of case studies developed by the author are included in Table 3. These can be easily modified and tailored for specific campus situations.

Another outstanding program, titled "Speak Your Mind" has been developed and implemented at the University of California at Irvine. The program is designed to be facilitated for a mixed audience, with approximately half being members of fraternities and sororities and the other half being members of campus GLBT organizations. The program is facilitated by four students—a fraternity member, a sorority member, a lesbian or bisexual female student, and a gay or bisexual male student. Student Affairs and/or counseling staff are available to provide support if needed. The participants are seated intermixed in concentric circles, with the facilitators standing in the center. After introductions and program instructions, a facilitator asks members of the GLBT community to respond to the question, "If there were something that you would like to never see happen or said again about your community, what would that be?"

Responses from Greek community members to the statements are permitted in this round. At the conclusion of the segment, the facilitator spends five minutes asking Greek students, "What did you just hear?" In the next round, a facilitator asks members of the Greek community what they would like never to see or hear again with regard to their community, followed by a similar chance

Table 3
Sample Greek Heterosexism Workshop Case Studies

CASE STUDY #1

Paul Boyd is a 23-year-old who decided to pledge a fraternity during the fall term. In addition to being older than a typical pledge, Paul is more mature, having served in the navy. One reason he selected Delta Omega Theta Fraternity was their progressive pledge education program. He wasn't interested in a pledge program where a 19-year-old might be ordering him around. Delta Omega Theta also had a reputation for having a superior intramural sports program and for having significant student government involvement—two of Paul's particular interests.

Paul immediately got very involved in the fraternity and was elected president of his pledge class. He was also a star player on the fraternity's football team, which finished in second place in the fraternity league. During a big brother/little brother retreat held three weeks before initiation, Paul revealed to those present that he was honorably discharged from the navy after acknowledging to his commanding officer that he is gay.

At the chapter meeting following the retreat, one of the brothers called for a "blackball" session, stating that he felt that homosexuality was "disgusting" and that no homosexuals should be allowed into the fraternity. According to the chapter's bylaws, only 3 negative votes are required to dismiss a pledge. Of the 44 secret ballots cast, 17 voted to blackball Paul. Paul's big brother informed him of the decision and confirmed that the sole reason for his dismissal appeared to be his homosexuality. After the other members of his pledge class learned of the situation, all 12 members of the pledge class quit in protest, although 4 were later convinced by their big brothers to return.

A reporter for the campus newspaper, who lives on the same residence hall wing as one of the pledges who quit, learns of the situation and decides to investigate it for a story.

1. You are the chapter president of Delta Omega Theta. Outline the steps you would take to handle this situation.

2. You are the Interfraternity Council president. The reporter from the campus newspaper calls and gives you the details of what has happened. The reporter asks, "What is the IFC going to do?" How would you respond?

CASE STUDY #2

Assume you are a member of Gamma Rho Kappa and (depending on your gender) are either the big brother or big sister to Chris. One of the exercises in your new-member education program is for each little brother/sister to have a discussion with his or her big brother or sister to discuss the true meaning of the fraternity's/sorority's creed. You and Chris are having your assigned discussion, and you are impressed with Chris's ability to understand and apply the creed to daily life situations. The three tenets expressed in the creed of Gamma Rho Kappa are fidelity, charity, and trust. Chris gives you a specific example of what each tenet means to him/her. When Chris comes to the final tenet, trust, Chris tells you that over the course of the semester he/she has developed a high level of trust in you that he/she feels comfortable sharing some very personal information that has never been shared with anyone else before. Chris then proceeds to tell you that he/she has recently come to the realization that he/she is gay/lesbian. You never had any

Table 3 (Cont'd)

hint of Chris's sexual orientation, so this comes as quite a surprise. Chris indicates that self-acceptance has been a struggle and that he/she is relieved to be able to talk with someone about the matter. Chris wonders whether any others should be trusted with this information. If you were faced with this situation, how do you think you would respond? What counsel would you give to Chris?

for the GLBT students to echo what they have heard. In the next portion of the program, anyone can ask a question to be answered by someone from the other community. In addition, the facilitators can ask questions to members of either community to follow-up on statements that have been asked. After the question/answer period has expired, participants are asked to close their eyes while the facilitators ask questions designed to get the participants to reflect on what they have just experienced and what they can do to help create a more harmonious and inclusive campus climate. There should be time afterward for the participants to mingle and continue the discussion on an individual level.

In developing programming on the issue of sexual orientation, another important constituency to involve is the volunteer alumni who serve in advisory roles to the chapters. Most of the time, it will be the chapter adviser that the students seek first for guidance when an internal matter arises, such as dealing with the homosexuality or bisexuality of a member. The Office of Fraternity and Sorority Relations at the University of California at Los Angeles has developed an ongoing Chapter Advisor Education Series to educate advisers on con-temporary campus issues and university resources. In the spring of 1995, as part of the series the office organized an excellent and well-received program titled "The Hidden Membership" dealing with the presence of GLBT members within chapters. Panelists included an openly gay staff member from the Office of Residential Life, a gay UCLA undergraduate member of a fraternity, and the author of this chapter.

Through strategic educational programming, Student Affairs staff and faculty members can help to change the homophobic and heterosexual culture of college social fraternities and sororities. In the process, the organizations can come closer to fulfilling the ideal of sisterhood and brotherhood.

CHAPTER 9

Coming Out/Coming Home: Black Gay Men on Campus

Michael J. Dumas

I cannot go home as who I am. When I speak of home, I mean not only the familial constellation from which I grew, but the entire black community: the black press, the black church, the black academicians, the black literati, and the black left. I cannot go home as who I am and that hurts me deeply.

—Joseph Beam (1986, 231)

As black gay men, we live fractured lives, along fault lines created by race, class, and sexual oppression. But we also live lives of struggle and resistance, in opposition to those forces of domination allied against our black male bodies that would dare love other male bodies. As an educator and researcher on collegiate culture, the primary space in which I act is the college campus. My concern in this personal/public project is with the lived experiences of black gay students; that is, how I/they/we construct meaning within any space on the campus and in relation to campus spaces. Broadly, this includes knowledge of self as a person and as a social and political being and consciousness produced through collective processes of dialogue and action.

In this chapter, I introduce Daryl Jones (not a real name), one of the students within a community of lesbian, gay, bisexual, and transgender (LGBT) people of color at a large public university in the midwestern United States. Most of our discussion is centered on coming out issues, since these are emergent concerns for Daryl as he makes decisions about his identity within the college community. I also critique dominant (white) discourses of coming out, suggesting that for many of us they only lead from one closet to another. Finally, I offer several implications for practice and present some recommendations that might help in our work with black gay college students. Although my analysis cannot be extended unproblematically to other student populations, the themes I address here are relevant in consideration of the experiences of black lesbian and bisexual women and other LGBT people of color.

TALKING WITH DARYL JONES

I met Daryl at the first meeting of a new campus organization for LGBT people of color. Skin the color of caramel, Daryl is an attractive 18-year-old first-year student from Detroit, where he grew up in what he characterized as a nice, middle-class city neighborhood, just a couple blocks away from a "bad" neighborhood. He has had little interaction with white people in his life; a single child of a single mother, he lived in a black neighborhood and attended predominantly black schools and a black church.

"I Had a Little Mark on My Neck"

Daryl came out to his mother this past summer in a teary "confessional." She had initiated the conversation, questioning his friendship with another male, who was in fact his boyfriend. "She asked me why I was hanging out with this gay guy; I just acted like I didn't know he was gay," Daryl explains. But then came *the* question, and since Daryl refuses to lie to his mother, the truth came out. She responded by invoking biblical indictments of homosexuality, interrogating Daryl to the extent that at one point he actually apologized for being gay. The religious assault was somewhat ironic, if not inconsistent; Daryl exhibits more of a commitment to his faith than she does. "She doesn't even go to church," he says. "I go with my grandmother."

Daryl returned home a few weeks ago for his mother's wedding. It was an intimate affair, in their own living room. Intimate enough, in fact, that his mother noticed the mark on his neck. I digressed for a few minutes to talk about his boyfriend, whom I already know, and we laugh about how small the community is. This digression is important. For all of us, and especially those just beginning to come out, talking openly about same-sex attractions and affections serves to validate our sexuality.

Pedagogically, talking about our sexual and affectional attraction to other men helps us become more conscious of how natural our desires are and how much we are entitled to love and companionship. I tease Daryl so we can tap into a certain happiness, an emotion that acts in opposition to the destructive emotions of guilt, shame and fear. Giddiness over boyfriends is not simply about joy but also about learning to resist heterosexist domination.

I didn't ask Daryl if he had hoped his mother would notice the mark on his neck, if he had intentionally *not* worn a turtleneck that day. Could the hickey have been a mark of resistance, a way to force some small amount of acknowledgment? Daryl loves his mother and hopes that one day she will understand.

For now, he's simply trying to avoid confrontation. He can't afford to live on his own this summer, so he'll be back at home in Detroit. Last summer, after he came out, she restricted his use of the phone and car. "It's her house and her rules." Daryl can only hope that, come May, the rules will have changed.

But for now, the site of the campus provides a distance from that which he has known: home, family, community. Student organizations, residence halls, and classrooms all provide spaces in which to tentatively explore new interests, identities, and affiliations outside of parental or community view. In the safety of his dorm room (at least when his roommate is gone), Daryl can be affectionate with his boyfriend; the very next day, he can go home to Detroit and enjoy time with family. The distance between home and campus becomes the distance between the warmth of that which is familiar and the desire to recognize a self we do not yet know.

"All Those Doubts Started Coming Back into My Head"

The significance of faith in Daryl's life cannot be overstated. To the extent that being a Christian provides joy for Daryl, it is also the source of much pain and frustration:

This past week, I've noticed, I'll be in the shower, and then I'll think "Thou shalt not lay with man as thou dost with woman" or something like that, and it's like popping into my head, and I'm like, is that my conscience or is that like—I don't know what it is. I don't feel guilty about it yet, but I could see feeling guilty about it. I really struggle with that.

Daryl's struggle is a very active resistance against his internalized notion of homosexuality as sin. On an intellectual level, he recognizes that the Bible is inspired by God but written by humans, with their own fallibility, and in specific historical moments, in which sexuality was understood and expressed quite differently than in contemporary society. He also points out that the canon has gone through multiple translations, so that it is difficult to know which interpretation is correct. "I'm not doubting God," Daryl stresses. "I'm doubting man. The Bible is good, I think. You just have to realize it was written by man."

If it were only a question of hermeneutics, Daryl could easily resolve conflicts between faith and sexuality. But being a Christian for Daryl is about sustaining a relationship with his God, family, and a community of faith. The black church, it must be remembered, has never been simply a religious body. It is also a space in which black people form supportive community structures and develop spiritual and material tools for survival in an antiblack world (Gordon, 1997). Daryl never speaks of abandoning the church or his faith. Instead, he struggles to locate the source of his own homophobia:

I'm becoming more and more comfortable with who I am. And I was comfortable with who I was before my mother found out, and then it's like after she found out and said all that religious stuff, all those doubts started coming back into my head. That's one realization I've come to: Any bad feelings I have come from outside; they are from outside forces. And that's where I found comfort before, because I didn't feel guilty feeling that way I didn't feel guilty.

Daryl's understanding that his negative feelings originate in the external sphere provides for him the consciousness that the problem is not within his own body. Still, he admits that the pressure to ingest guilt and shame is often more than he can bear:

But then, I mean, we're influenced. We're easily influenced. Even if you have a strong will, you can't deny that the world influences you. If everybody around you is saying that it's wrong, you're going to start thinking that the things that you're doing are wrong. And I'm not the most strong-willed person, so if my mother, who is very, very influential in my life, and my religion, which is also influential—just those two things, and those aren't the only things saying it's wrong—but just those two things, that's enough to plant a seed within me of guilt, saying that maybe this is wrong.

Daryl's struggle reveals the need for a pedagogy that will provide strength when we are weak. I refuse to believe he doesn't have a will strong enough to resist domination. Rather, I believe he needs—we need—to develop ways to understand our existence as black gay men that allow us to challenge, with a fierce love, those in our communities who would negate our lives.

"I Was Looking for a Little Bit More"

Daryl and I spent much of our time talking about coming out on campus. For most black gay men, and for Daryl, race acts to determine, or at least influence, how we experience coming out, from choices we make about the spaces in which we come out to how we envision what gay identity will mean in our lives. Early in September Daryl saw the flyer announcing a new supportive, informative, and social group for all LGBT people of color. Not one to join groups, he decided to attend because "I didn't have any friends here who I could talk to about these things." The campus does have several groups, but "there were no *black* people in those other groups," Daryl points out. "They were all white, not that there's anything wrong with that." In fact, Daryl says, he would have been comfortable in the general campus organization if it had simply been more diverse. "I was looking for a little bit more," he says, "for people like me." He also acknowledges that he was looking for other men to date and that he is generally not attracted to white men: "It comes from pride. I admire our characteristics; the way we look is beautiful to me. Their look is not attractive to me. But it doesn't mean I might not fall in love with a white man if that's who I love, but in initial attraction, I prefer black men, our features, strength, nobility. I think we're just a beautiful people."

The summer before he came to college, Daryl attended a few meetings of a Detroit group for black gay youth. He discussed with me his decision to participate in that group and tentatively articulates the significance of race in his search for spaces to come out. "I wanted to be around more gay people. I just wanted to meet other people, other black people. I guess it's the way you're raised and how you are. I guess you look for people who are like you, and you're more comfortable with people who are like you, for whatever reason."

After much more dialogue, Daryl acknowledged that his discomfort around white people may lead to changes in his behavior, including self-censoring of language. We talked about a few white people we know who are "cool with black people," but haunting questions remain: Is this white person talking down to me? What do they really think about black folks? Can I *really* trust them?

OUTING THE WHITENESS OF GAY DISCOURSE

Daryl spoke of his need for familial relations with other black people. During our discussion about coming out in the dorm, he expressed an interest in how the two (black) guys next door might respond if they were to find out. Thinking it was curious that he only mentioned his black floormates, I followed up:

M: Who lives on the other side of you?

D: Two white guys.

M: Hmm. I'm wondering why you didn't mention them.

D: Well, I don't care if white people know, but I don't know why I don't care. Maybe it's because the black guys are my people. I mentioned them because I would probably be more hurt if I was condemned by them than the other guys. Also, even though the black community is so big here, I'm worried that it will get around, and then my people will turn against me. I wouldn't want to be alienated from the black community. Then you really are alone.

Race matters here both in Daryl's desire to maintain humanity in the eyes of black people and in his ambivalence toward maintaining relationships with his white neighbors. However alienated Daryl may presently feel, he would indeed *really* be alone if he were regarded as less than human in the eyes of other black students on campus.

Black gay men and lesbians are situated differentially than white gay men and lesbians in relation to homophobia. Our investment in ending homophobia may be to strengthen our connections to other black folks and to affirm a space within black struggle. White gay men, especially middle-class and nonethnic men, tend to express their desires more individually (Monteiro & Fuqua, 1995). In Rhoads's (1994a) study, a collective "queer" identity becomes important, but this is still an identity that for black gay men individualizes them in relation to other black people.

Too often, oppressions are discussed as if they exist individually, as constructs of domination occupying completely separate spaces than other forms of domination. Sears (1995), for example, in an article titled "Black-Gay or

Gay-Black?" characterizes black gay men as "caught in the cross fire between allegiance to their racial heritage and to emerging gay communities" (p. 147). Even in this discourse that suggests that we are equally one and the other, black and gay exist in separate, conflictual spheres. I'm beginning to find this explanation wanting as I interview black gay men who have never lived one life in a black community, and another in a (white) gay community. More commonly, these men grew up within black communities and struggle to make sense of their sexuality within that cultural context (Monteiro & Fuqua, 1995). Their sexuality does not exist in binary opposition to their blackness. Rather, the conflict is with integration of sexuality into blackness. The difference here may seem subtle, but it is significant enough to abandon language that seems to decontextualize oppression and almost seems to accept the duality as given, implying that as an out gay person one should somehow be affiliated with a white gay community.

I am not trying to propose one essential black gay identity that is more ideal than any other. Nor am I suggesting that black gay men should consider race more important than sexuality. Rather, I advocate the radical idea that our identities are inextricably interrelated. As Seidman (1993) explains, "Individuals do not have a core gay identity around which race or class add mere social nuance. Rather, individuals are simultaneously gay, male, African-American, Latino, or working-class, each identification being shaped and shaping the others" (121). To speak of the simultaneity of identity is to acknowledge the black gay body, rejecting the quantitative notion that one identity is simply an addition to the other. We also bypass the seductive dualistic trap of measuring blackness and gayness against each other.

I find useful Phelan's (1977) reinterpretation of the meaning of coming out. Phelan, in her work on lesbians, "replaces the essentialist view of 'coming out' as a 'process of discovery' with an anti-essentialist view of 'coming out' as 'self-creation.'" Self-creation implies that we can develop our own ways of coming and being out, collectively and as individuals. These new creations do not exist outside the context of current discourses, social constraints, or material realities, but may be shaped against or in spite of them. In any case, the challenge is to engage in a self-conscious praxis of identity, in which coming out necessarily entails risk, conflict, and experimentation.

SUPPORTING BLACK GAY COLLEGE STUDENTS

For Daryl Jones, what has been important is finding a community. The campus organization for lesbian, gay, and bisexual students of color becomes important as a site of cultural production in which students find support in the process of self-creation. Students in the group should be encouraged to dialogue about their struggles to make meaning and to share with each other ways in which they've learned to resist domination in their own lives. Collectively, within this group, and within discussions specifically among black gay students, we might foster creation of a critical consciousness (Freire, 1970).

Clearly, organizations specifically for LGBT people of color should be supported and nurtured. Simultaneously, mainstream LGBT and racial/ethnic student organizations should initiate their own efforts to combat racism, sexism, homophobia, and other forms of oppression. The impetus should not be the presence or absence of lesbian, gay, and bisexual people of color in the respective organizations. Rather, students should act based on shared values of justice and a commitment to coalition building. Certainly, we cannot, nor should we, impose our values on students. Still, we can influence students through our actions and through engaging them in critical dialogue.

Many LGBT students of color may be more likely to affiliate with racial/ethnic student organizations. LGBT Campus Resource Centers and student organizations might do well to develop liaisons with offices and student groups that primarily serve students of color. The goal here is to serve as a resource to functional areas and racial/ethnic student groups, assisting them in addressing the needs and concerns of LGBT students of color. To be clear, I believe that LGBT groups have a responsibility to serve LGBT students of color. However, as I have stressed throughout this chapter, these students may not wish to participate in predominantly white organizations and activities. We need to find ways to make it safe for them to come out wherever they are, in ways that feel true for them.

"Multicultural," "multiethnic," and "minority" affairs offices must bear much of the responsibility. Staff should actively seek ways to support LGBT students of color through relevant educational and social programming and initiation of ally programs. Some events might be co-sponsored with the LGBT Campus Resource Center or campus group, but other activities should be initiated and sponsored by the multicultural office alone or in conjunction with professors and administrators who are broadly respected by students of color. One such activity might be dialogues or workshops specifically intended to bring together all students of color for discussion on racial and sexual identities.

At the end of one of our interviews, Daryl emphasized the impact of our discussions on his own thinking: "It's kind of stimulating, because I've thought of things I didn't think of before. When you talk about things, you really have to think. And sometimes you realize your thought pattern has changed in a matter of minutes. That's really stimulating for me." As educators and administrators, we need to begin acting to help black gay students in their own processes of self-creation. At the same time, we should continue to challenge our own thinking about how we engage in this praxis.

CHAPTER 10

Negotiating the Subtle Dance: Unique Challenges Confronting Lesbian, Gay, Bisexual, and Transgender Graduate Students

Timothy M. Matheney

Graduate students, whether they are law students or Ph.D. candidates in anthropology, encounter similar challenges. At both small private universities and large national research institutions, graduate students often struggle with funding their education, fulfilling program requirements, and finding a job after they earn their degree. Besides these universal experiences, however, lesbian, gay, bisexual, and transgender (LGBT) graduate students confront a unique set of challenges.

While LGBT graduate students are benefiting from much less hostile campus climates in recent years (D'Emilio, 1992), they can still be found performing, as one of the informants for this study contended, a subtle dance. In citing the phrase, Andrew,[1] who is pursuing his Ph.D. in a behavioral science, explained that his subtle dance involves trying to discern whether his sexual orientation is an issue with faculty, administrators, or peers. When it appears that being openly gay is a problem with someone, he'll avoid that particular professor's course or seek out friends in other social circles. For Bjorn, a Ph.D. candidate, the subtle dance involves the issue of the people with whom he shares his sexual identity. He very carefully avoids public disclosures that he is bisexual, preferring to come out to friends very selectively. Fiona, who is earning a master's degree, experiences the subtle dance when her parents visit: Her father does not know she is a lesbian.

LGBT graduate students are quite capable of negotiating the subtle dance. Most have been coping with issues of sexual orientation for many years. Yet as long as society's heterosexist presumption persists, they will face distinct problems. University administrators and faculty, many of whom are already easing the way of LGBT students, are uniquely positioned to enable sexual minority graduate students to thrive intellectually and personally during their graduate years. To facilitate this, I will offer suggestions on the experiences of LGBT students in universities about which I was informed by the literature, by interviews I conducted with LGBT students, and by my own experiences as a graduate student.

Creating an LGBT-positive graduate school environment should be a priority for administrators and faculty for a number of reasons. First, prejudice against LGBT people is a persistent problem. A Department of Justice report cited by D'Augelli (1989b) found that lesbians and gay men are the most frequent targets of hate crime in the United States. A 1990 poll of 128 four-year colleges and universities found that of the colleges reporting acts of intolerance on their campuses, sexual orientation accounted for the intolerance more than either race or ethnicity (cited in Sherrill & Hardesty, 1994).

Second, administrators and faculty should keep in mind that the experiences of graduate students while pursuing their degrees have consequences that extend beyond their commencement exercises. Graduate school is a particularly important time for the socialization of persons pursuing careers in medicine, law, academia, school administration, and business, among many other fields. As Friskopp and Silverstein (1995) contend in their study of gay and lesbian experiences at the Harvard Business School, "[T]he on-campus lessons heterosexuals learn about what it means to be gay in business and how the campus administration treats gay students are the models they take with them into the business world" (37). If graduate students see homophobia tolerated during their professional socialization, they will be more likely to tolerate it once they have graduated. Friskopp and Silverstein's (1995) study offers some evidence that administrators and faculty can make a difference. At the Harvard Business School, "the administration itself has initiated a number of policy changes that support those who are openly gay. As a result, many of those who have attended Harvard Business School in the 1990s are less fearful about being gay at work and are convinced that being out holds more benefits than disadvantages for their professional careers" (42).

CREATING A SAFE CLASSROOM

During the initial years of most graduate programs, the classroom is the locus of activity. Faculty instructors can make a significant difference in the lives of their LGBT students by taking affirmative steps to create a positive classroom environment. Instructors should begin with using appropriate terminology in class. For example, the terms *gay* and *lesbian* are preferred over *homosexual*; *partner*, *spouse*, or *significant other* are recommended in place of the gender-presumptive terms *husband* and *wife*. J. Smith (1995) notes that graduate faculty have primary impact on the safety felt by students who are deciding when and how to come out by discouraging discriminatory remarks and creating a safe space that provides overt evidence that (LGBT) students are accepted and appreciated.

Instructors can also declare that their classroom is a safe space for LGBT students by including readings on LGBT topics on their syllabi as well as by accepting sexual minority issues as legitimate subject matter for papers and theses. In general, Fiona, who herself looks forward to a career in higher education, has found that "doing these papers on queer topics" has been rewarding, but she finds she is forced to do "double the work that someone else might do." She has found that most of her professors lack background in LGBT research and theory, so "I have to build up everything starting from vocabulary all the way up to my main theoretical argument." In one class where she submitted a paper utilizing Queer Theory, her professor "blasted my paper in class for about twenty minutes, then finally said, 'You got an A.'" The professor is "very traditional, very old school. But she was very receptive to learning. She said she didn't understand it, but she wanted to learn." Department chairs should support the efforts of faculty and students—by providing travel and conference funds and funds for visiting professors, for example—to learn more about LGBT topics, Queer Theory, and related topics.

WHEN THE GRADUATE STUDENT TEACHES

When the graduate student is on the opposite side of the teacher's desk, the issues are rather different. All graduate students, regardless of sexual orientation, should be attentive to the use of negative stereotyping and derogatory comments in their classroom. Experienced and capable faculty and administrators should train graduate student instructors and teaching assistants (TAs) to respond appropriately in these situations.

As college instructors and TAs, graduate students are forced to negotiate a particularly subtle dance over the appropriate level of self-disclosure in their classes. Opffer (1994) states a strong case in favor of being out to one's students. She argues that educational researchers have found that self-acceptance and self-disclosure are particularly relevant to the classroom setting. Coming out, she says, "is essential to the mental health of teachers and students, can enhance both teaching and learning, can facilitate interpersonal and intercultural understanding, as well as provide accurate information and counter negative stereotypes. By coming out, lesbian and gay teachers can serve as positive role models and provide experientially based knowledge about lesbian and gay culture" (300).

An openly gay or lesbian instructor might be a powerful role model to a student struggling with his or her sexual identity. Opffer (1994) notes that their out instructor might be the first open LGBT person they know who is a healthy, productive professional.

Faculty and administrators should discuss appropriate levels of self-disclosure with TAs under their charge. In general, though, being open about one's sexual orientation appears to be the most optimal situation. Faculty and administrators can assist in this process by helping graduate students develop appropriate ways for coming out in the classroom. They might connect the graduate students with other openly LGBT instructors or provide them with appropriate reading materials. In her research, Opffer (1994) found that most of the college instructors in her study came out as a result of teaching lesbian or gay subject matter, whereas others addressed the issue in more casual discussion of current events, relationships, or philosophy.

My own experience in coming out in the classroom was very positive. After a great deal of thought about whether or not I should disclose my sexual orientation, I concluded that since there were no openly bisexual, gay, or lesbian faculty in my field at the university, it was important that my students encounter an "out of the closet" instructor. I chose to wait until I had a chance to get to know my students—and them me—without my sexual orientation being a factor: I was performing my own subtle dance. In the course of a discussion on teaching about varying family structures several weeks into the semester, I explained to the class that as a gay man my own family would not fit the traditional model. The students in the class might have been a bit surprised, but my self-outing did not affect my rapport with them. I was particularly pleased when a Muslim student approached me after class, thanking me for being open.

Bjorn, who is nearing completion of his doctoral program, is more reluctant to share his sexual identity with students. "I can see that some [undergraduates] whom I'm supervising might have some problem with my bisexuality, and it would affect our relationship." He points, in particular, to a religiously devout student who was experiencing personal problems. If she were aware of his bisexuality, Bjorn insists, she would not have sought his help. On the other hand, Bjorn has come out to a student who he knew is gay and undergoing counseling for personal and sexual orientation issues. Administrators and faculty can help LGBT graduate students make informed and situation-sensitive decisions about coming out in the classroom through a frank and open discussion of the topic.

MENTORING

The nature of graduate school places tremendous importance on the role of mentors in the lives of graduate students. Networking in a particular field, refining a research agenda, and negotiating university bureaucracies are facilitated by caring mentors. Fortunately, an LGBT graduate student's potential for finding a gay or lesbian or LGBT-friendly faculty advocate is much greater than it was two or three decades ago. As D'Emilio (1992) notes, "In 1970 there was not one openly gay or lesbian college professor in America" (133). Now, many institutions claim one or more openly gay or lesbian faculty members and many LGBT-positive faculty.

But even if an LGBT student experiences difficulty with finding appropriate mentoring on his or her campus, national professional groups are a valuable source of support and assistance. Faculty and administrators can assist LGBT graduate students by connecting them with the lesbian/gay caucuses in professional groups like the American Sociological Association, the Modern Language Association, the American Historical Association, and the American Educational Research Association. Now, most professional associations offer active gay caucuses (D'Emilio, 1992).

RESEARCH ISSUES

Despite the progress of the last 25 years, social and political pressures continue to keep some gay and lesbian faculty members in the closet and "discourage them, as well as graduate students, from doing [scholarly] work on homosexuality" (D'Emilio, 1992, 134). Graduate students seeking to conduct research on LGBT topics need the open support and encouragement of faculty and administrators. They need to be assured that their scholarship is considered a legitimate pursuit: And indeed it is important. As D'Emilio (1992) notes, "The expansion of scholarly production is a critical piece of any strategy for equality. Information, education, and ideas are powerful levers for social change, and as we have more information, we will be progressively empowered to act in the world" (135).

Yet at least one researcher, D'Augelli (1989b), is not optimistic about the prospects for such change. "Few faculty conduct research on lesbians and gay issues, and seldom represent a critical mass on any particular campus to initiate change" (p. 128). Even interested faculty may steer away from taking up LGBT research topics since they fear being labeled lesbian or gay, regardless of their actual sexual orientation. For the same reasons, they may tend to shy away from including lesbian and gay material in their teaching and fail to strongly support graduate students interested in pursuing LGBT topics. LGBT and LGBT-positive faculty need to exercise leadership in "carving out" a place for research on gay and lesbian issues in the academy; otherwise, "in such a power vacuum, top academic administrative leaders can define the limits of 'truth' by legitimizing or delegitimizing the concerns of lesbians and gay men" (D'Augelli, 1989b, 128).

From his experiences in graduate school, Andrew is convinced that many researchers are in fact dissuaded from pursuing sexual orientation research questions because of the stigma attached to bisexual, gay, and lesbian topics. He notes that when researchers allow their ethnicity or socioeconomic backgrounds to inform their work, they are affirmed by the academic world. "I feel like [bringing] my background as a gay man into research and scholarship hasn't been encouraged," Andrew said. "In fact, it's been discouraged and not seen as legitimate areas for research or as something that would assist me in my career path."

Other students expressed concerns about the stigma attached to the study of LGBT topics. Bjorn, who looks forward to conducting some research on LGBT issues, worries that researchers pursuing such topics are immediately pegged as solely "gay or lesbian researchers." Bjorn argues, "I think there should be a place for researchers to bring in their sexual orientation viewpoint into their research, but nobody seems to be doing that." He sees researchers at two extremes: There are those known as strictly "gay/lesbian/bisexual researcher[s]" and those who "just ignore the issues completely." Andrew insists that his interest in LGBT research topics is "a piece of the puzzle for me, but it's not the large picture." Andrew says, "It's a piece that I won't exclude from what I do as other people might, but it certainly isn't the central focus." Whether as a researcher or as a person, Bjorn maintains, "I don't think that's all that defines me is my sexual orientation." Tenured faculty, particularly those who are leaders in their disciplines, could help perpetuate better scholarly identities by welcoming and valuing research on LGBT issues from all scholars, not just LGBT researchers.

VALUING LGBT STUDENTS AS A SOURCE OF DIVERSITY

Just as the advancement of knowledge will benefit from greater diversity in academia, administrators and faculty have much to benefit by promulgating LGBT-positive policies in their graduate programs. LGBT graduate students are a rich source of diversity who can offer distinctive voices on a variety of issues, not simply lesbian and gay studies topics. Rarely, though, are LGBT students recognized and rewarded for their struggles with anti-gay prejudice and discrimination. "Queer students," according to Fiona, remain "the invisible minority" on many campuses. She attributes her own difficulties in adjusting to graduate school to a lack of institutional support. While her program offered special assistance to students of a minority race or ethnicity, its office of minority affairs never addressed problems encountered by members of a sexual minority.

Dan, another master's degree student, expressed disappointment that neither his program nor the university recognizes being LGBT as the basis for minority status in some situations. He particularly believes LGBT students should be eligible for some minority scholarships, as some universities have begun to do.

LGBT GRADUATE STUDENT GROUPS

LGBT graduate student groups, while somewhat different in function than an undergraduate LGBT group, provide important social and professional support. Such groups, often formed with the assistance of a university's LGBT Campus Resource Center, help LGBT graduate students connect socially and support one another professionally. LGBT graduate student groups in the United States pursue diverse missions: Some primarily organize social events and provide the means for networking, while others are service oriented. The LGBT student group at the Harvard Law School, for example, serves the LGBT community by providing research assistance to individual attorneys and advocacy groups working to further the rights of LGBT people and people with HIV. They have also organized public speeches and discussions on such topics as the experience of being an out lawyer and gay parenting. Faculty and administrators can encourage such groups by making office space and meeting rooms available and by providing funding comparable to that of other student organizations. Faculty and administrators can also demonstrate their commitment to an LGBT-friendly environment by attending the groups' activities and recognizing their contributions in official university publications.

THE EVOLVING NEEDS OF GRADUATE STUDENTS

As J. Smith (1995) so appropriately notes, university administrators, staff, and faculty should recognize that students at different points in their graduate education have widely differing needs. LGBT people applying to graduate school primarily need information. They need to be able to make an informed decision about whether a particular university would be a comfortable place in which to live and work. University staff responsible for admissions should be prepared to answer questions about the availability of LGBT-friendly housing, whether the university offers domestic partner benefits, the climate of the campus and area in which it is located, and the university's explicit anti-discrimination policies. Universities can prepare summary documents to inform LGBT applicants about these issues. Admissions personnel can similarly develop networks of LGBT graduate students to enable applicants visiting campus to get some firsthand observations.

Admissions staff might also refer potential applicants to *The Gay, Lesbian, and Bisexual Students' Guide to Colleges, Universities, and Graduate Schools* (Sherrill & Hardesty, 1994). For that volume, the authors surveyed LGBT students at 189 colleges and universities. The book includes information about the climate for LGBT students in a number of graduate schools.

Continuing graduate students, while still from time to time needing basic information, are more likely to value assistance in negotiating the university bureaucracy. Those LGBT graduate students with partners may need help in qualifying for spousal benefits like health insurance, access to married students' housing, recreational facility use, and even library privileges. Graduate students in their first or second year might also call on university administrators for support of LGBT student groups. For continuing students, a director of LGBT programming or designated LGBT advocate or ombudsperson would prove to be a valuable ally.

Graduate students nearing graduation have an entirely different array of needs, usually centered around career counseling. Faculty members should be sensitive to the unique factors that influence an LGBT graduate student's job search. Faculty should realize that the LGBT-positive qualities of an organization greatly influence a graduate students' considerations about taking a particular position. Any contacts that faculty and administrators can provide that would enable the LGBT student to make a more informed decision about whether or not to accept a job offer are obviously appreciated. LGBT faculty and recent alumni are particularly valuable resources. They can provide valuable advice about whether and when to come out during a job search as well as how to handle LGBT content on a resume or curriculum vitae.

University career counseling centers can also be important allies for the LGBT job applicant. They, too, can formally and informally connect graduating students and LGBT alumni in cities where the students are seeking positions. The career counseling center might consider placing an ad in the university's alumni magazine to build a list of names for LGBT contacts in other cities.

Underlying all the recommendations in this chapter is a student-centered approach to teaching, advising, and administration. Faculty and administrators who are sensitive to the unique needs of each graduate student in their charge are quite likely already employing many of these strategies. They realize that they can effect change in their institutions and in so doing improve the quality of life and education not just for LGBT people but for all graduate students.

NOTE

1. All names of informants are pseudonyms.

CHAPTER 11

Establishing a Visible Presence on Campus

Doug Bauder

Each of our lives is marked by some experience, some relationship, some situation that, in reflecting upon it, causes us a certain amount of pain or confusion, disappointment or embarrassment, and that we prefer to hide from ourselves and others. Part of human nature is to act as if such events never happened or as if such thoughts or feelings are not a part of who we are, to put them away as in a closet or other dark hiding place. When I was a young boy, I recall an older relative talking about someone in our family who had a "skeleton in his closet." I was led to believe that it was only the rare individual who had such haunting phantoms. As I grew older, I began to realize that simply wasn't true: All of us know what it's like to have something.

Many of us manage very well to keep those closet doors shut most of the time. After all, why do other people need to know everything about us? On the other hand, if the "secret" with which you are living is an essential part of your personhood—shaping the way you think and feel, how you see yourself in relationship to others, and, perhaps, even what you believe about ultimate things—and no one knows that part of you, that secret or skeleton can become a monster of enormous proportions.

I am often asked why I took on the job of coordinating Indiana University's first Gay Lesbian Bisexual Office, particularly when its establishment was met, initially, by controversy. My answer has much to do with a young man who lived in a closet—a closet that, in time, became a coffin.

Richard (not his real name) was a shy young man when I first got to know him, sitting in the pew with his family in the church I once pastored. It wasn't until I chaperoned an out-of-state youth event that I got to know Richard better. He was bright, articulate, sensitive, and he was funny. On a church-sponsored bus trip, he had his peers and me in stitches with his antics. Later, on the Sunday I bid a tear-filled farewell to my congregation in the midst of my own coming out, Richard's concern for me was genuine and unabashed. He was barely a man when I got to know him, but he had a wisdom beyond his years. When I left the community, he gifted me with a poster that now hangs in my office. "A friend," it says, "is a person who is for you always."

Richard and I corresponded several times after I had moved. During his first year of college I received a message from a friend who said, "Doug, I'm afraid I'm calling with some very sad news. Richard committed suicide yesterday afternoon." I couldn't believe what I was hearing. Richard had driven to a secluded area, hooked a hose from the exhaust into the front window, turned on the engine, and died. I was in shock. It made no sense. Richard had every reason to live.

I began to piece the puzzle together, to remember hints he had dropped, to recall that something seemed to be troubling him that he didn't even know how to express. I'm convinced that Richard thought he was gay and that he didn't want to disappoint his parents, couldn't imagine that his friends would understand, and assumed that the church would not be supportive of him. So where could he turn?

I fear that there are lots of other "Richards" out there with nowhere to turn. College campuses are unique places to begin to explore new dimensions of oneself. But if those discoveries are in conflict with values learned earlier in life, it can take an enormous effort to find the answers to the questions within. Support services for students struggling with issues related to sexual orientation are an essential part of this discovery, and campuses need to address this concern as more students decide that living in a closet is not an option anymore. What follows are some reflections on how Indiana University, after several years of study and survey, of planning and politicking, established a visible gay, lesbian, bisexual, and transgender (GLBT) presence on campus.

In the summer and early fall of 1994, the headlines in Indiana University's (IU) campus newspaper read: "Backlash against Gay Students Office," "Students Protest GLB Office Funding Switch," and "Divisive Issue Unparalleled in IU History." Within a few months after the GLBT Campus Office opened the headlines were reading "Over 300 Attend GLB Office Open House," "Newly Named Coordinator Wants to Build Bridges," and "GLB Office—A Place of Guidance." Today the office is boasting over 500 contacts every month—drop-ins, phone calls, letters, and e-mail, and, according to one university administrator, has "become a part of the IU fabric."

What is it that led to such a transformation in a relatively short period of time? Part of it is the fact that students and administrators had been planning for this service for over five years. Once the office was approved and the coordinator selected, other factors came into play, factors that I have come to refer to as The Ten Commandments—the "thou shalts" and the "thou shalt nots" of organizing a support service for GLBT students (see Table 4).

Table 4
Doug Bauder's Ten Commandments for Organizing an LGBT Support Services Office

1. Make up your mind.
2. Surround yourself with positive people.
3. Affirm the power of students.
4. Network, network, network.
5. Listen at least as much as you talk.
6. Be visible and supportive of other diversity issues.
7. Keep statistics.
8. Take advantage of technology.
9. Foster good relationships with the media.
10. Be aware of funding sources.

MAKE UP YOUR MIND

During my interview as a candidate for the Indiana University coordinator's position, an administrator stated that the new office demanded someone with skills in advocacy, counseling, and education. Each of the top three candidates had expertise in one of those areas. The administrator asked me, "Which of those areas do you see as the most important and why?" In reflecting on my response, it occurred to me that this was *the* most important question asked in the search process.

Considering the controversy surrounding the opening of the office and the problems that had been created with a breakdown in communication between individuals as a result of that controversy, I answered that I felt counseling was the most important role—that the new office needed someone who was a bridge builder, a networker, someone who communicated well, but also someone who had facilitative listening skills. Closeted students, as well as the most vocal activist, inevitably needed someone with some counseling skills, because the work we had to do demanded a supportive and affirming environment.

That may not be the situation on every campus. Different times and different circumstances demand different styles of leadership. What is important is to be clear about what is needed and to do a few things well, rather than try to be all things to all people. Some of the best advice I received was from chatting with my next door neighbor, a retired history professor at the university. He reminded me that people would be demanding a lot of me and expecting the office to endorse all sorts of positions. Be careful, he warned, of those who will seek to use the office to advance their own personal causes. Those words have been helpful in developing a clear vision for our work and a concise mission statement for our office.

SURROUND YOURSELF WITH POSITIVE PEOPLE

The establishment of a new office on campus, particularly one dealing with a controversial issue, demands that one pay attention—at all times—to the issue of public relations. On any given day, in answering the phone, in greeting a student who comes into the office for the first time, in attending meetings and receptions, in responding to inquiries from the press, a central issue is first impressions. It is about communicating that GLBT people are wonderful individuals to those who have a variety of strange ideas about homosexuality and bisexuality. We're talking about debunking the myths that have held us hostage for far too long.

Mindful that this work is tedious and at times terribly frustrating, it's important to be able to work in partnership with people of varied skills. It is equally important to work with men and women who have a positive outlook, a vision for the future, and a sense of hope. As I think of the good work we have accomplished during our early years of service here at IU, I am aware that people who are staff or volunteers are trustworthy, sensitive, flexible, and hardworking. And every one of them has a great sense of humor.

When you have spent several hours with someone struggling with issues about their sexual orientation, when you hear from a student who is considering leaving the campus because of harassment, when you agonize with a young person who is trying desperately to be honest and real with parents, at the end of the day it's nice to need to hear a colleague say, "You did a great job today."

We need to take the work we do very seriously, but we must not take ourselves too seriously. While wishing to hire staff or volunteers who are efficient, it is important to surround yourself with people who care as much for each other as for the work they are doing. When people think about the GLBT Office here on campus, hopefully images of Carol, Mike, Tony, Sophie, David, Jeff, and Erica come quickly to mind.

AFFIRM THE POWER OF STUDENTS

It was the hard work of students who served on various committees for several years: students who met with university administrators; students who lobbied legislators; and students who protested delays in its establishment who made the dream of a GLBT Office a reality at Indiana University. Their vision, passion, dedication, perseverance, energy, and, yes, even their patience must be credited with turning a series of recommendations into a suite of offices that function as a library, a counseling space, a computer center, and a gathering place for students struggling with their own identity and for students seeking answers to questions about GLBT issues.

It is still students who make a difference in our work, inspiring even the most jaded among us, to continue the fight. For example, several gay men were not allowed to donate blood at the Red Cross. It was a student who challenged the GLBT Anti-Harassment Team to compose a statement of value that was eventually adopted by the local Red Cross chapter. It affirmed all people and encouraged those not able to donate blood to contribute their time to the chapter's work. It was a small, but significant gesture of goodwill.

NETWORK, NETWORK, NETWORK

I cannot stress enough how important it has been for the success of our office to make the most of each and every opportunity to meet people from various walks of life and to help them consider the importance of being open to GLBT issues and individuals. During the early months of our operation, I spent a considerable amount of time visiting with key administrators, attending receptions, and participating in programs on campus and in the community. Our staff continues to divide its time among events around the campus and the larger community and to provide services in our own space.

Being a presence in public and being available in the office is a tricky balancing act but one worth the challenge. GLBT issues will be taken seriously when we build coalitions: The best way I know to do that is to meet people face to face, one at a time, sometimes on their turf and sometimes on ours. The people at IU who have been most supportive of our efforts over the months have been those who know us and understand our concerns.

LISTEN AT LEAST AS MUCH AS YOU TALK

Listening well to the people around us can both inform and inspire. It can also be a source of great healing in a climate where we are all dealing with anger, pain, fear, and frustration. Taking time to listen to another's story can also lead to great friendships—gifts we need to cultivate so that our sense of community continues to be enriched. Above all, listen to the students.

BE VISIBLE AND SUPPORTIVE OF
OTHER DIVERSITY ISSUES

If we as members of the GLBT community expect support from others, we must be visible and concrete in strengthening the work of other minorities in our midst. Is there a Black Cultural Center on your campus? Attend some events there. Do you have a Latino or an Asian group planning programs? Assist them as you are able. What about a group representing a religious minority? Get to know something of the meaning behind their observances and rituals and, where possible, become involved in supporting their efforts.

Last year, students from the campus Hillel organization planned an observance to remember the Holocaust. Mindful of the history of the pink triangle and the persecution of homosexuals along with Jews during that period, our office offered its assistance in planning this year's observance, so that it will be a program jointly sponsored. Similarly, work with the Black Cultural Center to organize a film series honoring the life of Audre Lorde or a reading highlighting the writings of James Baldwin. Working together on issues of oppression is essential if we really want to make a difference and create a climate of understanding.

KEEP STATISTICS

One of the most worthwhile things we did within the first few days of operation was to design a simple contact sheet that we would complete after every visit, phone call, letter, or e-mail message the office received. During the first month, we recorded 93 contacts. Within six months, we recorded over 500 contacts on a monthly basis, and we have maintained that level of activity. After a year of keeping fairly accurate statistics, we decided to limit our recording technique of specific contacts (see Table 5).

Citing monthly statistics quickly established our credibility with students, faculty, university administrators, state legislators, and the larger community. Accurate information underlines the need for GLBT services: Such data tend to silence the critics in our midst.

TAKE ADVANTAGE OF TECHNOLOGY

E-mail. Voice mail. The web. Resources are unending, and the information highway is filled with queer folks. The trick, of course, is to strike a balance between "surfing the web" and relating face-to-face with people. Activism is establishing some familiarity with the incredible array of resources (human and electronic) available on the Internet–crucial in order to provide educational materials and supportive services to students who are looking for information that will help them integrate their orientations with other aspects of their lives.

During one recent week, we had the opportunity to relate to two students in a more meaningful way as a result of our Internet contacts. Jason was anticipating graduation and had questions about how out to be on his resume. We suggested that he contact some of the new members of our GLBT alumni group via our listserv to get their reactions. In a matter of days he had several helpful responses from graduates around the country. Michelle was a senior in high school in a small rural community. She had thoughts of attending IU, having

Table 5
LGBT Office Contacts and Assistance

Contact	Assistance
Female undergrad who identifies as lesbian seeking information on a military career	We provided information on advocacy groups that work with various armed services.
Gay student who is affiliated with the Republican Party looking for support.	We suggested new book in library by gay Republican congressman Steve Gunderson and gave contact number for Log Cabin Club.
First-year student met to discuss issue of harassment in the residence hall.	We offered support and filed a report with Anti-harassment Team.
Spoke long-distance with mother and father of a student who came out to them prior to campus.	We provided support and gave them information on the PFLAG* group in their area.

*PFLAG is Parents and Friends of Lesbians and Gays.

heard it was relatively supportive of GLBT students. But it wasn't until after visiting our office, in response to our web page, (http://www.indiana.edu/~glbserv), that she decided this was the place for her college experience. GLBT students applying for admission, those anticipating graduation, and many in between have found added support through our office as a result of our Internet connections.

FOSTER GOOD RELATIONSHIPS WITH THE MEDIA

Establishing a good working relationship with reporters and broadcasters from campus and community newspapers, radio, and TV stations is a key element in helping people to gain greater insight into the importance of dealing with GLBT issues and in getting to know GLBT individuals. Discovering who might be respected, responsible, and perhaps, even supportive may take time, but once a solid relationship is developed with such an individual, your work will benefit from publicity that will be both accurate and positive. It is still true that the image that many people have of GLBT people comes from the media alone. It is imperative to make sure that image is balanced and fair.

BE AWARE OF FUNDING SOURCES AT ALL TIMES

Jim had attended IU over 20 years ago. He was now a professor in a small liberal arts college. Married, he was generally happy with his life, except for one thing: Nobody knew he was gay. Within a month after the Office opened, I received a call from Jim, asking if he could visit. He was going to be in town and wanted to stop by his old alma mater. He arrived on time and we went to lunch. He spoke about his struggles as a closeted undergraduate, the lack of support he experienced over the years, and his appreciation that the university was finally providing solid support for GLBT students. Before we parted company, he wrote out a check for $500 for our office. It was the first of many unsolicited offerings from students, parents, faculty or staff members, or alumni. The individuals with whom I have worked over the years in the GLBT community are among the most grateful women and men I have ever known. Providing them with a variety of opportunities to express that appreciation is mutually beneficial.

CONCLUSION

As I reflect upon the many and different individuals our office has served, the variety of programs we have sponsored, and the host of issues we have tried to address, it seems to me that our single most important function is simply *be-*

ing. It's being visible–providing a presence on campus—in a particular space and at various events. We are here, and we make valuable contributions to the campus and the surrounding community. Sometimes that needs to be stated in large and noisy ways, at other times quietly, but the proud presence of a GLBT Office in a specific setting is a statement by itself.

When I allow myself to think about my young friend Richard who chose to end his life rather than share his struggle, the phrase "Silence=Death" comes to mind. No one should have to struggle in silence any longer, particularly on a university campus where personal growth and well-rounded education are so highly valued. To provide a place of hospitality for those who have questions or concerns related to homosexuality, bisexuality, and transgender issues is no small thing: To provide a context for meaningful dialogue may make the critical difference in a person's life.

CHAPTER 12

Out in the Stacks: Opening Academic Library Collections to Lesbian, Gay, Bisexual, and Transgender Students

Michael A. Lutes and Michael S. Montgomery

Most library professionals, like the rest of society's heterosexual majority, have had little reason to question the biases in American culture against lesbian, gay, bisexual, and transgender (LGBT) persons or the ways in which personal reading needs and preferences are shaped by sexual orientation and gender identity (Aubrey, 1973). While educational institutions including libraries have adopted equal opportunity and multicultural policies, these policies have often omitted recognition of LGBT culture (Carmichael & Shontz, 1996). Within the library profession the issue has been largely ignored, and homophobia continues to be endemic in library school programs. As a result, the leadership of the library professional organizations and library school educators have seldom advanced the cause of rights for LGBT colleagues and clients, and thus libraries have failed to recognize a patron subculture that is identifiable and numerically significant (Carmichael & Shontz, 1996).

LGBT members of academic communities should reasonably expect libraries to meet their research and leisure reading requirements, as most libraries do those of racial, ethnic, or gender-based minorities on campus (Fischer, 1995). Librarians must meet this expectation with a vigorous commitment to free and equal access to libraries and information. Academic libraries should promote the search for knowledge that may interest, disturb, or engage the user and must recognize the diversity of their users and their users' needs (Gough & Greenblatt, 1992). Academic LGBT students, particularly, are "at risk" to homophobia inherent in society and to a paucity of supporting library materials. Consequently, libraries should develop a bias-free and balanced collection, and librarians must make an attempt to bring into the library collection as many points of view as possible (Tsang, 1990). In short, academic libraries should offer a full range of services and materials in order to meet the general information needs of the institution's LGBT communities and to support the intellectual requirements of LGBT studies courses in the curriculum (American Library Association, 1990; Bryant, 1995; Gittings, 1990; Owens, 1993). College and university libraries should not fall prey to common misconceptions: that only LGBT persons are interested in these materials; that LGBT library users are already well served; that there are no LGBT communities in the area; that stocking LGBT books endorses a particular lifestyle; and that LGBT books should be placed on restricted access (Gough & Greenblatt, 1992).

LIBRARY SERVICES

Optimal library service for LGBT people is achieved through the cooperation of technical and public services units. Cataloging, circulation, reference, collection development, and general administrative units all have important roles to play in its provision.

There are two ways in which cataloging departments have poorly served LGBT users: in call number classification and in subject cataloging. Of these, the former is the more difficult problem because its remediation would require a major restructuring of the Library of Congress (LC) system, the scheme most commonly used by academic libraries, and moreover because the ideal solution is unclear. In the LC ontology, bisexuality, homosexuality, transvestitism, and transsexualism are labeled "Sexual deviations" in LC's HQ74-77 social scientific "Sexual life" classes (Anonymous, 1996) and "Personality disorders" in its RC558 medical class (Anonymous, 1996). This taxonomic arrangement is clearly unacceptable—but whether materials on LGBT subjects would best be placed under some more general heading relating to human "Sexual life" (earlier in HQ) or under the rubric of other minority groups or lifestyles (perhaps somewhere in JK) is debatable.

With regard to subject cataloging, cataloging records should be kept as current and as full as is practically possible. Many LGBT readers are reluctant to approach an information or reference desk with their questions, so records produced with sensitivity to LGBT needs and concerns will make the materials represented accessible, without librarian intermediation, to even the shyest and most conflicted and closeted users. Only the latest Library of Congress subject headings should be used, and older, homophobic headings should be eradicated from the library catalogs (Berman, 1979). The term *homosexuality* did not appear in LC's list of subject headings until 1945, when it appeared as a cross-reference to "Sexual perversion," and it did not receive LC's sanction in its own right until the following year (Greenblatt, 1990). Since the late 1980s the official vocabulary of sexual orientation and gender identity has changed greatly (for example, "Homosexuals, Male" are now "Gay men," and "Homosexuals"—

specifically gay men and lesbians—are now "Gays"). A majority of academic libraries have tried to keep up to date with LC practice in various ways. The most desirable option, of course, is for all library catalogs to reflect only the latest LC practice, but this is not always possible. At Notre Dame and Princeton, for example, while the On-line Catalog of materials cataloged since 1979 reflects current usage, the older card catalog does not. In 1990 and 1991 Princeton's Catalog Division added a complex structure of *see* and *see also* references among the card catalog's homosexual headings (though its policies required it to decline a request to upgrade the obsolete, homophobic heading "Sexual perversion," the subject term under which the Library's oldest LGB materials were cataloged). While LC has made headway in keeping up with current terminology, problems continue to exist. For example, self-identified bisexual fathers find materials of interest under the heading "Gay fathers," whereas men and women who identify as cross-dressers must look for information under the dated term "Transvestites." Another difficulty is that a large portion of LGBT fiction is made invisible and irretrievable owing to the traditional academic library practice of not assigning subject headings to poetry, drama, or prose fiction. For example, Patricia Nell Warren's novel *The Front Runner* might be assigned "Gay athletes—Fiction," and Gore Vidal's *Myra Breckinridge* could be located under "Transsexuals—Fiction." Although often problematic (as in deciding whether a protagonist is "lesbian" or "bisexual"), adding appropriate subject headings to literary works would make them more accessible to users. Subject headings and cross-references should of course be reviewed periodically and changed as the LC ontology is revised and expanded in order to open ever wider the cataloging closet.

Circulation departments should adhere to professional standards regarding the confidentiality of library records. The American Library Association (ALA) in its policy manual "strongly recommends" that libraries "formally adopt a policy which specifically recognizes its circulation records and other records identifying the names of library users with specific materials to be confidential." The organization also holds as a point of professional ethics that "librarians must protect each user's right to privacy with respect to information sought or received, and materials consulted, borrowed, or acquired" (American Library Association, 1995, pp. 134, 137). In keeping with this policy, the practice at Princeton has in recent years been, for example, to deny requests by instructors who are investigating instances of possible plagiarism to turn over records of students' recent borrowings from the library. However, Princeton's circulation staff on inquiry may, problematically, reveal to a member of the university community the identity of the person who has charged out to her or him a particular, specified book. Notre Dame follows a similar policy, unless the borrower has requested a "closed record" status, which protects the user's confidentiality.

Reference department managers should see that their staff members are sensitive to the needs and concerns of LGBT users and acquainted with the major reference sources, in both paper and electronic formats, of value to LGBT users. Malinowsky (1988) provided the first major compilation of relevant reference materials, and several new sources (bibliographies, dictionaries, directories, and handbooks) are now being published every year. Moreover, at least one reference librarian should ideally be known within the department as a specialist in LGBT studies. Bibliographic handouts like research guides, pathfinders, and reading lists on LGBT topics should be developed, and a library web site relevant to LGBT studies should be created and key sites marked on the reference department's home page (Gough, 1990a, 1990b, 1990c; Gough & Greenblatt, 1992; Luckenbill, 1993; Montgomery, 1996).

All public service librarians and support staff can help to create a supportive and understanding atmosphere for their LGBT patrons. Staff should attend training and staff development programs that heighten awareness of LGBT issues and needs; there some librarians will have to come to terms with their own homophobia and recognize that service to LGBT users should be given as unreservedly as it is to other clientele. Librarians should learn never to assume heterosexuality—or anything else—about their library users. They should become clearly attuned to their users' needs and learn how to respond to them adequately.

Libraries can be made a neutral ground or "hate-free" zone for LGBT persons. Users wanting LGBT materials for whatever purpose should feel safe reading material in the collection and borrowing materials from it (Gough & Greenblatt, 1992). Some LGBT men and women may not feel comfortable checking out a book on sexuality from the library but would enjoy a safe, quiet space in the library where they can read it. The provision of such a space will have a pronounced effect on creating a positive self-image for those people who are not out or openly gay (Alyson, 1986). Also, LGBT persons need a central location where they can meet in a secure and nonhostile environment. Library administrators can demonstrate LGBT-friendly attitudes through outreach to the campus LGBT communities by offering specialized bibliographic instruction sessions and by mounting exhibitions of materials from the library's collection. Libraries can include alternative materials in bibliographic instruction and book discussions. Service points can distribute bookmarks that contain information on key locations of LGBT materials, specific subjects, gay literary figures, or the annual winners of the ALA's Gay, Lesbian, and Bisexual Book Awards or the Lambda Book Awards ("Lammies"). If the library has a small collection, a Union List may be feasible (Gough, 1990c).

LIBRARY RESOURCES

Academic library collections serve campus LGBT users to varying degrees. Some offer a wide array of materials in fiction and nonfiction, whereas others have less than a shelf of outdated, dusty works condemning or pathologizing homosexuality, bisexuality, and "gender dysphoria." Many libraries have not kept their collections current because of benign neglect or dwindling monetary resources. According to a survey conducted by *Library Journal*, libraries nationwide have continued to ignore LGBT materials in collection development: 14 percent of 250 libraries polled said their libraries carried no gay or lesbian titles; 50 percent owned fewer than 30; 26 percent fewer than 150; 13 percent between 150 and 500; and only 10 percent more than 500 titles (Bryant, 1995). Clearly, a large portion of library collections are out of touch with contemporary LGBT issues and inadequate to meet the needs of LGBT readers.

All academic libraries should provide basic book and serial resources, at both the popular and scholarly levels, on the theory and performance of diverse sexual orientations and gender identities. Sweetland and Christensen (1995) show the extent to which master's-level library and information science programs generally fail to educate their students about issues in LGBT librarianship, and other researchers have provided guidance for librarians. For example, Taraba (1990) and Taylor (1993) discuss general and theoretical issues of LGBT collection development, and Gough & Greenblatt (1990a) and Wayle (1991) offer recommendations for îcore collectionsî of gay and lesbian materials, lists that can be used for either collection building or collection assessment.

In the post-Stonewall era a gay and lesbian publishing market has grown and flourished (Carmody, 1992; Fein, 1992; Groff, 1993; Mann, 1995; A. McDonald, 1994; McMillen, 1992; Ponce de Leon, 1989; Streitmatter, 1995; Summer, 1992, 1993). While most books on homosexuality published before 1970 disparaged LGBT people, the newer books commonly offer a more positive depiction of LGBT life and liberation. Books that would have been rejected by mainstream publishers 25 years ago are now rapidly appearing in print and are eagerly sought by a growing readership. LGBT publishing has also been fueled by the emergence in the 1970s and the flourishing in the 1990s of academic LGBT studies (Brogan, 1978; DíEmilio, 1992a, 1992b; DíErasmo, 1991; Heller, 1990; Mohr, 1984; Ocamb, 1990; Rider, 1994; Saslow, 1991).

Creating a collection that supports LGBT identities and presents positive role models remains a primary goal of LGBT librarianship. Reading continues as one of the few private ways a person can gather information about sexuality (Fischer, 1995). Books have assisted a large number of LGBT persons in discovering who they are and finding their place in society. A basic function for libraries has been to ease the coming out process and to provide ongoing service with a degree of relevance similar to that allotted to other minority groups (Parkinson, 1987). This function affects not only LGBT library users but also heterosexual students and other researchers into the nature of human sexuality in all of its complex permutations. Issues such as AIDS, discrimination, domestic partnership, and sodomy law reform all have an impact on the LGBT communities and may also be of interest to others. Although there is often a wide discrepancy between what those in charge believe readers do or do not want to know and what circulation records reveal, all people are entitled to information that is nonjudgmental and bias free. Libraries must stock LGBT books as part of their role in the democratic process. In support of these efforts, academic librarians now have the full backing of our primary professional organization, the American Library Association, which in its policy manual states that the group "stringently and unequivocally maintains that libraries and librarians have an obligation to resist efforts that systematically exclude materials dealing with any subject matter, including gender, homosexuality, bisexuality, lesbianism, heterosexuality, gay lifestyles, or any facet of sexual orientation" and "encourages librarians to proactively support the First Amendment rights of gays, lesbians, and bisexuals" (American Library Association, 1995, 135).

Censorship can be a serious problem when libraries attempt to collect LGBT materials. It may occur at a number of different stages in the collection building and maintenance process (Tsang, 1990). Libraries may simply refuse to purchase certain titles because of controversial content. Sometimes obtaining materials through library book vendors is problematic: Some may stock no or very few LGBT titles, and orders may be backlogged for many months. Also prevalent is a lack of staffing resources or funds to purchase adequate holdings. Staff may lack adequate knowledge or training for choosing appropriate items. Once purchased and cataloged, books may be subject to stringent internal censorship; this may take the form of segregating all such materials to restricted access areas, which forces readers to request these items specifically and deters use. External pressure may be exerted by religious or political interest groups in an effort to ban materials from collections. Librarians charged with acquiring LGBT materials should resist others' recommendations or their own personal inclinations to purchase only "gay-positive" works and should also consider materials by authors unsympathetic to LGBT interests or concerns; for the histories and natures of homophobia, biphobia, and opposition to gender diversity cannot be studied or understood without documents representing those points of view, any more than racism can be studied without racist documents. LGBT librarians should therefore make sure that a representative selection of such materials is locally available, and suggestions that such materials be withdrawn from the collection should of course be vigorously resisted.

Tsang (1990) describes ways in which homophobic library workers can subvert efforts to build LGBT collections, and library supervisors must exercise some vigilance if they suspect such activities. Since LGBT items are at unusual risk for loss and mutilation at the hands of destructive homophobes and acquisitive homophiles alike, the collection should be periodically inventoried and replacement considered for missing materials. Libraries that maintain both public stacks and remote storage areas must establish guidelines regarding where materials will be located. Gittings (1978, 1990) describes how as a first year student at Northwestern University in 1949 her attempts to learn about lesbianism were thwarted by the total inaccessibility of homosexual materials owned by the library. Similarly, most of Princeton's books on homosexuality acquired before the 1970s were marked with an "L" and locked away to render them unavailable to all but the most persistent or resourceful undergraduates. Now such new acquisitions are placed, properly, in the open stacks of most college libraries, but LGBT collection managers must still make thoughtful decisions about whether to "unlock" older (often homophobic or scientifically outdated) materials and whether some newer items might still be at such extreme risk of depredation by friends or foes that they might best be shelved elsewhere for mediated access. Libraries with severe space constraints may selectively weed offensive and outdated titles, but all should maintain a balanced collection representing various sides of issues for research and archival purposes.

Collection management is a pivotal issue (Gough & Greenblatt, 1992; Taraba, 1990). Books on the shelves should be examined periodically and repaired, bound, and replaced as necessary. Libraries should conduct an ongoing review and formal assessment of the collection to determine whether it is adequately meeting the needs of the campus LGBT constituencies. Does the collection provide help to the sophomore who is struggling to come out? Does it support the curriculum and faculty research? How many nonfiction books of interest to LGBT people are on the shelves? How many reference books are there? How many LGBT journals, magazines, or newspapers does the library subscribe to, and do they satisfy local needs? Are there sex education manuals for lesbians, bisexuals, and gay men in the collection? What depth of coverage is there for LGBT fiction, poetry, and drama or for LGBT genre fiction such as mysteries, science fiction, and romances? Are there materials in a variety of formats (recorded music and oral histories, films, archival ephemera, and manuscripts as well as books and serials)? Is there a vertical file containing LGBT information?

Library managers can help build their collections by encouraging employees to select or recommend LGBT materials and if possible appoint a specific selector for these materials and create a fund sufficient for such materials' acquisition. The selector should be a person knowledgeable about LGBT history and culture and their artifacts in art, music, and literature, and one who has a working knowledge of small presses and appropriate LGBT selection tools. The person designated should also be sufficiently broad-minded to avoid supporting the needs of his or her own identity group at the expense of others': A gay male selector, for example, should not stint lesbians, nor should a bisexual ignore transgender needs. The results of such an appointment can be dramatic: In the six years following the assignment of LGBT selection to an interested librarian in 1990, the number of LGBT book subject headings in the Princeton On-line catalog increased from 980 to 3,047 (211 percent) and serial subject headings from 7 to 54 (671 percent).

A discrete collection development policy that explicitly includes LGBT concerns should be adopted and followed. The policy may articulate reasons why the library should collect LGBT materials and a historical overview of the collection (Taraba, 1990). The responsibility for collecting materials of various types should be clearly specified in the policy statement. Other subject bibliographers and liaisons should also be encouraged to include LGBT materials within their selection statements. The LGBT selector should develop procedures for dealing with complaints and inquiries (Gough, 1990c). The policy should define adequately the selection and purchase of fiction and nonfiction books, especially biographies, that address and mention sexual orientation as significant topical matter. A basic collection should include reference materials, histories of gay politics since 1969, legal rights handbooks, social science studies of LGBT lifestyles written by LGBT persons, both popular and serious literature, national and local periodicals, and recorded music and film (Wyatt, 1978).

To have a suitable selection of books, an LGBT selector must make a committed effort to stay abreast of what is published. The selector might place her or his name on mailing lists of prominent mainstream and small press publishers of LGBT books. He or she should contact gay, lesbian, and feminist bookstores and ask to be placed on their mailing lists: Such stores as A Different Light (Los Angeles, San Francisco, New York), Lambda Rising (Washington, D. C.), Giovanni's Room (Philadelphia), and Glad Day (Boston, Toronto) act as national mail-order centers for people lacking local gay and lesbian book dealers. Browsing shelves in bookstores and in other libraries can suggest new acquisitions for one's own institution. It may be useful to be placed on similar mailing lists maintained by antiquarian book dealers who search and sell LGBT literature, vendors such as Paths Untrodden (Seattle) and Books Bohemian (Los Angeles). One may join professional organizations such as the American Library Association's Gay, Lesbian, and Bisexual Task Force, whose clearinghouse distributes useful materials (Gittings, 1990), and participate in professionally oriented electronic mailing lists and listservs like GAY-LIBN. Professional review sources should be scanned on a regular basis; *Library Journal, Publisher's Weekly, Choice,* and *Bookseller* (United Kingdom), and newsletters like those of the ALA's Social Responsibilities Round Table and its GLBTF (Gay, Lesbian, Bisexual, Transgender, and Friends) are useful, as are such gay and lesbian journals as *Common Lives/Lesbian Lives,* the *Harvard Gay & Lesbian Review,* the *Journal of Homosexuality, LGSN: The Lesbian and Gay Studies Newsletter,* the *Lambda Book Report,* the *Lesbian Review of Books,* the *Women's Review of Books,* and national news publications like the *Advocate.* If the library does not have any of these items on hand, it should select at least a few for collection development purposes, or if necessary the selector should subscribe personally. Malinowsky (1990) and Katz and Katz (1992) are helpful in selecting journal titles. Selectors should also annually review the award winners of the ALA.-GLBTF and Lammy Awards against library holdings. LGBT bibliographies and other reference works can be employed to bolster the collection (Gough & Greenblatt, 1990; Malinowsky, 1988; Summers, 1995), as can collection-specific research guides (DeSantis, 1994; Fritz, 1995; Walker, 1990). Faculty, alumni, and student groups may want to donate books they have or offer to purchase items for the collection. Such liaisons can prove especially beneficial in filling gaps and in building a retrospective collection (Taraba, 1990). A *Library Journal* survey (Bryant, 1995) reveals that only 19 percent of college libraries reported having some communication with local LGBT groups, but informal gatherings, group consultations, and surveys can, along with users' requests, also provide valuable ideas.

CONCLUSION

Each year at the ALA's Gay, Lesbian, and Bisexual Book Awards ceremony, the recipients commonly begin their acceptance speeches with an anecdote illustrating how libraries influenced their own journeys of sexual self-realization. Often the point was that he or she felt entirely alone in same-sex attractions until reading about another gay male or lesbian in a library novel or discovering a book about homosexuality on a library shelf. Sometimes older authors will add that that initial encounter with, for example, Radclyffe Hall's *Well of Loneliness* or Edmund Bergler's *Homosexuality* was so appalling that they remained huddled in their closets for years afterwards. More recently, however, increasingly, the speakers will tell of finding LGBT fiction with positive characters and happy endings, or monographs that helped them to understand and accept their sexualities, or will describe an interaction with a librarian whose careful, matter-of-fact direction led them to those crucial works.

It is the responsibility—and duty—of academic librarians of all sexual orientations and gender identities to serve LGBT clientele by providing reference and research assistance, by ensuring a sufficiency of LGBT resources, by making the records of those resources easily accessible, and by guaranteeing professionalism and confidentiality in all library transactions. We hope that the suggestions offered in this chapter will aid other librarians in achieving these goals.

CHAPTER 13

Staying Connected: LGBT Alumni Groups

Jayne Thorson

Lesbian, gay, bisexual, and transgender (LGBT) people are creating an increasing number of alumni organizations on college and university campuses throughout the country. The potential value of these groups is remarkable, both in the magnitude of their impact and in the diversity of roles they can serve. This chapter will describe advantages and benefits of LGBT alumni groups, factors to consider when creating such a group, the importance of selecting visible projects and activities that are valued by the university, and several challenges that LGBT alumni groups are likely to encounter.

THE VALUE OF LGBT ALUMNI GROUPS

LGBT alumni groups are uniquely positioned within university communities. Although alumni groups typically function with a great deal of independence and exist outside of institutions' managerial hierarchies, they can nevertheless exert a strong influence within the universities. Among the nearly 200 LGBT alumni groups in existence, structures and activities vary widely. Yet all LGBT alumni organizations share one overarching strength: They are perfectly poised to serve as external, yet affiliated, voices for LGBT concerns within university communities.

LGBT alumni organizations have resulted from the efforts of several groups. Recent graduates who desire a means of staying closely connected to the university have spearheaded organizations on many campuses. At other institutions, organizational efforts have been led by not-so-recent graduates who seek a closer affiliation with the university or who are committed to improving the climate on campus for the students of today and tomorrow.

Irrespective of the groups' origins, all alumni organizations can benefit from the participation and contributions of alumni of all ages. This may be especially true for LGBT organizations, given the tremendous social changes that have occurred in recent decades and the accompanying differences in students' educational and social experiences. Older alumni can contribute to programs and activities in ways that were not possible when they were students, and younger alumni can gain a valuable perspective and appreciation for the history of their community.

The value of LGBT alumni organizations extends far beyond those alumni who are directly involved. Present and future students benefit from alumni support of existing campus resources and educational programs, as well as new initiatives established by alumni groups, such as scholarships or seminars. All alumni organizations have the potential to be influential in campus politics; this is especially true for LGBT groups as colleges and universities consider significant policy changes related to sexual orientation, such as the extension of staff benefits to employees' same-sex partners.

Alumni groups can be effective advocates for LGBT students. On campuses fortunate to have specific offices or a LGBT Campus Resource Center dedicated to LGBT issues, alumni groups can provide valuable support to students by augmenting the services and activities of the offices or centers.

CREATING A GROUP WITHIN THE EXISTING ALUMNI STRUCTURE

Most colleges and universities have well established alumni organizations and programs. While it is possible to create new LGBT alumni groups that are independent of the existing structures, there are many advantages to establishing groups within the larger organizations. First, it provides the new group with official standing. This cachet of approval may be particularly important for LGBT groups, which are more likely than others to find their validity questioned.

More concretely, there are numerous practical advantages to working within the existing structure. Alumni associations possess the machinery for publicity, events organization, fund-raising, accounting and bookkeeping, maintenance of records, and other organizational necessities. The more assistance any group can receive with these tasks, the more time and effort will be available for the important work that the group has as its mission.

It is possible to learn from the experiences of other alumni groups that work effectively within the organization, valuable lessons for any newly created group. Working within the larger organization may also result in the acquaintance of other interested and involved alumni who themselves are LGBT. Their talents and experience with other facets of the alumni association can be very beneficial.

Alumni associations vary among colleges and universities, so it is important to become familiar with the structure, activities, and support available from the association at your institution. It is also important not to be deterred by previous unsuccessful attempts to create a LGBT group within the official structure. Many such efforts were rebuffed several years ago for a variety of reasons, but the recent rapid increase in the number of LGBT organizations nationally has assuaged many early fears. When making a proposal, it will be helpful to include information from other institutions that have established similar groups, especially colleges and universities that closely resemble your own.

Unfortunately, it may still seem impossible at some colleges and universities to include LGBT organizations within the existing structures. This leaves little choice but to establish independent groups, a much more laborious process. United States military academies, such as West Point and Annapolis, epitomize the successful creation of LGBT alumni groups outside of the university systems.

BUILDING A MEMBERSHIP

Building a solid membership should be among the early priorities of any new alumni group. In addition to the obvious advantages of having more participants in events and fund-raising, the timely establishment of a significant membership will add to the group's credibility within the larger organization.

Two different but complementary strategies can be utilized to locate LGBT alumni of a college or university. Communications can be directed to groups of alumni to contact those who are LGBT. Conversely, LGBT groups can be addressed in order to contact those who are alumni. These approaches, while distinctive, are not mutually exclusive. Newly created LGBT alumni groups can benefit from utilizing both.

A rich source of potential new members is the larger alumni association. These alumni have already self-selected as individuals who are interested in having continuing contact with their alma mater. They are also easy to contact, since they regularly receive mailings from the association. Depending on the size of the institution, it may be possible to send all alumni information specifically about the new gay and lesbian group. If the institution is too large to make this feasible, the same information can be provided through routine publicity such as the alumni magazine or newsletter.

Similarly, graduating students are potential new members. The size and composition of the graduating class will determine the most feasible and effective method of communicating information about the alumni group. Sponsoring a reception for graduating students is an example of an activity that is extremely worthwhile in its own right and has the secondary benefit of increasing the group's membership. Of course, LGBT alumni groups should seek potential members from within their local LGBT organizations. Again, the optimal methods of communication will vary among institutions and communities.

Electronic communication, through local e-mail or the Internet, is becoming an increasingly widespread method of communication and is especially prevalent in colleges and universities. It offers unprecedented ease in communicating with large groups and can be used very effectively to reach alumni, students, and gay and lesbian individuals and organizations. Its lack of geographical restrictions makes it an ideal tool for reaching alumni in diverse areas of the world. Many LGBT alumni organizations maintain sites on the World Wide Web. At the University of Michigan (UM), for example, it is possible to become a member of the UM Gay and Lesbian Alumni Society (UMGALAS) by registering through the UM Alumni Association's web site. This site is also accessible from the web page of the university's LGBT Campus Resource Center.

SELECTING PROJECTS AND ACTIVITIES

The range of potential projects and activities for LGBT alumni groups is nearly unlimited. The type of activities selected will depend on the underlying mission of the group, whether it is a political, social, advocacy, or service group, or, more likely, a combination of these. A clear and succinct mission statement can serve as a valuable touchstone to keep the group on a consistent course.

Of the vast array, it is important to carefully choose a few projects for the group's first few years. Regardless of the group's mission, each of these selections should meet three criteria: Activities should be worthwhile, achievable, and enjoyable. That an activity should be worthwhile and achievable seems self-evident. And as is true of work within any volunteer organization, if it's not enjoyable, it won't get done. Nevertheless, these criteria can serve as valuable guideposts when deciding how to expend a group's limited time and resources.

In selecting projects, the criterion of being worthwhile is especially important for LGBT groups. The groups' mere existence is likely to be challenged, and they may face a level of scrutiny not experienced by other organizations. Especially in the first few years when new groups are most vulnerable, particular care should be taken to select activities that make clear contributions to the university community.

The relative visibility of various projects should also be considered. One of the benefits to current students of a LGBT organization is simply that it is there. Frightened and uncertain students may find comfort in the simple existence of a LGBT alumni group, even though they may not interact directly with the alumni organization.

Alumni groups can amplify their effectiveness and their range of activities by collaborating with other university organizations. An active alumni group can be a tremendously valuable partner for a LGBT Campus Resource Center or office. Mutually beneficial collaborations can be established with other university organizations as well. At the University of Michigan, in addition to working extensively with the UM LGBT Campus Resource Center, UMGALAS has cosponsored events with organizations such as the Career Planning and Placement Office, the Art Museum, and the Quilt Project.

One of the primary missions of the UMGALAS is to improve the campus climate for LGBT students. Consistent with this goal, the first major project selected was the creation of scholarships for students who have made valuable contributions to the LGBT community. The choice was made to award a greater number of smaller scholarships in order to recognize as many outstanding students as possible. Currently, two $500 scholarships are awarded each semester, and soon a third will be added. Several members of the board of directors serve as panelists for an annual symposium for LGBT students about job seeking, interviewing, and résumé preparation. (This symposium is cosponsored by the Career Planning and Placement Office and the LGBT Campus Resource Center.) As another service to students, UMGALAS is building a database of alumni in various professions who are willing to discuss career options with LGBT students.

For students, alumni, and the larger community, hosting a seminar on legal issues for same-sex couples, including wills, adoption, and powers of attorney, is very effective. Letters can be written to university officials discussing issues that are of particular interest to LGBT people, and publicly recognizing and thanking individuals who are especially supportive of efforts to reduce discrimination based on sexual orientation on campus is frequently long overdue and gratefully accepted.

Social events might include annual reunions and holiday parties, a theater series, a progressive party of musical performances, and an outing to a nearby city's art museum. These gatherings are enjoyable and serve additionally as valuable opportunities for building membership and fund-raising.

EXPECTED CHALLENGES

Unfortunately, LGBT alumni groups are likely to face several challenges that are not experienced by other groups. The politics of individual campuses are unique, but many LGBT alumni groups are likely to confront a number of common obstacles. While it is tempting to ignore them, the best strategy is to preclude as many as possible and to be prepared to deal with those that are unavoidable.

The confidentiality of mailing lists is not a problem that alumni associations are likely to have faced previously. Unfortunately, this can be a crucial issue for LGBT organizations. Each group will need to decide how this issue will be handled and may need to work with the larger organization to implement different record-keeping procedures. Most important, leaders within each LGBT organization must decide—prior to building a membership—what promises they are able or willing to make in this regard.

When the existence of the new organization is publicized, it is possible that the university may be threatened with a loss of financial contributions. The experience at the University of Michigan demonstrated that alumni making such threats were rarely those who were actually making donations. However, this is a situation that should be anticipated and appropriate responses considered. It may be useful to note the number of new or increased contributions that are direct consequences of the creation of the LGBT group, whether at your own institution or a peer school.

Finally, and most unfortunately, LGBT alumni groups must be prepared to face unfounded accusations of "soliciting" students. These allegations are best ignored, but groups need to anticipate them—and be prepared not to respond. Again, this speaks to the importance of including "worthwhile" as a criterion for any project undertaken, especially in the first few years of the group's existence.

CONCLUSION

The potential value of LGBT alumni groups is tremendous. With thoughtful planning, a few dedicated alumni can create effective organizations that are capable of contributing to real and lasting change within their university communities. And they can have a good time doing it.

PART III

Career Planning and Advising

CHAPTER 14

Addressing the Career Needs of Lesbian, Gay, Bisexual, and Transgender College Students

Simone Himbeault Taylor, Kerin McQuaid Borland, and Sharon D. Vaughters

Issues of sexual orientation for lesbian, gay, bisexual, and transgender (LGBT) students are influential in career decision-making, employment, and advanced educational pursuits. Students' sense of self and societal pressures interplay in their decision-making within a context of homophobia and heterosexism on campus, in the workplace, and in society. The purpose of this chapter is to describe how career offices can best assist the LGBT student population in making and implementing career decisions. From the perspective of career counselors and administrators in a comprehensive career office at a large multiversity (over 36,000 students), an underlying tenet of this chapter is the notion that if career services are enhanced for one population, the result will be enhanced services for all populations. Career issues for LGBT students, when integrated into total career services, allow the entire student population to become educated: In this way, neither services nor students become marginalized. From an organizational perspective, mission, goals, staffing, and training are the foundation for service and delivery mechanisms that ultimately make a positive difference for students.

This chapter will address three specific aspects related to working with LGBT students: career development and decision-making issues; strategies for creating an LGBT-friendly, inclusive career services climate; and issues for students making a successful transition from school to work, particularly regarding biases in the work world.

CAREER DEVELOPMENT AND DECISION MAKING

Positive career development interventions require an intentional focus on the complexity of individuals to be served and on the resources and systems designed to provide and support service delivery. These include understanding career decision-making processes, engaging in the accurate assessment of individuals, and introducing appropriate career decision-making intervention strategies to address the career development needs of LGBT students constructively.

Understanding the Career Development of LGBT Students

In addition to being competent in career development processes, providing knowledgeable assistance to LGBT students involves learning about the career development needs unique to this population. Sue, Arredondo, and McDavis (1992), in a call to the profession for multicultural counseling competencies, put forth necessary competencies regarding the knowledge, skill, and awareness needed for effective and ethical service to multiple constituencies. They suggest the practitioner/educator must be engaged in ongoing self-awareness, including gaining awareness of personal biases and how they may affect counseling and, in this case, programming and administration; knowledgeable about specific issues LGBT students face (i.e., how being a member of a minority group or multiple groups affects career decision-making); and skilled at intervening in effective and culturally appropriate ways. With these baseline expectations, the counselor/educator must become well versed in the career development and identity formation issues of the LGBT clientele.

Assumptions about the Career Decision Process. The primary assumptions about career decision-making center on the complexity of students, their issues, and the developmental processes required to reach an informed career decision. Career development models encompass identity formation and development, the impact of societal influences, culture, family of origin, and integrating information. Additionally, psychosocial, cognitive, behavioral, cultural, and spiritual processes all influence decisions as students examine what they desire from a career, their value systems, and environmental presses. When focusing specifically on LGBT students' career issues, complexity (and therefore interventions) will be heightened by introducing intricacies specific to this population, such as identity formation regarding sexual orientation.

LGBT Identity Formation. As for all students, identity formation for LGBT students follows a developmental path; as such, it is important to assess where the student is along this path. Cass's (1979, 1984) developmental schema describes stages of development as (1) identity confusion, (2) identity comparison, (3) identity tolerance, (4) identity acceptance, (5) identity pride, and (6) identity synthesis. A more recent model (McCarn & Fassinger, 1996) describes phases in lesbian development encompassing individual sexual identity as well as group membership identity. Career decision-making processes for LGBT students may also be influenced by other factors including effects of oppression, limited exposure to role models, internalized homophobia, and self-esteem and self-efficacy issues (Pope, 1995a; Prince, 1995).

Through such statements as "Straight people don't have to talk about their sexuality, why should I?," "Do you have a gay counselor on staff I could talk to?"; and "I'm not sure if I want to come out on my resume or in the interview," LGBT students offer clues about the phases or stages of identity in which they are operating. Understanding the developmental process allows career professionals to anticipate students' concerns and help them arrive at suitable career decisions. By doing so, the professional communicates knowledge and understanding, which, in turn, communicates safety and openness.

Individual Assessment and Evaluation. A knowledge base that integrates LGBT issues into career development processes serves as a springboard for individual assessment and for the realistic evaluation of the systems implemented to address career concerns. Assessment is the bridge to understanding the unique needs of individual students. In one-on-one situations (e.g., career counseling, mentoring), the practitioner's responsibility is to collect information about the individual's needs and to engage in goal-centered exploration aimed at heightening an understanding of self, career information, and the interplay of society and self. In group situations, greater responsibility is placed on students to assess and translate information independently. Groups represent a safe forum for LGBT students to test out the openness of an environment; it could serve as the first opportunity for LGBT students to explore the degree of acceptance and competency they will encounter in the career services office.

Implementing Career Decision-Making Interventions

Counselor success in assisting students with the career decision process hinges on helping them integrate information about themselves and their world in order to identify "satisfying" career options. Clarification of values, skills, interests, strengths, and weaknesses must come together with knowledge of the labor market, culture, or subcultures; awareness of the implications of a homophobic society; and support systems in order to reach an informed decision. A skilled practitioner will tailor interventions, providing appropriate challenge and support (Sanford, 1966).

Examples of interventions and strategies for implementation are offered in Table 6. The career services provider utilizing this information with LGBT students will have a solid foundation for constructing helping relationships. However, without a gay-friendly environment, LGBT students will be less likely to utilize services. Attention must be paid to examining tangible ways in which to deliver and convey inclusive career services on campus.

Table 6
Intervention and Implementation Strategies in Career Planning

Intervention	Implementation Strategy
Provide LGBT role models and allies who can articulate their decision and their work lives.	Mentors, case examples, panels, informational processes, interviews, "struggles," videotapes.
Discuss current and future self images.	Career counseling, career workshops.
Discuss key elements of career decisions, including concrete and individual elements, such as the labor market and personal style, personal meaning of work and success, balancing work and family, and dealing with homophobia in the workplace.	In person, e-mail discussions, counseling, brown bag meetings, collaborative efforts with academic and Student Affairs or counseling and career services.
Discuss how LGBT individuals add to a multicultural workforce.	Career counseling, career workshops targeting all students.
Discuss the skills, perspective, oppression, and implications of being part of an often invisible minority.	Career counseling, career workshops targeting all students.

CREATING A GAY-FRIENDLY,
INCLUSIVE CAREER SERVICE

Career offices may possess a strong theoretical understanding of the career needs of LGBT students, but it is the ability to translate theory into meaningful service delivery that distinguishes the intentionally LGBT-friendly office from one that simply serves this population among many. Essential to creating effective service delivery is possessing a clearly articulated set of goals that includes the goal of inclusiveness. In the same way that the mission serves as the cornerstone for the unit, a commitment to inclusiveness for all students forms the mortar for service. This needs to be clearly described in both the concrete long- and short-term goals established for the career office.

Hiring and Training

In an e-mail communication, a career professional indicated that while he counseled "gay" persons as part of his job, his own value system rejected homosexuality as morally wrong. Such attitudes are as prevalent in higher education as in other sectors; concern emerges when homophobic attitudes influence behavior resulting in an uninviting or intimidating environment for students. Thus, the hiring and training of informed, open-minded staff—secretary, paraprofessional, and trained professionals alike—help ensure that inclusive behavior is practiced on a daily basis.

Indeed, if service units value being representative of the populations they serve, hiring should reflect the campus diversity, including sexual orientation. This begins with writing an inclusive job description; posting vacancies in publications targeting diverse groups; and charging the search committee to stay true to the diversity mission of the unit. All new hires should be made explicitly aware of the values held by the unit so at the time of hiring they may evaluate their ability to uphold these standards within their own practice, regardless of personal beliefs. Ongoing training—readings, discussions, speakers—reinforces the organizational goals and provides professional development for working with diverse populations. In the end, there is no substitute for a tolerant, open-minded staff committed to building relationships with students.

Investing in Inclusive Service Delivery

Deliberate Programming and Resources. Targeted programming, resources, and service delivery are key in gaining credibility with any student population. Such targeting brings life to the organizational mission. Deliberate targeting means more than just offering a job search program and publicizing it in the LGBT Campus Resource Center; it is offering a program entitled "The Job Search: Perspectives for Lesbian, Gay, and Bisexual Students" and cosponsoring it with the LGBT Campus Resource Center or programming unit. It also means being attentive to representation by gender, race, and level of "outness," in all programming. Deliberate programming also means making LGBT issues ubiquitous, woven into examples reaching all populations. In this way, students both "closeted" and "out" may obtain helpful information and will know that an open environment exists for pursuing additional information discreetly, whereas heterosexual students will become more informed and better prepared to function in a multicultural workforce.

Targeted resource development means acquiring LGBT-oriented job search books for the career library and featuring regular displays showcasing these resources in a highly visible location so that *both* LGBT and heterosexual students are alerted to the needs of LGBT students. Deliberate service delivery means conveying a generic warmth to *all* students and personalizing messages using multiple means of access—outreach, focus groups, the media, and electronic means—to say "this career office wants to help you." Services operationalizing the goal of inclusiveness ensure that there is a genuine translation between word and deed, between expressed mission and the unit's "deliverables." Credibility is thus heightened in the eyes of students and administration.

Linking with Constituents. Time-intensive, often unseen efforts must be employed to create positive, tangible outcomes. These may include staff working with and educating other units. Such units might include faculty and staff in academic departments, central Student Affairs, or the LGBT Campus resource Center or programming unit where many students turn as a first contact. The career office's goal should be to create more ties with trusted individuals within the system: If these LGBT-friendly units and individuals are aware of the interest of the career office in attending to the needs of LGBT students, this will pave a word-of-mouth path that will extend across campus.

Because career offices function with one foot in academe and one foot in the world of work, career professionals have an obligation to educate and inform the employers with whom they interact. Employing organizations are not always fully versed in the legal and ethical implications of their activities. In addition to educating employers, some career offices find deliberate mechanisms for keeping employers aware of the importance of drawing from a diverse pool. For instance, University of Florida career fairs include student-led diversity receptions. This effort shows visibility and commitment to diversity to employers and students alike. Thus, in addition to educating students about their interactions with employers, career professionals carry the obligation to educate employers and advocate equal and fair employment consideration for all students. This education must be done in a way that builds on relationships and does not alienate the recipient. This is also one of the most compelling reasons for investing in the heterosexual student population regarding these issues: They will constitute a substantial portion of future leaders and employers responsible for ethical decision-making.

Maintaining an LGBT-Friendly Career Office

Listen to Students. While these strategies represent an array of options toward effective service delivery, what matters most is whether these efforts have made a difference. How will you know if your services are reaching LGBT students and are effective? Ongoing service evaluation through surveys, formal focus groups, and informal electronic communication will ensure that career services are successfully responding to the real—and changing—needs of the LGBT student population. There is no substitute for deliberately listening to students.

Engage in Climate Control. What *are* the qualities that make a difference in students' perceptions of a career office? Focus group data suggest that it is a complex combination of impressions of the environment, perceived openness of staff, and the relevance of actual services offered that work to create an LGBT-friendly image. One focus group highlighted the following: attention to inclusive language by staff and to nonverbals that convey acceptance, evidence of staff sensitivity (perhaps gained through training) to avoid offensive off handed remarks; evidence of an informed, knowledgeable, and skilled staff; targeted materials addressing concerns of LGBT students (e.g., a chart indicating whether organizations have a non-discrimination policy that includes sexual orientation or whether they offer domestic partnership benefits); reference to LGBT organizations in office-produced resources and programs (this is especially effective when providing examples or including gay organizations as illustrations); attention to visual image, by displaying work of notable gay artists or creating displays highlighting themes of interest to LGBT students; demonstrating visible ties to LGBT programming units, such as linking homepages; providing evidence of being LGBT-friendly through fliers, posters, and books displayed in the environment; and displaying "safe zone" indicators, such as a pink triangle or rainbow flag.

These efforts illustrate ways in which career offices may attend to their culture, climate, and services, conveying to LGBT students that they will not be marginalized. To the contrary, combined with knowledge specific to transitional needs of the LGBT student population, students will feel welcomed and respected. Relevant content knowledge follows; while the strategies discussed below are effective for all students, they are essential for the success of LGBT students in the transition from school to work.

THE SUCCESSFUL TRANSITION FROM SCHOOL TO WORK[1]

Because career education is the confluence of process and content for the practitioner and the student alike, the following section grounds career educators in the issues of transition out of academe. It offers concrete information on important success strategies for students to utilize in advancing in their chosen area. Success in seeking employment is based on targeting fields of interest, identifying skills valued in the workplace, and possessing the confidence to market oneself to an employer assertively. As with career decision-making, determining organizational fit requires all job seekers to engage in some degree of self-assessment. What do they seek in an organization's culture? Does the organization have a conservative or progressive philosophy? Questions related to organizational fit are especially important for LGBT students, for embedded in the question of organizational fit lies the question of "outness" as professionals within their employing organization.

Coming Out in the Job Search and in Professional Life: Personal and Organizational Considerations

The extent to which sexual identity is integrated into a professional setting is a personal decision directly linked to an individual's developmental progress and, often times, to an individual's professional experiences. For example, a lesbian job seeker may choose initially to be closeted but, as she becomes a more seasoned professional, may decide to be out, or, at a minimum, selectively out in the workplace. Informed career professionals know that personal and organizational characteristics influence whether or not individuals disclose sexual identity in a work environment. These characteristics may include comfort level with sexual orientation; extent to which one is out with heterosexual friends and family; support available from a partner or LGBT friends for coming out at work; degree to which the workplace is considered a nonhostile environment; and extent to which a coming out plan is developed (Friskopp & Silverstein, 1995).

Out in the Workplace? The following scenarios illustrate that implications are present for every choice made. "Joe," a bisexual finance major, has set his sights on a financial analyst position on Wall Street. Knowing that the types of organizations of interest to him tend to be more traditional and potentially homophobic, he decides not to disclose his sexual orientation to his prospective employer. In order to strengthen his chances for this position, Joe may decide to limit disclosure of his leadership experiences in an LGBT student organization and his independent study project on sexual discrimination in the workplace. This is a trade-off he is willing to make to get his career started. "Linda," on the other hand, decides that masking her sexual orientation would be artificial and cause her to move awkwardly into her first professional experience. She is in search of organizations that have demonstrated a commitment to diversity. Through her research she decides that organizations that include sexual orientation in their affirmative action statements are of interest to her. She will target these organizations, thus circumscribing her job search options. Joe and Linda represent extreme ends of an identity disclosure continuum. LGBT individuals may find themselves at different points along this continuum throughout their careers as they grow personally and make decisions that impact them professionally.

Researching the Organizational Environment

Many organizations are working to create inclusive and productive environments. Organizations addressing the needs of LGBT employees through instituting domestic partner benefits programs or including sexual orientation in their Equal Employment Opportunity (EEO) statements are clearly at the forefront in working to attract the most qualified individuals and to counteract homophobia actively. Organizations in this category may, in many instances, be safe settings for new LGBT professionals to begin their careers, regardless of if, how, or when they choose to disclose their sexual orientation.

Organizational Clues: Policy Positions. While there are many more inclusive organizations (in September, 1996, IBM joined the ranks of organizations offering domestic partner benefits) than there were even a few years ago, limiting a job search strictly to such organizations may prove to be an unnecessary–not to mention unrealistic–constraint. A next tier of organizations to explore are those that have directly addressed the needs of other minority groups–women, people of color, and those with disabilities. Reviewing EEO statements, sexual harassment policies, or an organization's implementation of the Americans with Disabilities Act (ADA) guidelines or the Family Leave Act are all indicators that an organization is committed to creating a positive environment for a diverse workforce.

Organizational Clues: On-the-Job Experiences. LGBT employees' daily experiences will be the ultimate test of an organization's openness to gay employees. What LGBT employees must be prepared to face are some of the "worst-case" scenarios in which knowledge of their sexual orientation, either self-disclosed or simply "suspected," creates barriers to becoming socialized and advancing within the organization. Situations ranging from isolation to being overlooked for advancement opportunities, to open "joking" or negative comments directed at gay community, to even more insidiously covert but subtle homophobia may represent the unfortunate realities in some workplaces. Policy development is one indicator of an organization's commitment to creating a welcoming environment for gay employees, but ultimately the goal is to find an organization that conceptually *and* practically makes the commitment a reality.

Thus, as LGBT students seek their first positions, there are several ways for them to evaluate the organizational environment. Specifically, as students approach the interview phase of the job search, they will want to consider organizational messages (in print or on a homepage) and to solicit information about the organization from others in the field. During the interview process, through interactions with current personnel, LGBT students will want to evaluate how the organization treats all its employees, paying particularly close attention to represented minority groups (Friskopp & Silverstein, 1995).

Strategies for Ensuring Career Success

Career professionals attentive to LGBT clients will go beyond merely providing students with the tools to make good career decisions and the resources with which to research viable options. They will also prepare students to make a successful transition by educating them about what to expect and how to continue grooming themselves for success. Drawing from the literature and practical experience, the following strategies for job success and related rationale for implementation are provided as examples that practitioners may want to use to educate their LGBT student clientele (Friskopp & Silverstein, 1995).

Build a Solid Skill Base or Area of Expertise. LGBT employees with solid skills and who make the effort to broaden their skill base will have greater opportunity to pursue employment in organizations that may offer a safe and supportive work environment. As new employees, they may look for opportunities to participate in projects with a broad scope that enhance their understanding of the organization and connect them with others (e.g., managers) not immediately associated with their daily responsibilities. Another key strategy is to engage in work that offers opportunities to stretch, refine, or develop new skills and to add to their knowledge base. By broadening their skill sets and organizational expertise, LGBT employees enhance their ability to move between departments and to increase their overall marketability.

Develop Mentor Relationships. New employees learn a great deal on the job. There are also some lessons less painfully learned through others, such as how to negotiate work relationships. Many times, finding a mentor and developing that relationship helps in charting a successful career path. By developing a trusting, supportive relationship with a seasoned professional (who may or may not be gay), LGBT professionals may engage in problem solving on workplace issues that can enhance professional growth while avoiding situations that could jeopardize advancement. The mentor and the mentee may know of each other's sexual orientation, but disclosure is not essential for the relationship to work. In many cases, however, as the relationship develops, the gay professional is likely to feel comfortable in disclosing his or her sexual orientation.

Engage in Professional Activities Outside the Workplace. Whether or not trust relationships develop naturally within the workplace, professionals outside the organization may fill a void and prove to be equally helpful and supportive. A new professional must realize that these relationships may take longer to develop. Extending beyond the workplace entails getting involved in the community—joining professional organizations (perhaps including gay professional associations) or capitalizing on an outside interest to expand social networks and interact regularly enough with other professionals for trust relationships to develop. The objectivity of an outsider can be an added benefit making it well worth the time invested in getting involved and making connections outside the organization.

Seek Opportunities in Supportive Locations. A final strategy for new professionals to consider is targeting geographic areas where supportive networks may be more readily accessible. Focus group insights indicate that a supportive community may be even more important than an LGBT-friendly work environment. Seeking locations in which gay communities are more widely known and accepted may ease the transition from student to professional. Gay communities in urban areas or on either coast may offer support that gay professionals find advantageous as they begin their careers. By locating themselves near an established gay community, new professionals may be in a better position to seek out necessary support systems. If, however, the employing organization is highly supportive, or as the gay individual develops into a more confident professional, geographic location may be of lesser importance.

These strategies are among many that informed career professionals will turn to in educating LGBT students. While these strategies are clearly effective for all in making a successful transition, they may be particularly relevant for LGBT individuals who may encounter discrimination in the workplace and in society.

CONCLUSION

A major emphasis in this chapter has been the importance and advantages of integrating LGBT students' needs into the total fabric of the career office's mission. LGBT students' trust and belief in career services will be reflected in how frequently they actually utilize the services. An additional measure of effectiveness will be hearing directly from the LGBT student population that they "matter" to the unit and to the institution. The benefit inherent in building quality services for one population is that, by definition, the career office will have increased the quality of services for all students. Success strategies that may be essential for one population can be similarly effective for another population. In addition, by educating the entire student body about the unique career needs of specific student populations on our campuses today, career offices will have helped prepare an entire generation of students to become contributing, successful, and ethical leaders in the multicultural workforce.

NOTE

1. The term *work* is used in this section to represent the transition into a job, graduate or professional school, or any next step a student may pursue.

CHAPTER 15

Becoming an LGBT Affirmative Career Adviser: Guidelines for Faculty, Staff, and Administrators

Roger L. Worthington, Saba Inez McCrary, and Kimberly A. Howard

Career centers exist on virtually all college campuses because career development is among the most important areas of personal growth that occurs during the college years. This is a crucial time for students to participate actively in their career development process. For many, the assessment of how race, class, gender, sexual orientation, and disability impact their career options is essential. During high school, lesbian, gay, bisexual, and transgender (LGBT) students are unlikely to have opportunities to explore the unique factors that impact their career options with a guidance counselor or other professional who has expertise in addressing LGBT issues, making it even more essential during college. Further, university faculty are commonly called upon to address many career choice and vocational development needs of the students with whom they work, particularly for students who are majoring in the faculty member's field of expertise. In the absence of LGBT-affirmative career agencies on many college campuses, the career needs of students belonging to sexual minority groups often ultimately fall on the shoulders of LGBT-affirmative faculty, staff, and administrators (FSAs). The purpose of this chapter is to present ways that FSAs on university and college campuses can become more effective in addressing the career development needs of their students. In it we will propose a model of the development of LGBT-affirmative attitudes and practices; describe the relationship of sexual identity development to the career development process; and identify the general career counseling and development needs of LGBT students.

BECOMING LGBT-AFFIRMATIVE: A DEVELOPMENTAL MODEL
OF ATTITUDES TOWARD SEXUAL DIVERSITY

We live in a sexually diverse world. LGBT people come from, live in, and contribute to all segments of society. We also live in a heterosexist and homophobic culture—one that denies the existence and contributions of LGBT individuals. In that context, all people are frequently assumed to be, and treated as though they are, heterosexual. Further, in denial of the complexity of human sexuality, heterosexuality and homosexuality are often mistakenly seen as dichotomous ends on a single continuum. Those who are not heterosexual are considered to be bad, immoral, deviant, maladaptive, sick, or depraved. This has been a persistent reality in the lives of gay men, lesbian women, and bisexual and transgender people. The oppression that accompanies sexual minority status impacts many facets of the lives of LGBT individuals, not the least of which are the educational and work domains.

Before addressing specific career counseling and development needs of LGBT students, it is imperative that readers have a foundation upon which to evaluate their attitudes toward members of sexual minority groups, as well as to understand the basis for the types of work environments LGBT students are likely to encounter. Attitudes toward sexual minorities vary widely between and among individuals. The basis for these differences can be partially accounted for by the degree of homophobia within different people. Homophobia has two commonly cited definitions: (1) the fear and hatred of homosexuality in others and (2) the fear of homosexuality in oneself. Both of these definitions can refer to LGBT as well as nongay individuals. Homophobia has become interwoven into the fabric of the dominant culture and, indeed, is part of the developmental socialization of all children in the United States (US). It constitutes a form of oppression that often goes undetected and is implicitly condoned. Overcoming these internalized messages can be difficult but not impossible. In fact, there is increasing attention to the mechanisms by which people develop positive, affirming attitudes and behavior about sexual minorities (i.e., Eliason, 1995a; Gelberg & Chojnacki, 1996). In order for FSAs to become effective in their efforts to facilitate the career development of LGBT students, they must (1) be realistic about the limitations imposed on them by their socialization into homophobic, heterosexist practices, (2) make a commitment to overcome that socialization, and (3) actively pursue experiences that facilitate their own movement toward that goal (Gelberg & Chojnacki, 1996). It is not only important for LGBT-affirmative FSAs to understand and utilize their knowledge of the issues faced by LGBT individuals, but it is equally important to consider their own development in becoming an LGBT-affirmative person.

Building on the work of Gelberg and Chojnacki (1996), Eliason (1995a), and others, we propose a model for the development of LGBT-affirmative attitudes and practices among heterosexuals.[1] Phases in the proposed model include: *passive conformity*, in which the person maintains a socially sanctioned, unconditional heterosexist/homophobic construction of the world; *revelation and exploration*, in which the person becomes aware that LGBT individuals exist in the world, having needs and experiences that may differ from one's own; the individual comes to question his or her assumptions about sexual minorities; *tentative commitment*, in which the person makes a tentative commitment to accepting LGBT individuals but without expending much energy to become fully aware of the concerns and realities of sexual minorities; *synthesis and integration*, in which the person begins to value, respect, and recognize LGBT individuals, consequently engaging his or her LGBT family members, friends, and associates, and comes to interact with the LGBT community more openly; and *active commitment*, in which the person begins to more fully incorporate the awareness achieved at earlier stages into her or his personal, professional, and political lives.

In reflecting on the various stages of development, individuals at each stage are likely to provide varying levels of quality in helping LGBT students who are seeking career guidance. Clearly, individuals in the passive conformity, and revelation and exploration stages are poorly suited for effectively advising LGBT students about any aspect of their lives. For these individuals, it is recommended that consultation or referral to a more equipped colleague be the strategy of choice. Further, while clearly more advanced than earlier stages, individuals in the tentative commitment stage need to be aware of their limitations, because their consciousness of LGBT issues is only newly emerging and may not yet reflect a level that will be optimally effective. Working toward one's own advancement through the stages is likely to have a positive effect on an individual's efforts to help LGBT and all students with their career concerns effectively.

This model of heterosexual attitudes toward sexual minorities can also be used to understand the nature of work environments to which LGBT students will be exposed. The vast majority of work and educational environments are composed of individuals who have unquestioningly adopted heterosexist, homophobic attitudes and behaviors (passive conformity). Increasingly, however, as larger numbers of LGBT-affirmative individuals enter administrative positions, employment practices are beginning to respond to the needs of LGBT workers. Reflective of that reality, Chojnacki and Gelberg (1994) have proposed four levels of work environment heterosexism: *overt discrimination*, in which both formal and informal policy exists to foster discrimination based on sexual orientation; *covert discrimination*, in which no formal anti-discrimination policy exists, and hiring and advancement favors heterosexuality; *tolerance*, in which a formal anti-discrimination policy exists, but no other support for LGBT workers is offered; and, *affirmation*, in which a formal anti-discrimination policy exists, and additional support is offered through actions such as extension of insurance to partners, employee sensitivity training on diversity, promotion of LGBT networking within the organization, and community support systems for LGBT people. At this level, LGBT employees are valued for the diversity they bring to an institution.

In adjusting to the reality of workplace heterosexism and homophobia, De Monteflores (1986) has suggested that LGBT individuals primarily cope by one of four methods: *assimilation*, or passing as a member of the dominant culture; *confrontation*, in which individuals face up to and address the differences; *ghettoization*, in which the person spends the majority of his or her waking hours within the confines of their sexual minority group; this may also involve flight to urban centers where tolerance is greater and invisibility can be maintained, as well as entrance into ghettoized career fields; and *specialization*, in which the person views himself or herself as superior and unique as a result of surviving the oppression of the majority. While some of these coping strategies may be more ideal than others, they occur within the context of an oppressive society, and each coping strategy must be adapted for the individual based on the context within which that person lives. To some degree, these coping strategies are likely to be a function of both environmental pressures as well as the sexual identity development of the individual.

MODELS OF GAY AND LESBIAN IDENTITY DEVELOPMENT

Most professionals of higher education are trained to think of students in developmental terms. Students are seen as entering the university in one developmental stage of growth and exit at another, their pathway through college life occurring within a relatively predictable sequence of developmental phases. Career development theories also encourage us to think of people as progressing through a series of stages toward the ultimate goals of occupational choice and work adjustment. Career development is often conceptualized as the person's progress toward the choice of a career field that is congruent with her or his personal interests, values, and abilities. Role models and mentors have been frequently identified as essential aspects of the development of positive work-related interests and values that prompt students to visualize their future in an occupational field. Work adjustment and satisfaction, then, become a function of the degree of match between the individual's work personality and important characteristics of the work environment. Until recently, however, theories of career or college student development have rarely addressed the social and psychological development of LGBT individuals.[2] It has become apparent that sexual identity development occurs concurrently with the formation of an individual's career self-concept (Elliott, 1993; Fassinger, 1995; Prince, 1995). With that in mind, we turn briefly to the description of models of gay and lesbian identity development as a prelude to the discussion of the career development needs of LGBT students.

There are several theoretical models of gay and lesbian identity development (i.e., Cass, 1979, 1984; Chapman & Brannock, 1987; Coleman, 1982a;

Faderman, 1984; McCarn & Fassinger, 1996; Sophie, 1985; Troiden, 1989). Most models of gay and lesbian identity development have similar features (Prince, 1995) and have been applied across gay men and lesbian women. Even though we acknowledge that differences exist between these groups, space limitations restrict our capacity to provide both. We have chosen to describe the model of lesbian identity development proposed by McCarn and Fassinger (1996) because it has qualities that make it less prone to criticisms often associated with other models, and Fassinger (1995) has applied this model specifically to the career development process. Their model "distinguishes two parallel, reciprocal processes—an individual sexual identity process involving the recognition and acceptance of same-sex attraction and lifestyle preferences, and a group membership identity process involving the confrontation of oppression and the acceptance of one's status as a member of an oppressed group" (Fassinger, 1995, 153). The distinction between these two processes is important because one's individual sense of self can be separated from the extent to which one identifies with, or actively and publicly participates in, lesbian or gay cultures. Fassinger (1995) describes four phases of sexual identity development that occur in each of the two branches: *awareness*, at the individual level involving an awareness of feeling different from the heterosexual norm, and at the group level involving awareness of different sexual orientations and the existence of heterosexism; *exploration,* at the individual level involving strong feelings about or a relationship with another woman (or women), and at the group level involving the assessment of one's feelings about lesbians as well as possible membership in that group; *deepening and commitment*, involving crystallization of choices about individual intimacy and sexuality, as well as increasing commitment to the lesbian and gay community; and *internalization and synthesis* of same-sex love and desire and membership in an oppressed group into overall self-concept (Fassinger, 1995, 153).

Specific influences of sexual identity development on career development and self-concept vary among individuals (Prince, 1995). However, because individuals in the midst of the identity development process are primarily focused on non-career aspects of identity (Fassinger, 1995), they are likely to have limited opportunities for exploration and definition of interests, values, and abilities, as well as the limited freedom to explore the suitability of various career environments openly (Prince, 1995).

BECOMING AN LGBT-AFFIRMATIVE CAREER ADVISER

Researchers have offered suggestions and guidelines for working affirmatively with LGBT students (Chojnacki & Gelberg, 1994; Croteau & Hedstrom, 1993; Croteau & Lark, 1995; Croteau & Thiel, 1993; Elliott, 1993; Garnets, Hancock, Cochran, Goodchilds, and Peplau, 1991; Hetherington &

Orzek, 1989; Morgan & Brown, 1991; Schmitz, 1988). The following is a brief discussion of some of the most important aspects of LGBT-affirmative career counseling to guide FSAs in developing LGBT-affirmative practices.

FSAs should work to understand their own feelings toward sexual minorities. We begin with this point because it is the cornerstone of an individual's choice whether to develop a career advisement relationship with LGBT students or to refer them to somebody who is more equipped to do so. Clearly, only FSAs who have thoroughly evaluated their own values and attitudes toward LGBT individuals and made a commitment to LGBT-affirmative practices should attempt to engage in the career exploration process with LGBT individuals. Still, even the most well-intentioned FSAs tend to retain harmful stereotypes about the personal characteristics of LGBT individuals if they have little contact or involvement with LGBT people in their daily lives. However, FSAs who have frequent contact and positive personal relationships with the LGBT people in their own lives are less likely to respond stereotypically to LGBT students; and they are probably less likely to use their relationships with LGBT students inappropriately to work out personal inner conflicts about sexual minority issues.

Since being LGBT is not a visible minority status, students will undoubtedly maintain their privacy about their LGBT status unless they feel comfortable coming out. Clearly, it is virtually impossible to engage in LGBT-affirmative career advisement unless the student is able to be out to the FSA. Therefore, FSAs should work to make their office environment safe and inviting of sexual orientation self-disclosure. It is important to recognize that if you speak and act like every student you encounter is nongay, then LGBT students will be more likely to choose to remain invisible in your presence. However, it is equally important to remember that disclosure of LGBT status is not a goal in and of itself. Being LGBT-affirmative means respecting the privacy and choices of the individuals with whom one works, and the student's status must be held with the utmost confidentiality. The FSA may be the only individual with whom the student is ready to share her or his LGBT identity.

LGBT students struggle with many of the same issues that confront heterosexual students. As such, it is important to balance both common and unique career concerns when working with LGBT students. Within that context, it is essential that FSAs be able to recognize when the sexual orientation of the student is central to the concern at hand and address issues of being an LGBT student directly. However, it is also essential for FSAs to be able to recognize when sexual orientation is peripheral to the issue at hand and to respond accordingly.

LGBT-affirmative FSAs should also strive to acquire knowledge about the wide-ranging needs of LGBT students and the issues relevant to LGBT career development. For example, having the opportunity to be out in the workplace is often important to LGBT individuals. It is also important to know whether the employer engages in LGBT-affirmative employment practices. Does the employer offer insurance and other benefits to the domestic partners of LGBT workers? Are there visible LGBT employees at all levels of the organizational structure, indicating the likelihood that the student will have the opportunity to move up the ladder?

FSAs should also gather pertinent information and locate resources designed to aid LGBT individuals in their career development. For example, LGBT-affirmative FSAs should have knowledge of anti-discrimination laws at the federal, state, and local levels. Although efforts to apply the guarantee of equal protection under the Fifth and Fourteenth Amendments to the Constitution have produced limited results, there are currently nine states (Wisconsin, Massachusetts, Hawaii, Connecticut, California, New Jersey, Vermont, Minnesota, and Rhode Island) and more than 100 cities and counties that include sexual orientation as a protected category in employment (Branson, 1995). This information could be vital for some LGBT students making important career decisions that have geographical considerations. FSAs should be aware of the existing laws in their own states and surrounding localities so that they might be able to offer that information to LGBT students considering career options. It is also important to identify LGBT resources and establish connections with LGBT individuals in differing occupations who are willing to be personal resources for students. FSAs should encourage students to examine the information gathered and the resources located. More important, however, FSAs should empower students to do additional research on their own regarding work environments and career options.

Additional reading of the literature cited above will inform the reader of the broad range of issues that are beyond the scope of this chapter. Further, FSAs should investigate the counseling and career centers on their campus to identify LGBT-affirmative counselors and career professionals who can serve as resources to themselves and their students. Information about the specific LGBT resources available on campus can be posted by LGBT-affirmative FSAs as a service to their students and reminder of their commitment to LGBT support.

CAREER ISSUES SPECIFIC TO GAY MEN, LESBIANS, BISEXUALS, AND TRANSGENDER PEOPLE

Many people speak and act as though LGBT people belong to a single, amorphous group when in fact there are clearly many differences among lesbian, gay, bisexual, and transgender people. This section is intended to communicate a brief set of issues that may be unique to each of these groups.

Lesbian Students

At times dual minority status may confer multiple levels of oppression on women who are lesbians, and can result in triple jeopardy for lesbian women of color or women with disabilities. Women are exposed to pressures to adopt stereotyped sex-role characteristics and frequently suffer hardships in the workforce stemming from sexism (including lower-status occupations, lower pay for equal work, and sexual harassment, among others). Lesbians must find ways to incorporate a healthy sexual identity while confronting these common difficulties. The multiple factors may be the reasons why lesbians are more likely than gay men to remain closeted in the workplace (Fassinger, 1995).

Gay Men

The tyranny of sex-role norms and socialization has an impact on the career development of men, making gay men particularly vulnerable to stigma and other difficulties as a result. Etringer, Hillerbrand, and Hetherington (1990) found that gay men scored the highest on both career uncertainty and dissatisfaction when compared to other groups. One possible explanation of these findings may be that the pursuit of work environments that satisfy the identity requirements of one aspect of self may sacrifice other requirements. For example, working in a gay-friendly environment may require the individual to sacrifice career objectives associated with values, interests, and abilities that are unrelated to sexual identity. Further, working in many traditionally male sex-typed jobs often requires enduring higher levels of homophobia or threats to safety than might otherwise be the case. As a consequence, some gay men may experience personal struggles that are normal reactions to the oppressive situations they encounter but may be perceived by others as pathological (Prince, 1995).

Bisexual and Transgender Students

Whereas there is limited but increasing literature on career development issues unique to gay and lesbian individuals, there is an almost complete lack of literature on career development issues unique to bisexual and transgender individuals. Bisexual students can often feel as though they do not belong to any community, rejected, marginalized, or misunderstood by members of other sexual minority groups, as well as heterosexuals. As such, identity issues become somewhat more difficult to resolve and may interfere in the process of career decision making in a variety of ways. Conversely, some bisexual individuals find it somewhat easier to engage in assimilation as a coping strategy because it is potentially more compatible with their lifestyle than it might be for other sexual minority groups.

While assimilation may be a viable coping strategy for gay, lesbian, and bisexual individuals, this option is much more difficult for transgender people, because gender identity is more visibly apparent than sexual identity. Thus, transgender students will have more difficulty avoiding stigma and homophobic reactions as a function of the visibility of their gender identity. It may be difficult for them to see themselves as transgender individuals achieving success and maintaining happiness. The transgender student may be posed with psychosocial difficulties ranging from a pervasive sense of ambivalence toward sexual identity and educational/career goals to rejections by friends, family, and community (Coleman & Remafedi, 1989). Support and acceptance, therefore, become crucial to the continuing development of transgender students.

CONCLUSION

In order for FSAs to be effective career advisers to LGBT students, they must (1) recognize and enact the belief that not all people are heterosexual; (2) have an awareness of their own beliefs, attitudes, and biases regarding sexual diversity in the world; (3) behave in ways that value and affirm LGBT individuals; (4) have basic knowledge of career development and counseling; and, (5) have specific knowledge of the career development needs of LGBT students. For some, the process of becoming an effective career adviser to LGBT students will require a personal journey of growth in becoming aware of their own attitudes toward sexual minorities. For others, the process will primarily require the development of career counseling skills and knowledge of the unique issues that face LGBT students in career decision making.

NOTES

1. While we do not assume that our readers are all heterosexually oriented, this section is written to address heterosexual attitudes toward sexual diversity because we are particularly concerned with assisting heterosexuals to become more competent in addressing the needs of LGBT students.

2. In reality, models of identity development for LGBT students almost exclusively address gay men and lesbians and unfortunately have not been effectively extended to bisexual or transgender people.

PART IV

Lesbian, Gay, Bisexual, and Transgender Health Issues on Campus

CHAPTER 16

Effective and Humane Campus Health and Counseling Services

Richard P. Keeling

Providing excellent health and counseling services for lesbian, gay, bisexual, and transgender (LGBT) students requires offering clinical, psychological, and prevention programs that are both effective (in purpose, content, and outcome) and humane (in format, pattern, and style). Effective and humane services will address the specific medical, emotional, psychological, and spiritual needs of LGBT students, with a commitment to understanding those needs in a careful and textured way that accounts for the influence of the campus environment, social norms, and the diverse psychological and cultural processes of "coming out." LGBT students will perceive effective and humane services as accessible, welcoming, affirming, and capable. The providers of those services will be well-trained, caring professionals who have sincerely examined their own attitudes about sexuality and are continuously working toward peace in the relationship among people of any sexual orientation. Prevention will be at the center of effective, humane programs, and the clinicians, counselors, and educators who work with LGBT students—both as individuals and as a complex community—will focus their efforts on implementing health promotion services that make real sense given the challenges, struggles, and opportunities that LGBT students face in the particular context of their campus. Effective, humane programs will be designed and implemented in close partnership with the campus LGBT community. All of these programs and services will be very visible, well integrated with other student services, and connected with community programs for LGBT people.

Health is not simply the absence of disease; it is a positive quality that includes both well-being and dignity. It is not measured adequately by medical parameters, and its determinants are not simply biological, or even personal.

The health of LGBT students is influenced not only by their personal knowledge and behavior, the diseases they may naturally experience, or the injuries that afflict them but also by both their internal psychological, emotional, and spiritual environment and the greater social and cultural context in which they live, learn, and love.

Homophobia is a critical, concrete, daily health issue, not just an abstract societal challenge. Prejudice against LGBT people infiltrates the lives, relationships, hopes, and dreams of LGBT students; it affects both choices about visibility (being "out") or behavior (sex, alcohol and other drugs, relationships, violence) and the unchosen tempests of stress, uncertainty, anxiety, and fear that complicate health, reduce the sense of well-being, and challenge personal peace. In the minds, bodies, and souls of LGBT students, homophobia is a felt reality, with physiological correlates. A true social illness, it sickens the hearts of people who hate, threatens the wholeness of LGBT persons, and weakens the bonds that hold all of us in community. To ignore the actual or potential harm done—both to individual LGBT students and to their collective sense of, and embodiment as, a community—by homophobic persons, institutions, religions, governments, and cultures is to neglect their most important health concern. To fail to address prejudice as a systemic LGBT health issue—no matter how good services for individual students may be—is to attend only to the trees and not to the forest. This is the central fact of health and counseling for LGBT students.

ADDRESSING THE SPECIFIC HEALTH
NEEDS OF LGBT STUDENTS

Several major misconceptions impede effectiveness in health and counseling services for LGBT students:

1. The most important health issue for gay and bisexual men is sexually transmitted disease (which grows from the incorrect presumption that having sex is the most important part of gay and bisexual men's lives).

2. Every student has equal risk of infection with the Human Immunodeficiency Virus (HIV)—the destructive legacy of attempts to make HIV prevention education more palatable by focusing on heterosexual individuals.

3. Clinicians and counselors can tell who is gay, lesbian, bisexual, or transgender—or, LGBT students will generally disclose their sexual orientation to their clinician or counselor.

4. Being gay, lesbian, bisexual, or transgender is the critical counseling issue for an LGBT student.

5. If we could just educate LGBT students better, they would have fewer health-related problems.

6. LGBT students are just like other students, except that they are sexually attracted to people of the same sex.

7. Childbearing is not an issue for LGBT students.

8. Being lesbian, gay, or bisexual is associated with certain psychopathologies or unusual health behaviors.

These errant assumptions reflect discomfort with LGBT students, a desire to "pathologize" them, and a deep cultural reluctance to know more about their lives. The best example of their impact on campus programs has been the virtual disappearance of LGBT concerns from many campus HIV prevention efforts— despite the clear epidemiological fact that among college and university students the overwhelming majority of people with HIV disease have been, and still are, men who have sex with other men.

The most important specific health issues for LGBT students are:

1.The psychological, emotional, spiritual, and physical consequences of homophobia.

2. Coming out.

3. The challenge of developing healthy, empathic, caring relationships.

4. Isolation from self, others, and community.

5. Concerns about and consequences of unprotected, unwanted, or unvalued sexual behavior, including, but not limited to, sexually transmitted disease and HIV infection.

6. Alcohol and other drug use and its negative impact on personal health and relationships.

7. Relationship violence.

8. Reproductive health concerns.

Effective health and counseling services for LGBT students specifically address these concerns through:

1. *Dedicated, persistent work—in partnership with other campus and community agencies—to identify, confront, and challenge homophobia in every aspect of campus and cultural life; celebrating National Coming Out Week; writing letters of protest or praise, as appropriate, to campus newspapers about events, statements, or activities that affirm or endanger LGBT students; and demanding inclusive language in all programs, written materials, and official documents.* If the institution does not include LGBT students, faculty, and staff in its non-discrimination policy, collaborate in advocating for adding such a clause. Support and attend concerts, lectures, seminars, and cultural events that notice, affirm, or appeal to LGBT students. Join in seeking employment—or student status—related benefits for the domestic partners of students, faculty, and staff.

2. *Specific counseling services that assist students at various stages of their process of coming out.* While many LGBT students are well served by a group format (variously intended as support or therapy), many others need, instead (or in addition) individual brief counseling or psychotherapy. Every campus counseling service should be prepared to offer both. While it is helpful and important to have specially identified counselors who provide LGBT-sensitive services, including the coming out and relationship groups mentioned herein, we cannot assume that all LGBT students will know of, or seek out, those counselors; every counselor (like every clinician and every educator) must be prepared to offer effective, humane services.

3. *Counseling services that do not presume that the fact of their sexuality is the only or dominant psychological issue for LGBT students.* This requirement does not contradict the previous one: It simply recognizes the diversity within the LGBT community on campus. For some students, coming out, while still an active, lifelong process, is no longer a major source of conflict, anxiety, or relational stress. An LGBT student should be able to receive excellent counseling about all of the other concerns that trouble many other students; anxiety, depression, attention deficit disorder, homesickness, loneliness, and turmoil in relationships are the great common ground of counseling issues among all students, LGBT or straight.

4. *Counseling services that do, on the other hand, take into account the specific needs created by being gay, lesbian, or bisexual, and the context that sexuality creates for other psychological and spiritual concerns.*

5. *Groups focused on building and nurturing relationships, organized with the distinct needs of men and women at their core; these groups are often best co-facilitated by a counselor and a health educator.* At the beginning of any such group's work, assess the needs of the students who wish to participate and adjust content accordingly. Expect a diversity of needs and be prepared, therefore, to provide a different focus in different groups over time.

6. *Good services for LGBT students who are the victims of sexual assault or relationship violence.* Most campus and community agencies that provide assistance after sexual assault, rape, or battering do not have specific programs for men or for victims of same-sex assault or violence. Locating sexual assault and rape service or prevention programs in women's centers creates substantial barriers—but greater barriers derive from our society's silence about same-sex assault or violence and from the absence of specific training on these topics for peer or professional counselors.

7. *Sexually transmitted disease (STD) and HIV prevention programs.* These include (a) "passive" sources of information and advice, such as LGBT-specific

pamphlets, brochures, and videotapes, available in both health and counseling service waiting areas, consultation and examining rooms, and offices; (b) references to LGBT students, relationships, and specific prevention needs in all programs for general campus audiences; (c) health communications projects (such as posters, articles in campus newspapers, or "table tents" in dining facilities); (d) carefully integrated prevention messages, delivered in a caring manner, during clinical visits for reasons related to sexual activity; and (e) outreach prevention "appearances" at LGBT social functions (e.g., dances), gathering places, or bars. In each case, the content and format of the prevention message should be responsive to the (recently and repeatedly assessed) needs and preferences of the LGBT student population and should be delivered in partnership with members of the campus LGBT community. It is especially important not to continue, without evaluation and modification, prevention programs that seemed to "work" for earlier generations of students but may feel dated—or even affrontive—to current ones; "condom awareness" activities, for example, were more relevant in the late 1980s, and "hot but healthy sex" messages seldom appeal to gay undergraduates in the late 1990s.

8. *Sensitive STD screening, diagnosis, and treatment services for LGBT students—which require that clinicians be both humane in their approach and skilled in providing the specific services needed.* STD evaluation and therapy are, numerically and epidemiologically, more common among gay and bisexual men, and bisexual women, than lesbians—but providers must not assume that self-identified lesbian students have no risk for acquiring STDs, since many women who currently identify as lesbian have, or have had, a diversity of sexual experiences. Many college health services offer a separate women's clinic for gynecological services; it is essential that the providers in those clinics not assume that (a) all women seeking gynecological care are heterosexual; (b) all women need contraception; (c) women who identify as lesbian are not interested in reproductive health issues, including conception and childbearing; or (d) anything about the recent sexual behavior of any woman (ask!). Similarly, clinicians serving male students must not assume that (a) all men are heterosexual; (b) men who self-identify as gay or bisexual are sexually active; (c) men who are sexually active with other men have anal intercourse; (d) men who do not self-identify as gay or bisexual do not have sexual encounters with other men; or (e) male students know what specific medical attention they need (such as what cultures to obtain, from what sites), given their sexual behavior. The essential "bottom line," of course, is that a caring, humane clinician will make no assumptions about any student's behavior or risks, but will, instead, ask gentle and appropriate questions to guide the medical assessments or interventions offered.

9. *Good information about alternative methods of conception and services for lesbian women who wish now, or eventually, to bear a child.* These questions

generally arise either in gynecological care visits or during counseling sessions, so both clinicians and counselors should be prepared to answer them and to make appropriate referrals for further assistance.

10. *High-risk drinking reduction/prevention programs for LGBT students.* Although no specific data define the precise prevalence or consequences of high-risk (also called binge, or problem) drinking among LGBT students as compared with other students, broad clinical and counseling experience suggests that being gay, lesbian, bisexual, transgender certainly does not prevent this problem—which is, in a general sense, the most important health issue on college and university campuses. Most high-risk drinking prevention programs, though, are not inclusive of LGBT students and concerns; while it is common to emphasize the connection of binge drinking to acquaintance rape, for example, there is seldom any reference to same-sex sexual assault or relationship violence. LGBT students, like other students, are at great risk for alcohol-related health and relationship problems, especially during the time of transition to college. Among LGBT students, the fear of "not fitting in," a desire to feel comfortable and accepted, and the hope of blurring their sense of difference may be key factors in the motivation to make drinking central in social and recreational experiences. On the one hand, excessive drinking may expose students' secrets (by reducing defenses against self-disclosure) or remove the inhibitions that otherwise would prevent their showing interest in another student of the same sex; these actions may be regretted.

11. *Alcohol and other drug assessment and intervention services that recognize the special needs of LGBT students.* Few campuses provide long term alcohol or other drug dependency treatment programs for any students, but many offer assessment and referral services for students whose drinking or other drug use has become a significant problem. Substance abuse counselors should know where to refer LGBT students for inclusive, sensitive evaluation and therapy.

ACCESSIBLE, WELCOMING, AND HUMANE SERVICES

The best campus services are useless and pointless for LGBT students if they are inaccessible, exclusive, and unwelcoming. The physical environment of health and counseling services (layout, furnishings, decor), the "tone" of their programs, and the inclusiveness and sensitivity of their paper and electronic materials (brochures, web sites, forms, handouts) are major factors that contribute to, or detract from, the impression of safety, inclusion, and welcome that are essential if LGBT students are to utilize, benefit from, and value clinical, counseling, and prevention efforts.

If LGBT students find no reference to people like themselves in the materials distributed or posted by health and counseling services, see no gay and lesbian magazines in the waiting rooms, have to search for LGBT-specific health promotion resources, and find no effort to include LGBT students in the ranks of peer educators (as examples), they will likely distrust reassurances that those services truly care about the needs of LGBT students. Ways to make health and counseling services accessible and welcoming include the following:

First, make every form (both paper and electronic) completed by students inclusive of LGBT students and their relationships. The preadmission health history form is an excellent opportunity to make a clear, institutional statement about providing good services to all students, including LGBT ones. Template clinical record forms used in medical (and especially in sexually transmitted disease or women's clinics) or in counseling services should not promulgate a heterosexual assumption.

Second, while there is controversy about the value of "gay safe" labels, signs, or decals on the office doors of certain staff members (because the presence of those insignia on some doors, but not others, implies that there is no "agency standard" of humane care for LGBT students, and suggests that providers who do not display the sign are not to be trusted—but that the agency tolerates that situation), it is nonetheless important to advertise, in some clear way, that health and counseling services are, in fact, safe for LGBT students. An understated, but directly phrased, sign on the registration desk (e.g., "This health service provides effective, humane care for all students regardless of sexual orientation") is helpful; a similar message should appear on the web site, in brochures about the pattern and format of services offered, and in descriptions of health and counseling services that appear in the college's student handbooks, catalogs, and orientation guides.

Third, Place a selection of periodicals that appeal to LGBT students among other magazines and reading materials in all waiting areas. A quick survey of LGBT students should identify the most appropriate and valued selections.

Fourth, make sure that health promotion brochures for LGBT students are included among other brochures in general racks and at all distribution points. LGBT students should not have to ask for these resources; they should be readily visible and accessible. Since many students whose primary affectional and sexual orientation is toward others of the same sex are not out during college, having these materials freely available, where someone need not self-identify as gay or lesbian to obtain them, is especially important.

Fifth, similarly, the representations of relationships in the text and illustrations of these materials—and of posters and other health promotion resources—should be inclusive of LGBT students. Strangely, in some health services, the only HIV/STD prevention pamphlets present are ones that picture opposite-sex relationships entirely.

Sixth, decorations in the offices, examining rooms, hallways, and waiting areas should also be inclusive. Too often, sports posters are the only "art" displayed. In selecting wall hangings, pictures, and posters, choose some that allude to LGBT issues, show LGBT people, or emphasize sexual diversity in the campus community.

Finally, in recruiting peer educators, search for some LGBT students—who are more effective as peer opinion leaders in their community than heterosexual students would be.

PREPARING AND TRAINING EFFECTIVE, HUMANE SERVICE PROVIDERS

The backbone of campus health, counseling, and prevention programs is the quality of the work done by the professional and support staff. Many LGBT students will turn to these services for support, understanding, and care. It is simply not adequate to have one, or a few, clinicians, educators, or counselors who are "known" to LGBT students as caring, skilled, empathic providers: LGBT students should expect that *any and every* clinician, counselor, and educator will be humane, caring, and interested in their concerns. No health or counseling service should continue to employ either professional or support staff who demean, insult, or otherwise harm LGBT students–individually, as a group, or systematically. Few counselors who exhibit racist attitudes would survive on today's campus, and a clinician who demeans women seldom becomes a long-term employee—but, still, homophobic clinicians and counselors are tolerated.

Research surveys have shown that LGBT patients commonly feel their primary care providers are homophobic and that one fourth to one third of both physicians and counselors frequently feel uncomfortable treating LGBT clients or patients (Hayes & Gelso, 1993; Rudolph, 1988, 1990). Although no such formal assessments concerning college physicians, nurses, health educators, and counselors are published, LGBT students generally share the perception that some (and in some places, most) professional staff in health and counseling services feel uncomfortable with LGBT issues and express that discomfort in a variety of direct and indirect ways (e.g. the physician who silently shakes his head when a student discloses that he is gay; the women's clinic nurse practitioner who seems baffled and tongue-tied when a student reveals that she is lesbian; the counselor who refers a gay student to another provider because he is "just not comfortable dealing with these things"). It seems likely that these incidents occur in numbers far beyond their reported frequency; LGBT students often feel humiliated, enraged, and damaged after the event occurs and may not want to file a formal complaint (a process that might, in their minds, only open them up to more harm). Any focus group—or informal interview—with LGBT students will typically unearth a series of descriptions of such incidents and a lot of emotion attached to them. Some clinicians and counselors are unfamiliar with, uncomfortable with, or disgusted by either the "street vocabulary" used to describe some gay or lesbian sexual acts or by the acts themselves. It never occurs to some service providers that anyone could be lesbian, gay, bisexual, or transgender or that heterosexual students engage in many of these sexual acts. And some clinicians and counselors are poorly trained in the specific medical and psychological issues that affect the bodies and minds of LGBT students.

The problem, of course, often starts before an LGBT student sees a counselor, physician, or other care provider. The receptionists at the registration desk, nursing or medical assistants who conduct students to examining rooms and prepare them for the visit, pharmacists who fill their prescriptions, laboratory technicians who draw their blood or accept their urine specimens, and clerks who secure the date and time of a return appointment all contribute to the net experience a student has using the facility and its services. LGBT students commonly report feeling "looked at," talked about, or laughed at by support staff; unsurprisingly, these feelings are more frequent among students who are more visibly "different."

Any LGBT student should be able to assume that every aspect of care provided through the campus health and counseling services will be decent, competent, and humane. To make that possible, first, in the orientation of all new staff members, supervisors and administrators should make clear that the agency serves a diversity of students and that it expects—and will make available training resources to assist—all staff members, of every job title, to contribute to providing a welcoming environment for LGBT students.

Second, both health and counseling services should survey LGBT users— and non-users, if possible—periodically to assess satisfaction and perceived quality of care and services.

Third, whenever complaints are made by LGBT students about insensitive remarks, offensive comments, non-inclusive language and services, or incompetent actions, administrators should take them very seriously, investigate the allegations fully, and respond to the complainant quickly and sincerely. If a complaint appears valid, there should be an appropriate and definitive supervisory action—including, if needed, either reprimand or referral for further training, as appropriate. Repeated infractions, like any others, demand more substantial punishments. Students should be made aware of the outcomes and the resolutions.

Fourth, periodically, both health and counseling services should utilize professional development time for presentations or discussions of LGBT-related topics and concerns.

Fifth, the clinicians, counselors, and educators (including peer educators) working in campus health and counseling services should conduct periodic personal assessments of their beliefs and attitudes about sexuality and sexual differences. There should be someone on the staff who is available to other employees who have concerns about LGBT issues, people, or services. It is far better for a homophobic staff member to "vent" to a peer than to serve a patient or client badly. This refuge, though, is not intended for repeated use; it is, instead, a kind of safety valve—and, once utilized, it should connect to further referrals for assistance.

Finally, if graduate or professional students or postgraduate trainees (such as predoctoral interns in psychology or residents in medical specialties) utilize health or counseling services for teaching and training rotations, it is essential that their orientation include training about LGBT concerns and information about the agency's commitment to providing inclusive, effective, humane services.

THE CENTRAL ROLE OF PREVENTION

The most pressing and important health issues for LGBT students are often not, in the usual sense, medical problems. As is true for most other students as well, the quality of life here and now, while on campus, is dependent on behavior decisions, the influences on those choices, and the social and cultural context within which life and learning happen. Prevention is therefore particularly important in institutions of higher education and should have a central role in health and counseling services for LGBT students—and for the community they comprise.

First, every clinical visit for a medical problem should include prevention messages, resources, and referrals, as necessary, to make another similar problem less likely. Each encounter between clinician and LGBT student is a prevention opportunity. It is essential, however, to develop enough strength in the relationship between clinician and student to permit a discussion of personal, and sometimes difficult, subjects.

Second, health services should allocate substantial proportions of their total resources (money, time, space, energy, and people) to prevention; doing otherwise is ignoring the most fundamental realities of college health. The same is true specifically of services for LGBT students. Offering even the most excellent clinical services for STDs is inadequate absent comparable attempts to prevent unwanted or unprotected intercourse.

Third, in designing prevention programs and assigning priority to different issues (sexual behavior, drug experimentation, binge drinking, relationship violence), educators should first listen to the voices of LGBT students—through surveys, focus groups, and structured and informal interviews. Find out what seems most important to them. Enlist them as collaborators. Take their advice seriously.

Finally, prevention efforts must take serious account of the enormous diversity of the LGBT population. Both men and women, younger and older, are at vastly different stages of coming out, connecting with the LGBT community, and developing relationships of all kinds. While it is true that limited resources do not allow health services to "be all things to all people," it is also true that prevention programs can, at least, take all people seriously and attempt to include their interests and needs in some way in their work.

COLLABORATION WITH OTHER STUDENT SERVICES, ACADEMIC PROGRAMS, AND COMMUNITY PROJECTS

Throughout this chapter, we have defined health broadly, noting its interdependent character and its connection to the sense of community and respectfulness on campus: It is a state of well-being and dignity. Health and counseling services, then, will do their best work on behalf of LGBT students when they do it in collaboration with other student service agencies and with community service organizations working with gay and lesbian concerns. This interconnectedness of programs both strengthens the safety net for LGBT students and models exactly the interdependence and wholeness that create and sustain health itself. In an era of limited (and sometimes declining) resources, sharing the work of building a safe place for LGBT students also makes administrative common sense. Residence life programs, disability services, international student and scholar offices, and community health departments and acquired immunodeficiency syndrome (AIDS) service organizations are all good examples of potentially cooperative agencies.

Likewise, collaboration with academic officers and faculty is vital. The influence of professors on the minds and memories of students is probably the greatest of all. Just as health and counseling services can promote academic achievement through removing barriers to learning and increasing flexibility of mind (by treating illness, relieving stress, or counseling about adjustment to college, for example), the academic experience can contribute something to health—once again, broadly defined. Professors and teaching assistants help determine the campus climate for LGBT students; if homophobic comments are common in classrooms (or other students shun study groups with LGBT students), classrooms will be fearsome places, teachers will seem dangerous, and the stress among LGBT students will increase. Counselors and health educators frequently can become advocates for LGBT students in noxious classroom environments; simply assisting a troubled student whose professor's harmful remarks, stereotypes, or assumptions misses the mark, in many ways, if it is not accompanied by systematic efforts to make those actions less accepted—and therefore less common.

CHAPTER 17

Coming Out in the Age of AIDS: HIV Prevention on Campus

Peter A. Newman

Owing to massive prevention efforts, often on the impetus of the lesbian, gay, bisexual, and transgender (LGBT) community, rates of new seroconversions for the human immunodeficiency virus (HIV) are declining among adult gay men. Gay and bisexual men have not fared so well; their rates of new seroconversions are on the rise. This chapter will address the critical importance of HIV and acquired immunodeficiency syndrome (AIDS) education and prevention for LGBT college students. Programmatic suggestions for effective prevention will be offered. A central theme of this chapter is that effective HIV prevention for LGBT college students must be conceptualized and implemented as part of a comprehensive programmatic response to the distinct needs of this population. Seven major points will be covered: Most college students are having sex and are at risk for HIV; LGBT college students are at greater risk for HIV/AIDS than heterosexual youth due to additional psychosocial risk factors; ethnic minority LGBT students are at a particularly high risk for HIV; developmental issues and coming out are integral to HIV risk and prevention; HIV prevention on campus must be part of a broader programmatic response to the social, cognitive and emotional needs of LGBT college students; peer involvement in HIV education and prevention for college students is essential; and lists of do's and don'ts for HIV prevention are provided.

COLLEGE STUDENTS AND HIV/AIDS

A recent White House report estimated that one in four new seroconversions for HIV is among youth aged 13 to 20 (Fleming, 1996). Two-thirds of adolescents in the United States (US) have had sexual intercourse by age 19, although less than 10 percent report regular condom use (Flora & Thoresen, 1988). Longitudinal data collected from college students from 1974 until 1991 found a 91 percent non-virginity rate for men and 76 percent for women, and only one third inconsistently practiced safer sex (Murstein & Mercy, 1994). Rates of condom use among college students failed to increase from the mid-1980s to 1991 despite the increasing prevalence of HIV and growing fears of AIDS. Sexually active adolescents have the highest rates of sexually transmitted diseases (STDs) of all age groups (Hein, 1993; Perry & Sieving, 1991). If one takes into account the average 10 to 11 year lag between initial infection and AIDS diagnosis, when considering that AIDS is the leading cause of death among 25 to 44 year olds in the United States (Centers for Disease Control and Prevention [CDC], 1996), it is also evident that many adults became HIV-positive during adolescence and young adulthood. In sum, college students are clearly at risk for HIV/AIDS.

LGBT College Students and HIV/AIDS

While college students are of an age group at risk for HIV, 70 percent of HIV-positive adolescents and young adults are male; one third of HIV-positive adolescent males aged 13 to 19 and 63 percent aged 20 to 24 years old are reported to have contracted HIV through male-to-male sexual contact (CDC, 1996). Several surveys of gay male youth have found that upward of 75 percent report being sexually active, whereas only 10 to 15 percent consistently used condoms for oral or anal sex (Lambert, 1990; Rotheram-Borus et al., 1989). Studies contrasting older and younger gay males have reported higher rates of unprotected anal sex among the younger group (Hayes, Kegeles, & Coates, 1990; Stall et al., 1992). Additionally, condom use is a preventive behavior that correlates negatively with most risk behaviors (Ku, Sonenstien & Pleck, 1992). What this means is that those young people who engage in the most sexual encounters, or who are substance abusers, are also least likely to use condoms. Finally, in a study specifically of gay male college students between 18 and 25 years of age, D'Augelli (1992b) found that even as the students were concerned about HIV infection and aware of the risks, some continued to engage in sexual risk-taking behavior.

Together, these statistics speak to an alarming risk for HIV among gay and bisexual male college students. While gay and bisexual male youth have disproportionately high rates of HIV, young women are increasingly at risk. In the last decade, the incidence of new cases of HIV in women has doubled from 9 percent to 18 percent, with young women at the greatest risk (CDC, 1996). More than twice as many new cases of AIDS in 1995 were among women from 13 to 19 (40 percent) as compared to women over 25 (18 percent).

What remains critical is that despite the disproportionate risk for HIV infection among gay and bisexual male young adults, and the increasing risk among women, the meager sex education and condom information offered to youth is most often based on a heterosexual model. Further, most research on HIV/AIDS in adolescents and young adults denies the existence of LGBTs among this population (Sussman & Duffy, 1996). This is a recipe for disaster.

There are several substantive reasons for the elevated risk for HIV/AIDS among LGBT college students, as compared to their heterosexual counterparts. Understanding the nature and mechanisms of these risks is essential to developing effective prevention strategies and allows one to appreciate the necessity of a broad programmatic response targeting these populations.

LGBT youth, as contrasted with heterosexuals, experience intense cognitive, social, and emotional isolation (Hetrick & Martin, 1987; Malyon, 1981). These forms of isolation have specific relevance to HIV-related sexual risk-taking behaviors among college students and present obstacles to prevention as well. *Cognitive isolation* refers to a lack of accurate information about what it means to be lesbian, gay, or bisexual and a lack of positive role models. Social isolation results from a sense of feeling different from the "norm" and distancing from peers and family. Feeling unable to share feelings about sexuality with family and friends openly results in emotional isolation as well. The experience of isolation and stigma is common among LGBT youth.

Specifically with regard to HIV/AIDS, cognitive isolation results in a dearth of accurate information about HIV and its transmission. This isolation may distance one from feeling oneself at risk and may promote the belief that HIV is a disease only of adults. Alternatively, the equation of gay men and AIDS may lead gay male youth to believe AIDS is inevitable. For lesbian youth, there may exist the erroneous belief that they cannot contract HIV, even though they may at times have sex with men. Lesbian youth may experiment with unprotected sex with gay men, both unconsciously believing gay people cannot become pregnant (Hunter & Schaecher, 1994). One pilot study found that 75 percent of young lesbians engaged in intercourse with young, often gay, men as well as sex with other women (Hunter, Rosario, & Rotheram-Borus, 1994). Another risk factor is that young people may use anal sex as a form of birth control, even as it presents a risk of HIV transmission (Catania et al., 1989). Confusion also arises for bisexual male youth, who may believe that because they are not gay, they are not at risk for HIV. Lack of access to accurate information, and lack of forums to discuss these issues and their sexuality, may greatly increase the risk of contracting HIV for LGBT college students.

Social and emotional isolation render both lesbian and gay college students vulnerable, though it becomes important to address the differential developmental paths of lesbians and gay men. For young women, loneliness and isolation may result in their seeking out a relationship with another woman, and then withdrawing into the relationship to the exclusion of other friends and sources of support (Krestan & Bepko, 1980). Particularly for young women who do not have available a lesbian community, and who lack social support, more dependent and enmeshed relationships may result (Lewis, 1994). This may in turn lead to further isolation from peers and renders the relationship itself quite vulnerable, with potentially deleterious effects on social support. Not only may young women who self-identify as lesbians experiment sexually with men, but pregnancy may at times even function as a means to hide sexual orientation (Hunter & Schaecher, 1994).

Differences in the psychosocial developmental trajectories of gay and lesbian college students have distinct ramifications for HIV-related risk behavior (Hunter & Schaecher, 1994). Social and emotional isolation for gay male college students may lead to their going to bars or other venues in which they have heard other gay men can be found. Their cognitive isolation gives homophobic media depiction of all gay men as hypersexual, and of gay male relationships as nonexistent, greater credibility. Often the meetings in the venues of which young gay men are aware may promote sexual contact. With this sexual contact seen as the only means for affirmation of their being gay, these young gay men, even if they know about safer sex, may give in to having unsafe sex with other men so as to avoid further rejection. Gay male college students, some of whom may seek out sexual intimacy (much as their heterosexual peers), may fear being stigmatized and ostracized if they are seen with male companions in their college dorms, or shared houses, and so may be driven to more furtive and underground sexual encounters, which generally entail greater risk of unsafe sex than situations in which sexual negotiation and refusal are greater possibilities.

Ethnic Minority LGBT College Students and HIV/AIDS

African-American, Latino, Asian-American, and other ethnic minority LGBT youth face all of the isolation described of other LGBT youth, but their experience is often compounded by living between three worlds (Chan, 1989; Icard, 1986; Morales, 1990). First, they face the homophobia and discrimination of the dominant heterosexual culture, compounded with racism. Second, as opposed to heterosexual ethnic minority youth who may greatly benefit from the support of their ethnically similar parents and the larger ethnic community, LGBT youth may feel a sense of alienation from their own ethnic community due to homophobia. They may experience support around their ethnic identity, but not in being LGBT, and may either hide their sexual orientation or distance themselves from their ethnic community. Third, ethnic minority youth frequently do not experience the larger LGBT community as home, due to the racism that exists in this often European American–dominated culture.

The confluence of these negative social phenomena, and the feeling of not belonging anywhere, may exacerbate the process of identity development and may render self-esteem and social support particularly tenuous for ethnic minority LGBT college students. AIDS knowledge may be high, but the motivation and capacity to act on that knowledge may be negatively impacted by feelings of alienation, low self-esteem, and lack of social support. It is also necessary to consider that some ethnic minority LGBT youth may have developed considerable resiliency having earlier dealt with ethnic identity development in a largely hostile society. Another possibility for some youth of color is that LGBT issues may not be as salient, nor as stressful, as compared to living in a racist society. Feeling compelled at times, however, to declare one's allegiance (e.g., "Are you black or are you gay?") is a stressor (Washington, 1995) not faced by European American LGBT youth. The variety of psychosocial stressors and social vulnerabilities experienced by ethnic minority lesbian and gay youth likely contributes to the overrepresentation of African-American and Hispanic youth and young adults in HIV/AIDS statistics (CDC, 1996; Rotheram-Borus, Rosario, Reider, & Koopman, 1995).

HIV prevention and education must differentially target ethnic minority LGBT youth, who may not relate to messages developed for European American youth. Ethnic minority LGBT youth may have distinct experiences, some of which alienate them from the dominant culture. One significant factor is that more African-American and Latino men who have sex with men identify as bisexual than in the European American community (Rogers & Williams, 1987), suggesting that bisexual men must be specifically targeted as at risk in these populations. There also exists a legitimate and historically based mistrust of the dominant European-American culture, and of the health care system in particular, that must be addressed for prevention to be effective (Thomas & Quinn, 1991). Research has also specifically underscored the distinct language and meanings around sex, and sexuality, used by African-American gay men and the need to make HIV prevention culturally relevant (Mays, Cochran, Bellinger, & Smith, 1992).

Issues around language and acculturation are also strongly relevant for Latinos and Asian-Americans, as well as international college students, necessitating targeted prevention. Latinos who are more acculturated have more accurate knowledge about AIDS (Marin & Marin, 1990), although they also evidence increased HIV-related risk behavior, such as drinking (Caetano, 1987), as compared to less acculturated Latinos. There are also culture- and gender- specific obstacles to prevention (as well as strengths) among Latinas, as assessed in a survey of Chicana/Latina university students (Flores-Ortiz, 1994), which must be addressed in culturally competent interventions.

Culturally appropriate HIV prevention programs acknowledge the culture of participants and seek to work within that culture to identify behaviors and values that reduce risk (Freudenberg, 1994; McLean, 1994; Schinke, Botvin, Orlandi, & Schilling, 1990; Singer et al., 1990).

COMING OUT AND HIV-RELATED RISK-TAKING BEHAVIOR

Another critical aspect of LGBT identity development, and one that is distinct from that of heterosexuals, is coming out. The coming out process has several ramifications for HIV-related risk behavior, and its prevention. Coming out is usually understood as psychologically beneficial, in that LGBT people eliminate, or lessen, the dissonance caused by the lack of congruence between public and private personas (Vincke, Bolton, Mak, & Blank, 1993). There are several aspects of this process, including recognizing oneself as lesbian, gay, or bisexual, making one's social and emotional attraction to persons of the same sex public, the reactions of one's social environment, and the subsequent adjusting of social relationships. The development of an LGBT identity and the need to express one's newfound identity are part of the coming out process.

While the internal psychological adjustment that accompanies coming out may indeed be positive, coming out into a hostile environment can also bring with it a variety of new stressors. On the one hand, coming out can decrease risk-taking behavior in that one who is less psychologically vulnerable, with a more intact sense of self esteem, is more likely to practice health-promoting behaviors (Vincke et al., 1993). Alternatively, coming out can expose one to greater stress, which increases sexual risk-taking behavior—and particularly if sex is perceived as the expression of one's newfound gay identity, as is characteristic for some gay youth (Rotheram-Borus & Fernandez, 1995; Vincke et al., 1993). One may also experience increased social ostracism and the loss of social support, which may impact greater drug use and increased sexual risk-taking behavior. Coming out, then, must be conceptualized as a transactional process between the individual and the environment, and one in which social support is crucial. Social support is correlated with greater self-esteem, as well as the implementation of preventive behaviors for HIV in gay and bisexual youth (Rosario et al., 1995). Greater social support has been found to be linked directly to decreased risk for HIV among African-American adolescents (St. Lawrence. Brasfield, Jefferson, & Allyene, 1994).

A distinct challenge that has not been faced by previous cohorts of LGBT youth is that of coming out in the age of AIDS. For young gay men, the belief may exist that AIDS is an inevitability. I have argued elsewhere that, tragically, for some gay youth who have never known adolescent and young adult life without AIDS, and who have witnessed the decimation of the older gay community, becoming HIV-positive may have become a normative milestone in the coming out process. In the context of AIDS, coming out and seeking intimacy are vastly complicated by fears of illness and death that manifest for the individual, as well as for family, significant others, and friends (Paradis, 1991). Some gay youth "now perceive themselves as potential carriers of death, and others have become severely anxious about contracting the disease" (Isay, 1989, 68). Interventions must combat the confounding of being gay and having AIDS, in addition to providing social support and HIV-negative adult gay male role models for HIV-negative gay youth.

A final and critical aspect of coming out of relevance to HIV prevention lies in its developmental trajectory. The median age of first male-male sexual intercourse is 15 years old (Griensven, Koblin, & Osmond, 1994), whereas the median age of coming out is often in later adolescence or early adulthood. While there is considerable variability in the ages at which these developmental milestones are attained (G. McDonald, 1982)—in part as a function of societal changes over time—generally coming out for gay men has been found to follow first sexual experience by roughly four years (Roesler & Deisher, 1972). Gay men are also reported to first act on their sexual feelings an average of five years earlier than lesbians (Riddle & Morin, 1977). Of particular importance for HIV prevention, gay men tend to act on their sexual feelings two years prior to understanding what it was to identify as gay, whereas sexual activity for lesbians tends to occur four years after understanding the term *lesbian*.

It cannot be emphasized enough that many LGBT youth experiment with opposite-sex activity and engage in same-sex sexual behavior well before self-identifying as lesbian, gay, or bisexual (de Monteflores & Schultz, 1978). Additionally, some young gay men who engage in sex with men and who dismiss their sexuality may also deny the risks of their sexual behavior (Coleman & Remafedi, 1989).

The implications of the trajectory of coming out regarding sexual behavior are twofold. First, if HIV/AIDS education and prevention are situated solely in LGBT programs, they will often be accessed too late. Second, while it is imperative that HIV prevention be included in LGBT programs, and so made accessible and relevant to LGBT college students, HIV education and prevention (that is lesbian– and gay–affirmative) must also occur as part of other medical, psychosocial, and educational programs that recognize the variable nature of sexual behavior and particularly among college students who may not seek out, or may assiduously avoid, LGBT-designated programs.

HIV PREVENTION FOR LGBT COLLEGE STUDENTS

Given the often intense isolation experienced by LGBT youth, and the various aspects, both positive and potentially conflicted, of the normative coming out process, it becomes imperative that HIV prevention for LGBT college students be situated as just one aspect of a larger programmatic response to the distinct needs of this population. Research confirms the potential for negative sequelae of the coming out process, including increased alcohol and drug use and increased sexual risk-taking behaviors (Vincke et al., 1993). These possible negative outcomes are largely the result of stigmatization and decreased social support when coming out is undergone in a hostile environment, rather than the results of individual psychological problems experienced in a vacuum. One study found that young gay men (under 25) who did not belong to a gay organization had significantly higher levels of unprotected sex than young gay men who were connected to a gay organization (Ridge, Plummer, & Minichiello, 1994). These findings underscore the critical nature of LGBT-affirmative social support for LGBT college students and link social support directly to sexual risk-taking behavior and prevention.

Peer Involvement in HIV Prevention

In conceptualizing HIV prevention as one aspect of a holistic approach to the physical and mental health of LGBT college students, peer involvement in HIV prevention becomes crucial. There are several distinctive advantages to the involvement of LGBT college students themselves in preventive interventions (Perry & Sieving, 1991).

One indicator of the need for peer involvement in prevention programs is that AIDS knowledge and condom know-how have consistently been found to be insufficient in effecting behavior change (Hingson, Strunin, Berlin, & Heeren, 1990; Kegeles, Adler, & Irwin, 1988; Rickert, Jay, Gottlieb, & Bridges, 1989). LGBT college students must personalize AIDS information: perceive the threat to themselves and appreciate that they are potentially at risk (Hansen, Hahn, & Wolkenstein, 1990; Hunter & Schaecher, 1994). One misconception, at times fostered by public health officials, and adults in general, is that AIDS is an adult disease. LGBT college students can best internalize prevention messages if these messages are presented as relevant within their own frame of reference. A primary means of accomplishing personalization is through the use of peer educators (Perry & Sieving, 1991)—other LGBT college students, both HIV-negative and HIV-positive.

The inclusion of HIV-positive youth in peer interventions is important both to make AIDS real for college students and to show those students who may already be HIV-positive that there is life after a seropositive test result. It is imperative, however, that HIV-negative LGBT youth have HIV-negative role models to combat the belief, particularly among young gay men, that AIDS may be inevitable (Odets, 1994) and to avoid a perspective that glorifies life with HIV/AIDS. HIV-negative peer educators must be prominent in peer prevention efforts. It is also necessary to include ethnic minority college students, as well as lesbians, in peer prevention efforts, so as not to promote the illusion that HIV is exclusively a gay white male disease. Engaging a diverse and multicultural group of peer educators is integral to making the message relevant from within the students' own frames of reference. Given the larger context of cognitive isolation, the modeling of preventive behaviors by similar LGBT peers is imperative as it reinforces an appropriate frame of reference and the belief that "I can do it, too."

Another benefit of peer models is that LGBT peer educators and counselors promote the diffusion of prevention messages among other LGBT college students (Fisher, 1988; Kelly et al., 1991). Simply put, information is more likely to get out to the target population, through both formal and informal channels, if members of the population are included as an integral part of the intervention itself. Again, members of the lesbian community and communities of color are essential to effect broad diffusion.

LGBT peer involvement in HIV prevention also has salubrious effects on peer norms. Research consistently reveals the significance of peer norms in influencing the behavior of youth, and safer sex behaviors in particular

(Fishbein & Middlestadt, 1989; Jemmott, Jemmott, & Fong, 1992). By creating a community of peers involved in LGBT campus programs, one can institute and support a norm of safer sex and a norm supporting frank discussion of sexuality and sexual behavior.

Incorporating college students across all stages of planning, implementation, and evaluation of programs targeting their peers is an essential component of insuring that programs meet the needs of the students as they perceive them and that they remain relevant to those needs. The process of involvement itself is also empowering and affirmative.

Peer-facilitated discussions and role-plays among LGBT youth, in both gender mixed and gender separate groups, are an integral aspect of prevention as they engage college students in thinking about their behavior and in practicing skills to be used in potentially vulnerable situations. It is also critical that a nonjudgmental atmosphere be created, enabling young people to discuss, without shame and guilt, the inevitable slips that occur in safer sex. Limited research comparing peer-led and adult-led AIDS education programs has found that while adult and peer leaders were both effective in promoting knowledge gains and attitude change, more questions were asked of peer educators (Rickert, Jay, & Gottlieb, 1991). Dialogue and interaction constitute a critical dimension of engendering safer sex behavior and also model communication between potential sexual partners—critical to preventive behaviors.

PREVENTION DO'S AND DON'TS

Do's

1. Effective HIV prevention and education for youth includes cognitive, affective, behavioral, and environmental components (Flora & Thoresen, 1988).

2. Specific components of successful prevention programs include the development of accurate knowledge; building behavioral skills in condom use; building and practicing sexual negotiation and sexual refusal skills (for which role-play is helpful); open dialogue; social and emotional support; and teaching how to enjoy safer sex.

3. Use of peers is integral to effective HIV prevention for LGBT college students.

4. Differential programs targeting lesbians, bisexuals, gay men, and persons of color are necessary so as to make the messages relevant, comprehensible, and culturally appropriate. Further, the target population of the intended intervention should be involved in the creation of the intervention.

5. General sex education, anatomy and physiology, and STD education are also imperative for prevention efforts, particularly as much sex education to which college students have been previously exposed is situated in a heterosexist and nondialogical model.

6. The availability of condoms is crucial. Positive attitudes toward condoms are meaningless if one has little or no access to condoms. The distribution of free condoms by student health services and LGBT organizations, in the context of health and prevention

programs, also serves an important symbolic function in suggesting that it is okay to talk about sex and AIDS.

7. Confidential or, better, anonymous HIV-antibody testing, with the provision of pre- and post-test counseling, should be available. Students should be able, without fear of breaches of confidentiality, to find out their serostatus.

8. Access to a community of LGBT college students, and out LGBT adult role models, is essential. Social support and modeling are critical environmental components of effective prevention.

9. LGBT-affirmative medical and psychosocial support is important for both those who are HIV-negative and HIV-positive.

10. The availability and accessibility of alcohol and substance abuse education and treatment are crucial. While sharing unsterilized needles during injection drug use can directly transmit HIV, noninjection drug use and alcohol use are strongly implicated in greater sexual risk-taking behavior among adolescents and young adults (Bowser, Fullilove & Fullilove, 1990; J. Johnson, 1990–1991; Koopman, Rosario, & Rotheram-Borus, 1994; Stall, McKusick, Wiley, & Coates, 1986).

11. Prevention is not a one-shot deal but requires a sustained and integrated effort. The pressures surrounding college life, and the stresses of being a young LGBT person in an ambient culture of homophobia, are ongoing. Coming out, rather than a discrete event, is also an ongoing process. So, too, should prevention be ongoing. Additionally, the phenomenon that some gay men who previously practiced only safer sex return to unprotected sex also underscores the need for sustained prevention strategies (Hart, Boulton, Fitzpatrick, McLean, & Dawson, 1992; Stall, Ekstrand, Pollack, McKusick, & Coates, 1990).

12. Well-meaning adults involved in AIDS education and prevention need to periodically reassess our own views and prejudices regarding LGBT youth, sex, intimacy, and HIV/AIDS. It may be humbling to remember that as adults we have myriad difficulties with sexual relationships, sexual negotiation, and safer sex. Many of us are products of a homophobic and sexphobic culture and at different stages of working it through.

Don'ts

1. Homophobia and erotophobia must be removed from AIDS education and prevention. Stereotyping and moralizing about LGBT persons, and denigrating sex, is counterproductive. These cut off, rather than engender, open communication, in addition to impacting self-esteem and self-efficacy negatively.

2. Misrepresentation is to be avoided. College students know when they are being lied to—as in that sex with a condom feels better than without or that condoms are unilaterally fun. Such misrepresentation only furthers cognitive isolation and breeds mistrust. Trust is foundational to education and prevention, as well as intimacy.

3. Scare tactics are ineffective and counterproductive in attempting to promote safer sex. Fear may contribute to a sense of nihilism or rebellion that, in fact, promotes risk-taking behaviors. Scare tactics may also support the disempowering belief that HIV is an inevitability.

4. Censorship of information and discussion, and judgmentalism are to be avoided. The inculcation of shame and guilt is also contrary to supporting self-esteem and discourages frank and open discussion of actual sexual behavior and the difficulties that may accompany safer sex. Open and frank dialogue is optimal.

5. Encouraging sometimes unattainable standards of behavior may be counter-productive. Abstinence may be a natural and healthy choice for some students and should be supported if it is consonant with the student's goals and values. Postponement of sex is another viable option for some college students. On the other hand, the data presented earlier make it clear that most college students are having sex. Demanding unattainable, restrictive codes of behavior for those for whom they are not relevant often counterproductively results in impulsive acting-out behaviors that are more apt to be unsafe than planned or less guilt-ridden sexual encounters (Odets, 1994).

6. Being overly directive or authoritarian serves to disempower young people, the opposite of what is aimed for in helping them to be reflective decision makers. Disem-powerment is contrary to building self-efficacy, sexual negotiation skills and critical thinking.

7. Overreliance on testing as a cornerstone of prevention is paradoxical, as it in effect may communicate that seroconversion is an inevitability. One takes a test over and over so as eventually to pass (Odets, 1994). Testing is only one aspect of comprehensive prevention.

CONCLUSION

This chapter has presented HIV-related risk-taking behavior and HIV prevention in a social context. Frequently health promotion, and HIV prevention in particular, is divorced from sociocultural context. Our prevention strategies are most often based on individual-level models of decision making and risk behavior. Nowhere is this less appropriate than in dealing with LGBT youth. In acknowledging the social context of isolation, discrimination, and coming out, and in underscoring the power of social support, it is clear that social– as well as individual-level aspects of HIV-related risk-taking behavior must be addressed for prevention to be relevant and effective. From this socially contextualized perspective it is also evident that HIV prevention must be instituted as a sustained component of a comprehensive and proactive programmatic initiative to facilitate the overall health and well-being of LGBT college students.

In acknowledging the social context of LGBT identity development and campus life, and of sex and HIV/AIDS, one need not, however, assume the individual is a passive subject. The framework of this chapter advocates that we maintain a balance between individualistic and social conceptualizations of health behavior and sexual behavior. Within the context of social and environ-mental forces, individuals make choices—some more or less informed and free than others. As difficult as it may be, with even the best prevention programs, and with the greater experience and knowledge we may wish to impart as adults in earnestly wanting to help, decisions as to sexual behavior lie with the students with whom we work, not with us. We can offer education and encourage frank discussion of beliefs and values about life, sex, and intimacy, but ultimately young adults must make their own decisions as to what constitutes an acceptable level of risk (Odets, 1994). Our role is to empower LGBT college students to make the most informed and beneficial choices for themselves.

CHAPTER 18

Gay, Lesbian, Bisexual, and Transgender Students with Disabilities: Implications for Faculty and Staff

Ric Underhile and John R. Cowles

The Americans with Disabilities Act of 1990 (ADA) provides civil rights to persons with disabilities. An individual with a disability is defined as a person who has "a physical or mental impairment that substantially limits one or more of the major life activities of such individual; a record of such an impairment; or being regarded as having such an impairment" (Americans with Disabilities Act of 1990, S. 3). Faculty, staff, and administrators (FSAs) are encouraged to become familiar with the breadth of coverage provided by this legislation. It is unfortunate though not unusual to hear reports of college personnel defending a lack of campus accommodation by assuming compliance to be the sole responsibility of the disability support office.

The ADA is a comprehensive legal document; interpreting it is no easy task. Professionals working in educational settings can save valuable time and increase service efficacy by requesting brochures that summarize relevant passages of the ADA. Integrating this legislation into staff and faculty in-service workshops or presentations reduces the potential for embarrassing and hurtful debates between students, parents and professionals. Gaining familiarity with accessibility and reasonable accommodations allows faculty and staff to become knowledgeable about issues related to people with disabilities (PWDs).

While PWDs are protected by the ADA, persons who are gay, lesbian, bisexual, or transgender (GLBT) have not yet been granted civil rights equal to those of other citizens of the United States. As a result GLBT PWDs may seem fearful, angry, or difficult. A typical reaction by faculty, staff, and administrators may be to attribute these feelings or behaviors to the student's disability. GLBT students often endure severe stress due to the constant self-monitoring and assessment of social safety necessary to survive in an environment where judgment and hatred of GLBT persons are loudly condoned, while safety and support are quiet and discreet. Hostility and harassment of GLBT college students are well documented (Comstock, 1991; D'Augelli, 1993; Herek, 1989).

Faculty, staff, and administration may say, "But we do not have any GLBT students with disabilities on campus." This is a common fallacy. Until a safe zone has been established, these students will not come out and, hence, will not have their needs met. College personnel have the responsibility to be proactive in destroying the myth of invisibility; indeed, some GLBT students will not persist on an unsafe campus, which defines the issue of retention among GLBT students.

Many times, PWDs are objectified as merely the sum of their parts, while GLBT students are diminished to a set of sexual behaviors. Gaining appreciation of these complex cultural minorities is a first step in understanding the student in your office. Do not look at sexuality or disability as something that needs to be fixed. "If they could only find a cure for" is an oft heard lament. Neither GLBT persons nor PWDs need to be fixed because sexual orientation and disability do not break them, but negative attitudes do contribute to a "broken" feeling. Proactively building bridges between the GLBT and the PWD communities sends a powerful message of cultural appreciation. Colleges and universities that support GLBT students through student groups and Campus Resource Centers have the advantage of being able to utilize students as community liaisons. In college communities where GLBT student groups do not exist, the initiation or creation of partnerships with community centers is an often neglected opportunity. Many GLBT PWDs want to be connected to both communities on and off campus. The social isolation felt by these GLBT PWD students can be ended by participation in one or both of these communities. Students will remain in school if they feel a connection to and support from the campus environment.

This chapter will focus on strategies that may increase campus awareness of GLBT PWDs. However, years of socially endorsed oppression leaves long-lasting impressions on these students. The experience of being different is magnified during childhood. In his autobiography *Breaking the Surface* (1995), Greg Louganis provides candid examples of growing up with multicultural stigma: "I usually told them I didn't want a fight. They would call me a 'sissy-boy faggot.' They'd say, 'See, we knew you were retarded.' I would want to fight back, and of course I'd get my ass kicked" (36). His dark, Samoan complexion, dyslexia, and peer-induced fear of being gay left him with feelings of isolation so great that he attempted suicide by age 12. Educators, though often silent, are not naive to the experiences of students like Louganis.

Educational environments provide the backdrop against which many persons live much of their early lives. Persons who experience themselves as different from those they see within their environments are at great risk of internalizing negative self-thought: "The others are normal. I am not like the others; therefore I am not normal." For GLBT PWDs, the isolation that begins in elementary school often continues into college. This occurs because as sexuality becomes more known to the individual, marginalization seems to increase, whereas visible support decreases. As a dual minority, GLBT PWDs are unique due to the high probability of teachers, peers, and other family members not appearing to be like them. This prevalent lack of shared culture often creates a visible, yet unspoken, barrier and, ironically, a sense of invisibility.

Young adults embarking on a college career often are in a constant state of self-criticism. Understanding, recognizing, seeking out, and joining in with supportive peers constitute a necessary social aspect of college life. The feeling of being an integral part of a larger group often is first an antecedent and then a complement to academic success. Social and physical barriers—real and imagined—often decelerate or prevent GLBT PWDs from integrating successfully into peer activities (McAllan & Ditillo, 1994).

A young bisexual professional student who uses a wheelchair shared what the university faculty and staff could do:

Just listen and know that we exist. Don't shun us. Some people shun us because we have disabilities; some shun us because we are gay, lesbian, and bisexual. Some people will "double shun" us. As a student it can be hard because you want to attend meetings for students with disabilities and you want to attend GLB student meetings. There are different political agendas, being pulled in different directions. As a student, I only have so much time. I have to study. (Personal communication, October 22, 1996)

This student provides great insight into the challenge of integrating and balancing support services. It seems that university systems have often dissected minorities. It is as though GLBT persons belong in one place and PWDs in another. Professional counselors and persons working in Student Affairs are just now beginning to realize the necessity of being trained to work most effectively with persons maintaining dual, triple, or even quadruple minority status. This reality has been satirized in *The Sad Story of Zoe Rastus-Canard* (Bethell, 1993) in which a hearing-impaired African-American lesbian who uses a wheelchair struggles to find employment along with her lover/interpreter. This satirical essay exposes the "culturocentristic obstinance" of persons reticent to hire GLBT PWDs.

From the perspective of the individual, sadness, isolation, and depression are likely. This may result in either a lack of academic success or for many, a need to overachieve. GLBT PWDs may feel shameful of their "beings" and therefore become "human doings," often working themselves into isolated exhaustion. The academically high-achieving college student is often the one who stays alone on weekends and hides away in study carrels (Beane, 1981).

Academic retention is a serious concern to professionals in higher education. Many colleges and universities have begun to create and implement programs that target urban, racial minorities, and "at-risk" youths. The matriculation of an individual who is at high risk of attrition is often an expensive and labor-intensive effort. Certainly laborious invitations with subsequent refusals to acknowledge persons with particular academic, personal development, and accessibility needs are expensive exercises in administrative self-defeat.

Students with disabilities may feel hesitant to ask for support (Fichten, Goodrick, Tagalakis, Amsel, & Libman, 1990). Academic support services can be more proactive in creating feelings of acceptance and safety for GLBT PWDs. This can be done through the routine inclusion into activities supported by student organizations, residential life, athletics and university counseling services. Faculty sponsors, staff, and students participating in both disability and GLBT support services are often relegated to one or two annual campus-funded events. This furthers the stigma of belonging to a special population. Annual luncheons and cultural pride events should be highlights of the year, not lonely attempts by "members of the choir" within the campus community. GLBT PWDs should be provided overt opportunities to take part in campus social and academic events.

University counseling services have the responsibility and opportunity to increase their knowledge of and availability of services to GLBT PWDs. It is not difficult or unreasonable to expect at least one counselor or social worker to be professionally knowledgeable about both sexuality and disability. Counseling is proactive and consequently necessitates that professional counselors are supported in their quest for additional education in regard to GLBT PWDs. This can be accomplished through the participation in and presentation of workshops, becoming familiar with community support groups, and investigating written and alternative format materials for students, faculty, and staff.

To facilitate academic and social success, faculty and staff can and do play a role in the lives of GLBT PWDs. It is the responsibility of faculty and staff to become aware of GLBT PWDs. Once awareness is achieved, faculty and staff must challenge their own stereotypes of sexuality and disability. Some of those stereotypes include the notion that the disability led to sexual orientation; persons with disabilities do not have sex; students are not sexually responsible; students with physical disabilities are mentally impaired; and people with disabilities cannot have children or, if they do, that their children will have disabilities.

Students with disabilities have for too long been desexualized. This desexualization leads to a feeling of dehumanization for many GLBT PWDs. On campus the desexualization and dehumanization of GLBT students with disabilities lead to other issues such as isolation, depression, and lack of academic persistence.

Many GLBT PWDs choose to belong to both the GLBT and disability communities on campus, and faculty and staff can facilitate this potentially empowering experience. Faculty and staff are encouraged to participate in campus groups and organizations for students with disabilities and GLBT students. The young bisexual professional student was quite clear in saying what was needed from faculty and staff: "Faculty and staff have an obligation to support students in these groups. Those that are gay and or disabled need to come out, if they can, and provide us with positive role models" (personal communication, October 22, 1996). Faculty and staff can and do provide valuable support to GLBT PWDs.

Another support faculty and staff can provide is the creation and/or identification of a network for GLBT PWDs. On those campuses where GLBT and disability support groups do not exist, faculty, staff, and students can create and build networks. Such networks provide a safe place for students to "find someone like me." This network can come from many areas on campus: GLBT faculty and staff—particularly those with disabilities—can play a vital role in the network for GLBT students with disabilities. As discussed earlier, student organizations for GLBT students and students with disabilities are excellent networks. These resources are as diverse as the students served by them. Some students will need to know if the LGBT Campus Resource Center or local community center is accessible. Others new to the area may need to know if there are "gay appreciative" interpreters, personal care attendants (PCAs), counselors, and doctors. The information needed by this population is inexhaustible.

Although groups and networks are vital to the academic and social success of GLBT students with disabilities, individualism must not be forgotten. Some students may have needs that cannot be met by a group or resource network. By considering individual students' needs, students will feel they are in an open, accepting, and safe environment. This acceptance is perhaps the most important responsibility faculty and staff can offer.

GLBT services along with disability support services must also be more multiculturally sensitive to GLBT PWDs. For example, within the gay deaf community, sign language has been enhanced to provide vocabulary for gay slang (Kane as cited in Erting et al., 1994). Although it is imperative that professionals increase their knowledge of cultural diversity, the experience of the presenting client is paramount—GLBT PWDs may be black, Asian, men, women, transgender. The pathway to affective support is through sensitive listening, being knowledgeable about the many avenues of cultural communication, and the ability to embrace, without judgment, the diversity of the individual.

RECOMMENDATIONS

The following recommendations are provided so that college faculty, staff, and administration may increase appreciation of cultural diversity on campuses.

After Opening Your Mind, Open Your Space and Make Sure It's Safe

FSAs should be aware that GLBT PWDs do exist on campus. FSAs can become more accepting of these students and make the spaces around them safe and accessible. Safe spaces have signs and symbols that let the student know it's okay to be themselves. These signs may include rainbow flags and stickers, pink triangles, and others. Accessible means physical and personal access: Can the student get to you? Is your office physically accessible for a student with a disability? Are you accessible as an ally to the GLBT PWD community? Maintaining a "person first" attitude is the initial step.

Get to Know a GLBT PWD

Students who are GLBT PWDs are understandably hesitant to come out to FSAs or to ask for help. Making yourself accessible sends a message of safety, challenges stereotypes, and increases cultural support in the campus community.

Organize a Support Group for GLBT PWDs

These support groups may be a joint effort between disability services and GLBT services or may act independent of these services. FSAs along with interested students will need to start these groups and provide leadership and support to continue as student interest wanes and then increases again. Counseling centers, student leadership groups, and community centers can provide leadership and locations for a variety of support or discussion groups.

Encourage and Promote Workshops on Sexuality of Persons with Disabilities

Counselor education programs, student health centers, and social work programs often include human sexuality workshops, seminars, or classes. FSAs can communicate and work along with these departments to incorporate information about GLBT PWDs. The information learned through these venues can be disseminated throughout the campus to establish a more inclusive campus community. Many campuses have weeks that celebrate and educate, such as Disability Awareness Week and Coming Out Day/Pride Week. Such educational forums are perfect opportunities to present programs on disability and sexuality, including issues relevant to gay, lesbian, bisexual, and transgender students.

Encourage and Assist GLBT Students with Disabilities to Join with Other GLBT Campus Resources, But Also Permit a Separate Group If Desired

Many students have been raised with the cultural message that "different is not normal." This is true for GLBT students as well as for PWDs. It is wrong to assume that GLBT students have not internalized homophobia or that students with disabilities do not believe the myths surrounding PWDs. FSAs have the responsibility to confront and destroy hurtful, inaccurate stereotypes. This can be accomplished by hosting diversity panels that are inclusive of individual student groups as well as through separate support groups.

Faculty, Staff and Administrators Must Monitor the Quality and Character of the Campus Climate for GLBT Students with Disabilities

Keeling (as cited in Ryan and McCarthy, 1994) points out that service providers have an obligation to monitor the quality and character of the campus climate. This is particularly true for GLBT students with disabilities. Historically, both students with disabilities and GLBT students have had unmet needs. Faculty, staff, and administrators can change this by tracking the campus climate toward incorporating GLBT PWDs.

Increase Service Potential by Cross-Training Staff so that at Least One Professional or Paraprofessional is Able to Provide Information to GLBT PWDs as Well as Other Persons Who are Culturally Represented within the Campus Community

Disability support services are notoriously understaffed. FSAs can increase staff productivity and student retention by implementing in-service training sessions that explain a few basic concepts about the ADA. This alleviates the embarrassment of having students with disabilities defend themselves to uninformed staff. A series of workshops that present and discuss the challenges experienced by GLBT PWDs can greatly enhance the experience of students and FSAs.

Assist With Finding Gay-Friendly PCAs, Interpreters, and Other Support Personnel

Students who are GLBT PWDs spend an inordinate amount of time assessing the belief systems of potential service providers. Creating, maintaining, and making available references of personal care attendants, interpreters, and other support staff who are known allies to GLBT PWDs allow these students more time to learn.

Educators may be struck by the administrative ease with which many of these recommendations may be implemented. All of the components for assurance of physical safety, psychological well-being, and academic success are within our reach. It is our responsibility to take hold of them and send an intentional message of appreciation and commitment to gay, lesbian, bisexual, and transgender students with disabilities.

CHAPTER 19

Transitioning on Campus: A Case Studies Approach

Karen Nakamura

This chapter is designed for faculty, staff, and administrators involved with a transgender student who is "transitioning" on campus. *Transitioning* is the process of moving from one gender to another—male to female (MTF), female to male (FTM), something in between or neither—and is the stage at which transgender and transsexual students need the most support and advocacy. By definition, transitioning is a public event, and as a supportive administrator, faculty, or staff member, you will deal with various critical moments in your student's transitioning process. Be assured that most of these are temporary road bumps and that with your help and guidance students can successfully transition while on campus.

This chapter presents case histories based on actual incidents at university campuses, followed by analysis and discussion. The information has been gathered over the course of several years as part of a larger anthropological investigation of transsexual life narratives. In order to protect those involved, names of individuals have been changed and institutional identifiers removed. The case histories have been divided into three sections: peer issues such as bathrooms, residence hall issues, and violence against students; faculty problems—such as classroom interaction; and administrative issues such as name and gender changes and health plan issues.

PEER PROBLEMS I: BATHROOMS

As manager of the student radio station, Christine's transition was very public. The administrator of campus affairs heard over the grapevine that some female students objected to "a man in their bathrooms." The administrator talked with Christine and she agreed to use the only unisex bathroom on campus—the faculty bathroom in the administrative building. Unfortunately, a key was required to access this bathroom, and it was not available during non-business hours.

Bathroom issues are perhaps the most difficult to deal with as an administrator. You must balance the needs and desires of the transgender student as well as the complainants. An egalitarian compromise should be reached. Normally, people don't really pay much attention to who is in the next stall, but this often changes when "there is a man in the women's bathroom." The targets of bathroom problems are usually male-to-female transsexual or transgender students, although many butch lesbians or other masculine-appearing women also complain of being harassed in the women's room, despite being biological women.

For many non-transsexual women, the women's bathroom provides a psychological refuge from sexism and male harassment in the workplace. They may see the introduction of an MTF transsexual or a masculine woman as an unwanted intrusion of "male presence" into their "last safe haven." Interesting, men seem to rarely care about "women in the men's room." Transsexual men joke that this is the result of the unspoken male rule of "no talking or eye contact in the men's room," but it may also be due to the cultural invisibility of FTM transsexuals.

The administrator in Christine's case leaned too far in protecting the rights of an anonymous group of complaining students. The administrator never talked to these students to discuss why they were uncomfortable and what compromises they might be willing to make. Forcing Christine to use only one bathroom on the entire campus is unfair to her because it places the burden of responsibility wholly on her shoulders. You should be careful about relying on unverified rumors or complaints as the basis of your actions. Talk to all of the parties involved and decide on a mutually agreeable solution.

When one of his graduate students transitioned from male to female, Professor Roberts heard from his office staff that other students were uncomfortable with the idea of Jennifer using their bathroom. When he pressed the staff workers for more details, he found out that it was actually the office workers who were uncomfortable; no students had come forward with a complaint. Professor Roberts discussed this issue with both the transitioning student and the office workers. The compromise was reached that inside the three-story building that housed the department Jennifer was free to use the female bathrooms on the first and third floors but would not enter the one on the second floor, the one closest to the administrative offices. Since no one else on campus had com-

*plained, Jennifer was free to use any other bathroom outside of the depart-
ment. No student ever did come forward with a complaint.*

There are many variables in the bathroom problem. If the student passes well
as a female (again noting that female-to-male transsexuals rarely encounter
complaints), then things usually run smoothly. However, the rights of students
should not be contingent on their ability to pass a beauty test. Keep fairness in
mind when balancing everyone's needs and desires. The period of discomfort
for people usually only lasts a short time until they become used to the new
situation; impermanent problems don't require permanent sanctions.

Discuss with the transgender student whether he or she is worried about
campus security being called if a complaint does arise. There are some options:
Advise campus security ahead of time of this student's needs; give the student a
letter of authorization (see Table 7) so that the student is not stuck alone if an
incident occurs after hours; and handle such situations on an ad hoc basis. A
campus security lieutenant reported that in all of her years of service, security
had never been called in to deal with transgender students—these incidents usually worked themselves out by themselves. Be sure the student is comfortable
with whatever you agree on.

Table 7
Letter of Authorization for Transgender Students

To Whom It May Concern:

*Jane Doe (student id #123-456) has formally requested a change of name and gender,
which the University has accepted. From now on, he is to be referred to as John Doe. All
of his student records should be changed to reflect his new name and gender. Mr. Doe is
to be accorded all rights and privileges accorded to other male students. I thank you in
advance for your cooperation.*

Dean TS Garp

PEER PROBLEMS II:
RESIDENCE HALL AND OTHER ISSUES

*Rachel wrote to me over e-mail. She was living in an all-male dorm in a state
university in the Midwest. She hadn't transitioned yet because she didn't feel
safe in her environment. She hadn't even come out to her roommate who she
described as a "football thug." She felt stuck and was extremely depressed.*

It is extremely important to create a safe environment in which a student
may transition, but unfortunately many colleges still have many single-sex residence halls; any change in gender also means a change in housing. Trying to

cope with housing and roommate problems along with psychological, family, and other issues can often be overwhelming for a student. Many transgender students feel that they relinquish all rights and privileges because of their transsexuality. You can take important steps to act as their advocate and mitigate the problem.

Just as with the bathrooms, the ideal situation would be to find the student a room in a dorm with mixed units and private bathrooms/showers. The student should not be forced to room with a person because of gender or other issues, nor should they be situated on a single-sex floor if they do not identify as a member of that sex. Other problems also arise if the student wishes to engage in sports, use locker facilities, or join a fraternity or sorority. These issues can be handled in a similar fashion to the bathroom problem. In all of these discussions, you play a vital role as the mediator between the rights of the transgender student and those of his or her peers.

The period between semesters is often a good time to plan any change in housing status. Explore various options with the student, including off-campus housing. Be careful to make it clear to the student that he or she is not "being thrown off campus" for being transsexual. If a student doesn't feel comfortable in his or her peer environment, talk about what steps could be taken to improve the situation. You can host a group "talk-in" or invite a guest speaker, both of which can help lessen any worries other students might have or dispel any misconceptions surrounding transsexuality.

PEER PROBLEMS III: VIOLENCE ON CAMPUS

Rich transitioned from female to male just over a year ago. He encountered various problems ranging from other students who refused to use his desired name and pronouns to those who yelled out slurs at him from passing cars. He also received threats on his answering machine.

Violence against transgender students is a very real problem in campus settings. Unfortunately, because of their visibility, transitioning students make easy targets for hate crimes. You should set a firm campus policy of "zero tolerance" with this type of violence or other forms of harassment. If your campus code of conduct does not already protect sexual orientation and gender identity, make steps toward including them. Make sure that this policy is conveyed to campus security and provide training regarding lesbian, gay, bisexual, and transgender (LGBT) issues. If you don't already keep track of hate crimes against LGBT students, start now. Notify the campus about relevant policy changes or clarifications.

Many transgender students are ashamed of their status and hate the public gaze that is cast on them. As a result, they might be unwilling to report incidents because they don't want to "cause more trouble." Stay proactive in order to maintain the civil rights of these students. Administrators, faculty, and staff often do not realize the degree to which they are the role models for the rest of the campus. If you show total acceptance toward the student and his or her new status, those around you will be much less likely to make it a problem.

If a student in transition relates problems with his or her peers, talk about what can be done. Again, a group discussion led either by yourself, the student, or a guest speaker can solve many minor problems. If you think the problem might lie with a particular group of students such as a sports team or a Greek house, talk with their supervisor about whether or not a sensitivity workshop may be useful. You can model these workshops after those based on lesbian and gay issues since many of the problems are similar.

FACULTY AND STAFF PROBLEMS: CLASSROOM INTERACTION

Jaime came into the Ombuds' office with a problem. One of her professors refused to call her by her new name and consistently used the pronoun "he" when referring to her. This happened both inside the classroom and outside and was extremely uncomfortable for Jaime since she saw herself as well into the transitioning process. She felt that it "outed" her to students that might otherwise not have known she was transsexual. The Ombuds listened to her problem and then asked if she had raised it with her professor. Jaime responded negatively since the professor seemed so belligerent toward her. The Ombuds told Jaime that before her office would act on this officially, Jaime should talk to her professor directly. Jaime reluctantly agreed and talked to the professor. It turned out that the professor, far from being hostile, was very curious about Jaime's transition. Additionally, he was confused about how he should refer to her, especially since he had known her for two years prior to her transition. He was glad that she had raised the issue, and although an occasional "he" still slipped from his mouth, the situation improved immensely.

Transsexual students are often disappointed after their transition when people still refer to them with their old name and pronoun. What they do not realize is that this is due more often to ignorance than malice. Many non-transsexual people simply lack information that could balance their fears and concerns.

Faculty should recognize the visibility and authority of their position. If other students hear the professor using the inappropriate gender and pronoun toward the student, they may start to refer to the student this way as well. Unintentionally "outing" a transgender student in front of an entire class may lead to harassment or violence at a later date. It is important to clarify with the student what name and pronoun he or she would like people to use. This may change during the transition process. For example, one student originally named "Chris" first changed her pronoun designation from "him" to "her" and then at a later date changed her name to a less gender-ambiguous one. Administrators play an especially vital role in keeping everyone informed of these changes as they occur.

Because most of these problems are due to ignorance or misunderstanding and not malice, having the student talk to the individuals involved is often the best solution. If the student fears reprisal, it may be appropriate for him or her to be accompanied by you, a staff member, or a fellow faculty member. It may also be appropriate for a student to discuss the matter with the faculty chair or administrator and ask for the issue to be brought up during a faculty meeting where the student's intentions can be presented in a public forum and questions answered. As a colleague supportive of the student, you can often aid this process with a well-placed, friendly phone call. Be sure to ask the student before taking any action, however, since you don't want to act without his or her knowledge and consent.

ADMINISTRATIVE ISSUES I:
NAME AND GENDER CHANGES

Ben went into the registrar's office to change his name and sex officially. The staff woman at the desk was quite bewildered and told him, "You can't do this; only the dean can let you do this." He went to talk to the Dean of Student Affairs, who was immediately confrontational. The dean told Ben that university policy mandated that he would only be allowed to change his name and gender if he had a court-ordered name change and a letter from his doctor confirming that a sex-change surgery had taken place. Ben asked to see where this policy was written, but the dean refused to show it to him.

Within reasonable limits, the university should be willing to let students use the name that they wish to on their identification (ID) cards. From a simple administrative standpoint, it causes much less hassle if the gender of the person who is taking classes matches the name on the ID card. There is nothing to be gained by taking the hard-line stand on a name change. One possible alternative is an ID card with a first initial, last name, and no gender specification. This may be especially appropriate for students who are still questioning their gender status. It is very important to let former students change their student records after graduation. Not only is this good public relations toward a possible alumni donor, but it may also be critical for employment or graduate school purposes. The last thing a transgender person wants is for their past to suddenly spring forward when someone conducts a background check.

Since many students work or drive cars, you might encourage them to file for a legal name change so that they can change the name on their social security card and driver's license as well. Many states allow common-law name changes, which means students can change their name simply by declaring their new name in a public forum such as a newspaper. Most of the remaining states allow name changes through a simple legal process through probate or other civil courts. Usually, lawyers are not necessary for this process, and there is a small $50 to $100 court handling fee.

In no circumstance should a university require students to have surgical sex reassignment in order to change the gender on their student records. Sex reassignment surgery is an extremely arduous process that involves at least a year of preparatory therapy during which the individual is recommended to live as the gender of his or her choice in a "real life test" (difficult if your ID does not match your test gender), major surgery, and an expensive medical bill. Because surgical techniques are constantly improving—and student finances only improve with time as well—nothing is gained by forcing a student to hasten into surgery simply for the correct bureaucratic designator.

Ask the student if he or she would like a letter from the administrative office stating his or her new name and gender. Such a letter (see Table 7) can often smooth faculty and staff acceptance of the student's new identity.

ADMINISTRATIVE ISSUES II: HEALTH CARE

The student health plan at Becky's university specifically rejects "transsexual surgery or treatment." In reality, the doctors at the health plan have been helping her with her hormone regimen, and the pharmacy has been covering these costs as well. She doubts that the university will cover her sex reassignment surgery (if she gets it before graduation), but upon hearing that other transsexuals have been able to get coverage, she has thought about hiring a lawyer to help her push her case.

Many university health plans, like Becky's health plan above, contain a line that denies coverage for transsexual-related health costs. Often these are the result of concern that the university is funding a voluntary or cosmetic surgery. It is important to distinguish between hormonal treatment and sex reassignment surgery in these cases. We will discuss hormonal treatment first and then sex reassignment surgery. All of the issues surrounding health care become considerably more difficult if the student is a legal minor. This chapter assumes that the student is at least 18 at the time of treatment and is capable of informed consent.

Hormonal Treatment

While it is not the university's job to interfere with the doctor-patient relationship, it is reasonable for the primary care provider of the student to require that the student talk with the mental hygiene specialists before beginning hormone treatment. There is a detailed "Standards of Care" (SOC) for transsexuals released by the Harry Benjamin International Gender Dysphoria Association, which requires such a psychiatric evaluation before treatment. However, many in the transsexual community challenge the Benjamin SOC because it forces transsexuals to declare themselves as mentally ill before they can receive treatment. They rightly argue that no other medical treatment—even those of a drastic nature such as tubal ligation, vasectomies, or breast implants—requires the approval of a mental hygiene specialist.

In terms of reimbursement, universities and their health care insurers should not single out any group for differential treatment. Transsexual students on hormonal therapy require much the same treatment, hormones, monitoring, care, and respect as postmenopausal women or men with low testosterone levels. The cost of these hormones and monitoring fees is negligible, often not much more than the monthly "Pill" and yearly gynecological exams for biological females. There should be no reason why your health plan should not cover at least hormonal treatment for transsexual and transgender students. Hormonal treatment has immediate but reversible (within reasonable time limits) effects on the body and, together with living as the new gender full-time, is ideal for gauging whether surgery is desired or appropriate.

Sex Reassignment Surgery

Many transsexual advocates have been successful in removing the "transsexual surgery" clause from health plans—often by filing suit against health plan insurers. Although the usual defense is that sex reassignment surgery is a voluntary and cosmetic procedure, the courts since 1979 have been finding in favor of the plaintiffs. In the landmark *Victoria L. Davidson* V. *Aetna Life & Casualty Insurance Co.* (101 Misc. 2D 1, 420 NYS.2d 450 [Sup. Ct. 1979]), the court ruled that the surgery "cannot be considered to be of a strictly cosmetic nature" and that the "sex change operation of the plaintiff is of a medical nature and is feasible and required for the health and well-being of the plaintiff."

Nevertheless, transsexual surgery is an expensive and dramatically life-changing process. It is usually accompanied by irreversible sterility. Like any major step, it should be aided by good counsel and careful thought. The best advice for transsexual students is to take their transitioning slowly and to not feel rushed or pressured from any source. The university can greatly aid in this process by making the real-life test of living as the new gender as comfortable as possible.

POSTSCRIPT: YOUR ROLE IN THE PROCESS

You and the university have an important responsibility to provide a student with a safe and supportive environment during her or his transitioning. College is a wonderful time for self-exploration, and many people come to understand their transsexuality during this period. However, it is not an easy path to take since transsexuality is a long-term process with many short-term crises. Quite a few authors have compared it with the emergence of a butterfly from its chrysalis. As a supportive faculty, staff, or administrator, you can help students plan for the long term, cope with emergencies as they arise, and watch them fly off with their new wings.

CHAPTER 20

Campus Sexual Assault Prevention and Awareness Centers: Addressing Same-Sex Dating Violence

Joyce Wright

Studies show that dating violence affects at least one in ten teen couples. Among college students the figure rises to 22 percent, equivalent to the rate for adults (Gamache, 1991). Rape by acquaintances accounts for 85 percent of rapes reported to rape crisis centers (Koss, 1988), and the majority of victims are between the ages of 16 and 24. These statistics clearly indicate that rape and dating violence are major sources of violence in young adult lives. However, in spite of awareness programs around issues of sexual and dating violence, the realities of dating violence among lesbian, gay, bisexual, and transgender (LGBT) students remain invisible, creating the illusion that dating violence among LGBT people does not exist. For college students to confront the violence that may be in their lives, they must be knowledgeable about and feel safe enough with your campus's sexual assault prevention and awareness center staff to be open about their sexual identity and their relationships.

This chapter will discuss education and intervention strategies that may be helpful in addressing dating violence in the relationships of LGBT students. It will also address the need for a safe and welcoming sexual assault prevention and awareness center on your campus.

CONFIDENTIALITY

Confidentiality is a critical issue for LGBT students. Public awareness of private relationships is a particular fear in a college community where everyone seems to know everyone else. In the state of Michigan, rape crisis centers can provide complete confidentiality for any client except when there is a threat of homicide, suicide, or child sexual assault of a minor by an adult. In order to establish trust and support, it is necessary to provide staff and space where confidentiality can be ensured. The best solution is to have a well-trained staff and office space in a public building that offers many other services where people may come for diverse purposes.

ACCESSIBILITY

The experience of coming to a sexual assault prevention and awareness center can be daunting, especially for the first-time student. A primary goal of the center is to minimize the possibility of extreme discomfort beyond that which is inherent in students' personal situations. Accessibility involves finding a place that is physically accessible to individuals of all abilities, that does not seem threatening after dark, and near public transportation or within walking distance of student housing.

The office space should offer a comfortable atmosphere with homelike furniture and cheerful colors. Pictures, posters, and reading materials should reflect the faces and experiences of the students coming for assistance. The staff should also reflect the diversity of the community for whom you are providing services. It is extremely important to train and sensitize the office staff about the range of feelings and experiences of those coming in for assistance or calling on the phone.

Make arrangements with your LGBT Campus Resource Center for an extended staff training and development program. Such networking is also an excellent way to cosponsor programs on issues of same-sex dating violence or co-facilitate an LGBT support group. These methods will help to establish your agency as an accessible and safe place for LGBT students.

STAFF

Depending on the size of your organization, a good staff mix would include professional counselors (Master of Social Work [MSW] or Psychologists), paraprofessionals such as MSW interns, volunteers (students or staff), and support staff. At least basic counseling skills are necessary when building relationships with LGBT students seeking help. Such skills would include the ability to listen empathically, to validate the student's experience, and to respond to the concerns and issues he or she raises.

It is also important for the staff to have knowledge and understanding of same-sex dating violence and how classism, homophobia, sexism, and racism are connected to such violence. An excellent preparation for your volunteer staff is a 30 to 40 hour training program on these issues plus additional inservices throughout the academic year. These volunteers would then be responsible as peer educators for presenting education/awareness workshops, staffing the crisis line and helping to publicize agency-sponsored events.

SERVICES AND PROGRAMS

Services available to students should include, but not be limited to, a 24-hour crisis line; crisis intervention support; individual counseling; advocacy in academic, medical, and legal arenas; and support group counseling. Education and awareness programs should be offered campus-wide to foster understanding, to inform the campus community about dating violence and same-sex dating violence, to train staff to respond to appropriately same-sex dating violence victims, and to end the isolation of victims. These programs must use explicit definitions and descriptions of control, intimidation, and physically/sexually coercive behavior. They must consistently stress that dating violence occurs between women and between men as well as between men and women.

CONCLUSION

Addressing issues of violence in intimate relationships is difficult for anyone. For LGBT students the barriers of silence and invisibility make disclosure even more complicated. It is important that same-sex dating violence be clearly defined, that available services be explained, and that confidentiality is emphasized. Only through coordinated efforts will we give voice to the silence that perpetuates the violence.

PART V

Lesbian, Gay, Bisexual, and Transgender Issues in Athletics

CHAPTER 21

Creating Safe Space in College Athletics

Katya Salkever and Roger L. Worthington

The creation of safe space is a difficult and complex process. Within many athletic departments, formidable barriers stand in the way of change. It is essential that these barriers be addressed in order for progress to occur. Some of these barriers include the prevalence of homophobia and heterosexism in athletics (Hargreaves, 1994); myths about homosexuality in student athletes and coaches; the lack of visible and accessible lesbian, gay, bisexual, and transgender (LGBT) role models for student athletes; and the omnipresent focus on winning, recruiting, and team image at the expense of creating and maintaining a safe and healthy atmosphere for all athletes. These obstacles can be diminished through a three-step program designed to eradicate homophobia and teach tolerance and appreciation for sexual diversity. Safe space can be developed for LGBT athletes through the establishment of (1) an anti-discrimination/anti-harassment policy, (2) educational programs, and (3) support services. The purpose of this chapter is to address the barriers to full participation in sports by LGBT students and to outline the components of safe space.

BARRIERS

Homophobia in Athletics

Homophobia—the irrational fear and/or intolerance of homosexuality (Murray & Matheson, 1993)—exists in many facets of college life. Intercollegiate athletics is heavily plagued by homophobic words, actions, and attitudes. Because homophobia instills fear of discrimination caused by the stigma of the LGBT label, LGBT athletes are often fearful of derision if they come out, and straight athletes are frequently afraid of falsely being labeled as gay if they do not participate in oppressive acts. If athletic departments fail to address homophobia, the hateful and fearful actions and assumptions are strengthened and confirmed by silence. This type of atmosphere of silence then encourages further homophobia and heterosexism and forces LGBT athletes and coaches into a situation of lies and denial. No one is able to avoid the widespread effects of the culture of fear, prejudice, and hatred.

Some visible results of homophobia can be evidenced in the following occurrences: Women are reluctant to participate in athletics for fear of being labeled a lesbian (Killion, 1994); teams are divided between LGBT and straight athletes, causing rifts and discomfort (Hargreaves, 1994); spectators yell homophobic remarks to denigrate players on opposing teams (Griffin, 1993); coaches are fired or are not hired because they are gay or lesbian (Hargreaves, 1994); players are stripped of their scholarships because of their sexual orientation (Brownworth, 1994a); and coaches refuse to recruit suspected LGBT athletes (Killion, 1994). All of these events take place in sports at the intercollegiate level. The atmosphere created by homophobia colors the experiences of all athletes, coaches, and administrators. Discrimination limits opportunities for growth and success, denying LGBT athletes the chance to recognize their potential and future in athletics. Until homophobia is confronted, the collegiate athletic experience cannot provide a true understanding of individual strength, trust, respect, and teamwork.

Myths about Homosexuality in Athletics

In collegiate athletics, cultures of homophobia and heterosexism have created numerous myths about homosexuality and sport. Many false ideas are learned and reinforced through established societal norms that define masculine and feminine ideal types. Other misconceptions occur because of the strong bonds and the intense friendships formed between teammates. These harmful and oppressive ideas are rarely addressed by athletic departments, leaving many questions unanswered and biased attitudes unchallenged. Such ignorant and biased views become accepted as unquestioned truths. Typical myths include the following ideas: Gay men are never athletes (Griffin, 1993); female coaches are always lesbians; gay men do not excel in power sports like football, hockey, basketball, and baseball; lesbian athletes and coaches try to convert team members to lesbianism (Murray & Matheson, 1993); male gymnasts and figure skaters are always gay (Griffin, 1994); softball is a lesbian sport (Killion, 1994); and, all LGBT athletes will always make sexual advances towards their teammates (Murray & Matheson, 1993).

These notions perpetuate false assumptions, discriminatory words and actions, and stigmatization. Over time, ignorance, fear, and slanted observations have further solidified these myths, making them difficult to dismantle. These powerful, biased ideas force athletes to take action to avoid the stigmatization of homosexuality perpetuated by the myths. Such actions include: A straight softball player quits the team because softball is maliciously labeled "the dyke sport on campus"; a bisexual student refuses to play ice hockey because he believes he cannot succeed at physical sports; a lesbian soccer player separates herself from her teammates, fearing they will discover her sexual orientation; a diver decides not to try out for the team because the coach is gay; and a lesbian coach favors only straight players, wanting to establish a straight team image. In each scenario a student misses an opportunity for learning and development because of the fear of discrimination, humiliation, or violence. In the end, all students fall victim to the power of the myths, unable to freely think, practice, play, or compete on teams supportive of the growth of all athletes (Griffin, 1994).

Lack of Visible and Accessible LGBT Athletic Role Models

Because of the silence and invisibility created by homophobia and hetero-sexism, LGBT student athletes often have great difficulty finding and identifying LGBT role models and mentors. Many coaches decide not to reveal their LGBT identity for fear of losing their jobs and their reputations (Griffin, 1993). LGBT team captains and student leaders are often hesitant to discuss their sexual orientation due to fear of losing the respect of their teammates. Pro-fessional athletes often choose not to identify themselves publicly as homosexual because they might lose contracts, endorsements, and professional standing (Killion, 1994).

LGBT athletes are hard-pressed to find heroes. They cannot identify LGBT idols from their childhood. In the past, homosexuality was never discussed and therefore could not be included in the profile of an athletic legend. Today, student athletes can rarely gain strength and affirmation from the triumphs of the few present-day LGBT superstars. Absent from television spot light, cereal boxes, and clothing labels, few out LGBT athletes become household names. The dearth of heroes, both past and present, leaves young LGBT athletes without a sense of community or an understanding of their history.

This striking absence of LGBT athletic role models sends out the alarming message that respect and success can only be achieved by straight or silent athletes. To establish a formidable, universally admired reputation, an athlete must display a mainstream image. Openly LGBT athletes suddenly become labeled as poor role models and less worthy athletes (Griffin, 1993). In this glaring void of positive images, LGBT athletes in collegiate sport struggle to affirm a positive identity.

Winning at All Costs and the Protection of Team Image

Athletic teams serve as highly visible representatives of the character and mission of their university. Coaches and athletes function as ambassadors to their sport, athletic program, and their college. Outsiders observe an athletic team's ability, success, and personality to gain familiarity and understanding of a school. These powerful assessments and ideas are projected to prospective students, influential alumni, surrounding communities, and the media. As a result of the pressures of the spotlight, team success and image become primary goals for many athletic departments. Each team hopes to represent its school with a victorious all-American team (Killion, 1994); Each individual team member is expected to act in accordance with these goals, regardless of whether they are misrepresented or stifled in the process. This focus rarely serves the best interests of LGBT athletes.

In many different ways, LGBT athletes become silenced on their own teams (Brownworth, 1994b). For example, many coaches assume heterosexuality when adopting motivational techniques, using LGBT slurs to punish and berate unsuccessful or weak players (Griffin, 1994). Players reinforce these ideas similarly using epithets and jokes to insult opposing players and slacking teammates. LGBT athletes suffer the assault of these homophobic remarks regardless of to whom they were targeted.

LGBT athletes face additional hardship in the protection and presentation of team image. A team is expected to appear straight regardless of the sexual orientation of its individual members. Coaches and teammates only acknowledge the existence and presence of straight partners of athletes. Gay male athletes considering revealing their sexuality often receive foreboding signs of rejection (Pronger, 1990). Many coaches of women's sports fear their team will be tagged with the lesbian label. In response to their fears, some coaches use negative and homophobic coaching and recruiting practices. For example, prospective recruits are told a team does not and will not have any LGBT participants (Brownworth, 1994a). LGBT players are ostracized and discouraged from continuing to compete. LGBT athletes face the unfair choice of keeping quiet, quitting, or losing scholarships (Hargreaves, 1994). Without some form of protection from this oppression, LGBT athletes will continue to be marginalized in college athletics.

CREATING SAFE SPACE

The first step in combating homophobia is to recognize that it exists in all places and with all people. Everyone has been influenced by the homophobic ideas held in our society. To varying degrees, even LGBT individuals have internalized these societal standards. These assumptions and prejudices are impossible to escape completely. It is therefore highly essential that every individual department member examine his or her own feelings of homophobia and questions about homosexuality (Griffin, 1994). They might ask themselves the following questions: Do I label an athlete's sexuality according to his or her sport? Do I assume that many female athletes and coaches are lesbians? Do I assume every male athlete is straight? Have I expressed any opinions on homosexuality to my players? Do I laugh at LGBT jokes? Do I discourage LGBT insults? Do I consider the comfort and safety level of my LGBT athletes?

As these questions are examined, each coach or administrator can begin to assess his or her own homophobia or heterosexism, pinpointing ideas and assumptions that need to be changed. The changes can first be represented with the establishment of administrative policy (Griffin, 1994). Then, through educational and training programs, athletic department members can learn how to undo their own homophobia. Once the unlearning process begins, the coaches can then address the elimination of homophobia on their teams while providing the support, services that meet the needs of their LGBT athletes.

Administrative Policy

The first step to combating homophobia must be initiated by the athletics administration. By adopting a mandate that requires the acceptance of diversity, a statement is made to the entire athletic community. The most effective manner to initiate this statement of change is to develop departmental policies that address homophobia and prejudice. These anti-discrimination, anti-harassment, pro-diversity policies will begin to create safe space for all athletes, coaches, and administrators. The key facets of strong administrative policy include expanding and enforcing an anti-discrimination statement to include race, gender, and sexual orientation (Griffin, 1994); an anti-harassment statement forbidding the use of words and actions to intimidate an individual because of their race, gender, or sexual orientation (Griffin, 1994); a statement regarding the protection of LGBT individuals in all employment decisions based on race, gender, or sexual orientation, including hiring, promotion, salary increases, or termination; and a statement of commitment to diversity pledging continued efforts toward the acceptance of all athletes. These four ideals lay the groundwork for a strong statement against racism, sexism, and homophobia. An environment providing comfort and safety of all athletes can be built around this policy.

It is important that both students and staff have some influence on the formulation and establishment of these policies. Input can be solicited from student leaders, coaches, and administrators. It might be helpful to examine existing policies in other area athletic departments. Athletic department policies should be consistent with, or extend beyond, university-wide anti-discrimination policies. Policies need to be explained to all students, staff, and administrators and should be displayed in the guidebooks and team rules and regulations. At home games, event programs should contain a statement prohibiting spectators from engaging in sexist, racist, or homophobic remarks, and announcements of such can be made over the public address system.

In order for the policy to be effective, consequences for infractions of the policy must be established. Specific guidelines and procedures need to be outlined to deal with policy violations. This solid stand against intolerance makes a strong statement of commitment to acceptance of diversity in athletics. With the backing of an anti-discrimination, anti-harassment, employment protection policy, the athletic department establishes a commitment to creating safe space for LGBT athletes.

Educational Programs

The next step in the movement toward the creation of safe space is the establishment of educational and informational programming. Educational programs serve to help athletes and staff to identify and combat homophobia while learning about the situations and needs of LGBT athletes. Numerous learning opportunities can be accessed through an array of athletic department programs, presentations, and offerings. Here a number of these programs are highlighted to illustrate an educational agenda that, in combination, can reach a varied and widespread audience. The possibilities are not limited to the examples that are discussed in this section.

Forum Presentation. A panel of LGBT athletes are brought together to answer questions and lead a discussion on diversity in athletics. Panelists can include both past and present LGBT athletes from your own or neighboring universities. Each individual talks about their personal experiences as LGBT athletes. In the telling of each individual's story, the following questions can be addressed: When do athletes face homophobia? What are visible and invisible effects of homophobia on both LGBT and straight athletes? How have coaches, administrators, and fellow athletes been effective in curbing homophobia? What are some of the highlights of competing as an LGBT athlete? What words or actions make LGBT athletes feel comfortable on their teams?

By presenting a panel of LGBT athletes, the audience begins to recognize that the LGBT athlete is a teammate, classmate, or friend who is forced to face the prejudices of homophobia in his or her athletic experiences. Each individual can then acknowledge the positive and negative effects of his or her own actions, while recognizing individual steps that can be taken to foster safe space.

Speaker Presentations. Outside speakers are invited to present on various topics relating to the LGBT experience in collegiate athletics and beyond. In a lecture atmosphere a student can quietly and anonymously gain important information and support through the experiences, stories, and advice of others. By connecting the college life and experiences beyond graduation, students will be presented with the long-term and omnipresent effects of homophobia. This can then lead them to consider the importance of their actions in the creation of safe space. Simultaneously, LGBT athletes can identify role models and recognize successful LGBT athletes. A speaker series might include a bisexual athletic alumna highlighting how competing as an athlete helped her career; a gay professional athletic referee telling about homophobia in the pros; a lesbian coach presenting on how homophobia and heterosexism forced her to lose her job; a transgendered sports management consultant talking about sports marketing in the alternative media; the parent of a gay collegiate soccer player discussing the struggles her son faced competing as an out gay athlete. Through this forum of formal speaker presentation, the athletic student population and athletic department staff can benefit from the exciting and sometimes high-profile experiences of those working and competing in the sports world.

Group Discussion and Problem-Solving Sessions. The group discussion and problem-solving program provides students with real and imaginary problems surrounding homophobia, heterosexism, and diversity in athletics. The students and staff work in teams to discuss the problems and identify solutions that might be effective. The scenarios will encourage individuals to consider the perspectives of others. The following are four examples of possible scenarios.

1. You are a sophomore athlete. You recognize that one of your first-year teammates is struggling with the dilemma of coming out to the team. What can you do to help your teammate decide whether she or he comes out?

2. You are a senior captain. Your coach continually uses homophobic slurs to insult or motivate his players and to cultivate an aura of non-tolerance on the team. You feel what he is doing is wrong. What do you do?

3. You are the coach of the tennis team. In confidence, one of your players comes out to you. What steps do you take to provide support for your player?

4. You are an assistant athletics administrator. An alumnus gives you a donation for the department but says he doesn't want money to go to the "queer teams." How do you handle this situation?

When presented with these problems, every participant in the athletics program is forced to confront real issues of homophobia present in all levels of the department. This method of education is a hands-on, concrete experience designed to encourage reflection and action.

The key to the success of the educational programs is majority participation and active involvement. For some events mandatory participation might need to be required to ensure department-wide exposure. Certain speakers, panels, and discussions might be included in the agenda of team activities to encourage team communication and support. Additionally, a strong administrative backing of the entire educational package will convey the importance of the issues. It is essential that the messages of tolerance, diversity appreciation, and safe space for all athletes be heard by the entire athletic community.

This combination of forums, speakers, and discussions will provide extensive information, viewpoints, and experiences of gay students in college athletics. As knowledge is gained, ignorance and prejudice can be lessened, providing a more sensitive atmosphere. All of these changes will serve to benefit the relationships of teammates and the comfort and growth of all athletes.

Support Services

The last step needed to create safe space for LGBT athletes is the provision of student support services. LGBT athletes face extreme isolation and struggle because of the silence and stigmas surrounding homosexuality and sport. It is essential that the athletic departments provide advising, group support, mentoring, and resource referral to alleviate some of the distress and meet the emotional needs of individual LGBT athletes. Administrators, coaches and fellow LGBT athletes can fill these roles as advisers, listeners, role models, and supporters. However, in order for these individuals to feel comfortable in their support roles sufficient preparation and training must be provided. Through workshops, role-plays, and information exchange, a coach, administrator, or fellow athlete can learn to answer questions, listen to problems, and provide referrals to LGBT athletes who are in need.

Coach as Adviser. When students are struggling with issues or problems in their lives, they often turn to their coaches for support and guidance. In the player's eyes, a coach is an individual who knows them well, sees them daily, yet can provide objective opinions because he or she is not involved in the social and academic portions of a student's life. It is important for coaches to display an open door policy to their players, to ensure healthy individuals and strong player-coach relationships. This means a coach must be prepared to listen to a player discuss a wide variety of topics, including issues of sexual orientation and homophobia.

For many coaches these issues are difficult to hear, let alone discuss. The culture of silence and homophobia makes many coaches wary of the consequences or stigmas attached to addressing and advising on topics of sexual orientation. In order to dispel these fears and discomforts, the entire coaching staff should receive some form of preparation or training in the form of workshops or role-play sessions. Through increased situational discussion and administrative encouragement, coaches can become more at ease in the advisement of students struggling with sexual identity, discrimination, and homophobia.

As advisers, the coaches should not consider themselves as counselors. They may not have the training or expertise to deal with the psychological issues facing an LGBT student athlete. The primary goal of the coach as adviser should be to listen to the troubled player, expressing concern and support. The coach should help the player consider and evaluate her or his needs for services without presuming that the student will want or need additional help. If more help is required, the coach should provide the student additional campus options for taking further steps in addressing his or her concerns. Coaches should have a list of referrals on campus that are targeted to meet the needs of LGBT students, including peer support and discussion groups on campus; faculty/staff or coaching mentors; student advisers and student affairs personnel designated to address LGBT issues; athletic department health services advisors who are trained to deal with LGBT problems; and counseling and career services on campus, especially LGBT-friendly counselors.

Each of these resources can provide crucial advice and support to LGBT students. They are also able to present students with off-campus support options.

It is essential that coaches provide the avenues for finding the resources when a player expresses the need for guidance and support.

Peer Support Group. For many LGBT individuals the most important support comes from LGBT and LGBT-friendly peers. On most campuses, one or more LGBT peer support groups meet regularly for student discussion, support, and socialization. Because LGBT athletes often function in a separate social circle from the general LGBT communities on campus, general LGBT support groups often do not meet the needs of the LGBT athletes. What may be needed is a support group that specifically targets the issues surrounding being an LGBT athlete.

By forming a Queer (LGBT) Athletes Alliance, or QAA, LGBT athletes and allies will have a forum for peer discussion and support. QAA can provide a weekly, biweekly, or monthly outlet to trade stories, voice grievances and struggles, and find common bonds between individual athletes. This group does not need to be run through or by the athletic department. It is possible that counseling services, the LGBT Campus Resource Center, or the Office of Student Affairs might provide the space, funding, and organization necessary for such a group to work. Regardless of who provides the resources, the formation of a QAA group would serve the needs of LGBT athletes searching for peer alliance and fellowship in a safe space and atmosphere.

Mentor and Role Model Program. LGBT athletes often need support not only from their peers but from adults in the college and surrounding community. A good way to establish this support is through a mentorship program. This program matches LGBT athletes with LGBT coaches, administrators, faculty, staff, and community members who can provide guidance and leadership through an understanding of past LGBT experiences. Because many LGBT athletic staff members do not feel safe disclosing their sexual orientation, the pool of possible mentors should stretch to LGBT faculty, staff, and administrators who were college athletes as well as LGBT athletic alumni.

Once assembled, this group of mentors could provide individual, informal guidance and support for LGBT athletes. Through such an established program, personalized services and community relationships could be forged benefiting both the LGBT athletes and the college as a whole. The athletes would gain the double advantage of feeling supported in the community while finding role models who demonstrate the triumphs and successes of LGBT athletes in the college community and in society.

Support services for LGBT athletes are essential for the creation of safe space in intercollegiate athletics. The services will help the student body, athletic staff, college, and local community provide support to further the growth, development, and health of LGBT athletes. The provision of coach as adviser, a QAA, and a mentor program creates a network of support for LGBT athletes utilizing resources, student alliance, and adult role models.

CONCLUSION

Athletic departments must take action to create safe space in college sports. What has traditionally been an arena of bias, discrimination, and silence can be transformed into an open, safe, supportive environment. However, overcoming decades of oppression and discrimination will require a long-term commitment to provide safe and supportive environments for all student athletes. Through self-evaluation the entire university community can clarify the barriers that exist in homophobia and heterosexism and move toward increasing levels of acceptance and affirmation. Change can be created using administrative policy, educational programs, and support services. Through the establishment of these three aspects of safe space, LGBT athletes can benefit from resources, allies, protections, and services. With time, the use and support of these programs can build a safe, comfortable, friendly space for athletes of all sexual orientations.

NOTE

The authors would like to thank Linda Scott and Jennifer Price for their input and comments on drafts of this chapter.

CHAPTER 22

Heterosexism and the Lesbian Label in Women's Intercollegiate Athletics

Susan R. Rankin

> In sports the L word is lesbian, and everyone—homosexuals and hetero-
> sexuals—lives in fear of being called a lesbian because it is used to discredit
> and disqualify people.
> —Donna Lopiano, executive director, Women's Sports Foundation
> (Brownworth, 1994b, 82)

Concern about homosexuality is a powerful force in sport. It has resulted in an intimidating pressure to deny the existence of lesbian, gay, bisexual, and trans-gender (LGBT) people in athletics and to "closet" those who are there. The issue of lesbianism in sport is so controversial that few women, gay or straight, will speak about it. Their fears are not unfounded: Being perceived as a lesbian in women's athletics carries the same stigma as *being* a lesbian. Coaches and administrators fear negative recruiting, job loss or not being hired for jobs, and challenges to their credibility. Student athletes fear ostracism, lack of playing time, and scholarship loss. Despite the National Collegiate Athletic Associ-ation's (NCAA) mandate that "the Association shall promote an atmosphere of respect for and sensitivity to the dignity of every person" (NCAA Manual, 1993, ix), the heterosexist climate in college sports is a painful reality for nearly every athlete, coach, and administrator in the country. While in recent years several professional sports figures such as Martina Navratilova (tennis), Greg Louganis (swimming), Rudy Galindo (figure skating), and Muffin Spencer-Devlin (golf) have identified themselves as lesbian or gay, the world of high-profile intercollegiate athletics has produced no such role models. This does not mean, however, that LGBT student athletes, coaches, and administrators do not exist in college sports.

As far back as I can remember, I have been involved in organized, competitive athletics. I played basketball on my grammar school team and softball in the parks league, and I competed in high school, college, and the Women's Fastpitch Major League of the Amateur Softball Association. I spent the last 16 years coaching at a Division I institution that is recognized nationally for its stellar intercollegiate athletics program. Also, for as far back as I can remember, I have identified as a lesbian. In recent years, I have been an outspoken advocate for LGBT equity in higher education, particularly in intercollegiate athletics. Through my own experiences, through the perceptions of my colleagues and student athletes, and through interviews with coaches and players across the country, I have discovered that the negative impact the heterosexist climate has on both straight and LGBT members of the athletic community is clear.

The victimization of LGBT people in the academic community is well documented (Berrill, 1990; D'Augelli, 1989a, 1989c; Herek & Berrill, 1990; Rankin, 1994). Research shows that anti-gay prejudice prevalent on college campuses obstructs the pursuit of knowledge and creates a hostile climate that allows, or countenances, victimization (Rankin, 1997). As a microcosm of the university, the environment in athletics mirrors the prejudicial climate evident on campus. Brownworth (1994b) noted, "Sports may be the most homophobic arena in the United States today." While the heterosexist climate affects all LGBT athletes, coaches, and administrators, this chapter will focus on lesbians and bisexual women in college sports through investigating the construction of the lesbian label in sport and its contribution to the heterosexist climate prevalent in intercollegiate athletics; examining the experiences of lesbian and bisexual coaches and student athletes in intercollegiate athletics and their impact on sustaining a heterosexist climate; and suggesting intervention strategies that may assist in improving the climate.

SOCIAL CONSTRUCTION OF THE "ATHLETIC CLOSET": THE LESBIAN LABEL IN WOMEN'S ATHLETICS

Historical Context

In an excellent history of American women in sport, Cahn (1995) wrote:

Women's very participation in sport has posed a conundrum that Americans have grappled with for more than a century. Beginning in the late nineteenth century, women made determined efforts to break down barriers to female athletic involvement. They claimed sport as a right, a joy, and a signal aspect of women's emancipation. These attempts elicited both approval and scorn, generating a series of controversies that spanned the century. The controversies surrounding female athleticism broached fundamental questions about the content and definition of American woman- and manhood. (3)

While some people celebrated the woman athlete as the embodiment of modern womanhood, others branded her "mannish" or lesbian. Women were cautioned about the "masculinizing" effects of sport, such as deeper voices, facial hair, and overdeveloped arms and legs. The intent of these warnings was to temper and control women's sport participation and to keep women focused on their "natural" and "patriotic" roles as wives and mothers (Lenskyj, 1986). To abate the stereotype of the "mannish," and therefore lesbian, athlete many women in sport accommodated to pressures that they demonstrate their femininity and conform to gender conventions inside and outside of sport.

"The tension between sport and femininity led, paradoxically, to [women's physical] educator's insistence on women's right to sport and on inherent differences between female and male athletes. Balancing claims of equality and difference, early physical educators articulated a woman-centered philosophy of sport that proposed 'moderation' as the watchword of women's physical activity" (Cahn, 1994, 9). Several generations of women professional physical educators sought to protect the reputation and health of female athletes by devising separate, less physically taxing versions of women's sports. In effect educators created a respectable "feminine" brand of athletics designed to maximize female participation while averting controversy. "Moderation provided the critical point of difference between women's and men's sport, a preventative against the masculine effects of sport. It was this philosophy, with its calculated effort to resolve the issue of mannishness, which guided the early years of twentieth century women's athletics" (Cahn, 1995, 9).

Ironically, the institutionalization of heterosexism in sport was initiated in part by women leaders in sport. "Intentionally, or not, policies designed to mollify a homophobic public merely added to the institutional bulwark that privileged heterosexuality and condemned lesbianism" (Cahn, 1995, 184). The strong cultural associations between sport and masculinity made women's athletics ripe for emerging lesbian stereotypes. Despite women's sports advocates' attempts to "prove" the heterosexuality of themselves and their athletes, such as mandating feminine dress and conduct codes, this strategy did little to suppress the lesbian stigma of women's sports.

Sexism and the Lesbian Label

In recent years, feminist scholars have begun to analyze the experiences of lesbians in sport (Bennett, Whitaker, Smith, & Sablove, 1987; Birrell & Richter, 1987; Cahn, 1995; Griffin, 1992; Hall, 1987; Lenskyj, 1986; Messner & Sabo, 1990). These authors share the perspective that women's participation in sport is a threat to male domination—an issue of power. "In a sexist and heterosexist society, women who defy the accepted feminine role or reject a heterosexual identity threaten to upset the imbalance of power enjoyed by white heterosexual men in a patriarchal society" (Bryson, 1987, in Griffin, 1992, 252). According to Pharr (1988), homophobia is a powerful political weapon of sexism. The lesbian label is used to define the boundaries of acceptable female behavior in a patriarchal culture. Lesbians challenge traditional gender roles and the patriarchal structure of society; hence, they are labeled as deviant and stigmatized by society (Bryson, 1987; Griffin, 1991). In the case of lesbians in sport, not only are they challenging traditional gender roles; they are doing so in a male-dominated environment (Knoppers, 1992). Since women's sports have been labeled as "mannish," and therefore lesbian, activity, women in sport are particularly sensitive to the use of the lesbian label to intimidate (Griffin, 1992). This challenge threatens the power and privilege enjoyed by men in sport and thus leads to increased incidence of prejudice and discrimination.

The feminist foundation for examining the experiences of lesbians in sport is predicated on these beliefs: (1) sport is a patriarchal institution and is considered a masculine domain in our society (Bryson, 1987; Griffin, 1994; Lenskyj, 1990; Messner, 1988); (2) negative perceptions of lesbians are perpetuated in the sport environment (Blinde & Taub, 1992a, 1992b; Griffin, 1992); (3) there exists an institution of sport-promoted compulsory heterosexuality (Lenskyj, 1990); and (4) the previous conditions lead to the creation and maintenance of a hostile environment for lesbians (Krane, 1996). One wonders, then, what is the impact of the lesbian label on women in intercollegiate athletics, and how does it contribute to the heterosexist climate?

IMPACT OF HETEROSEXISM AND THE LESBIAN LABEL ON WOMEN IN INTERCOLLEGIATE ATHLETICS

Women heard for decades that they should not participate in sport. Historically, athletic competition was considered "dangerous," creating large muscles and threatening women's ability to bear children. Today women are warned that if they are involved in competitive sport, they will be identified a lesbian. Tara VanDerver (USA Olympic women's basketball coach) commented that "a lot of different things have been used to keep women out of athletics. [The lesbian label] is one of them" (Cart, 1992, C1). Lesbian coaches and athletes face a unique set of circumstances not experienced by their heterosexual colleagues. In intercollegiate athletics, to be lesbian and an athlete is to be the target of anti-gay prejudice.

As noted earlier, the victimization of LGBT members of the academic community is prevalent on college campuses. Recently, the discrimination and harassment faced by lesbians in athletics have also been documented (K. Brown, 1991, 1992; Brownworth, 1994a, 1994b; Krane, 1996). The incidents range from physical violence and verbal harassment to more subtle discriminatory behaviors such as ostracism and lack of opportunity. One coach said, "One of my players stayed late after practice for some extra work. Some football players walked by and started yelling some anti-gay names. She protested, and they beat her up (lesbian coach, personal communication). An administrator noted, "Some athletic directors screen applicants for coaching positions and administrative jobs based on perceived sexual orientation [they] simply hire women who have husbands or hire male coaches to avoid dealing with the lesbian label for women's teams" (athletic administrator, in Mott, 1996, 18). An athlete shared, "I was the starting shortstop at my college for three years. My senior year, I decided to come out and march in the local pride march. That spring, I was cut from the team" (lesbian athlete, personal communication). Another athlete said:

> She [the coach] said it the first day of practice in my first year. Lesbians are not welcome and indicated that if she found out she would take away their scholarship. I remember at the team meeting in my second year I was so afraid that it was going to be like the first. She made the point very strongly. It was a very negative statement. I just remember it affected me. Of the meeting, all I remember is that one moment. That sticks in my mind. It will be in my mind forever. (lesbian athlete, Cart, 1992, C1)

These examples typify the subtle and overt forms of anti-gay prejudice that are evident in women's athletics. Heterosexist comments are a symbolic form of violence and serve as a constant reminder of the threat of physical assault or other forms of discrimination, such as being cut from the team, being ostracized by teammates, not getting a job, and so on (Garnets, Herek, & Levy, 1992). Altman (1993) suggested that it is the more subtle forms of discrimination and oppression that are most disconcerting. These types of actions are more difficult to avert and, in turn, perpetuate the heterosexist environment in sport. According to Blumenfeld (1992), heterosexism "diverts energy away from more constructive endeavors" (13). In the case of women in sport, this diverted attention has a limiting effect on both straight and lesbian athletes as they strive to excel in a restrictive climate.

Silence and Invisibility Fueled by Fear

In response to the stigma of the lesbian label and the threat of anti-gay prejudice, many lesbians in sport decide to remain silent and invisible. For example, Babe Didrickson, one of the greatest women athletes in history, never publicly avowed her relationship with Betty Dodd.

> Her lack of self-acceptance and articulation was a loss to a generation of lesbian women who yearned for a self-proclaimed lesbian hero. Her silence does not make her less of a person. It simply makes her a survivor of a generation and a culture constrained by unrealistic images of men and women and sometimes violent homophobia. In this arena she was human, vulnerable, and afraid. For all her courage, bravado, and fiercesomeness, she ultimately chose silence. (Cayleff, 1995, 265)

The inducements for a woman to reveal her lesbian life to a national audience are few; the reasons for silence, many. Fear is rampant in women's college sports, according to both athletes and coaches. Some say that lesbians, and the homosexual image, are destroying women's sports. Others say the stereotype is simply a mechanism to keep women out of sports and it is heterosexism that is ruining women's sports. What both sides share is fear—fear of talking about it, fear of being accused of it, fear of those who are different.

Pat Griffin, a pioneer in the area of homophobia in women's athletics, noted that lesbians have always experienced discrimination in sports and that such discrimination affects all women in sports. Women fear that if they are perceived to be lesbians they will not be hired or they will lose their jobs. There is real fear that athletes will be dismissed and that coaches will use negative recruiting techniques. Grffin admonishes that all this takes place amid a huge balnt of silence. (Griffin, in Mott, 1996). In a recent study of lesbian athletes, Krane (1996) suggested "[T]hrough concealing behaviors, silencing their lesbian identity, and compartmentalizing their lives, athletes constructed an appearance that would allow them to fit in with their teammates in what was perceived as the least aversive manner" (29). None of the lesbians interviewed in Krane's study felt safe enough to be completely open about their lesbian identity. Learning to hide one's lesbian identity is a necessary strategy in order to endure in a heterosexist environment. A golfer shared, "When I got to college in 1974, the other golfers told me to stay away from the coach, she was one of 'them.' I thought, who do they think I am? Silence was the safe way to operate in those days" (Lipsyte, 1991a). A straight athlete said, "I don't really have any problem with homosexual athletes, coaches, or sport psychologists. But I do resent the fact that their silence and secrecy causes others to think that all of us are homosexual. It is more of an image thing: how they affect my image is my biggest problem with it" (non-LGBT athlete, Rotella & Murray, 1991, 356). A lesbian athlete told this story:

> I remember someone shouting yelling out "you Dyke" or "you Butch" and every woman on the team shuddered. I shuddered too. It was just so exposed. You know, you're taking a shot, and you can't hide your strong arms. But the thing was, there were no lesbians on the basketball team that I knew of. It was just the kind of thing that people said about women players. And I think that's part of why there is so much fear of it. The straight players don't want people thinking they're gay. (Lesbian athlete, Brownsworth, 1994, 83)

The lesbian label and subsequent silencing of lesbians in sport serve to foster the heterosexist climate in college athletics (Krane, 1996; Palzkill, 1990; Peper, 1994). For example, in 1988-1989, the NCAA conducted a survey to examine what women in intercollegiate sports believed were the barriers in their college athletic careers. Of those surveyed at 180 institutions, 75 percent of the women administrators said they were aware of existing stereotypes that might be perceived as barriers to attracting or retaining women in athletics. When asked to specify the "barriers," 54.4 percent said their involvement in sports led others to assume that they were gay (National Collegiate Athletic Association, 1991).

Consequences for Being Out in Athletics

The issue of homophobia in college sports was raised publicly in March 1991 by Rene Portland, head basketball coach at Pennsylvania State University. Coach Portland articulated what many had been saying in private. It usually happened the first practice of the year—sometimes it was later—but it always happened. Portland would gather her players and state her team rules: "[N]o drinking, no drugs, no lesbians" (Cart, 1992). To be open about one's sexual orientation means the possibility of being benched, losing a scholarship, or being ostracized by teammates. "It [Portland's policy] pushes more women into the closet, it pushes more issues under the rug. I've seen young lesbian women get married just to get a coaching job. And I've heard athletic directors say, 'If we have lesbians here, I don't want to hear about it' " (women's athletic director, in Lipsyte, 1991a).

The lesbian label also affects the visibility of lesbian coaches in that very few lesbian college coaches can be out in the workplace. In addition to the anti-gay prejudice experienced by out lesbian coaches, negative recruiting is also used against those who are perceived to be gay. While it is against NCAA rules to "negatively recruit," that is, to disseminate negative information about another coach or school, the practice is prevalent. Coaches say privately that this is what happened a few years ago when a letter was reportedly circulated among the nation's top women basketball prospects. The letter contained a list of supposedly gay and straight women's coaches and warned prospective student athletes away from the lesbian coaches. More recently, a male amateur softball coach from California circulated a list of allegedly lesbian women on a softball Internet listserv: He said they were "killing the sport of softball." These actions underscore the fact that the perception of lesbianism is used as a threat in recruiting female athletes. One coach said, "I know she is one of the best players in the country but there is no way we are going to recruit her. I hear she is a lesbian and she would just destroy our whole team. Besides, she would kill our recruiting for next year. Other coaches would use it against us" (coach, Rotella & Murray, 1991, 355). A lesbian coach ironically stated, "I try to discourage lesbians from my teams. It isn't necessarily that I'm against lesbians. I'm a lesbian myself. But I think there's a stigma attached to the game itself when there are too many lesbians involved" (lesbian coach, Brownsworth, 1994b, 77). An associate athletic director shared: "The real panic is in women's inter-collegiate sports. Athletic departments don't even like to run workshops on sexual and gender issues, they think it will be used against them in recruiting. There's homophobia, of course, but I think it's basically a power issue, another way of controlling women" (associate athletic director, Lipsyte, 1991a, C1). Another athletic director said, "Yes, it [negative recruiting] is used. There are coaches who are terrified it will be used against them. There are athletic directors who are terrified it will be used. I would hope that parents would view a coach who would resort to that sort of recruiting technique as being desperate" (associate athletic director, Cart, 1992, C1).

Lesbian coaches who are out fear the consequences their openness may have on their coaching careers. In addition to the possibility of losing talented prospective athletes due to negative recruiting practices, lesbian coaches also face losing their positions or relinquishing their credibility with their athletes and peers. Further, they may have to deal with these issues with little or no support from their athletic administrators, who themselves may be lesbian. In my 16 years as a head coach, several of my colleagues were fired or pressured to resign from their coaching position due to their sexual orientation. Such horror stories are well known throughout the coaching ranks and fuel the fear and subsequent invisibility of lesbian coaches. Personally, I found it very difficult to function in a heterosexist environment as an open advocate for LGBT equity. While I was not dismissed from my position, I feel my credibility with many of my athletes suffered. This eventually led to my decision to resign from my position. Unlike men's athletics, where head coaches are fired and hired on a daily basis, women coaches who leave a position rarely return to the profession.

In summary, a heterosexist climate is prevalent in intercollegiate athletics, revealed in the subtle and overt harassment and discrimination experienced by women athletes, coaches, and administrators. Krane (1996) suggested, that "understanding the experiences of lesbian administrators, coaches, and athletes, and the impact of those experiences, can lead to the development of appropriate strategies for combating [heterosexism] in collegiate sports" (16). Based on this suggestion, the next section will investigate possible strategic interventions to improve the current climate in intercollegiate athletics.

A CHANGING CLIMATE IN ATHLETICS?

Enforcing the Silence

It is evident that the silence and invisibility surrounding the lesbian issue in women's sports are deeply ingrained at all levels in women's intercollegiate athletics, from student athletes to coaches to administrators. Griffin (1992) noted, "We [women in sport] have responded to questions about lesbians in sport with silence, denial, and apology" (261). Such widespread silencing reflects the heterosexist climate in sport and the fear associated with the lesbian label. This "strategy of silence is counterproductive to efforts to dispel or minimize the impact of the lesbian stereotype. Not only does silence disallow a direct confrontation with those who label athletes lesbian, but it also perpetuates the power of the label by leaving unchallenged rumors and insinuations. Moreover, the fear, ignorance, and negative images that are frequently associated with women athletes are reinforced by this silence" (Blinde & Taub, 1992a, 159).

The refusal of leaders in women's sports to address the lesbian issue may be partially due to women coaches and administrators themselves being victimized by the lesbian stereotype. Thorngren (1990) reported that the lesbian label was a significant source of stress for women coaches and impacted on several domains of their lives (social life, recruitment of athletes, searching for and retaining coaching positions). "If our goal is to defuse the lesbian label and strip it of its power to intimidate women in sport, then we must break the silence. [O]ur failure to speak out [against heterosexism] signals our fear, ignorance, and discrimination that flourishes in silence" (Griffin, 1992, 261).

What steps can we take to challenge the heterosexist climate? Building on the recommendations in the literature, three themes for strategic transformation emerged: (1) structural changes; (2) formulation of inclusive policies, and (3) educational efforts. The intervention strategies are summarized and presented in Table 8.

The Private Impacts the Public

The pressures for lesbians in sport to keep their lesbianism a private and invisible matter forces them to restrict their public interactions with their colleagues and student athletes. S. Woods (1992) commented on how defining sexual identity as a personal and private matter acts to deflect institutions away from developing non-discrimination policies on the basis of sexual orientation. "When sexual orientation is viewed from this perspective, the institutional forces that shape and define oppression are not questioned. [T]he onus of change is placed on the individual and not the system. This stance allows heterosexual coaches and administrators to appear liberal and tolerant with regard to lesbian issues without having to recognize and address both the personalized, sociopolitical, and institutionalized aspects of heterosexism that renders many of their colleagues invisible" (114–115). This emphasizes the need for heterosexual coaches and administrators to reflect on their own implicit support for, and acceptance of, heterosexism on their campus. Griffin and Genasci (1990) argued that taking action against heterosexism is the responsibility of all women in sport, regardless of their sexual identity.

The implementation of the interventions suggested in Table 8 indicates the athletic administration's visible support for the LGBT community and its commitment to providing a welcoming climate for its LGBT members. Providing a climate that is welcoming and celebratory of difference provides a safe environment for lesbian athletes, coaches, and administrators to be out. Research by Herek (1986) and Rankin (1994) indicated that contact with out lesbian and gay people who embrace their sexual identities reduces anti-gay prejudice. According to Griffin (1992), increased lesbian visibility is one of the most effective tools in combating heterosexism in women's sports. If athletic administrations can provide welcoming, inclusive environments that foster the visibility of lesbian athletes, coaches, and administrators, then perhaps the lesbian label in women's sport will finally begin to lose its power.

Table 8
Strategies for Change in Athletics

Structural Change

- Create an LGBT student athlete support group.
- Actively advocate the recruitment of LGBT athletes and coaches.
- Use inclusive language in all athletic venues.
- Visibly support current LGBT staff and student athletes (for example, attendance of athletic director/coaches at National Coming Out Day and LGBT Pride Week rallies and activities).

Policy Inclusion

- Include sexual orientation in university nondiscrimination clause.
- Include sexual orientation in policies and other written materials produced by the athletic department (media guides, sport camp information, ticket policies, facility policies, etc.).
- Include in "athletic department code of conduct" that anti-gay prejudice (both subtle and overt) will not be tolerated.
- Develop policies and procedures for reporting anti-gay prejudice in intercollegiate athletics (note that issues of confidentiality are especially important for student athletes).
- Develop policies and procedures for responding to anti-gay prejudice.

Educational Efforts

- Develop diversity training programs inclusive of sexual orientation for administrators, coaches, and student athletes (mandatory for all new employees and in-coming first year students).
- Incorporate sexual orientation into education programs for student athletes
- Conduct educational workshops on issues of sexual orientation for academic athletic advisers, medical staff, athletic trainers, strength and conditioning coaches, managers, and so on.

CHAPTER 23

Athletics and Gay Male Identity: The Loneliness of the Long-distance Runner

Dan Bauer

Any college faculty member or administrator who seeks to improve the lives of gay and lesbian students cannot overlook the athletic arena. While the 1980s and 1990s entailed significant infusion of gay and lesbian visibility into popular culture, the world of college athletics remains a bastion of inhospitality to gay and lesbian students, whether or not those students participate in sports. Particularly at small liberal arts colleges, where student athletes may compose anywhere from one fourth to two thirds of the student body, this policing function against gay identity is particularly curious and problematic. The athletic arena is so charged with concern for the well-being of students, and also with a palpable obsession with physical appearance, as well as the corollary of such vanity—sexual desire. In fact, of all the places on campus where compulsory heterosexuality is enforced, athletic complexes are notorious for breeding an atmosphere where social space for lesbian, gay, bisexual, and transgender (LGBT) students and LGBT college athletes is restrictive and cold and where homosexuality is only alluded to as a locker room joke.

Unfortunately, the world of college athletics is a mirror image of professional athletics. Magic Johnson, for example, stressed the claim that he contracted AIDS from heterosexual contact or drug abuse. Why do the specifics of his infection matter? Regardless of the actual configuration of his sexual desire, why does he feel compelled to portray a public heterosexual image? Because in the athletic world, any other explanation, including homosexual contact, is simply unthinkable. Accusations of same-sex contact need to be explained away in order to reproduce existing social conditions, to cast Johnson as "normal." Johnson's explanation carries on athletics' long, rigid tradition of public identification with heterosexual identity and marginalization of gay identity (or to para-phrase Johnson, "rest assured, folks, I didn't get it *that* way").

While the age of AIDS has brought out numerous publicly gay non-sports figures, athletics project a strictly heterosexual world view where LGBT people are made invisible and silent: With the exception of Olympic diver Greg Lou-ganis, our society lacks well-known, self-professed gay male athletes. Further-more, because athletics maintains an oppositional view of the world, we depend on Johnson's heterosexual orientation to legitimate our belief that the butt-patting and warm embraces seen on the playing floor are divorced from any possible same-sexualized interpretations. In other words, "Anything but *that*" (and it's important to the heterosexual normalizing function of athletics that gay interaction or gay identity remain euphemistically nameless and therefore "dif-ferent" or "odd"). Is it any wonder, then, that we *seem* to have so few gay ath-letes on our teams? Quite simply, there is no social space for gay athletes to in-habit.

While gay athletes do need enlarged social space on our campuses, the pur-pose of this chapter is to argue that our athletic teams are filled with closeted gay men in need of special consideration. Undoubtedly, there are some gay ath-letes who may fit in this category, and I will elaborate on their needs, but I will do so only in the larger context of how athletics can help us to understand gay identity so that that identity may more easily be claimed by *any* student on cam-pus. In my view, discussion of gay identity cannot be separated from discussion of campus athletic programs because our athletic programs create for students a kind of belonging—which is an essence of identity. This role is so overwhelm-ingly positive for successful athletes that it often lives on in the minds of spec-tators and teammates long after the athlete has graduated or left the institution. When the successful athlete is a student on campus, he has a coveted social power that is based on an elaborate system of awards and honors, thus providing an example of what French sociologist Pierre Bourdieu (1991) would call a "rite of institution." Athletic participation and/or success "consecrates," to use Bour-dieu's terminology, "because it transforms the representations others have of [the successful participant] and above all the behavior they adopt towards him and because it simultaneously transforms the representation that the invested person has of himself" (119).

Successful college athletes are lionized; the unsuccessful are often laughed at, disrespected, or humiliated. In fact, perhaps the most potent social function of college athletics is the way they create and circulate well-known positive and negative public identities. If we as college faculty and administrators can use the social power of athletics to the benefit of gay students, we will be tapping into our campus's most potent vehicle for (1) promulgating identity, (2) for making students feel they belong, and (3) for transforming negative representations into positive ones. These three functions, I will argue, are at the heart of what we as faculty and administrators should do to improve the lives of gay and lesbian students.

The few gay students who infiltrate the vocally heterosexual world of athletics find themselves marginalized away from chances for a public proclamation of gay identity, thus successfully insulating themselves from their deepest curiosity and their most authentic selves. The price of athletic participation is often high—alienation from gay people and, for gays, sometimes alienation from one's own possibly liberating sense of self. Greg Louganis (1995) said he considered suicide when he was a senior in high school. He even wrote a suicide note, explaining his reasons, except he left out the overriding reason: the overwhelming sense of rejection he felt all around him for the homosexuality that was inherent in who he was. Throughout a subsequent visit to a counselor, he kept his sexual orientation to himself, and he did not return to the counselor for a second visit. He writes, "The replacement for therapy for me, as always, proved to be my diving" (92).

Louganis's insight applies to many who live daily with the lack of social space for gay people: They seize upon some substitute to bolster their self-esteem. Athletics provides an ideal surrogate, even though the replacement value we find in athletics may be more of an escape than it is a true validation of the parts of ourselves we want most to be approved.

I was in Seattle and accidentally found an arch rival from my college athletic days. We did not recognize each other at first, but when we did, we found that we each knew well the other's life. He had been the team captain and top runner on a National Collegiate Athletic Association (NCAA) national championship cross-country team, yet his description of his motivation for running was so that he "would be tired all the time." His reasoning was that if he was too tired to think about who he was as a gay man, then he could claim some other more socially acceptable identity. I do not use his name in this chapter because he would, after nearly ten years, still prefer that his "true" story not get back to his alma mater and his old teammates. These athletic perspectives illustrate how athletics can demonstrate what researcher I. H. Meyer (1995) has called "hyper-vigilance," which is a continual monitoring of behavior to avoid discovery or harm.

Athletics is a complex set of social practices, discourse structures, economic arrangements, and cultural institutions that inspire identities characterized by self-esteem, self-worth, and cultural value. Masters and Ogles (1995) found that "[V]eteran marathon runners are primarily motivated by a 'marathon social identity'" (69). Kishton and Dixon (1995) documented the relationship between sports camp participation and positive changes in self perception. Finkenberg and Moode (1996) show that men believe that athletics leads to enhanced social status and high status career opportunities. Because athletics is a complex way of affirming student identities, we also see identity as something that is learned. Just as college courses teach new identities—immersing people in the difference and newness of academic disciplines and professional discourses–so can colleges affirm gay identity without significant alterations or overhaul of current practice.

While coaches or athletic administrators may never admit it, sports is perhaps our most powerful societal force for constructing positive identity. In fact, athletics serves the often invisible social function of arbitrating between "winning" and "losing" public identities. While many coaches refer to their work as merely cultivating "proper attitudes" among their athletes, the influence held by those coaches extends far beyond the actual arena or locker room. Long before little boys are conscious of any "choice" they may have in the range of public identities they may choose for themselves, they are subject to an overwhelming set of cultural forces, including athletics, that normalize rigid expectations and parameters of masculinity and heterosexual identity.

In an especially powerful scene from the film *Torch Song Trilogy*, Harvey Fierstein responds memorably to his mother's suggestion that he should leave all references to his sexual orientation "in the bedroom, where it belongs," suggesting that his strong awareness of his sexual identity is a "sickness." He says, "You want to know what's sick? That after all these years, here I am still trying to justify my life." Fierstein's play expresses an important truth in illustrating that to be queer means to suffer from what Bergman (1991) calls a crisis of authority, or an inability to have one's words and one's stories be immediately valued. Lesbian and gay college students know well that to proclaim a queer identity means to spend years attempting to explain away attacks against one's personhood, to explain why telling our narratives as gay people does not constitute merely "talking about sex," when proclamations of heterosexual identity, such as weddings, are seen as "news" or, in the case of some writer like Jane Austin, are seen as "great literature." Queer narrative does not enjoy the cultural privilege that other forms of narrative have attained, and until that fact changes, gay and lesbian college students will continue to be silent and continue to use athletics as a way to hide from their queer identity.

Bourdieu's (1991) theory regarding rites of institution reminds us that positive identity has two principal parts: the private and the public. The first part is shaped and molded by the second. LGBT students are apt to remain silent and isolated—consider suicide or alcohol or drug use—because despite the increased public awareness of LGBT people and issues, they lack familiar public narratives that inscribe, normalize, and liberate them away from the private realms of silence and/or euphemism. Despite the increased visibility of LGBT people in movies or on television, LGBT students still have experienced countless negative subtle and not-so-subtle messages about how LGBT people "really are." Fear of being publicly labeled a "fag" in junior high or high school will often keep gay men from even thinking about adopting a private gay identity internally; the public diatribes by the religious right about the so-called gay lifestyle reinforce the oddity, the shame, the inferiority of gay identity. As I work with students who make reference to gay people, I am constantly reminded of the way this myth of a gay lifestyle has inculcated an uncritical sense of Other in most students' perceptions of gay people. When I question students to define the gay lifestyle, they are hard-pressed to do so. They have often seen enough evidence of gay existence to know that LGBT people are varied and individual, yet they still cling to this phrase, which suggests a kind of monolithic gay existence. No wonder gay students hesitate to embrace either a public or private LGBT identity when that identity is so often drained publicly of any room for variety or individuality.

Despite the fact that students use the word *gay* rather than *homosexual*, when asked, they still tend to define gay people in sexual terms—as people who have sex with others of the same sex. For a gay student who is celibate and isolated away from a gay identity, this notion of active sexual behavior as the defining mark of gay identity works to keep him from associating his own identity with that perceived sexually active identity that is foreign and false for him.

In "The Names We Give Ourselves" Martha Gever (1990) discusses a gay filmmaker who creates a work that fails to explore explicitly gay themes and asks whether or not that work should still be considered "gay" Her discussion reminds us that being gay is not necessarily an identity that inherently excludes other identities, but too often students do proclaim other identities as a way of obscuring their gay identity. The important lesson to learn from athletics is that self-knowledge and self-esteem are important components in formulating "winning" identities, but more importantly, athletics teach us that identity is about more than self-knowledge. It also takes public proclamation.

As long as LGBT students are "relegated" to a ghettoized campus club, then gay identity will never gain the kind of mass exposure that it needs in order to relieve LGBT students of the need to stay silent and otherwise claim other non-gay identities. As long as the only safe space relegated to LGBT students is within a curriculum or within an office in the student programs realm, then LGBT identity will still remain less understood and less visible. Until we teach that LGBT identity is more than sexual identity, our LGBT students will continue to feel less than accepted.

To pursue athletic success, or an athletic lifestyle, means to engage in commonplace self-evident goals that need no justification, no apology, or no defense. To best help gay and lesbian students, then, we should draw on what we already know from the athletic worlds. We must work toward a world where narratives of LGBT identity are as self-legitimizing as are narratives of athletics competition. In a sense, we need to remind all LGBT students to live as if they were athletes.

PART VI

The Faculty and the Classroom

CHAPTER 24

Queering the Curriculum or What's Walt Whitman Got to Do with It?

Saralyn Chesnut

Those of us who work with young lesbian, gay, bisexual, and transgender (LGBT) college students generally agree about the obstacles they must surmount in order to thrive during their college years and to emerge at the end ready to enter and succeed in the adult world. Like their heterosexual counterparts, these young men and women must adjust to a new environment and separate from their families; at the same time, they are under intense pressure to fit in socially and to perform academically. Further, the traditional undergraduate years are "a key time for identity development in general. [S]tudents are faced with many areas in which they need to reconsider their self-perceptions, develop new skills, and master developmental tasks" (Levine & Evans, 1991, 1). The stress of college is multiplied exponentially for a young person developing an identity as a gay, lesbian, bisexual, or transgender person—regarded as sick, immoral, or both by many Americans—in a college environment where LGBT people are tolerated at best, despised and reviled at worst, and encouraged, in many overt and covert ways, to keep silent and remain invisible (Massachusetts Governor's Commission on Gay and Lesbian Youth, 1993; Obear, 1991; Rutgers President's Select Committee for Lesbian and Gay Concerns, 1989; Thorson et al., 1991).

The good news is we know what young LGBT people need in order to thrive during their college years. We know that they need acknowledgment, affirmation, and support *as LGBT individuals*, both from their institutions and from individuals within those institutions. We know that they, along with students who may be struggling with their sexual identities, need adult LGBT role models, access to objective information, and a community of peers in which they can feel comfortable as they explore their options. We know what can happen when these needs go unmet: Students become depressed and withdrawn, their academic performance suffers, they may turn to substance abuse to deaden their feelings, and in extreme cases, but all too often, they resort to suicide (Evans & Wall, 1991).

On most campuses, the job of meeting the developmental needs of students—indeed, of being concerned with their psychological and emotional well-being at all—is relegated to the Student Affairs division, while academic affairs is assigned the task of promoting intellectual growth. However, I will argue that an academic area, LGBT/queer studies, benefits LGBT and questioning young people on college campuses not only intellectually but psychologically and emotionally as well. Looking at these benefits makes clear that the emotional, psychological, and intellectual components of students' development are interdependent and that faculty and Student Affairs personnel must work together to create a safe, supportive, and intellectually rich campus environment for LGBT and questioning students. This is not the only reason LGBT/queer studies is valuable; already, work in the field has made enormous contributions to our understandings of sexuality within history and culture; it has also produced information of enormous benefit in countering myths and misinformation about LGBT people today. However, the focus here will be on how LGBT/queer studies can help young college students develop positive LGBT identities, and thereby enhance their emotional and psychological well-being. I will discuss LGBT/queer studies as an academic discipline. I will then consider ways in which LGBT/queer studies courses directly and indirectly affect LGBT identity development. Finally, I will describe measures that can be taken to make LGBT/queer studies available on college campuses.

THE EMERGENCE OF LGBT/QUEER STUDIES

It may seem odd to claim that LGBT/queer studies is a relatively new academic field, since "homosexuality" has been an object of study within the fields of sexology, psychology, medicine, and sociology for over a century. However, the new field of LGBT/queer studies that has emerged over the past 25 years encompasses a broader range of academic disciplines, from literature to law, gender studies to genetics. Further, LGBT/queer studies situates the study of homosexuality within an overall study of how sex and sexuality have been understood, expressed, and represented in diverse cultures and throughout history, and how these categories relate to other social categories that organize individual and collective identities (Duke University Coordinating Committee for Lesbian, Gay, and Bisexual Studies, 1995; Evans & Wall, 1991; Thorson et al., 1991).

From the broader perspective of LGBT/queer studies, our society's binary opposition homosexuality/heterosexuality (with bisexuality somewhere in between), the background against which many earlier studies of homosexuality were conducted, itself becomes an object of inquiry. Has Western culture always categorized sexuality according to whether sex acts occur between members of the same gender or opposite genders? Has the gender of an individual's sexual/affectional partners always been regarded as a defining component of that individual's identity? Do all cultures categorize sexuality and identity in this way now? Do all cultures recognize only two genders, and more generally, how does the organization of sexuality in specific cultures relate to the organization of gender?

Such questions force us to see categories like man, woman, heterosexual, and homosexual not as natural and universal (and thus immutable) but as culturally and historically specific. They lead to further questions about how categorizations and characterizations of sex and sexuality affect, and are affected by, a society's science, art, theology, literature, and relations of power, including those based on gender, race, and class. As the editors of one of the first lesbian and gay studies anthologies put it, "[L]esbian/gay studies intends to establish the analytical centrality of sex and sexuality within many different fields of inquiry. [It] attempts to decipher the sexual meanings inscribed in many different forms of cultural expression while also attempting to decipher the cultural meanings inscribed in the discourses and practices of sex" (Abelove, Barale, & Halperin, 1993, xvi).

As an inherently interdisciplinary field, one of whose aims is to bring to light a body of knowledge and a set of perspectives that have long been absent from the academy, LGBT/queer studies follows in the footsteps of African-American studies and women's studies. Like these fields, LGBT/queer studies seeks to go further than merely to add new information and perspectives to existing ones, for what it adds challenges existing orthodoxies and requires the rethinking of long-unspoken and unexamined assumptions (Abelove, Barale, & Halperin, 1993, xv; McNaron, 1991). LGBT/queer studies is often seen as most closely aligned with women's studies, in part because the categories of gender and sexuality are so closely linked in Western culture—a link embodied in the political alliance between LGB and transgender people (transvestites, drag queens, transsexuals), built upon the common ground these groups occupy as transgressors of gender norms, transcenders of gender boundaries.

The terminology that describes this field varies widely. Some LGBT/queer studies courses are offered in women's studies or gender studies programs; other courses or programs are titled Lesbian and Gay Studies; or Lesbian, Gay and Bisexual Studies; or the more cumbersome Lesbian, Gay, Bisexual, and Transgender Studies. The term *queer* is sometimes used as shorthand for LGBT, and *queer studies* is often a synonym for LGBT studies. Some scholars and activists, however, prefer not to use *queer* at all, and others give it different meanings: *queer* sometimes describes a radical, anti-assimilationist stance taken by LGBT people, and sometimes includes not only LGBT people, but all people who "dissent from the dominant organization of sex and gender," or, taken still further, all people who "are using their experience of marginalization to produce an aggressive critique of the prevailing social system" (Duggan, 1995, 165–66). In recognition of this terminological variation, I use the encompassing term *LGBT/queer studies* here. (See Escoffier [1992] on five often-contradictory paradigms that currently underlie work in LGBT studies; and Abelove, Barale, and Halperin [1993] on the difficulty of adequately describing this fast-changing field.)

LGBT/QUEER STUDIES AND LGBT/QUEER IDENTITIES

The contested meanings of the term *queer* signal the political dimension of LGBT/queer studies: As the academic wing of a movement for social change, the field both influences and is influenced by the larger movement. Like women and racial and ethnic minorities before them, LGBT/queer people see the academy's exclusion of their concerns and perspectives as yet another manifestation of their exclusion from the mainstream in society. Members of these marginalized groups have pointed out that those who fit what Audre Lorde (1984, 116) calls the "mythical norm" in the United States—for our purposes, those who are white, male, and heterosexual—have until recently had disproportionate power to determine what counts as knowledge, what should be spoken and written about and taught to young people. In the post-Stonewall era, as many LGBT people have emerged from silence and invisibility to fight openly for social and legal rights, those within the academy have not only focused attention on the needs of LGBT students and employees but have also claimed the right to break the intellectual silence and repression that have discouraged teaching and publishing on openly LGBT/queer topics (D'Emilio, 1992).

The Politics of Silencing

The academic silence that has prevailed until recently is an extension of what Robert Rhoads terms the "politics of silencing" that LGBT people encounter in virtually every aspect of our lives (1994a, 101). The politics of silencing works in two ways. First, anti-LGBT prejudices enjoin LGBT people to remain silent and invisible *as LGBT people* or risk rejection by friends and family, loss of jobs, housing, children, and verbal and physical assault. Furthermore, society itself maintains a silence about LGBT people and issues and renders us invisible by its heterosexism: the assumption that everyone is (or should be) heterosexual. A subtle form of heterosexism was played out on our campus recently when in a residence hall "ice-breaker" exercise students were asked to answer a series of questions as they thought their roommates would. One of the questions was "What would you do if you found out your roommate is a lesbian?" After virtually every student said she would be very uncomfortable, the staff who had organized the exercise simply moved on to another question, oblivious of the fact that one student in the room *was*, in fact, a lesbian and that she was left feeling hurt and frightened.

In the classroom, the politics of silencing takes the form of overt homophobia when students make derogatory remarks about LGBT people and professors fail to challenge them, or when professors themselves perpetuate myths and stereotypes about LGBT people. (I still remember when one of my professors in a graduate course asserted that lesbianism exists only when women become too strong and men too weak, so that women are forced to turn to one another!) More commonly, though, heterosexism reigns in academic courses, so that the existence of LGBT people and issues is never even acknowledged. Professors of American literature teach the poetry of Walt Whitman without pointing out its homoerotic elements; courses on social movements never mention the movement for LGBT rights; lectures and articles on the Holocaust neglect to include gay men and lesbians among its victims. In the face of this powerful silence about LGBT lives and issues, only the rare student will be sufficiently self-confident to risk speaking up *as an LGBT student.*

How can LGBT/queer studies counteract the politics of silencing and facilitate the development of positive LGBT identities among students? It may be helpful first to define some terms. By *LGBT identity* I mean that aspect of a person's total identity that defines him or her, to self and at least some others, as lesbian, gay, bisexual, or transgendered, as those terms are used within his or her social setting. A positive LGBT identity denotes "acceptance of and satisfaction with" an LGBT identity (Miranda & Storms, 1989). Sexual identity is distinct from sexual behavior or even sexual orientation in that not everyone who engages in same-sex sexual activity or experiences romantic/erotic feelings toward members of the same sex identifies as lesbian, gay, or bisexual. Similarly, not every transsexual, transvestite, and so on, identifies as a transgender person. I should note here also that there are significant (and under-researched) differences among LGBT people in terms of how they develop and experience their identities, although their shared status as members of what US society regards as sexual minority groups makes it possible to discuss them together as I do here.

The development of a positive LGBT identity is a lifelong process rather than a onetime event. Most researchers describe several stages in the process but note that individuals may cycle through one or more stages more than once and may never reach the final stage, attainment of a positive LGBT identity. For example, one researcher describes the final stage as "commitment," or "acceptance of self and a serenity towards one's status and life," but notes that "commitment is always somewhat inconsistent, strengthened or weakened at various points and contexts by personal, social, or professional factors" (Troiden, 1989, 68). Research has shown, however, that a positive identity as lesbian or gay is positively correlated with psychological health in lesbians and gay men (Miranda & Storms, 1989).

Breaking the Silence

Given the fact that a positive identity as LGBT contributes to psychological well-being, how can we on college campuses help to minimize the inter- and intrapersonal conflicts that work against the development of a positive LGBT identity? Clinicians have identified two strategies that may help lesbians and gay men successfully resolve these conflicts: self-labeling and self-disclosure. Self-labeling, or internalizing a sense of oneself as an LGBT person and integrating that aspect of self into one's total identity, helps to minimize intrapersonal conflict by preventing the compartmentalizing of feelings and behavior. Self-disclosure, or "coming out" to others, minimizes the conflict between one's self-perception and others' expectations (Miranda & Storms, 1989). Moreover, all youth need external validation and a strong sense of self-worth in order to feel safe enough to explore their psychosocial options fully. Finally, "an expanding horizon of potential identities" is crucial, especially for minority youth (Jackson & Sullivan, 1994, 97). As Jackson and Sullivan summed, the adolescent and young adult years are

above all else a transition to a more complex set of roles which have to be integrated into the totality of the self. It is a period in which we practice and hone relationship skills. All of this rests on a belief in one's own future and on the integrity of self-definition. [The] obliteration of possible positive identifications and role models is dangerous for all minority youth. (98)

By counteracting the politics of silencing, LGBT/queer studies can supply many of the requisites for a relatively smooth passage from adolescent questioning and exploration to development of a positive LGBT identity. The following are among the benefits young LGBT people can derive from exposure to LGBT/queer studies.

Validation and Self-Esteem

As one professor of literature notes, the very act of teaching LGBT literature is subversive, for it "effectively undermines the long-standing cultural notion that homosexuality is and should remain 'unspeakable' and 'untouchable'" (Cady, 1992, 89). The same may be said about the very existence of LGBT/queer studies. Particularly on a college campus, where intellectual pursuits are valued over any other, discussions, lectures and courses on LGBT/queer people and issues are in themselves validating for LGBT/queer people.

LGBT/queer studies also validates and empowers LGBT students as individuals, increasing their self-esteem. As LGBT or questioning young people encounter materials about various LGBT identities and communities, and gain a broader perspective on how different cultures have categorized gender and sexuality, they begin to realize that our society's definitions and negative views of sexual minorities are neither infallible nor inevitable. They learn specific information with which to challenge and counter specific anti-gay myths and stereotypes. Further, since heterosexual people's level of anti-LGBT prejudice decreases as their knowledge of LGBT people increases (D'Augelli, 1989; D'Augelli & Rose, 1990; Obear, 1991), classes that bring together LGBT and heterosexual students allow LGBT students an opportunity to win support from their heterosexual peers. LGBT students often report increased self-esteem and empowerment on their evaluations of LGB studies courses: for example, one young lesbian wrote, "I evolved from being timid (terrified) into someone who spoke up a lot in discussion and felt comfortable" (Duke University, 1995, 37).

A SAFE ARENA FOR SELF-DISCLOSURE AND EXPERIMENTATION

One of the most devastating aspects of the injunction to remain silent and invisible is that LGBT young people are denied the freedom to talk openly about their feelings and experiment openly with new ways of being. It is in part by experiencing their own and others' reactions to new roles, ideas, and behaviors that young people develop a sense of who they are and what they want. By providing for the open exchange of ideas and opinions about sex and sexuality and creating a space within which LGBT youth can express themselves, verbally and behaviorally, *as LGBT youth*, LGBT/queer studies can enrich the developmental experience of all students, especially of LGBT and questioning ones. Again, this is reflected in students' evaluations; on our campus one student wrote, "I loved going to [my LGB studies class] knowing that everyone knows I'm gay, and it's cool. [I]t was a safe place to talk about issues that really affect my life, and those places are hard to find."

Positive Role Models

Identity development is, in part, a process of identifying with and internalizing aspects of one's external reality, including aspects of the external identities of others. In the absence of positive role models, young LGBT people may identify with the negative stereotypes of LGBT people as, for example, emotionally immature, mentally unstable, depressed, and lonely. They may see their own future possibilities as narrow and bleak. Self-labeling as LGBT will be a source of conflict or shame, leading to lowered self-esteem. Contact with healthy, productive, and fulfilled LGBT adults—and peers—is therefore one of the most important conditions for the development of a positive LGBT identity. Nor do role models always have to be "real" people; fictional characters and historical figures can also provide positive role models (Jackson & Sullivan, 1994). LGBT/queer studies, whether taught by an LGBT person or an informed and enlightened heterosexual, offers a plethora of role models and a range of ways of being and acting in the world on which young people can draw as they explore and develop their own identities.

MAKING LGBT/QUEER STUDIES
AVAILABLE ON YOUR CAMPUS

Given that LGBT/queer studies affects, as we have seen, not only the intellectual but also the psychological and emotional health and development of LGBT students, it should be clear that providing emotional and psychological support for LGBT students is not the work of Student Affairs professionals alone. The provision of courses, lectures, and other means of presenting LGBT material and perspectives should be viewed as part of an overall strategy for improving a campus climate for LGBT students. Some of the measures described below will help build the groundwork for schools whose ultimate aim is a minor concentration or degree program in LGBT/queer studies and offer some exposure to LGBT/queer studies on campuses where a full-fledged department or program is not feasible. Many of them also offer an opportunity for students, Student Affairs personnel, and faculty/academic administrators to work together.

Besides meeting students' needs more effectively, working together just makes good sense for LGBT people; it increases their pool of available resources, financial and other; it creates community among people who may otherwise rarely come into contact with one another; and it brings to bear diverse skills, experiences, and points of view. Student Affairs personnel, for example, generally have skills in organizing and publicizing events and programs; students may be adept at negotiating the red tape involved in getting student government funding for speakers, and so on. The measures I describe here can be implemented cost effectively if they are planned by a broad range of people who come together to think creatively about how to maximize existing resources.

Establish a Lecture Series in LGBT/Queer Studies

An ongoing lecture series in LGBT/queer studies can bring to campus several speakers each academic year for lectures, afternoon colloquia, and informal meetings with interested scholars. Funding can come from one or more academic departments, student groups, and students affairs offices. A committee made up of students, faculty, and Student Affairs personnel should meet regularly to plan the series and organize and publicize the specific events.

Offer a Faculty Development Seminar

A more ambitious—and expensive—undertaking is to organize a semester-long or year-long faculty development seminar in LGBT/queer studies, led by a faculty member on campus who has worked in this area or by visiting scholars. Ideally, faculty who attend the seminar should be given partial release time from teaching. The idea should be to encourage the incorporation of knowledge and insights from LGBT/queer studies into mainstream courses. If necessary, the cost can be lessened by offering a shorter seminar, perhaps lasting only a few weeks, or asking participating faculty to teach their normal course loads.

Make Sure Research Materials are Available

A campus-wide committee should be charged with making sure that books and journals in LGBT/queer studies are available in the campus's main library. In addition, on campuses where an LGBT Campus Resource Center exists, this office should maintain a library and subscribe to journals and periodicals, and should also when possible make computer terminals available to students who want to access information on the Internet. Where an administrative office does not exist, a student group may subscribe to journals and periodicals and even maintain a library, with support from faculty and interested Student Affairs professionals.

Use Existing Faculty and Graduate Students to Offer Courses in LGBT/Queer Studies

In addition to mainstreaming LGBT/queer studies, schools should offer courses specifically in this field where feasible. LGBT/queer studies courses may be offered in virtually any academic department where a faculty member or graduate teaching assistant has the knowledge to teach them: English, women's studies, anthropology, biology, theology, humanities, history, genetics, law, business, theater, music—the possibilities are myriad. Where possible, an interdisciplinary introductory course should be offered, preferably co-taught by faculty in different traditional academic disciplines. When several courses have been developed and approved by the curriculum committee in the appropriate area, it is then possible for faculty to coordinate what they are teaching and when and eventually to develop a course sequence, laying the groundwork for a minor or major in LGBT/queer studies.

Offer Student Writing Awards for Work in LGBT/Queer Studies

To encourage student work in LGBT/queer studies and increase the visibility of LGBT students and studies, graduate and undergraduate writing awards can be offered for papers written in LGBT/queer studies or other courses, dissertation chapters, conference papers, and so on. Ads publicizing the awards should be placed in the student newspaper, and campus-wide publicity should be extensive. The committee to evaluate submissions should bring together faculty, students, and Student Affairs personnel, with the awards given at a public ceremony of some kind (on our campus we have an annual Pride Banquet at which the awards are presented by the president of the university).

Organize Brown-Bag Lunch Discussions in LGBT/Queer Studies

Simply by reserving a room and publicizing it, anyone can organize a brown-bag lunch and discussion group in which students, staff, and faculty who are interested in LGBT/queer studies come together at regular intervals to read and comment on one another's work, or simply to read and discuss books or articles in LGBT/queer studies.

Encourage the Hiring of Faculty in LGBT/Queer Studies

Faculty and others who are interested in developing an LGBT/queer studies program should also encourage the hiring of faculty whose specialty is specifically in one or more areas of LGBT/queer studies. Once courses are being taught and student interest has been documented, departments that are hiring can be approached and encouraged to seek someone with an expertise in this area or to allocate one or more faculty lines to a position in LGBT/queer studies.

Many of the measures described above require only a small outlay of funds; however, they do require time and a coordinated effort on the part of those interested in promoting LGBT/queer studies. As students, Student Affairs professionals, and faculty work together, it should become increasingly clear that a campus-wide, integrated approach to meeting the needs of LGBT and questioning college students benefits everyone involved. Students will benefit most of all, as their emotional, psychological, and intellectual needs are met and they are given what every young college student deserves: a chance to grow and thrive in a safe, supportive, and intellectually challenging environment.

CHAPTER 25

Lesbian, Gay, Bisexual, and Transgender Students in the College Classroom

Kristen A. Renn

How college faculty address, or fail to address, issues of sexual orientation in their classrooms has a significant impact on the learning environment for students who identify as lesbian, gay, bisexual, or transgender (LGBT). By introducing LGBT topics, supporting academic inquiry in LGBT-related areas, and creating a welcoming classroom for students of all sexual orientations, faculty contribute not only to students' academic success but also to the development of a positive self-identity. By engaging in homophobic harassment and heterosexist behavior, faculty perpetuate negative stereotypes, validate the hatred and violence perpetrated against LGBT people, silence LGBT voices in their classrooms, and inhibit LGBT students' learning.

In this chapter I will describe how learning theory can be used to understand LGBT students' experience in the classroom, and strategies will be suggested for faculty who want to improve the quality of their teaching with regard to LGBT issues and students.

THE CLASSROOM CLIMATE

We know that LGBT students experience significant negative consequences when they are exposed to violence and harassment on campus (Comstock, 1991; D'Augelli, 1989a; Governor's Commission on Gay and Lesbian Youth, 1993; Kurdek, 1988; Myers, 1993; Norris, 1992). The classroom—the place on campus reserved for the free and respectful exchange of ideas—should provide an oasis from this seemingly constant barrage of anti-LGBT harassment, violence, and invalidation. Unfortunately, this is not the case. In 1993 the Select Committee on Lesbian, Gay, and Bisexual Concerns at the University of Minnesota reported testimony from undergraduate and graduate students who described the "humiliating and demeaning environment" (15) they experienced both in the classroom and in pursuit of their academic program of study. Students told of occasions when faculty made derogatory jokes, minimized or denied the contributions of LGBT people, and denied, made light of, or dismissed as irrelevant the sexual orientation of artists, scientists, or historical figures. Students also reported incidents of professors making overtly hostile or demeaning comments, including some implying that violence against LGBT people is justified and deserved.

At Brown University in 1989, the Faculty Committee on the Status of Sexual Minorities reported that 66 percent of LGBT students feared harassment or discrimination by classmates, 40 percent feared harassment or discrimination by professors, 60 percent did not feel safe being open about their sexual orientation in class, and 53 percent censored their academic speech, writing, or actions in order to avoid anti-gay harassment or discrimination. Of all students, gay or straight, in the Brown survey, 10.5 percent reported occasionally hearing faculty make negative remarks or jokes that denigrate LGBT people.

While overt victimization of LGBT students is clearly a problem on campuses and in classrooms, students encounter other negative experiences resulting not from conscious acts of aggression but rather from a passive stance on the part of faculty. LGBT students' needs are unknown, unmet, or ignored by well-meaning but uninformed individuals. Paradoxically, in a study at Oberlin College, Norris (1992) found that students, faculty, and staff of all sexualities expressed strong positive attitudes toward their LGBT peers and colleagues, but these same LGBT people were subject to widespread harassment and violence. In explanation, Norris presents evidence that while these supportive students and employees are not the same people who are engaging in specific anti-gay actions, they are not actively preventing or discouraging these activities. By not acting to interrupt the pattern of LGBT victimization these students and employees are contributing to it.

Even if faculty wish to become more informed about LGBT issues, many institutions do not provide them opportunities to do so. In the Oberlin study 55 percent of heterosexual faculty and staff expressed interest in learning more about LGBT concerns, history, and culture (Norris, 1992). A graduate student told the University of Minnesota Select Committee (1993): "As a teacher, I have received no support or training for dealing with homophobia in the classroom. I have been discouraged from discussing my concerns about this, again through the discomfort and ignorance of my colleagues and faculty. Homophobia should be an issue in training all TAs(teaching assistants)" (20). Another student said, "It would also be a good idea to sensitize faculty in all disciplines to the fact that many of their students are not heterosexual. In examples they give in class, or in their assumptions about their students, they should be aware of this" (23).

Increasingly, LGBT students are benefiting from support and encouragement from faculty. Academic programs, individual courses, or projects within existing courses and curricula are having a significant impact both on LGBT students and on the attitudes of their non-LGBT peers (Chesler & Zuniga, 1991; D'Augelli, 1992a; McLaughlin & Tierney, 1993; Mohr, 1989; Stevenson, 1988). Campuses that support openly LGBT faculty and staff create an environment of acceptance where faculty can serve as role models for all students (Massachusetts Governor's Commission on Gay and Lesbian Youth, 1993).

LESBIAN, GAY, BISEXUAL, AND TRANSGENDER STUDENTS AS LEARNERS

There is currently no evidence to support the idea that LGBT students learn differently from their heterosexual peers. Assuming that LGBT students learn in the same ways that their classmates do, four pillars of learning theory—involvement, motivation, emotion, and constructing meaning—remain critical elements in the teaching environment. What is different for LGBT students are the realities of victimization on campus and some of the life experiences they bring into the learning environment. Their learning experience may be inhibited or enhanced by faculty' attitudes and behaviors regarding LGBT concerns.

Involvement

The degree of an LGBT student's involvement in academic and extracurricular activities could easily be influenced by an atmosphere of intolerance or an atmosphere of support for LGBT issues. According to A. Astin (1993), a teacher is competing with all of a student's other academic subjects, extracurricular activities, work, home or residence life, relationships, and overall psychological development for a finite resource of student time and energy. LGBT students, as shown by D'Augelli (1989b), the University of Minnesota Select Committee (1993), and the Massachusetts Governor's Commission (1993), are required to spend time and energy, because of the harassment they face, every day above and beyond that of their heterosexual peers. Following Astin's thesis, this additional time and energy is taken from the reserves available to fuel other areas of involvement, such as academic life. Therefore, LGBT students may be less involved or not participating in the campus community.

On the other hand, claiming an LGBT identity may provide some students with additional opportunities for involvement on campus and in the classroom. As students seek to understand their own lives, they may be especially interested in academic work concerning LGBT issues in history, literature, science, psychology, or other areas, which is similar to the struggles of other groups such as women or students of color. Faculty who support these interests and provide opportunities for students to work on them may have an additional "hook" to stimulate student involvement.

Motivation

McMillan and Forsyth (1991) present a heuristic model of motivation in which motivation is influenced by what students believe is important (their needs) and what they believe they can accomplish (their expectations). Therefore, a student with a high level of need or a strong interest in learning who believes that she can accomplish her goal will be very motivated and involved. Her classmate experiencing the same degree of need but little belief that he will be successful will be far less motivated or involved.

College students' needs are identified as self-actualization, achievement, competence, self-worth, and goals (McMillan & Forsyth, 1991). D'Augelli (1992c) and Uribe and Harbeck (1992) imply that before college LGBT students may have had fewer opportunities than their peers to fulfill these needs. They may have received specific messages about homosexuality from family and others that lead to a diminished sense of competence and self-worth (Sloane, 1993; Uribe & Harbeck, 1992).

Just as LGBT students bring a variety of needs to the classroom, they also bring a variety of expectations. McMillan and Forsyth (1991) identify four factors within the category of expectations: self-efficacy, previous experience, success of others, and feedback. Since students' evaluations of their ability to achieve influences their level of effort in learning (McMillan & Forsyth), decreased expectations could undermine LGBT students' academic performance.

Some LGBT people come to college with increased expectations of success. A study by the Massachusetts Governor's Commission on Gay and Lesbian Youth (1993) found that 45 percent of males and 25 percent of females were harassed or attacked in high school or junior high school because they were perceived to be lesbian or gay. Therefore, many of the LGBT students who come to college immediately after high school have already surmounted more obstacles than their heterosexual peers.

Emotion

According to Brookfield (1990), students use their emotions as learning devices—surprise, excitement, pride, anger, embarrassment, anxiety, and grief for lost certainties. Brookfield recommends that faculty pay attention to the emotionality of the learning situation and work with, rather than against, students' emotions. Tiberius and Billson (1991) summarize a number of studies dealing with the emotionality of the student-teacher interaction. They specifically mention the need for a sense of security within the educational process. The harassment and violence to which LGBT students sometimes are subjected present a serious challenge to developing this sense of security. The Brown (1989), Minnesota (1993), and Oberlin (Norris, 1992) studies showed that some LGBT students do not see the classroom as a refuge from their fear of being victimized. Miller (1994), while advocating for classrooms where conflict among different viewpoints becomes central to the teaching-learning process, warns against establishing "an environment that is relentlessly threatening, where not feeling safe comes to mean the same thing as feeling terrified" (396).

Fear is not the only negative emotion LGBT students might experience in the classroom. Dismayed by the absence of lesbian and gay curricula, LGBT students report that anger and frustration interferes with their learning (Crumpacker & Vander Haegen, 1987). Bensimon (1992) discusses the anxiety and alienation experienced by women who are forced to maintain a public-private dichotomy between their assumed heterosexuality and their actual lesbianism. Though her article focuses on lesbian faculty, the emotions may be generalized to include closeted LGBT students as well.

Faculty can provide a sense of empowerment to out or closeted LGBT students by including LGBT history, culture, and experiences in the curriculum. They may provides access to such information that many students are generally denied educationally. When faculty include these topics, and support individual student's interest in them, LGBT students have the opportunity to feel excitement, pride, and other positive emotions in the learning process.

Construction of Meaning

While learning theory indicates both negative and positive implications for LGBT students in the areas of involvement, motivation, and emotion, it also is helpful for faculty seeking to assist students to connect with new information. Construction of meaning consists of two basic elements: *un*learning false theories and paradigms and learning new ones. There are several different models for understanding cognitive growth and the construction of meaning, but most focus on how the learner takes in new information and either fits it into existing paradigms or comes to reject existing paradigms, creating new mental structures in their place.

There are many opportunities to capitalize on the unique experiences and insights these students amass as they come to understand and live out their lives as lesbian, gay, or bisexual people. Faculty are in positions to affect the lives of LGBT students and their peers by helping them *un*learn incorrect ideas they may hold about various sexual orientations.

For many students, college represents the first opportunity to explore their sexual orientation and the implications of identifying as LGBT (D'Augelli, 1989d, 1992; Sloane, 1993). Students who seek to make meaning of new academic material by connecting it to this salient aspect of their identity may be discouraged from doing so by faculty who are not aware of the importance of LGBT issues to the student or of the possibilities for building connections and meaning based on LGBT development, culture, or experience. In some cases discouragement may be passive or unintended on the part of the teacher, but in other cases, it may be the result of the teacher's open disrespect for LGBT people and/or lesbian and gay studies. In either case, the teacher is missing or denying an opportunity for the student to make new connections and to learn.

The development of an LGBT identity gives students opportunities to learn new paradigms and models for understanding the world. They interpret their academic surroundings differently from their heterosexual peers (Ghaill, 1991). Whether or not they identify publicly, LGBT students who identify personally have a heightened consciousness of self versus others (D'Augelli, 1992) that may influence the way they create cognitive structures or the elements to which they attach meaning. As they come to see themselves as healthy, normal, and productive, they challenge and unlearn negative messages they have internalized about LGBT people (D'Augelli, 1992; Massachusetts Governor's Commission, 1993; Uribe & Harbeck, 1992). These students are not strangers to the process of reformulating information into new structures.

In order to support students' efforts to make meaning and to connect with course material, faculty need to know what students already know (Angelo, 1993). Understanding the gap between students' existing knowledge and their learning goals provides faculty with insights into what might motivate student learning and how students might make meaning of new material.

IMPLICATIONS FOR PRACTICE

Knowing that faculty are able to influence student involvement, motivation, emotion, and meaning-making, and knowing that LGBT students' education is further influenced by the unique needs and experiences they bring to the classroom, thoughtful practitioners may wonder what they might do to advance these outcomes. The intersection of learning theory and the reality of LGBT students' lives points to ways to reduce the victimization of these students and to use LGBT issues to increase learning for all. The question of how to implement LGBT-inclusive teaching is illustrated, in part, by pedagogical and curricular initiatives already taking place in a handful of colleges and universities. The purpose of this section is to provide both basic direction and potential resources to address these issues.

What Might Faculty Do Differently?

Teach to Reduce Victimization of LGBT People. Faculty should participate in the following: Recognize and interrupt homophobic harassment when it occurs; refrain from anti-LGBT jokes, derogatory remarks, and personal attacks on LGBT students; call prompt attention to both malicious and unintended homophobic remarks by students; and, create a classroom climate that supports dialogue, debate and disagreement within a context of personal respect.

Work to Increase Visibility of LGBT Issues and People. Faculty should incorporate LGBT material in the curriculum of "mainstream" courses and support the development of queer studies curricula; conduct research on LGBT topics; support visible LGBT faculty and staff as role models for students; and for heterosexual allies, use privilege to work for institutional change.

Support Students in their Academic Exploration of LGBT Issues. Faculty should encourage all students to research and write about LGBT issues; become a knowledgeable resource for students doing LGBT academic work; and learn more about LGBT issues by attending campus and community events as well as LGBT sessions at academic conferences.

How Can Faculty Implement Changes?

For faculty to accomplish curricular changes, there are a number of existing curricular initiatives. Chesler and Zuniga (1991) present a model for introducing a unit on homophobia to a sociology class. Crumpacker and Vander Haegen (1987) give examples from their sociology, history, American studies, and women's studies classes. D'Augelli (1992c) describes his unique approach to teaching a course on lesbian/gay development at Pennsylvania State University. Myers (1993) writes about her experience teaching an undergraduate Lesbian Studies course, and Grossman (1990) discusses LGBT issues in leisure and recreation studies. A significant amount of work has been done in the area of introducing LGBT issues in writing courses. Personal narratives are seen as a means to bring silenced lives into the academy (Tierney, 1993a) and to write unheard voices into the story (Fontaine & Hunter, 1993). Other ideas for institutional or individual change may be drawn from the multicultural teaching literature (see Myers, 1993). Finally, students themselves have ideas about how LGBT issues might be brought into the classroom. Ask them.

CONCLUSION

Through their teaching, service, and scholarship, faculty can improve the climate for LGBT students in their classrooms and on campus. Faculty concerned with student involvement, emotion, and motivation need to understand why and how to interrupt patterns of victimization, as well as how they might use LGBT students to enhance student learning. They need also to examine their own attitudes for conscious and unconscious biases and to be aware of the ways in which their inadvertent collusion with harassers and/or their support for LGBT students affects the learning environment. By supporting LGBT students' learning goals, college faculty can name the unnamed realities, make audible the silent voices, and make visible these invisible students within the academy.

CHAPTER 26

Homophobia in the Scholarly Climate: Campus Attitudes toward Women's Studies Students

Bonnie J. Morris

The cost of homophobia is indeed steep when students and postgraduate scholars perceive that an entire academic field is "lesbian" turf and, hence, swiftly dismiss its curriculum as marginal to the undergraduate canon. Certainly, campus homophobia hurts and impedes the gay or lesbian student. But as an educator and historian, I'm also concerned with the ways in which homophobia detracts from the scholarly climate *all* students share. Having taught women's studies and women's history for over ten years, I can attest that the fear of being labeled a lesbian is one of the primary deterrents to undergraduate enrollment in women's studies courses.

No other academic field—barring actual gay and lesbian studies, of course— is so fraught with unflattering stereotypes about the presumed sexuality of its majors. The harassment of first-time women's studies students by their peers typically includes derisive comments such as, "I didn't know *you* were a man-hater," "Are you going to become a lesbian now?" and "I can't see you becoming one of *them*." A substantial amount of energy is wasted in responding to such comments, with the disturbing result that many students who are excellent historians elect to go no further in women's history research. This, I contend, is a problem to which all faculty must be alerted.

There are three types of homophobia that continue to impede the academic climate for women's studies on campus: the lesbian-baiting of students who demonstrate any interest in women's issues; the vulnerability of women's studies professors mentoring both lesbian students and their homophobic peers; and the absence of relevant scholarship in lesbian history in most undergraduate and graduate studies on women. While I will address each concern, it is the harassment of students interested in women's issues that has the greatest impact on would-be women's studies majors, minors, and graduate students.

A CASE STUDY IN CAMPUS LESBIAN-BAITING

I became aware of homophobia as a campus climate issue while serving as an assistant professor of women's history at St. Lawrence University. St. Lawrence, a small, private liberal arts college, offers women's studies courses for both history and gender studies concentrations. During the two years that I taught there (1992–1994), I grew increasingly concerned that otherwise outstanding students were being deterred from their interest in women's history because of strong peer disapproval; most often, this disapproval—from boyfriends, sorority sisters, or roommates—was couched in homophobic language. In spring of 1994, I included an unusual writing assignment in my women's history survey course. I asked the students (35 or so, one third of whom were male) to maintain a journal throughout the entire semester, recording attitudes, jokes, and stereotypes about women's studies they observed on their college campus. The results were an astonishing outpouring of incidents. Lesbian-baiting was by far the most significant problem confronting female students who desired to participate in any course addressing women's achievements in history or literature; and the cost to one's reputation increased if one attended any event offered by the campus Women's Center. That the overwhelming majority of the Women's Center residents were heterosexual—in fact, I knew of only two lesbian students at St. Lawrence—never prevented critics of the Center from applying the lesbian label to any female student who crossed its threshold. Not surprisingly, my students' journals indicated their reluctance to be involved with workshops or student programs sponsored by the Women's Center, even when the topic interested them or was relevant to their research papers. I learned from my students' journals that even enrolling in my courses was an invitation to slander, although, surprisingly, *my* reputation as a scholar and popular teacher never suffered in this equation.

Why the emphasis on Lesbian as Other in a community with no real lesbian population? Just as contemporary Poland, for example, has seen an increase in Jew-baiting despite the postwar absence of any sizable Jewish community, it is possible for lesbian-baiting to flourish in an environment minus lesbians. Such was the case at St. Lawrence University. No visible lesbian community existed—only the very separated lives of perhaps three lesbian professors, counting myself. But as my students' journals indicated, fighting off lesbian-baiting took up an absurd percentage of social time and effectively served to discourage female students from the mildest of feminist pretensions. No matter how many male suitors regularly called for their steady girlfriends at the Women's Center, other female students were instructed by their own boyfriends not to visit that "lesbian house"; no matter how few active feminists existed on campus, feminists and their implied undesirable lesbian aspect were the primary target of anger in casual student commentary.

According to their journals, students in my courses were routinely asked by their sororities to remove textbooks for my course from public space, such as coffee tables or hallway shelves, on the grounds that women's history titles made "bad impressions" on male visitors and hinted that the sorority had become a "dyke house." Several of my students experienced altercations with boyfriends who threatened them verbally for studying "lesbian crap." Those of my students who did reside in the Women's Center were awakened at 4 A.M. one spring morning by male student intruders shouting "Dyke!" and throwing torn-up pornography into the living room. Graffiti on meal trays, desks, and library carrels accused all campus feminists of being "man-hating dykes." One of my students who sought refuge from male harassment by inquiring about an all-female residence hall regretfully chose not to take a nicely appointed room because her boyfriend informed her that it was located on "the dyke floor." The pervasive impact of homophobia extended even to campus housing allocations. Such experiences wasted my students' time and mental resources.

From my group exercise of journal keeping, I learned that as long as the label *LESBIAN* is accepted as the worst thing one may be called, female students will struggle to maintain behaviors that place them above suspicion—and this goes far beyond having a proven boyfriend handy. It means refusing to get involved in activities with other women or in activities, courses, or campus programs placing woman's experience at the center. It means an active *female* participation in name-calling and lesbian baiting of other women. What was most revealing to me, as an educator, was the commonly held belief among non-women's studies students that only women with a *sexual* interest in women could possibly care about women's history, culture, legal standing, economic location, athletic accomplishments, artistic innovations, and so on. Assuming that only lesbians would enroll in a course with the word *woman* in the title, for example, perpetuates the conundrum that men studying the history of men is serious scholarship, but women studying the history of women is lesbianism.[1]

Let us concede that women's history might indeed attract students who personally care about women. This would include lesbians; but why would heterosexual males be exempted from the same fascination? After all, they will, presumably, marry women, be employers or employees of women, and raise daughters. In attempting to deconstruct these ideas about exactly who benefits from studying women's history, I once pointed out that the conservative viewpoint—which honors the "traditional" family—would direct *all* students to learn the history of motherhood and childbearing conditions in modern civilization. And much of a good women's history or women's studies curriculum is just that: an overview of our foremothers' survival under harsh socioeconomic conditions. But at many universities, student contempt for an academic focus on women is an extension of contempt for women, period.

Curiosity about feminism is the bridge that takes hitherto non-baited women into the realm of homophobia. At St. Lawrence's predominantly white and Christian campus, with its homogenous student population, gay-baiting was the only cultural form of name-calling many students experienced, and thus I distinguish lesbian-hating from other forms of hostility, such as racism. The lesbian identity is something *implied*; if one is female, one may be accused without proof. By contrast, it is unusual to be called by racist names when one is white. Any woman can be named a lesbian; it is a reputation waiting to happen.

Suzanne Pharr is the best-known scholar on this subject. Her text *Homophobia: A Weapon of Sexism* (1988) explores the problem of defending, or "credentialing," one's sexuality when challenged by men with the power to defame. To understand this problem, one need only look at women in the US military. A parallel exists in the campus hierarchy of reputation, where concerns about lesbian-baiting determine many undergraduate women's choices.

In part, the fact that a women's studies course attracts a primarily female enrollment creates criticism. Feminine space (private) has traditionally been viewed as less important than masculine space (public); since the second wave of feminism, gatherings of women have been perceived as subversive, especially when the women present are engaged in defining and interpreting their own cultural conditions. To be fair, most women's studies courses do include a particular viewpoint: the viewpoint that men have, historically, held excessive power over women's legal, academic, and economic opportunities. Because feminist scholarship is critical of male power, of male protection of women, of male-dominated institutions (such as religious bodies) rendering significant decisions on women's lives sans female representation, there is a popular conclusion that feminists do not want men in our lives. This is another connection to implied lesbianism; and every one of my female students at St. Lawrence University noted in her journal that her boyfriend feared "losing" her to the male-bashing outlook of women's studies.

THE VULNERABILITY OF FACULTY IN
MENTORING LESBIAN STUDENTS

From the first moment a St. Lawrence freshman informed me to my face that "Gays aren't human," I elected to put a human face on the problem of campus homophobia and came out publicly as a lesbian early in my second teaching semester. I never experienced a single incident of overtly anti-lesbian harassment from the history students who continually re-enrolled in every course I taught. As a professor, a grown-up, my own life was so separate from the undergraduates' lives that I didn't "count" in their peer hierarchy. In fact, I provided an opportunity for them to show tolerance of *me*: Toni Armstrong Jr., who works with the Gay, Lesbian and Straight Educators Network (GLSEN) counteracting homophobia in public schools, has called this the attraction of strangers to any person who is forthcomingly authentic. Sadly, however, students' willingness to accept a lesbian professor does not necessarily translate into a willingness to show tolerance toward one another. It is almost impossible for faculty to comprehend the social world in which students spend their four years, as our own undergraduate experiences always recede a generation or two into the past. What *is* possible is for the extreme hatred toward lesbians and gay men to be addressed by students themselves. Yet most well-intentioned peer programming to this effect reaches an audience already in agreement; the hostile rarely attend, and mandatory lectures on tolerance have been very poorly received by undergraduates.

One effective tactic I have used in class discussion is to remind those present that while I have the temporary power to grade their work, they, as voters, have a much larger power to put me and all gay or lesbian educators out of work forever, should they support such referenda. This has helped spark discussion about the personal and economic fallout of false name-calling in a society that still denies jobs and child custody to lesbians. I have also labored to make my women's studies syllabi visible, available to prospective students ahead of time, in order to correct notions that only "male-bashing" is taught, or that only a certain kind of student is welcome in the women's history classroom. These practical solutions, applied at St. Lawrence, appeared to prove most beneficial to straight males.

THREATS TO RELEVANT SCHOLARSHIP IN LESBIAN HISTORY

Having demonstrated the stereotyping both students and faculty of women's studies endure, I'll raise a third concern: the risk of incorporating even minor information on gay and lesbian history in the women's studies classroom when so many critics are poised to crow, "See? That's the real agenda of women's studies." The stoic scholar does not care what the uninformed and often biased critic thinks, but students, again, pay the price. They pay the price when lesbian history is included, for their parents may threaten to stop payment of tuition, and their boyfriends may respond abrasively. And they pay the price if lesbian history is excluded, because the 10 percent who are indeed lesbians lose any opportunity to receive academically sanctioned information about their heritage.

There is little pre-college preparation for an adult curriculum in women's history. The discipline is isolated from younger Americans, and first appears as a college "elective," thus ghettoizing women's studies programs apart from departments that continue the study of subjects introduced in secondary school. This serves to politicize the subject Woman as trendy or, in recent language, "politically correct." Hence the impetus for formalizing scholarship on women and reducing its revolutionary reputation. Making women's studies competitive with traditional scholarship requires proving academic credibility. Regrettably, a focus on the history of lesbian identity and community detracts from the "normalizing" of the discipline, and normalization is indeed an objective for more conservative scholars in women's studies/history (Christina Hoff Sommers, Gertrude Himmelfarb, etc.) Thus, it is possible for a doctoral student in women's history to spend six years at an excellent institution and receive a Ph.D. in US women's history without once encountering a course or curriculum addressing lesbian history.

Tentatively requesting greater background in lesbian history is the greatest risk for a women's studies student, as it confirms the most hostile attitudes surrounding her work; and, again, her mentor in academia may be but marginally more informed, considering the lack of graduate training in lesbian studies. A heartbreaking dilemma for a women's studies professor occurs when an outstanding student, preparing to publish a scholarly paper with a lesbian theme, inquires, "Do you think I should list this on my resume?" In fact, many women's studies students and faculty colleagues I know maintain two separate vitae: one with lesbian publications included, the other doctored out of professional concerns for homophobic response. A useful workshop for women's studies students would include open discussion of how faculty and scholars in the field have handled this dilemma.

CONCLUSION

This overview of three interconnected concerns—lesbian-baiting and the awareness of homophobia, the vulnerability of mentoring role models, and the threats to relevant lesbian scholarship–was designed to bring awareness to the unique issues of women's studies students. A lesbian identity is often assumed by others when considering one's motives for taking women's studies courses, which can be daunting to the first-year women's studies student even if she *is* a lesbian. Indeed, economics or communications majors are seldom put through a comparable discussion of their academic work. This kind of fallout from homophobia continues to affect all women in college who seek to learn more about women in history.

NOTES

1. Administrators and department chairmen, regrettably, often contribute to this phenomenon. In one interview for a tenure-track position in women's history, I was actually directed by the history program chair not to prepare courses with the word *woman* in the title, lest male students be discouraged from applying; at a different interview for a visiting position at a state university, the dean began our discussion by asking me whether I felt there would be "any need" for women's studies in the future. I cannot imagine such comments being directed at a professor of African-American studies, for example. Students are quick to pick up administrative contempt for the women's studies discipline and to devalue its curriculum accordingly.

CHAPTER 27

Faculty and Staff Mentors for LGBT Students: Key Responsibilities and Requirements

Beth Kraig

Who am I? What can I do with my life? Do I have any skills that separate me from the crowd? Can I find a job that enables me to serve others, or should I focus on making money? Will I have to work at a job I hate, and find satisfaction in my personal life? And what about that personal life—is somebody going to love me? Should I concentrate on having fun while I'm in college, or should I look for a life partner? And how do I know which is which—what distinguishes the "fun date" from the "lifelong love"? I want to be happy in my life. Is that possible?

As a professor at a "New American University," one that provides liberal arts programs and professional training to students in an atmosphere that encourages faculty and staff to serve as mentors, I spend a great deal of time talking with students about the questions above. I have many such conversations with heterosexual students, whose identities do not preclude their having doubts about their futures. And I have such conversations with lesbian, gay, bisexual, and transgender (LGBT) students, who face an uncertain future with the knowledge that social prejudices and legal discriminations will almost certainly shape some of the decisions that they make in their lives. My interactions with students of various sexual identities have informed and inspired me as an openly lesbian faculty member. I have discovered that students of all identities hunger for discussions about life and especially want to ask questions about how those of us who are a little older came to fill our current roles.

Parents of a gay student with whom I have worked closely recently wrote me a note in which they thanked me for serving as a "role model" for their child. I pondered the meaning of that phrase. Almost certainly, their son is not going to study history (my own discipline), nor is he likely to pursue a career as a college professor. It is possible that he will enjoy gardening and reading, two of my favorite avocations, but I suspect that his parents weren't suggesting that connection. Certainly I hope that he will develop personal relationships that enrich his life as much as my own partnership enriches mine; but, again, I think that his parents had something else in mind. I think that they were saying that they were glad that their son had discovered that in a large, complex world people can and do care about one another. People at their son's college had taken the time to see his many attributes and to affirm his sexual identity, and because of that, their son was more certain that he could reach out into the world and contribute.

And yet, for those LGBT people who work as staff members or faculty at a college or university, receiving the occasional "thank you" note from parents may seem an inadequate reward, given the challenges that being openly LGBT might bring. Why should one risk the kinds of criticisms, condemnations, or perhaps threats to one's job that might ensue if one "comes out" on campus? Will there be more rewards than the "thank you" note? How much will LGBT students benefit from having openly gay, lesbian, and bisexual mentors? Even more practically, what does one *do* to serve as an open "role model"?

ASSESSING THE NEEDS AND RISKS

For LGBT faculty and staff who wish to serve as mentors to LGBT students, a first question to answer is whether others are already out on campus or might be willing to come out. Obviously, if your campus has a non-discrimination policy that includes sexual orientation, the atmosphere may be more conducive to honesty. If there are out staff and faculty, but they do not seem actively involved with student support services, it still will be useful to meet with them to discuss the campus climate and determine their reasons for pursuing other interests and goals. Before considering mentoring, does the institution reward faculty and staff for serving as mentors, or does it see such work as a distraction from scholarship, teaching, or other duties? Do those individual out staff and faculty simply believe that their gifts and interests lie elsewhere? Discussing such questions with others can provide a valuable body of knowledge that will make it easier to decide if, and how, to begin serving as a mentor.

Are there others who would like to work with you to develop mentorship for LGBT students? Colleagues will be invaluable, and their presence will almost certainly constitute one of the "rewards" of serving as a mentor. Identity issues should also be addressed, with reference to forming a "big tent" of open LGBT staff and faculty who will work with students. Differences of race, ethnicity, religion, and gender (among others) should be considered.

Lack of a non-discrimination policy covering sexual orientation may not denote a "dangerous" environment but could be testimony to an absence of openly LGBT members of the community (often it is the presence of such people that brings the issue of a non-discrimination policy to the table and the opportunity to pursue a policy might be seen as one of the rewards of coming out). If such a policy is not in place and there are no openly LGBT staff or faculty, are there other signs of support for LGBT people? For example, while no faculty or staff were openly identified as LGBT members when I was hired by my employer, a campus pastor was leading a confidential support group for LGBT students. Our university has a religious affiliation, and the Campus Ministry office enjoyed a central role at our institution. The presence of a gay-affirmative group there suggested to me that there would be probable administrative support for out faculty and staff.

It is hard for me to imagine the institution that has no need for openly LGBT mentors, given the likelihood that all institutions have LGBT students. But how great is the need at your institution? Colleges in major urban areas with lively and diverse LGBT programs and community groups may have less need for strong mentor programs than do those located in smaller cities or towns, where there are fewer obvious signs of community support and activities for LGBT students. In fact, in more remote areas, the need for campus programs may be great, indeed; is it probable that LGBT students will have *no* support if they don't find it at their college or university?

Are the support programs at your institution currently led by heterosexual people, and if so, what message does this send to LGBT students? Certainly the contributions of heterosexual allies should be applauded when they serve to affirm and strengthen the security and confidence of LGBT students. However, absence of LGBT mentors may tell students that older members of their identity group "don't care" or "have to hide." In the former case, LGBT students may learn that heterosexual people care more about their needs than other LGBT people; this is a damaging message that surely undermines the idea that LGBT people can form communities and provide guidance, insights, and friendship to one another. In the latter case, closeted LGBT faculty may be "teaching" LGBT students to hide and thus implicitly may be suggesting that LGBT people are inferior to heterosexual people and should accept such inferiority as a matter of fact.

Realistically, anti-gay leadership at some colleges and universities will make it difficult in the extreme for LGBT staff and faculty to be out. Such circumstances raise tricky ethical questions. Can staff and faculty at such institutions serve as mentors in confidential ways, through unauthorized groups that meet without official campus status? Will LGBT students benefit from such options, despite the problematic elements of staying closeted and seeing their mentors operating in the closet? Perhaps in such circumstances, LGBT staff and faculty can work with students to identify and assess the political and personal value of being openly LGBT and suggest strategies for achieving out status, even as such a status may not be feasible in the immediate future at particular institutions. Ideally, in such situations, LGBT faculty and staff may be able to identify a few heterosexual allies and work with them to advance community awareness of the need for a safer environment for LGBT people. Such steps would show to LGBT students that their mentors are pursuing change and may encourage the students to push for change as out alumni.

INTERACTING WITH LGBT STUDENTS

If LGBT staff and faculty are willing and able to come out and serve as mentors, how can they initiate this process? Does one buy a pin saying "ROLE MODEL" and start wearing it to work each day?

Obviously, volunteering to work with (or to start) a campus organization for LGBT students and allies is a first step toward discovering opportunities to serve students. Most colleges and universities require student organizations to locate faculty or staff advisers, and openly LGBT faculty and staff can volunteer to fill such positions.

Student groups exist to serve student needs, so it is vital that supportive staff and faculty assess the ways in which they can be useful, rather than assume that students are in need of "supervisors" to tell them what to do. In reality, faculty and staff may provide very useful services (especially with relation to knowing names and details of university administrative bodies, having acquaintances in various parts of the college or university, etc.). However, most students already know how to be "bossed" by faculty or "corrected" by staff; LGBT students are not likely to tolerate such tactics just because they come from gay, lesbian, or bisexual faculty and staff. *Listening* is a key. Offering one's services in a supportive and subordinate role will also be appreciated. Take instructions—don't give them.

That said, often because of their greater institutional knowledge and awareness of particular institutional customs or procedures, LGBT staff and faculty may be able to guide students in helpful ways. Mentors may offer advice, if they are prepared to have it be rejected, altered, or ignored. Students of traditional college age (17–23) may also value the greater knowledge of LGBT history, cultures, and issues that faculty and staff mentors may possess, as long as they can participate in a learning process (rather than listen to long lectures that shut down conversation). Similarly, LGBT mentors will quickly discover that there is much to learn from students, who, growing up as LGBT people in the 1980s and 1990s, may have had dramatically different experiences as children and adolescents from those of the mentors. Reciprocity should be a hallmark of the first stages of forming relationships between LGBT mentors and students and should remain a priority in all later stages.

Beyond campus groups (LGBT and allies), LGBT mentors and students can meet in a variety of contexts. Like all students, LGBT students should be encouraged to participate in activities like sports, social events, cultural programs, campus publications, and social justice groups. Such activities are often in need of staff or faculty advisers, and again, LGBT mentors may volunteer their services in such capacities.

For example, what benefits accrue when an openly gay staff member serves as adviser to Amnesty International? Why should an openly lesbian faculty member work, for instance, as faculty editor of a student publication? Clearly, such voluntarism sends a number of important messages. First, it demonstrates to LGBT (and other) students that LGBT people have wide-ranging interests and want to serve the larger communities of which they are members. Second, when LGBT staff or faculty are holding such positions, LGBT students will almost certainly feel that they can participate in groups and programs without being as much at risk of rejection or condemnation as might be the case were no openly LGBT mentors on the scene. Third, the LGBT mentor is sending a message to LGBT students: This can be, and perhaps should be, your future. Your world should not be limited because of anti-gay or antibisexual prejudices. LGBT students may justifiably be frustrated with the notion that their future service to society should come only through LGBT organizations and movements; while such work is vital, not all LGBT people prefer or plan to pursue it. At the same time, most colleges and universities try to inculcate the practices of good citizenship, of community engagement in their students. LGBT students should be supported and encouraged in developing such habits without feeling that their assistance will only be valued by other LGBT people.

LGBT faculty (and in some cases, staff) may also support LGBT students in their academic work and thus provide valuable academic mentorship. In some cases, and especially at larger institutions, there may be openly LGBT faculty in most or all departments, which may facilitate the opportunity for LGBT students to develop better understandings of their major areas of study through discussions with a mentor. Smaller universities and colleges often do not have the resources to provide regular courses on gender and sexuality, but individual faculty members may provide independent study opportunities to interested students; through such avenues, LGBT faculty can support LGBT (and other) students who wish to study—for example—LGBT authors, legal issues for same-sex couples, or bisexuality in Native American cultures. It may even be possible for mentors to work with students to construct individualized majors or minors in queer studies if there is an institutional mechanism for the creation and approval of such individualized programs.

SHARING LIFE STORIES

I recall that some of my favorite professors from my undergraduate days were those who would drop a personal anecdote into a lecture or would stand and chat in the hallway about their own hobbies or experiences. These are "real people," I would think, and not just Ph.D.s imported from another planet. Many of us can remember such moments, and sometimes they provided learning opportunities that greatly extended our intellectual and personal growth beyond that which occurred directly in our academic studies.

LGBT students are especially in need of opportunities to talk with LGBT mentors about life, love, and the mysteries of the future. As I noted at the beginning of this chapter, many students (regardless of their sexual orientations) are asking a host of important questions as they pursue their academic work, and I have had numerous conversations with heterosexual students about their hopes, fears, and plans. However, heterosexual students can avail themselves of dozens or hundreds of role models regarding their sexuality, personal lives, and places in society. Most heterosexual students have heterosexual parents or adult guardians who serve as role models in some capacity. In contrast, most LGBT students will not have parents or adult guardians who share their sexual identity and may have had few or no opportunities to talk with older LGBT people about their lives.

The opportunities for such discussions may emerge through campus activities (for example, at meetings of the campus LGBT & Allies group), but may also extend into larger contexts, including off-campus ones. Most heterosexual students are familiar (from grade school onward) with the larger lives of their teachers; a teacher's husband may be the local Little League coach, or perhaps a teacher and his family attend the same synagogue or church that the student's family attends. LGBT students may have little or no sense of the larger lives of LGBT mentors, and this is a gap that the LGBT faculty or staff member can begin to fill. Take your partner to a concert on campus, and invite LGBT students to sit with you. Plan a potluck or pizza party at your home and invite the campus LGBT & Allies group. Participate in the nearest AIDS Walk or take a group of students to the nearest Gay Pride festivities—and bring your family if you have one.

Some LGBT faculty and staff members may still avoid such situations, especially if there are off-campus activities involved, to avoid stimulating any inferences that the LGBT faculty or staff person is "picking up" students. Appropriate attention to faculty-student or staff-student relationships is now a part of most campuses, and many colleges and universities have detailed policies that speak to the question of intimate relationships between authority figures on campus and students. Nevertheless, heterosexual faculty and staff seldom avoid inviting students over to their homes for pizza because of such policies; nor are such policies intended to stifle friendly relationships between faculty, staff, and students. However, LGBT people recognize that a lingering element of anti-homosexual prejudice centers on the myth that LGBT people are "predatory" and especially prone to pedophilia. Responding to the possibility that such prejudice still is harbored by colleagues, some LGBT people may avoid any interactions with students that vary from the strictly academic.

But this sends harmful messages! LGBT students learn to accept false stigma, rather than to challenge them. LGBT students miss out on the valuable opportunity to see older LGBT people in their larger contexts, with partners, in families. By responding to the lingering stigma by avoiding connections between their personal and work lives, LGBT faculty and staff are shortchanging themselves and shortchanging their students. This is especially true if the college or university involved is one that emphasizes families as parts of larger communities. At my university, for example, faculty regularly invite students to join them in informal study or chat sessions at their homes (usually with family in attendance), and it is commonplace for faculty families to be involved in activities related to the larger mission and outreach of the university. When possible, the university often hires the legal spouses of faculty and staff; many children of faculty and staff attend the university. In such an environment, the larger ways in which personal lives and working lives can intersect (to the benefit of the individual involved and the community) are part of the "teachings" of the university. LGBT students would miss such teachings if only heterosexual faculty and staff were to demonstrate them.

As individual students wish to discuss particular and specific aspects of a faculty or staff mentor's personal life, the mentor must set his or her own limits. Obviously, policies pertinent to sexual harassment should be considered, as should necessary limits between one's intimate life and one's work life. I have never had students ask me questions about the intimate physical aspects of my partnership, and I don't anticipate that such questions will ever be asked; in the very largest sense, though, I probably share details about my personal life that some of my colleagues might not wish to discuss with students. At the same time, I know that some of my heterosexual colleagues *do* share stories about their personal lives with students in ways that are illuminating and informative for students who wish to consider issues of commitment, mutuality, and two-career couples. Perhaps the best guideline in this regard is to trust one's own sense of comfort about self-revelation and to take some clues from students' needs. We live in a society in which students of all sexual orientations seem hungry for examples of happy, mutually satisfying, and productive family relationships, and LGBT mentors who can speak to such a need may be serving many students if they do so.

SUPPORT FROM THE INSTITUTION

As noted above, institutions that create policies through which LGBT members are made to feel welcome, safe from discrimination, and affirmed will probably be rewarded with LGBT faculty and staff who serve the communities' needs well. Such policies are not sufficient, however, if they are not accompanied by public and constant statements of support for LGBT members of the campus. Administrators who include phrases like "gay, lesbian, bisexual, and transgender" when referring to the diverse constitution of the campus community are reminding people of the existence of LGBT people in that community. Funding for speakers and other programs that deal with LGBT people and issues also shows that the institution genuinely honors its LGBT members. If institutions lack such policies and practices of support, LGBT mentors may wish to pursue them—in part, because the network of support will be useful and of service to the LGBT faculty and staff, and in part because such activism within the workplace will demonstrate to LGBT students how important (and necessary) it is to work toward equality on the job.

Individual heterosexual administrators, faculty members, and staff may also do much to facilitate the contributions of LGBT mentors. If the mentors' job evaluations include sections that pertain to community service or service to students, supervisors should acknowledge that the mentorship of LGBT students makes valuable contributions in such a regard. Supervisors may also recognize that LGBT mentors (especially if most LGBT faculty and staff remain closeted or uninvolved) will be disproportionately responsible for serving the larger needs of LGBT students; accordingly, they may seek to lighten the LGBT person's workload in other areas, if possible, or may at least acknowledge the heavy load that the LGBT mentor is carrying. A number of studies about the heavy workload of other minority identity faculty and staff (such as African-Americans and Asian-Americans) attest to the demands that colleges and universities may unwittingly place on the few "representatives" of a particular marginalized group. Too often, the individual LGBT person is serving on committees that address a range of diversity and equity issues, and may also be heavily involved in programming and planning activities that serve diversity needs on the campus. Add to this the time-consuming work of mentorship, and it's no wonder that the LGBT mentor may find time and energy to be in short supply. Official attention to that kind of job stress may reduce the possibility of burnout and do much to sustain the efforts of LGBT mentors.

Finally, heterosexual colleagues can increase their own knowledge of LGBT issues and make mentorship of LGBT students a part of their work. When students learn about heterosexism or anti-gay laws in a heterosexual colleague's class, they are more affirmed in their status as members of the community. The well-educated heterosexual colleague is much less likely to ask an ill-informed (and possibly inflammatory or insulting) question of an LGBT colleague. Similarly, the well-informed heterosexual colleague will understand why an LGBT faculty or staff person may spend many hours each week in service to LGBT students, rather than imagine that such work is unnecessary or frivolous. Most LGBT people speak of the loneliness they experience when heterosexual colleagues "don't get" the fact that LGBT people are often angry and frustrated by social prejudice and legal discrimination; that "loneliness" is quickly dissipated when a heterosexual colleague correctly and astutely speaks to such problems and acknowledges appreciatively that their LGBT colleagues are grappling with them.

IT'S WORTH IT

Some students with whom I have worked have received internships with the Human Rights Campaign and National Gay & Lesbian Task Force; others are active in local organizations that pursue equality for LGBT people; still others are in graduate school, beginning their careers, or engaged in service work. All of the students with whom I have worked have delighted me with their energy and integrity, and amazed me with their stamina and creativity. I often describe my work as a role model or mentor as simply trying to clear some debris from the paths that these students are so well prepared to travel. I am not a guide or a leader, but I can be an assistant as they rightfully assume the roles that society should come to expect from them.

CHAPTER 28

"Do We Have to Call It *That*?!" Planning, Implementing, and Teaching an LGBT Course

Jean H. Thoresen

If a community of clinical or legal professionals insisted on maintaining willful ignorance about a subject that involved 10 percent of their client population directly, and another one third indirectly,[1] that decision could arguably be viewed as malpractice. Ignorance of *any* subject on that scale in academia should be unacceptable as the functional equivalent of malpractice, so long as the function of the university is to dispel ignorance and replace it with accurate and adequate information. Therefore, lesbian, gay, bisexual, and transgender (LGBT) related courses belong in mainstream university curricula. About 10 percent[2] of the general population, and probably an equal percentage of students, is lesbian or gay, and the academic community, as well as the larger community, needs to respond to that fact in terms of research, scholarship, and teaching for those disciplines in which the study of lesbian and gay people is a legitimate topic for inquiry and in terms of serving students in all disciplines and the college or university community in general in an effective way.

Ideally, we on campus should not only become accustomed to that idea; we should embrace it. We are, after all, the people in the place where things that cannot or will not be easily discussed elsewhere are legitimate topics of discussion. That's what academic freedom means. Academic freedom means not just freedom for faculty to teach but freedom for students to learn. Three quarters of a century ago, the Supreme Court held that among the "privileges long recognized at common law as essential to the orderly pursuit of happiness" was "the right of the individual to acquire useful knowledge" (*Meyer v. Nebraska* [1923]). That central rationale in our cultural definition of freedom provides an initial stance for introducing a course on lesbianism and homosexuality into the college or university curriculum. Ignorance is unacceptable per se.

Some people might say, "Well, we cover that *stuff* in other courses." Traditionally, that has meant the Sociology of Deviant Behavior, or perhaps Abnormal Psych. The first important point in planning an LGBT course is to make sure that the topic is not subsumed under some denigratory heading such as *deviance* or *abnormality*. That may indeed be some individual faculty's or administrator's view of an appropriate designation, but it is long since out of date. The American Psychiatric Association removed homosexuality from its list of mental disorders in 1973.[3] For a college or university to relegate a topic to categories of deviance or abnormality is to stigmatize individuals who take an interest in such a topic, those who choose to teach about it, and even more important, students who are finding their ways to their own identities within the context of the campus community. How can a lesbian or gay student come to a positive sense of self when a defining characteristic of that person is denigrated officially by the very institution to which the individual has entrusted herself or himself? The presence of an LGBT course is a serious signal to students that who they are and what they do are legitimate and acceptable within their environment.

If there is no Queer Studies Department on your campus (and there is not on the vast majority of American campuses), then there needs to be a "home department" for such a course of study. An interdisciplinary approach may be advantageous for a number of reasons, some of which will be discussed below, but it is also true that in eras of declining budgets and curricular constriction, courses with no "home" and therefore no built-in advocates may be most vulnerable, and therefore an LGBT course will benefit from a departmental domicile.

The same point is analogously true of "Special Topics" designations within departments.[4] Such a designation implies, first of all, that the material covered is not integral to either the discipline or the Departmental conception of itself, that it may drift in and out of the curriculum in a haphazard fashion, that the topic needs to be considered only "on occasion" or "as needed." Such an assumption marginalizes an offering substantially. Such a designation often means that a course will be offered only once, or only once in a while, or only when the "regular" (i.e., "important") courses have been covered. It also suggests that individual faculty who teach such a course are not offering anything of permanent or substantive value and discourages faculty participation in the course, particularly under Damoclean conditions of tenure and/or promotion, when faculty are perhaps less willing to take chances, less willing to risk having their career interests defined as tangential or undesirable. It is even possible that under such conditions, offering an LGBT course will somehow be seen as a "radical"[5] action, potentially embarrassing to an administration, or as a possible cause of controversy, and thus make the offending professor inconvenient. It would not be the first time that faculty have suspected that fiscal constraints can be transformed into constraints on inquiry and academic freedom. It was Max Weber who first pointed out that sociology, often considered a radical discipline, and one that often challenges uncritical acceptance of the status quo, is the "science of inconvenient" facts. Under conditions of scarcity, it may not seem wise to be involved in inconvenient activities.

Being an LGBT faculty member, and being willing to introduce an LGBT course into the curriculum, is an important step; it may also be a somewhat dangerous one. First, and probably most obvious, is the question that may be raised as to the individual's sexual orientation. If an LGBT faculty member seeks to introduce an LGBT course, it is my opinion that formal engraved announcements to the entire campus as to one's sexual orientation might as well be sent along with the application to create the course; everybody will suspect or assume that one is gay. On a campus without adequate non-discrimination policies or employment protections, a faculty member would have to think long and hard before putting her or his career on the line in that manner.

Even if one is out, however, it may be somewhat dangerous on a curricular level to have such a course identified as belonging to a particular faculty member. That may mean to other faculty or administrators that the course is more about politics and/or personal identity than it is about a legitimate subject of academic inquiry; that makes both the course and its inclusion in the curriculum suspect, and it may also call into question the motives and academic priorities of the professor who offers it. Is she or he putting politics above the academic mission of a department or the institution? Is he or she serious about the academic content? Does she or he have expertise other than simply being lesbian or gay?[6]

One solution to this problem, and the one that I think is both professionally responsible and necessary, is to have a course designed so that both LGBT and straight faculty can teach it, and have a colleague, either gay or straight (whichever you are not), available who will commit to teaching the course as a part of her/his regular elective rotation. An alternative solution may be to construct a course that is inherently cross-disciplinary. At Eastern Connecticut State University, for example, we have a 200-level course called "Lesbian Culture," which is cross-listed in English, sociology, and women's studies and can therefore serve as an elective for credit in any of those majors. The course is team-taught by an English professor and a sociology professor, one a lesbian, one straight. This validates the principle that an LGBT course is not part of some "special" category of offering that is somehow other than/less than, again, the "regular" offerings of departments and the university as a whole. Both of these options avoid the possibility that the course is seen as "nothing but" a collection of anecdotal war stories based on personally interesting but academically suspect experiences alone.

A related curricular option may be the integration of the course with offerings and/or requirements in other departments. For example, undergraduate programs that offer a bachelor's in social work are required to provide opportunities for students to gain information about sexual orientation.[7] An LGBT course can fill such a need, without having to be offered by the Social Work faculty themselves. A LGBT course might also be included as one of a set of electives from which health and physical education or psychology majors must choose to provide analogous beneficial information about diversity and populations at risk.

A word about the syllabus: Once a course is established and included in the regular curriculum, what should it include? On one hand, the answer is simple: whatever is analogous to the academic content of any other course in the curriculum. On the other hand, such an answer may be obvious, but is incomplete. Students come into many courses such as math, English literature, US history, with some knowledge that has been presented within their previous education. That knowledge is probably neither inaccurate nor derogatory. In an LGBT course, much of what a student thinks she or he knows will not be from academic sources, as very few courses in high schools ever acknowledge the existence of lesbians and gay men. What "knowledge" a student may have is often a steamy stew of caricatured stereotypes and misinformation. So there needs to be some corrective information that accurately presents the material. Here, traditionally "academic" work will help a great deal.[8] In addition, however, both gay and straight students often want to know what it's like to be lesbian or gay. LGBT students especially may need such information in spite of the ubiquitous presence of the topic on talk shows and in the popular media; many students cannot identify with the people who appear in such contexts and really need to know something about how to "do" gay. It is almost guaranteed that they have not had many socially approved ways in which to "practice" being who they are. For these students, in particular, first-person accounts such as Preston's (1991b) *Hometowns* or the coming out stories in Cassingham and O'Neil's (1993) *And Then I Met This Woman* are good resources. There are also some novels, for instance, Forrest's (1995) *Curious Wine,* that provide a good basis for discussion of lesbian identity. For gay men, an autobiographical work such as Paul Monette's (1992) National Book Award winner *Becoming a Man: Half a Life Story* can serve a similar purpose. Both fiction and nonfiction can work well to engender empathy with the lives of lesbians and gay men. Also, it is useful to provide information on the coming out process, especially to parents, through works such as Fairchild and Hayward's (1989) *Now That You Know* for both gay and straight students, the former because they really may need the help, given the prevalence of coming out during the college years, and the latter so that they can understand what it is like to have to present to parents and others an aspect of self of which parents and friends may have been totally ignorant. For most lesbians and gay men, talking with their parents is a crucial part of their becoming who they are, and it is an important part of their lives for others to understand.

Syllabus development is an integral part of any course but may be particularly significant when lesbians and gay men may be among the "client group" of students who will take an LGBT course, looking for information, guidance, and understanding that they may not be able to find anywhere else in the campus community. Because of misinformation and stereotypes, the value of outside speakers is probably more useful in an LGBT course than in many others. Living, breathing gay people often make the most difference in developing critical thinking in such a course, in helping students to examine whether their preconceptions and what they think they know actually corresponds with the reality of the lives and experiences of lesbians and gay men. In many areas of the country, active speakers bureaus may be a good source of such speakers.

There is always a risk that outside speakers may be seen as merely the "Queer for a Day" and that without an ongoing presence of LGBT people, outside speakers may appear somewhat "exotic." It is in that context that LGBT faculty become a particularly valuable resource: They are not going to go away. They provide direct evidence of the existence of LGBT people on campus, thus signaling the safety factor to students. They can also become an ongoing resource to LGBT students who really do need someone with whom to talk in a nonclinical circumstance.

Courses exist in contexts: within departments, within schools or divisions of universities, within the culture of the university itself, and within the society as a whole. To start at the most global level, it is more plausible to offer an LGBT course in a state where same-sex sexual behaviors are not criminalized than in one in which they are and where teaching about LGBT issues or individuals will not call into question anything about the personal identity or legal status of the instructor. It is easier still to offer such a course in a state that has lesbian and gay rights laws on its statute books. It is more plausible still to offer such a course on a campus that has a strong statement of non-discrimination, explicitly including sexual orientation as an impermissible ground for differential treatment. It is easier still to offer such a course when sexual orientation is protected as a basis for employment within the university. It is more plausible to offer such a course on a campus that has an active group of out LGBT faculty and an officially sanctioned LGBT Campus Resource Center. The campus environment and structure signals to *everybody* the sincerity of the university's commitment on the part of administration and faculty to fair and equal treatment of LGBT members of the academic community, as well as their willingness to see LGBT inquiry as a legitimate part of the curriculum.

Implementing an LGBT course also involves some sensitivity to student concerns about the larger contexts in which they live, which are probably not involved in other course selections. There is an ironic and inherent contradiction in the fact that accurate labeling is both academically desirable and a statement of institutional courage and equity and that, at the same time, students live in a world that extends beyond the campus gates. There are two main issues for students. The first and most important issue for many LGBT students is their concern at questions that may arise from parents or family members if "Sociology 208—Homosexuality and Lesbianism" appears on their transcripts. Many of those students take such a course precisely because they need and want the accurate information. After all, they probably have had few avenues open prior to college to pursue such information in safety. They know that they need to know.

But they do not want to come out to their parents by way of a grade report sent home.

A second issue involves future employment, especially in a sensitive area such as K-12 teaching or physical education. Will a student's job chances be jeopardized if a principal or school board member sees "Sociology 208—Homosexuality and Lesbianism" on the student's transcript? Certainly, in a state where homosexual behavior is criminalized, or in a state without laws protecting the employment rights of LGBT people, if the writing on the transcript raises even the merest whiff of suspicion as to the personal identity of the student, the student's chances for a job might well be compromised; the same is probably true in reality even in states that have legal protections. Why did you take such a course? may not be a neutral question. Intellectual curiosity alone may not be deemed a sufficient answer. If a student is not gay, questions are raised that are inappropriate to that individual. If a student is gay, what then? Can the student duck the question if asked directly? Will the presence of the course on the transcript cause the question to be asked, which otherwise would not have been asked? And, of course, lying is not an option; perjury on an application for employment, or in an interview, is almost always, and justifiably, grounds for not hiring an applicant or subsequently dismissing an employee who has already been hired. So the LGBT student has nowhere to turn in honesty and safety.

The solution we have used at Eastern is to allow an optional "smokescreening" of the course title. A student who makes a request of the Registrar may choose to have Sociology 208 listed as "Sociology—Special Topics" rather than "Homosexuality and Lesbianism." This is a poor solution. It does not accurately represent the student's actual course work and level of information about a topic that *ought* to be advantageous to students within disciplines such as education or social work. It is, perhaps, craven acquiescence to a particular presumptive political or moral point of view to smokescreen the course title. But we have not been able to ascertain other alternatives that protect a student's privacy and her or his future employment possibilities. Until we can change bigotry on a societal scale, such evasions seem reasonable or even necessary. I am still unsettled as to the ethics of such an action; the paradox of such a solution, in a context in which one of the purposes of Sociology 208 in the curriculum is to signal a safe and welcoming environment for lesbian and gay students, is a terribly cruel irony.

Just as students live within a larger context, so, too, do colleges and universities as institutions. There are constituencies "out there": parents, boards of trustees, state legislatures. The question of "Do we really have to call it *that*?!" was raised at Eastern by a colleague in a Curriculum Committee meeting when I first presented the proposal for our course "Homosexuality and Lesbianism." He was concerned about the content, as it was morally offensive to him to have consideration of what he considered to be perversion included in an approved course of study. Additionally, however, he suggested that inclusion of the specific words in the college catalog might prove troublesome; he wondered whether parents might wish to prevent their children from attending our institution, or whether the state legislature might withhold funds from us on the basis of the inferences that he felt could be drawn from the information provided by our having to list the course by that title in official publications.[9] He probably was not the only person present who was questioning the wisdom, if not the necessity, of the "H" and "L" words; he was merely the most troubled, or perhaps the most honest. He asked; I replied: "Yes." There was no further discussion as to the title of the course, and it was unanimously approved for inclusion in the college curriculum.

The "naming" of things is important. We know that to name something is to own it, to create it, to construct it. An LGBT course is a valid academic endeavor. It concerns LGBT issues, lifestyles, and individuals. It is here as are LGBT people in our society. To evade or deny that reality—and the course content—is dishonest. It suggests that some topics or subject areas are or ought to be taboo on a university campus. It suggests that some euphemism is reasonable or necessary. It devalues the subject, the students who are interested in it, and the faculty whose professional and pedagogical expertise include the subject matter.

The course needs to be present, it needs to be a regular offering, and it needs to be offered regularly. This is how our "serious" academic work is presented, to our universities and our students, and to our other stakeholders as well—parents, trustees, state legislatures. And it needs to be called what it is. Here are suggestions for basic strategies in implementing an LGBT course:

1. Work first to create a state-wide and campus-wide climate in which such a course will be viewed as unexceptional.

2. Justify the course on the same sorts of academic and pedagogical grounds as you would any other; there *are* no, other grounds that are appropriate and fair, and which will (or ought to) work.

3. Make sure that you or some other LGBT faculty member do not "own" the course. Such a perception can lead to defensive reactions about why the course exists.

4. Find ways to integrate the course into extra-departmental curricula so that it benefits many students.

5. Make sure that the faculty member(s) who will teach the course has appropriate *academic* credentials, and do not try to smokescreen personal or political experience as academic.

A last point about the value of yes and no answers. When individuals ask in one way or another, "Do we have to call it *that*?!" they are often inquiring, sometimes from truly agonized positions, about the validity of LGBT people in their worlds. Often they are coming from traditional perspectives and may feel that their worlds and their values are under increasing threat, that there is some sort of a "slippery slope" down which culture in the US is descending, and that the academy is the last bastion of legitimization of approved formal topics of study. If LGBT people can breech these walls, there's probably nowhere they cannot go.

This is a real conundrum for academics who honestly do not understand why diversity is an important part of the current university. But in one sense, at least, their agonized *cri de coeur* is also a last gasp, one final bleat of protest, and need not be answered with specificity because it is not actually a request for rationale or information but precisely that last gasp. These individuals are not looking for reasons but for recognition that they have tried, symbolically at least, to bar the gates and protect the walled city, perhaps even Winthrop's (1985) "city on a hill,"[10] that they believe represents and is represented by Western culture as they understand it, in some constricted ethnocentric vision. Providing a mountain of detail as to reasons will not help them with their dilemma.

The best answer to the question?

"Yes."

NOTES

1. Lesbian and gay people are variously estimated to make up from 4 to 12 percent of the population of the United States, using data from the original studies by Kinsey. Pomeroy, and Martin (1948), and more recent data by Weinberg and Williams (1974), Bell and Weinberg (1978), and Paul, Weinrich, Gonsiorek, and Hotvedt (1982). If we include families of LGBT individuals as being affected by one's sexual orientation, then one third of the population is a reasonable estimate overall.

2. These numbers can be, and have been, argued endlessly, both in the scholarly and the popular media. I do not wish to reiterate those arguments here and have selected numbers that I believe to be competently and professionally derived.

3. See the American Psychiatric *Association's Diagnostic and Statistical Manual of Mental Disorders* (*DSM*) (1980). The actual decision to remove homosexuality from the category of mental disorders had been made earlier (1973), but the *DSM-III*, which replaced the *DSM-II* (1968), was not published until 1980. It included the category of "Ego-dystonic Homosexuality" [302.00] (*DSM-III*, 1980, 281-282), which included as a "feature" of the disorder that "physical satisfaction [as a result of homosexual relationships] is accompanied by emotional upset because of strong negative feelings regarding homosexuality" (281). The issue of how an alive, awake, aware, and attention-paying member of our culture could avoid such negative feelings regarding homosexuality was left unaddressed.

4. But please note the exception that may seem appropriate at individual request, as discussed later in the text.

5. The etymology of *radical* means to get to the root or heart of something (Gove, 1986).

6. Simply *being* lesbian or gay *cannot* be a credential for teaching an LGBT course; the expertise, including whatever combination of academic background, teaching experience, and research participation that applies to the selection of *any* professors on a particular campus, should, in my opinion, *not* be altered and *especially* ought not to be diminished or minimized in faculty selection for an LGBT course.

7. The current *Handbook of Accreditation Standards and Procedures* (1994) from the Commission on Accreditation of the Council on Social Work Education in "The Accreditation Standards and Self-Study Guides" provides that "[e]ach program

[B.A./B.S.W.] is *required* to include content about population groups that are particularly relevant to the program's mission. These include, but are not limited to, groups distinguished by race, ethnicity, culture, class, gender, sexual orientation, religion, physical or mental ability, age, and national origin" (M6.6 [Diversity], CSWE, 1994, 140), and further that "[p]rograms of social work education *must* present theoretical and practice content about patterns, dynamics, and consequences of discrimination, economic deprivation, and oppression. The curriculum *must* provide content about people of color, women, and gay and lesbian persons" (M6.8 [Populations-at-Risk], CSWE, 1994, 140).

8. Suggestions include Lillian Faderman's *Odd Girls and Twilight Lovers* (1991), Bell and Weinberg's *Homosexualities: A Study of Diversity Among Men and Women* (1978), and McWhirter and Mattison's insightful *The Male Couple: How Relationships Develop* (1985).

9. For the record, in the 16 or 17 years since the course has been listed—under the full title of "Homosexuality and Lesbianism"—there has never been, to my knowledge, any expression of objection or concern transmitted to any member or representative of the university by anyone: parent, legislator, or others.

10. "For we must consider that we shall be as a city upon a hill." See John Winthrop's "A Model of Christian Charity." (1985).

PART VII

Administration and Policy

CHAPTER 29

Bending Toward Justice: Examining and Dismantling Heterosexism on College and University Campuses

Brian L. Watkins

> When we get to homophobia and heterosexism, the thinking gets cloudy and people find themselves lost in a fog, unable to find their way through to the other side. Many things cause this fog: fear, misinformation, lies, stereotypes, and religion. It is my belief that once we conquer heterosexism, we will be able to begin to put our society and world into an order that does reflect "liberty and justice for all."
>
> —Blasingame, 1992, 47

We in higher education bear witness to the dawn of a new millennium, especially in regard to gay, lesbian, bisexual, and transgender (GLBT) issues. With the recent ruling in Hawaii barring the state from prohibiting same-sex marriage, higher education must be prepared to deal with the aftermath. But are we? Such a ruling by the Hawaii courts will certainly have ramifications far beyond its own state systems and will, in fact, impact colleges and universities nationwide. Universities will need to extend the same health and housing benefits to same-sex partners as those provided for married couples of the opposite sex. The time has come to address same-sex unions by welcoming them into our institutions. Will such measures, however, rid college and university campuses of the systemic problem of heterosexism?

Of the more than 3,000 institutions of higher education in the United States, approximately 250 include sexual orientation in their affirmative action statements (National Association of Student Personnel Administrators [NASPA], 1993). Even fewer institutions offer the same benefits to domestic partners as are offered to married couples (American College Personnel Association [ACPA], 1995). Despite the increased acceptance of GLBT people—and community, college, and university policies prohibiting discrimination on the basis of sexual orientation—heterosexism is rampant on our campuses. According to Berrill (1992; as cited in Slater, 1993a), "anti-gay prejudice and violence are serious problems at many colleges and universities. In 1989 alone, a total of 1,329 anti-gay episodes were reported to NGLTF [National Gay and Lesbian Task Force] by lesbian and gay student groups on just 40 college campuses" (185). In a survey of GLB students conducted by Sherrill and Hardesty (1994), 40 percent of the 1,464 respondents "indicated that they do not feel completely safe on their campuses, with 57 percent saying that their schools do nothing in response to [GLB] hate crimes occurring on their campuses" (10).

When an institution does not respond to hate crimes and other negative incidents affecting GLBT individuals, a clear message of intolerance echoes across the campus. The messages sent by leaders of our colleges and universities can be deliberate and explicit. In 1994, a dean of the Yale Divinity School, which prohibits discrimination based on sexual orientation, signed a statement that discussed the "threat posed by the gay-rights movement to the 'heterosexual norm.' Among other things, it stated that homosexual partnerships should not be considered the moral equivalent of marriage [and] argued that some discrimination was necessary in society" (Mooney, 1994, A39); thus, discrimination against GLBT people is justifiable.

The purpose of this chapter is to define heterosexism, highlight the ways in which heterosexism is manifested on college and university campuses and the impact this form of oppression has on the entire campus community, and provide specific actions administrators and faculty can take to eliminate heterosexism. While most of this chapter could be spent citing specific programs and successful efforts on college campuses to combat heterosexism, it is imperative that people have a thorough understanding of what heterosexism is and the pervasive nature of this form of oppression. Then, and only then, can we work to eradicate it.

UNDERSTANDING HETEROSEXISM

Heterosexism Defined

The term *homophobia*—"the irrational fear, hatred, and intolerance of people who are gay, lesbian, or bisexual" (Obear, 1991, 39)—is frequently used to describe the prejudice heterosexuals have toward nonheterosexual people; however, despite common acceptance and usage of this term, *heterosexism* more accurately describes the attitudes and behaviors of many heterosexuals regarding GLBT people. As Pellegrini (1992) demonstrated, "*homophobia* may not be the most useful way either to name or to conceptualize the diverse practices—from physical violence to verbal insinuations—that seek to deny or efface outright the existence and integrity of same-sex love" (44). While heterosexism may be accompanied by homophobia, there is no necessary connection between the two (Jung & Smith, 1993). As Jung and Smith (1993) noted, an individual who is heterosexist might not be homophobic and an individual who is homophobic might not be heterosexist. Heterosexism is equivalent to sexism and racism while homophobia is analogous to misogyny and bigotry (Jung & Smith, 1993).

Heterosexism, as defined by Jung and Smith (1993), is a "reasoned system of bias regarding sexual orientation [that] denotes prejudice in favor of heterosexual people and connotes prejudice against bisexual and, especially, homosexual people" (13). Herek (1995) elaborated by defining heterosexism as a system of denial, denigration, and stigma towrads any non-heterosexual behavior, relationship, or identity. Utilizing these definitions, heterosexism, then, is a reasoned system of bias regarding sexual orientation that denotes prejudice in favor of heterosexual people and denies, denigrates, and stigmatizes any non-heterosexual form of behavior, identity, relationship, or community.

It is apparent that the definition of heterosexism is very similar to that of homophobia; however, it is the discriminating *actions*, based on prejudices, that help to define heterosexism. Like its counterpart racism, heterosexism is systemic. The dynamic of power that plays out in heterosexism enables heterosexuals to discriminate against GLBT people. For example, some institutions of higher education, where no legislation exists to prevent discrimination based on sexual orientation, are legally allowed to discriminate against any GLBT individual in hiring and admissions practices.

Neisen (1993) wrote, "When our institutions [and individuals] knowingly or unknowingly perpetuate these prejudices and intentionally or unintentionally act on them, heterosexism is at work. [And heterosexist] acts interconnect when heterosexist individuals discriminate and institutions passively allow and foster the continuation of such discrimination" (50). Rather than elaborate further on the definition of heterosexism, it may be useful to examine the ways in which everyone is affected by heterosexism, as well as highlight the manifestations of heterosexism in higher education in an effort to better understand its definition.

How Heterosexism Hurts Everyone

In 1992, Warren Blumenfeld edited the text *Homophobia: How We All Pay the Price*, which highlighted the ways in which heterosexism, or *homophobia* as defined by Blumenfeld, hurts the members of the heterosexual community. While GLBT people are "marginalized and disenfranchised" by heterosexism, this form of oppression serves "the dominant group [heterosexuals] by establishing and maintaining power and mastery" over the nonheterosexual minority (8). Despite the privileges assumed by heterosexuals as a result of this power, they, too, pay a price. As outlined by Blumenfeld, heterosexism hurts heterosexuals in the following ways:

First, heterosexism locks people into "rigid gender-based roles that inhibit creativity and self expression" (8). Consider the female college student wanting to major in civil engineering, a role traditionally filled by men, or the male college student hoping to major in nursing, a role traditionally held by women. Both students face external and internal conflict for choosing two gender-based areas of study. Regardless of the fact these students possess valuable skills for their desired profession, they choose an alternative career in an effort to resolve the external and internal conflict caused by heterosexism. The male student, fearing being labeled "gay" because he wants to be a nurse, chooses a more "masculine" career. Likewise, the female college student, facing harassment from her peers, adopts a more "feminine" role.

Second, heterosexism "compromises the integrity of heterosexual people by pressuring them to treat others badly, actions contrary to their basic humanity" (9). Harper (1992) wrote of the similarities between heterosexism and racism and reflected on what fugitive slave and abolitionist Frederick Douglass called the "dehumanizing effects of slavery" (57). The victims, according to Douglass (as cited in Harper), were not only black slaves but also whites whose position of power "corrupts their humanity" (57). Similarly, the prejudice, discrimination, and harassment directed toward the nonheterosexual minority cause heterosexuals to behave in a way that corrupts their humanity.

Third, heterosexism "greatly restricts communication with a significant portion of the population" (Blumenfeld, 1992, 9–10). Blumenfeld pointed out that heterosexism forces heterosexuals who may know someone who is gay, lesbian, or bisexual to be closeted about their friend or family member. For example, parents with a lesbian daughter may refuse to disclose this fact to others due to heterosexist conditioning. In addition, college and university faculty in some institutions face retribution for any mention of homosexuality as "positive" and "acceptable" in class (Carmona, 1994); thus, delivery of true information about GLBT people is denied, and false information and stereotypes are perpetuated. As noted by Jung and Smith (1993), "[T]he dishonesty, secretiveness, manipulation, hatred, and ostracism fostered by heterosexism undermine the development of healthy social interaction" (95).

Fourth, heterosexism can be used to "stigmatize, silence, and, on occasion, target people who are perceived by others as gay, lesbian, or bisexual but who are in actuality heterosexual" (Blumenfeld, 1992, 11). Vazquez (1992) wrote, "[W]omen who are not identified by their relationship to a man . . . who like or are knowledgeable about sports, or work as blue collar laborers" are likely to be labeled "lesbian" at least once in their lives (161). Likewise, single men who hate sports or design flowers or wear an earring are likely to experience "fag bashing." Countless reports describe the violence directed toward heterosexuals who were victimized as a result of being perceived as gay or lesbian by others. According to the Community United Against Violence (CUAV), an agency that serves the victims of anti-gay and antilesbian violence, "3 percent of the over three hundred victims seen by CUAV each year identify as heterosexuals" (as cited in Vazquez, p. 160).

Finally, heterosexism "inhibits appreciation of other types of diversity, making it unsafe for everyone because each person has unique traits not considered mainstream or dominant" (Blumenfeld. 1992, 13). As demonstrated previously, heterosexism promotes negative stereotypes, based on physical traits or gender roles, associated with GLBT people that affect both the non-heterosexual minority and the heterosexual community. Thus, heterosexism inhibits appreciation of diversity.

How Heterosexism Impacts the Campus Community

A University of Oregon report stated that "the university environment is neither consistently safe for, nor tolerant of, nor academically inclusive of lesbians, gay men, and bisexuals" (cited in Tierney, 1992, 43). In a 1990 survey conducted by *USA Today* and People for the American Way, several colleges and universities stated that sexual orientation accounted for most acts of intolerance on their campuses (Sherrill & Hardesty, 1994). Coming "face to face with 'otherness' is a risky proposition" (4) and contributes to an inherent fear of and prejudice against those who are different. It is this prejudice and belief in the superiority of heterosexuality that contribute to the acts of violence toward GLBT people on college and university campuses.

In addition to violence, heterosexism is also manifested in higher education in curricula development. Many college and university faculty members are working to combat racism and sexism by rearranging course curricula, while failing to eliminate heterosexist materials and validate the contributions of gays, lesbians, and bisexuals (Obear, 1991). McNaron (1991) pointed out that "many professors, especially in departments of literature and the humanities, hide the fact of a given author's homosexual orientation in order to preserve the myths surrounding some of our white Western culture's most prominent literary giants" (20). After all, how many students learn that Socrates, Plato, Aristotle, Walt Whitman, Willa Cather, and Virginia Woolf, to name a few, have all had same-sex relationships (Jennings, 1994)?

Student social organizations and college programming also contribute to heterosexism. Many student organizations, especially fraternities and sororities, promote heterosexual date nights while overlooking the fact that there may be a lesbian, gay, or bisexual individual who wishes to bring a same-sex date to the event. Advertisements for dances and social events on campus typically feature a heterosexual couple rather than a same-sex couple. Furthermore, college programming rarely, if ever, includes any movies, dances, or entertainment of a GLBT nature.

Financial aid for GLBT students is an important issue, especially if the student's parents have relinquished all ties with their son or daughter. For a dependent student whose financial aid is determined by the amount of money made by the parents, aid for college expenses becomes a problem. Due to government-regulated policies, financial aid offices are unable to recognize this dilemma, and the student may not be able to meet his or her financial obligation to the college or university; thus, the student may be unable to continue his or her education.

Several heterosexist policies also affect GLBT faculty and staff in regard to health benefits, living quarters, and employment procedures. For example, only 60 colleges in the nation offer "soft" benefits (such as the use of library, recreational facilities), while only 30 colleges offer "hard" benefits (full medical/dental) for same-sex domestic partners of GLBT university employees (R. Davidson, personal communication, March 30, 1995). These small numbers demonstrate the lack of importance and value placed on same-sex domestic relationships by the heterosexual majority.

In addition to the denial of health care benefits, "most college and university campuses have [heterosexist] policies regarding live-in professionals" (Cullen & Smart, 1991, 189). In residential life positions and in married-student housing, heterosexual couples "are granted the right to live together. [Y]et these same privileges are denied to gay, lesbian, or bisexual partners" (189).

In regard to employment by and admission to colleges and universities, discrimination on the basis of sexual orientation is not prohibited by law. Although several colleges and universities have added sexual orientation to their statement on non-discrimination, thousands of other colleges have yet to adopt such a policy. In institutions that do not legally protect the rights of GLBT people, discrimination based on sexual orientation is acceptable; and many colleges and universities that include sexual orientation in their nondis-crimination statements continue to allow this discrimination to occur. Such practices and the lack of protective policies for nonheterosexual minorities prohibit GLBT individuals from enjoying the same privileges and equal benefits as heterosexuals.

Heterosexism pervasively harms entire university communities. As stated by Jung and Smith (1993), "Heterosexism, like racism and sexism, creates deep resentments and frustrations that eventually erupt with destructive destabilizing consequences hinder[ing] the ability of people—heterosexuals, bisexuals, and homosexuals alike—to address together the questions of how to develop sexual behaviors that honor and respect each person's sexual identity while contributing to the well-being of larger society" (95).

Institutions of higher education, where community should be both fostered and celebrated, must recognize the effects of heterosexism—especially on GLBT individuals—and work to eradicate this deplorable, systemic form of discrimination. Allowing heterosexism to endure will continue to erode the very standards of community that colleges and universities profess to uphold. Eliminating heterosexism from academia will take the efforts of every member of the community, particularly those who are in positions of power.

STEPS TO DISMANTLE HETEROSEXISM
ON COLLEGE CAMPUSES

First, institutions of higher education must ensure equitable treatment of every member of the college community, regardless of race, gender, sexual orientation, religion, nationality, age, socioeconomic class, or physical ability, in an effort to ease human suffering and provide the best possible educational experience for all. As demonstrated in the previous section, heterosexism is damaging and harmful to GLBT people and to heterosexuals. Thus, the college community must ensure the rights of all individuals. Unless colleges and universities actively protect the rights of the nonheterosexual minority, heterosexism will continue to plague the academy.

Second, administrators, faculty, and staff must develop moral courage (Tierney, 1992). Being morally courageous means being vocal, condemning harassment and discrimination, and advocating for the rights of the GLBT community. As Pharr (1988) acknowledged, having the courage to speak out against heterosexism may result in loss of privilege. However that loss may reveal itself, the benefits for GLBT people, as well as the entire academic community, will be far greater. As educators, we have been granted "the extraordinary privilege of thinking critically as a way of life," and as critical thinkers "we should be astute enough to recognize when a group of people is being mistreated systematically" (D'Emilio, 1990, 18). This kind of critical thinking is a privilege that will never be lost.

Tierney (1992) stated, "In educational communities, we have an obligation to speak out on issues of social justice. [T]he president, administrators, and faculty need to speak up and denounce attacks against any individuals on their campus. [I]f we cannot expect moral leadership from the president and faculty [and administrators], then who can we expect it from?" (46). Not only should administrators *vocalize* their support for the GLBT community; they must also take *action* against intolerance and work to educate the campus community.

Third, in keeping with the spirit of moral courage, GLBT administrators, faculty, and staff need to "rethink their silence and invisibility" (Tierney, 1992). Heterosexism is not a battle for heterosexuals alone. Gays, lesbians, bisexuals, and transgenderists must also play a role in initiating dialogue and eradicating heterosexism. One of the most important ways we can do this is to come out of the closet. Sullivan (1995) stated that "while it is not in some sense fair that homosexuals have to initiate the dialogue, it is a fact of life. Silence, if it does not equal death, equals the living equivalent" (186).

Some, many of whom are heterosexual, have stated that being in the closet is a choice and that GLBT people should feel fortunate that they are able to hide and revert to a safe place. But the closet is not a place of safety; it is a place of fear. The closet is not a luxury; it is a place of dishonesty and denial. There is no choice involved when a gay, lesbian, or bisexual individual remains closeted by heterosexuals and the heterosexism rampant in society. Gays, lesbians, and bisexuals do have a choice, however: to rethink their invisibility and come out of the closet as gay, lesbian, or bisexual individuals.

Research shows that when a GLBT individual comes out to a heterosexual family member, coworker, or friend, the heterosexual individual's heterosexism decreases (Tierney, 1992). Thus, when a GLBT faculty member or administrator comes out to his or her colleagues and students, opportunity for education escalates with increased tolerance. Cullen and Smart (1991) both agree that "for heterosexuals, gays, lesbians, and bisexuals alike, visibility is imperative if any education and role modeling is to take place" (185).

Fourth, institutions of higher education must actively work to eliminate heterosexual privilege, as evidenced in the following ways: spousal memberships to college health clubs, pools, and other recreational facilities (Washington & Evans, 1991); health care benefits and insurance; social activities geared toward heterosexuals (Washington & Evans, 1991); ability of heterosexual married students to qualify as financially independent of their families; "married" student housing; live-in positions for heterosexual couples; and the list goes on. Equitable treatment must be given to all individuals regardless of sexual orientation.

Finally, recognizing the visible and educational role of administrators and faculty, these individuals must "take an activist stance to counteract the misinformation about GLBT people that many members of the university community have, the cultural prejudices that are still endemic in the United States, and the growing problem of hate-motivated incidents" (D'Emilio, 1990, 18). This can be accomplished in the following ways:

First, action by administrators and staff to "face their own homophobia and *wish* to erase it from their emotional vocabulary" (McNaron, 1991, 22). These individuals must recognize how their own thoughts and actions perpetuate heterosexism and wish to eliminate such behavior. For example, the belief that domestic partners do not "deserve" the same privileges as married couples is heterosexist and must be challenged.

Second is sensitization of residence life staff regarding GLBT issues (D'Emilio, 1990). This would include educating staff on such issues as identity development, coming out to others, forming connections with other GLBT individuals, and being victims of harassment and hate crimes. Residence life staff work closely with many students and need the knowledge and skills necessary to provide support and create an affirming environment for GLBT individuals, and to combat heterosexism in the residence hall.

Third is a quick response to incidents involving harassment and/or discrimination (D'Emilio, 1990). Administrators and staff must not only include sexual orientation in the campus harassment policy but must also develop a clear protocol for confronting such incidents (see Berrill, 1992). Hate crimes and discrimination are not to be tolerated in any form and administrators and staff must respond immediately and efficiently.

Fourth is regular programming that appropriately represents the diversity of the entire campus community. This would include, but is not limited to, campus lectures, guest speakers, entertainers, films, and social events that represent women, people of color, GLBT people, various religious traditions, and so on.

Fifth is the hiring of personnel, especially in counseling positions, who foster self-acceptance rather than self-hatred (D'Emilio, 1990). Staff members, especially in areas of student development, who consistently work with students must affirm GLBT individuals rather than degrade, devalue, and dehumanize. This will foster self-acceptance of a GLBT identity and ease psychological discord and shame caused by heterosexism (Neisen, 1993; see also Herek, 1995).

Last is the development of a GLBT Campus Resource Center to be utilized by all members of the college and university community. This office would serve as the primary clearinghouse for GLBT educational resources, such as videos, books, and pamphlets, would provide support services for GLBT individuals, sponsor GLBT cultural events, compile GLBT hate crime statistics, and conduct training sessions for the campus community on GLBT issues and heterosexism.

FROM COWARDICE TO COURAGE

The steps presented in this chapter to combat heterosexism represent a beginning to eradicate heterosexism in higher education; yet without each, heterosexism will continue to damage the entire academic community. Our endeavors in academe must involve the pursuit of truth, and until members of the college and university community can cease the perpetuation of misinformation about gays, lesbians, bisexuals, and transgender people, the idea of truth will remain a quagmire.

Community, according to Naylor, Willimon, and Naylor (1994; as cited in Willimon & Naylor, 1995), is a "partnership of people committed to the care and nurturing of each other's mind, body, heart, and soul through participatory means" (145); and "real communities must be grounded on a foundation of *equality* and *justice*" (151). The mistreatment of GLBT students, faculty, and staff on our campuses is unethical and unjust and is antithetical to the process of developing and fostering a community in which every member is engaged in the search for meaning (Willimon & Naylor, 1995). Heterosexism does nothing more than undermine community and encourage injustice.

Institutions of higher education and, more important, those who have leadership roles must desire to create positive change and work together to combat heterosexism in academe. Higher education will not rid itself of heterosexism simply by including sexual orientation in statements of non-discrimination. Ending heterosexism will take efforts at all levels, by individuals who value community and who have the moral courage to stand against injustice and appreciate the fullness of diversity. As Tierney (1992) stated, "A diverse community does not merely tolerate difference; it honors it, while encouraging dialogue and cooperation" (43). Through dialogue and appropriate action, administrators and faculty can provide the leadership necessary to dismantle heterosexism and create a healthy learning environment for every member of the college community.

CHAPTER 30

The Campus Climate Report: Assessment and Intervention Strategies

Susan R. Rankin

> When those who have the power to name and socially construct reality choose not to see you, or hear you, whether you are dark-skinned, old, disabled, female, or speak with a different accent or dialect than theirs; when someone with the authority of, say, a teacher describes the world and you are not in it, there is a moment of psychic disequilibrium, as if you looked in a mirror and saw nothing. Yet you know that you exist and others like you—that this is a game with mirrors. It takes some strength of soul—and not just individual strength, but collective understanding—to resist this void, this non-being into which you are thrust, and to stand up, demanding to be seen and heard.
> —Adrienne Rich, 1980

Academic institutions are on the forefront of the creation of knowledge, and academic communities expend great amounts of effort in fostering environments where the creation of knowledge is nurtured. This effort is undertaken with the understanding that institutional climate has a profound effect on the community's ability to excel in research and scholarship. However, recent research indicates that prejudicial acts against lesbian, gay, bisexual, and transgender (LGBT) students, faculty, and administrators have surfaced with alarming frequency (D'Augelli, 1989a, 1989b, D'Emilio, 1990; Rankin, 1994). LGBT members of the academic community are subjected to physical and psychological harassment, discrimination, and violence, which obstructs the achievement of their educational and professional goals. This chapter will discuss the importance of campus climate in providing an atmosphere conducive to maximizing the creation of knowledge, review the current national climate for LGBT members of the academic community, and propose strategies for implementing change.

WHY STUDY CAMPUS CLIMATE?

Institutional climate is defined as "current common patterns of important dimensions of organizational life, or its members, perceptions of, and attitudes towards, those dimensions" (Peterson & Spencer, 1990, 31). The major features of climate are its primary emphasis on common participant views of a wide array of organizational phenomena that allows for comparison among groups over time; its focus on current patterns of beliefs and behaviors; and its ability to change (Tierney, 1990).

Kuh and Whitt (1988) suggest that the environment of an institution has a significant impact on its members, who, in turn, contribute to the creation of that institution's environment. Therefore, creating and preserving a climate that offers equal learning opportunities for all students and academic freedom for all faculty—an environment free from discrimination—should be one of the primary responsibilities of educational institutions. The necessity for creating a more inclusive, welcoming climate on college campuses is supported by several recent national education association reports.

Boyer (1990), writing for the Carnegie Foundation for the Advancement of Teaching and the American Council on Education, suggests that in order to build a vital community of learning a college or university must provide an environment where students and faculty work together, where freedom of expression is protected and civility and dignity are affirmed, where equal opportunity is deeply valued, and where the good health of all is absolutely supported. In addition, the Association of American Colleges and Universities (1995) challenges higher education institutions to create and articulate a commitment to inclusion, fairness, and equality. It proposes that colleges and universities commit to developing inclusive environments in which all are welcome, valued, and heard equally. The report suggests that in order to provide a framework within which a vital community of learning can be built, a primary mission of the academy must be to create an environment that ideally cultivates diversity and celebrates difference.

Research examining campus climate focuses on the beliefs and behaviors of members of the academic community. The body of literature regarding institutional climate suggests that the attitudes, beliefs, and behaviors of faculty and administrators significantly contribute to the climate of their institution (Rankin, 1994). As subcultures within the institution, faculty and administrators are the most enduring institutional members and thus can most directly influence organizational strategy or changes in academic management practices. In addition, faculty have a significant impact on the development, maintenance, and/or modifications of students, attitudes and values (Astin, 1990; Kuh & Whitt, 1988;

Pascarella, 1980, 1985). In an extensive review of the literature, Pascarella and (1991) conclude that individuals who attend college "change their value and attitudinal positions in a number of different areas," and "they do so as a consequence of attending a college or university and not simply in response to normal, maturational impulses or to historical, social, or political trends" (325).

In summary, the creation of a welcoming climate is conducive to fulfilling the missions of institutions of higher education, and members of the academic community both contribute to and are impacted by the campus environment. A climate that is welcoming, supportive, and inclusive will allow for the creation and dissemination of knowledge. It follows then that an examination of the climate for LGBT members of the academy is warranted.

AN ASSESSMENT OF HETEROSEXISM IN HIGHER EDUCATION

Heterosexism

Heterosexism is the assumption of the inherent superiority of heterosexuality, an obliviousness to the lives and experiences of LGBT people, and the presumption that all people are, or should be, heterosexual. Based on the ideology of heterosexism, or what Rich (1980) calls "compulsory heterosexuality," a systematic set of institutional and cultural arrangements exist that reward and privilege people for being or appearing to be heterosexual while establishing potential punishments or lack of privilege for being or appearing LGBT.

Like racism, sexism, and other ideologies of oppression, heterosexism is manifested both in societal customs and institutions and in individual attitudes and behaviors (Herek, 1990). I suggest that both the subtle and overt forms of harassment and discrimination experienced by LGBT persons on college campuses are supported by institutionalized heterosexism (Rankin, 1994).

Campus Climate Reports

In response to the victimization of LGBT individuals reported on college campuses, a great deal of research was conducted focusing on the climate at colleges and universities for LGBT people. For example, for several years the National Gay and Lesbian Task Force (NGLTF) documented reported incidents of harassment and violence against LGB students around the country. In 1988, 1,411 anti-gay incidents including threats, vandalism, harassment, and assault were reported to the NGLTF. When asked if anti-gay violence had increased on their campus since the previous year, 32 percent responded affirmatively (Berrill, 1989a). Additionally, Reynolds (1989) pointed out that gay men rated the climate at the University of Virginia lower than straight men with regard to emotional support, intellectualism, change, and innovation. Several university administrators appointed ad hoc committees or task forces to investigate the institutional climate for LGBT members of their academic community. Thirty campus climate reports were compiled and examined for this chapter.

Building on a strategy developed by LaSalle and DeVries (1993), each report was reviewed, and the purpose, methodology, findings, and recommendations identified. Each institution's purpose for assessing the campus climate was unique, prompted by a particular set of circumstances occurring on that campus. For example, at both Vanderbilt University and Pennsylvania State University, the reports were developed in response to the universities' investigations into adding sexual orientation to the non-discrimination policy. In contrast, at the University of Massachusetts at Amherst and the University of Oregon, a history of aggressive, highly visible anti-LGBT harassment prompted the assessment. Further, at the University of Illinois, an assessment was prompted by the chancellor's rejection of a proposal to amend the university's Code on Campus Affairs and Regulations to address discrimination based on sexual orientation. The chancellor stated that there was a lack of compelling evidence of this being a problem. In summary, this review indicates that the impetus for conducting a campus climate assessment is in response either to incidents of harassment or to an awareness of a lack of equity.

The methodology used to examine the campus climate was also varied. The methods utilized were generally influenced by the purposes and goals of the committee as well as the type of questions the institution was examining. Of the 30 college and university reports reviewed, 13 conducted surveys, 6 conducted focus groups or interviews, and 5 opted for a combination of both quantitative and qualitative methodology (6 reports did not indicate their method of assessment). Just as there were a variety of stimuli for writing the reports and various methods employed to complete the assessment, the population sample also differed. For example, the University of Arizona queried 600 faculty and staff regarding their perceptions of the campus climate for LGBT people. In contrast, the University of Massachusetts conducted three surveys purposefully sampling LGB students, resident assistants, and student service personnel. Open forums and public hearings where all members of the academic community were encouraged to share their voice were held at Vanderbilt, Rutgers, and the University of Wisconsin at Madison. Pennsylvania State University and the University of California at Davis conducted extensive interviews with LGBT faculty and staff.

While it is difficult to compare the investigations due to differences in research methodology, instruments, and samples, it is clear that anti-LGBT prejudice is prevalent in higher education institutions. For example, in studies where surveys were used as the primary tool, the data indicated that LGBT students are the victims of anti-gay prejudice ranging from verbal abuse to physical violence to sexual harassment. According to Harry (cited in Campbell, 1991) anti-gay incidents "have a greater impact on its victim than do other forms of victimization. These include higher levels of depression and withdrawal, increase in sleep difficulties, anxiety and loss of confidence. Further, an extraordinary percentage of victims report serious interpersonal difficulties with friends and significant others" (7). It is also important to note here that a major limitation of prevalence studies of anti-gay violence is that many crimes go unreported. Fearing further victimization, many LGBT victims do not report anti-gay crimes; therefore the number of actual incidents of violence and harassment are probably much higher than reported (D'Augelli, 1995; Herek & Berrill, 1990). This concept is supported by the findings of this study where between 50 to 90 percent of those who responded noted that they did not report every incidence they experienced.

In those investigations that utilized qualitative data, analogous findings were reported indicating the invisibility, isolation, and fear of LGBT members of the academic community. For the professor, counselor, staff assistant or student who is gay, lesbian, bisexual, or transgendered, there is the constant fear that should their sexual orientation be discovered, they will be ostracized, their careers will be destroyed, or they will lose their positions. While the reports indicate differences among the experiences of these individuals, their comments indicate that regardless of how "out" or how "closeted" they are, all expressed fears that prevent them from acting freely. Three themes emerged from the interviews, focus group comments, and open forum statements presented in several of the reports and will be briefly reviewed.

Invisibility/Ostracism. Institutionalized heterosexism on college campuses creates an oppressive situation for LGBT persons. The university environment negates their existence, thereby promoting further invisibility. The fear of rejection has a tremendous impact on the way that these individuals lead their lives. "I have tenure, but if the faculty in my department found out that I am a lesbian, I would be ostracized" (faculty member, Penn State, 1994). "What has to be the most painful to me is the invisibility I have had to face as a gay student. I have often felt unwelcome in the place that is my home. What I can say is that except for the university gay community, I have not participated in campus life. It may be an unwritten rule, but it is clear that gays are not welcome in fraternities or on athletic teams" (undergraduate student, University of Minnesota, 1993). "At work, I am not a human being. At 5:00 PM, that's when I can be who I am. I remember thinking about finishing school and starting work as being a freeing experience. Now I know better; it makes me bitter at the University and the world" (LGB staff, University of Colorado at Boulder, 1991).

Isolation/Self-Concealment. In order to prevent what they anticipate will be their colleagues' or peers' rejection, many LGBT members of the academic community choose to conceal their sexual orientation. As one faculty member noted in Tierney (1992) that hiding sexual orientation is necessary for survival. To protect themselves from discrimination, LGBT persons do a lot of lying. The university climate communicates the message that being honest about one's sexual orientation may have direct negative effects on salary, tenure, promotion, and emotional well-being, so they choose to remain in the closet, where it is safe. "An untenured faculty member has been afraid to attend meetings of the Faculty/Staff Lesbian, Gay, Bisexual Caucus for fear that senior colleagues might hear about it" (Tufts, 1993). "I completed your survey at home so no one would see me" (LGB staff, University of Colorado at Boulder, 1991).

University Consequences. The university suffers from its own heterosexism. Talented LGBT students, faculty, and staff feel "forced" to leave the university, and students (both LGBT and heterosexual) are deprived of role models and academic growth. "I'd be scared to be an advisor to the lesbian, gay, and bisexual student association because that is being too obvious. I am close to tenure, and I don't want them to find a reason not to give it to me" (faculty member, Penn State, 1994). "A student enrolled in a history of sexuality course told the instructor that her roommates tried to talk her out of it because 'only lesbians take that course" (Tufts, 1993).

Heterosexism is a form of prejudice that conspires to render LGBT people invisible. Indeed, most LGBT members of the academic community are invisible: Due to fear of harassment and discrimination, we deliberately conceal our sexual orientation. The pervasive heterosexism of the university not only inhibits the acknowledgment and expression of LGBT perspectives; it also affects curricular and research efforts. Further, the contributions and concerns of LGBT people are often unrecognized and unaddressed—to the detriment of the education not only of LGBT students but of heterosexuals as well.

In summary, the results of the climate studies reveal two important themes. First, institutions of higher education do not provide an empowering atmosphere for LGBT faculty, staff, and students—an atmosphere where their voices are heard, appreciated, and valued. Second, and perhaps more significantly, the results suggest that the climate on college campuses acts to silence the voices of its LGBT members with both subtle and overt discrimination. D'Augelli (1989c) wonders, "Why hasn't this problem made its way through the usual streams of anointment as a campus 'problem'? The answer is locked in 'the closet' of lesbian and gay life on campus. It is a 'closet' inhabited not only by self-identified lesbian, gay, and bisexual students, faculty, and staff, although they constitute most of the inhabitants; it is also shared by heterosexual people on campus who know the needs of lesbians and gay men but do not speak out on their behalf" (129). The final section of this chapter will examine the strategies for change suggested to deinstitutionalize heterosexism.

STRATEGIES FOR CHANGE

The recommendations provided in the campus climate reports have several implications for policy makers and program planners in higher education. In order for institutions of higher education to welcome the complexity and richness of the world of the twenty-first century, there is a need to shift basic assumptions, premises, and beliefs in all areas of the institution—only then can behavior and structures be changed. In the transformed institution, heterosexist assumptions are replaced by assumptions of diverse sexualities and relationships; these new assumptions govern the design and implementation of any activity, program, or service of the institution. This sort of transformative change demands committed leadership in both policy and goal articulation. New approaches to learning, teaching, decision-making, and working in the institution are implemented. It will demand the forming of relationships between individuals who are radically "other" to each other. These transformed assumptions, premises, and beliefs will provide the environment with the catalyst for change.

A synthesis of the recommendations suggested in the 30 campus reports reveals four areas where climate change may be influenced: structural transformation; policy inclusion; curricular integration; and educational efforts. A summary of the recommendations is provided in Table 9.

Table 9
Summary of Recommendations for Changing the Campus Climate

Structural Transformation
Creation of an office for LGBT concerns
Creation and identification of a designated safe, social meeting place
Integration of LGBT presence in university documents/publications (grievance procedures, housing guidelines, application materials)
Active recruitment and retention of LGBT persons and allies
Creation of an LGBT alumni group within the existing alumni organization (such as a special interest group)
Creation of documentation form in Police Services for reporting of hate crimes against LGBT persons
Creation of a standing LGBT advisory committee

Policy Inclusion
Inclusion of sexual orientation in the institution's non-discrimination clause

It is important to note some challenges that may occur when trying to implement the recommendations. The implementation phase is the most crucial in transforming the campus climate. Is the administration supportive? Is there fiscal support? As noted earlier, change demands committed leadership in both policy and goal articulation. Are those administrators who have the power and authority to make decisions making public and affirming statements? Are the resources available to implement the recommendations? Are the recommendations presented in the university's strategic plan? The other key players in transforming the campus climate are faculty and students. Are they involved in the planning and writing of the recommendations? Tierney and Dilley (1996) argue that rather than focusing exclusively on surface-level issues—faculty appointments, an inclusive curriculum, a gay-friendly environment—that structures need to be "disrupted." "If one assumes that the structures of knowledge in part have defined normalized relations that have excluded homosexuals, then one needs to break those structures rather than merely reinvent them" (22). To quote Audre Lorde, "The master's tools will never dismantle the master's house" (1984, 112).

One wonders if the implementation of policy changes and more inclusive curricula and service programs will indeed improve the campus climate or if, as queer theorists suggest, we need to disrupt the existing structures. Regardless of the path, higher education has as its mission the creation of knowledge and must provide an environment to nurture that quest.

CHAPTER 31

Extending Benefits for Students' Domestic Partners

Richard P. Keeling and Ferdinand J. Schlapper

Increasing numbers of institutions of higher education are extending certain benefits to the domestic partners of their students. These "fringe benefits," which derive from either student status or employment, encompass a wide range of access, programs, and services, including health insurance, eligibility for residence in campus housing, use of campus recreational facilities, and tickets for athletic or other events. There is great variation among institutions in the kinds and extent of benefits provided.

The absence of these benefits, particularly health insurance, is a serious deficiency that affects the lives and welfare of lesbian, gay, bisexual, and transgender (LGBT) students; it clearly demonstrates that the committed relationships of LGBT students are "less than" those of married students and, therefore, contributes to a negative campus climate while simultaneously causing extra expenditures and unnecessary stress for LGBT students. Health insurance, for example, is far more expensive for a long-term same-sex partner than it is for the spouse of a comparable heterosexual student, who is eligible for the campus-sponsored health insurance plan. Married heterosexual couples can almost always be accommodated in college housing; LGBT partners usually must arrange to live apart or pretend to be "roommates." Efforts to correct this deficiency often generate significant controversy and pressure from governing boards, alumni, and local politicians. In the campus community, there is frequently ardent opposition as well. However, every institution of higher education has a responsibility, in the spirit of justice, to respond equitably and fairly to the needs—and relationships—of the LGBT members of its community. Failing to attend to these concerns implicitly violates all college and university non-discrimination policies that prohibit discrimination based on sexual orientation.

We take as our starting point in this chapter the assumption that the committed relationships of LGBT students are as valuable, and as deserving of support, as heterosexual marriages. Colleges and universities that share that perspective will endorse benefits for domestic partners. The successful implementation of inclusive benefit plans for students' domestic partners requires addressing the following five major issues: defining, verifying, and documenting a domestic partner; deciding what benefits to offer; managing controversy and the politics involved; undermining mythologies about the cost of these benefits; and developing both a strong network of allies and a flexible strategic plan.

DEFINING, VERIFYING, AND DOCUMENTING DOMESTIC PARTNER STATUS

A progressive view of domestic partnerships holds that what is asked of domestic partners should be neither more nor less than what is asked of married couples. That is, proving the existence of a domestic partnership should be no more complex or demanding than proving the existence of a marriage. Students who claim to be married for benefits reasons are seldom, if ever, required to produce a marriage certificate as evidence of their relationship: Students who affirm they are married are considered to be exactly that. At the same time, married students, in the process of enrolling a spouse for insurance or other programs, usually acknowledge through signing a form that the information they have provided is true. Later, if it turns out that a marriage really did not exist, benefits may be denied. It is, therefore, important that institutions of higher education establish criteria by which domestic partnerships can be defined, verified, and documented—even if those institutions have no intention of verifying the relationship a priori. Requiring that domestic partnerships be certified in some manner is sometimes an intermediary step (for political reasons) that expediently reduces resistance to implementing benefits plans.

Students should be able to verify, document, or certify a domestic partnership through evidence of an interdependent relationship, or by demonstrated compliance with local regulations for registration as domestic partners. Typically, the student would sign a statement certifying that the domestic partnership exists and is valid. These statements usually incorporate a definition that includes two people: who meet a minimum age requirement; are living together on a continuous basis; neither of whom is married or has another domestic partner or is related by blood in a manner that would bar their marriage in their state of residence; who are sharing an exclusive personal relationship; and can provide evidence of financial interdependence. This interdependence can be demonstrated by joint banking accounts or credit cards, shared lease or mortgage contracts, reciprocally named beneficiaries on insurance policies, or records of shared household expenses. Obviously, the process of certification is much easier for colleges and universities located in communities that have in place domestic partnership statutes and registration procedures—though the presence of those procedures does not relieve the institution of all responsibility to develop its own policies, since the community domestic partnership registration is usually available only to persons who also claim permanent residence in the local jurisdiction (which many students cannot).

A key decision will be whether the benefits provided to domestic partners are available only to same-sex couples or also to opposite-sex couples who choose not to marry legally. Some will argue that an inclusive policy should not discriminate against any domestic partners (so opposite sex couples should be eligible, too), while others feel strongly that domestic partner status and benefits should be limited to gay and lesbian couples who do not have the option to marry. There are valid points to both perspectives, and the institution will ultimately need to defend its final position. For purposes of this chapter, the important point is to make domestic partnership benefits available to LGBT students.

IDENTIFYING BENEFIT CATEGORIES, RESTRICTIONS, AND LIMITATIONS

The most important—and the most controversial—of possible benefits for domestic partners of LGBT students is health insurance. Some colleges and universities require that all students (or all international students) have health insurance; most strongly recommend it, and many sponsor a specific insurance plan. In addition, some students have access to health insurance as a fringe benefit of their employment as teaching or research assistants on campus. The costs of health insurance continue to rise, and understandably, institutional administrators are concerned about any change that might raise premiums. On the other hand, many campus health and Student Affairs staff are equally concerned about the impact of illness or injury on uninsured, or underinsured, students and their spouses, partners, and families.

Most health insurance plans for which domestic partners are eligible offer benefits that are comparable or identical to what is provided to legally married spouses. These benefits usually include hospitalization, surgical, accident, and major medical coverage; certain levels of inpatient or outpatient mental health and alcohol or other drug-related services; obstetric and maternity care; operative dental services; vision care; and prescription drugs. Insurance plans available to students—and therefore to their spouses or partners—vary extensively in the details of benefit levels, deductibles, copayments, and exclusions of preexisting conditions.

An important consideration is whether to extend rights under the Consolidated Omnibus Budget Reconciliation Act (COBRA) of 1985 to these partners, in order for the plan to be truly comparable and equal to what is provided for married spouses. Coverage under COBRA would provide a domestic partner with access to the same health insurance plan for a transitional period of time after a change in eligibility status (student is no longer enrolled or the relationship is terminated).

In addition to health insurance coverage, other benefits that institutions of higher education may offer the domestic partners of their students include family housing; access to and privileges to use the resources of campus libraries; access to recreational facilities and eligibility for classes and locker or equipment rentals; tickets for athletic and cultural events; use of institutionally affiliated travel agencies; and check cashing privileges. There are few risks and marginal direct costs involved in offering most of these benefits. Often, therefore, approval of them can be achieved through a much simpler, less scrutinized process than is true for health insurance. It may be as simple as review and approval by the appropriate campus advisory or oversight committee.

DETERMINING OPTIMAL POLITICAL
AND PUBLIC RELATIONS STRATEGIES

Some benefit plans have been quietly extended to domestic partners without much public attention or fanfare to avoid controversy, debate, or potential policy reversals. This "under the radar" approach has the advantage of letting a plan get a foothold before it is attacked—but it does not mean that benefits are extended without required approval from regulatory agencies (such as the state insurance commissioner or insurance regulatory board, for health insurance). At the other end of the spectrum, some institutions have proudly publicized these progressive policies in a forthright, direct manner and braced for any negative reaction (which was usually forthcoming). These strategies have varied from institution to institution, depending on the benefit category (health insurance is much higher profile than facility access), the current analysis of campus and external climate (when the legislature is in session may be a poor time for a state university to announce its decision to provide health insurance to domestic partners), and the resolve and clout of the initiators of the policy change.

Neither bombast nor enthusiasm will overcome statutory reality, nor will it prevent eventual judicial review. Some institutions have valiantly taken leadership roles in implementing health insurance benefits for domestic partners, attracting national attention (and a combination of acrimonious criticism and warm praise) in the process—only to discover that their action raised serious questions about the statutory definition of spouses, or dependents, or partners that prompted, eventually, judicial review and, in some cases, court rulings that overturned the campus plan. A skilled review of the legal and statutory conditions in the state should precede any college or university's extension of benefits to domestic partners, and the conclusions of that review may help determine both what kinds of benefits are feasible now and how "public" to be about providing them. (It may also stimulate a plan for political action to alter the statutory barriers that are identified.) The political ramifications of drawing public attention and scrutiny to the proposal can have devastating effects—but, in a democracy, what changes without debate? Is it wiser to be aggressive, "fight the good fight," and push public discourse (at the risk of short-term losses), or to quietly effect incremental change and gradually shift the established norms?

If an "out front" public relations strategy is chosen, the institution should be prepared with prewritten op/ed pieces, carefully written press releases, statements from senior officers, testimonials from students, and the opinions of experts in health insurance to support its position.

PROVIDING RISK ASSESSMENT
AND COST ANALYSIS DATA

The concern of dramatic cost increases and risk exposure related to benefits for domestic partners is predominantly concerned with the extension of health insurance coverage. Health insurance underwriters were initially hesitant to cover domestic partners because of their lack of claims experience with this population and the absence of control over the risk pool. An unstated, but clear, worry was that many gay men would enroll partners who had human immunodeficiency virus (HIV) disease—and that those partners would incur high medical costs as a result. Most early plans therefore imposed a 3 to 5 percent premium surcharge to insure domestic partners in anticipation of additional medical services claims. In fact, though, these insurers found that the claims experience of domestic partners was comparable to, if not lower than, that for married couples—and the premium surcharge was accordingly eliminated within several years. The potential financial risk of treating an acquired immunodeficiency syndrome (AIDS) patient was discovered to pale actuarially in comparison to the 22-year-old female with a complicated pregnancy, the 55-year-old male suffering a massive heart attack, or the 27-year-old, male or female, with a serious, complex injury.

Additionally, the claims experience for domestic partners has been minimal because of the low enrollment rates for this group. Colleges and universities offering health insurance coverage for students' domestic partners have typically encountered an enrollment rate of less than 1 percent. This may reflect the percentage of LGBT students who are in long-term committed relationships; are comfortable with public knowledge of their sexual orientation; have domestic partners who do not have access to other health insurance and feel a need to be insured; and have the financial resources to pay for the coverage. When health insurance is not mandatory, a substantial minority of students will choose not to carry it, banking on their current good health as a kind of insurance against the uncertainties of the future; it is, then, not surprising that many healthy domestic partners would make that same net calculation. Extending benefits to domestic partners in any of the other categories would impose either a minimal additional cost on the institution or would actually increase revenues through user fees.

DEVELOPING A BROAD FOUNDATION OF SUPPORT

In July 1996, the University of Maryland System's Gay and Lesbian Faculty and Staff Association issued a press release reporting that

[T]he 16-member University of Maryland System (UMS) Board of Regents has overwhelmingly rejected three recommendations from its own ad hoc committee regarding the extension of benefits to domestic partners of UMS employees. After months of academic research, informative public hearings, and enlightening correspondence, the committee concluded that extending benefits to domestic partners would have significant value for the UMS. The committee presented its 11-page report and recommendations on April 12, 1996. At Friday's public meeting, two full months after the report's release, many regents demonstrated a lack of familiarity with both the committee's report and the most basic principles of the issues. With little discussion on any of these measures, the regents swiftly rejected the committee's recommendations. [M]embers of the UMS Lesbian, Gay, and Bisexual Staff and Faculty Association said they were saddened and embarrassed by the Board of Regent's failure to act with leadership and courage. They feel that the institutions of the UMS are now in a poor position to honor the university's expressed commitment to equity and diversity in higher education. Additionally, members of the group believe that the UMS will find itself less competitive in its ability to attract and retain outstanding faculty and students.

The sequence of events that occurred in Maryland during the summer of 1996 has been repeated in various ways multiple times on college campuses across the country. The issues are thoroughly researched, a broad spectrum of perspectives is captured, relevant data are collected, comparative analyses with peer institutions are conducted, and summary reports with thoughtful, justifiable recommendations are submitted—and then rejected summarily by an administrative or governing board that, for political and/or personal reasons, has no intention of substantially reviewing the proposal, much less actually approving it. Should the proposal make it through the review of the governing board, it may still be "shot down," in the case of state colleges and universities, by insurance commissioners, the legislature (usually through its committees), or the governor. And regardless of previous battles and their outcomes, any plan to benefit domestic partners may eventually come up for court review if it is challenged on statutory or constitutional grounds.

It is for these reasons that the success of any process of providing inclusive benefits to the domestic partners of LGBT students is critically dependent on formulating strategic plans for identifying allies, confronting barriers, reducing resistance, and building a foundation of support. Different benefit plans will have varying degrees and depth of support from groups on and off campus.

These groups of potential allies may include students, faculty, staff, labor unions, alumni, local editorial boards, selected politicians, and representatives of peer institutions. It is a mistake to assume that all LGBT students (or, for that matter, LGBT faculty, staff, or community citizens) will support benefits for domestic partners; some gay and lesbian activists oppose any strategy that seems to blend, or assimilate, same-sex relationships into society's traditional structures, and other LGBT persons may feel threatened by the political ramifications of the required debate. It is important to search for, find, and affirm common ground—such as the need to get as many people insured as possible—in order to create the largest potential coalition of support. Focusing on benefits for domestic partners as a "gay issue" will, unfortunately, probably limit the interest of some potential supporters.

The broader and stronger the foundation of support, the more difficult it will be for any governing body to dismiss proposals for inclusively extending benefits to domestic partners. Where state institutions are concerned, this means that the support of other campuses in the same system matters a great deal. A single institution can be easily disregarded, labeled politically correct, and portrayed as a renegade; it is much harder to write off a group of institutions that have reached consensus. One of the strongest vehicles for building support is a statewide, or systemwide, organization of counterpart officers—e.g., the health service directors, counseling center directors, senior Student Affairs officers, deans of students, or housing directors. Important, too, are connections off campus; since community hospitals may have to care for uninsured individuals, they may be interested in advocating for more insurance coverage for more people. The city or county medical society may help for the same reason. Employee benefits officers at local corporations that have extended benefits to the domestic partners of their staff are invaluable.

As noted earlier, though, no amount of support or enthusiasm prevents judicial challenge and review. When a good analysis of extant law and regulations reveals deficiencies that will weaken attempts to include domestic partners in health insurance, for example, proposed plans should be accompanied by a series of advocacy efforts designed to change the language of law or regulation as needed—truly a long term process. This caution does not imply that institutions should let uncertainty about future interpretation prevent them from attempting to make progress in providing benefits for domestic partners—only that those uncertainties should elicit a long-term commitment to changing the legislative landscape.

CHAPTER 32

A Giant Step Toward Equality: Domestic Partner Benefits

Jayne Thorson and Raelynn J. Hillhouse

A major advance in gay and lesbian rights during the 1990s has been the extension of staff benefits to employees' same-sex domestic partners. Hundreds of corporations, municipalities, governmental entities, and colleges and universities have included gay and lesbian partners along with heterosexual spouses as recipients of employee benefits.

This chapter will focus on the extension of domestic partner benefits at colleges and universities. It will discuss the rationale for the provision of benefits to employees and for the inclusion of employees' domestic partners; the cost of extending benefits, including no-cost benefits, expenses associated with health insurance, and a mechanism for predicting costs; criteria for determining eligibility of domestic partners; residual tax consequences of domestic partner benefits; and the option of including heterosexual unmarried partners.

Over sixty American and a dozen Canadian colleges and universities have extended benefits to employees' same-sex partners. The trend among colleges and universities has spanned private and public institutions across the continent, including such diverse schools as Massachusetts Institute of Technology (MIT), Antioch University, University of Iowa, Bowdoin University, Harvard University, Mission College, North Dakota University, Princeton University, Florida International University, Wellesley College, Tufts University, Pomona College, and the University of New Mexico. At essentially all of these institutions, the extension of benefits has occurred since 1990.

WHY BENEFITS?

Colleges and universities, like other employers, provide various services, opportunities, and benefits to their employees and, in the case of colleges and universities, their students. These benefits are provided for two basic reasons: to attract and retain the most highly qualified employees and to establish a positive working and learning environment. Benefits are extended to employees' same-sex spouses and their dependents for the same reasons.

As educational institutions have increasingly recognized the value of a diverse intellectual community, many have implemented policies that prohibit discrimination against lesbians and gay men. A growing number of colleges and universities include sexual orientation in the non-discrimination clauses of their bylaws and in their equal opportunity statements; extending benefits normally provided to spouses of employees to same-sex partners is a logical step in achieving such a goal of inclusion. Spousal benefit policies that exclude same-sex partners convey the impression that the families of gay and lesbian employees are somehow inferior and less deserving than the families of married employees. When made aware of the facts regarding compensation (of which employee benefits are a significant component) and access to university resources (including housing), university leaders are forced to acknowledge the significant inequalities in compensation and opportunities between their employees who have same-sex partners and employees who are legally heterosexually married. Thus, the provision of benefits to same-sex partners becomes a matter of upholding university commitments to non-discrimination and equal opportunity.

Typically, some benefits have been extended to the married spouses and dependents of employees. These spousal benefits are of two types. Some, such as health insurance, recreational facilities privileges, and tuition waivers, are extended directly to employees' spouses and dependents. Other benefits, such as dependent care leave and bereavement leave for the death of a spouse or family member, are provided to employees who are legally married. Clearly, it is advisable to include both categories of spousal benefits when considering the extension of benefits to same-sex domestic partners.

In addition, common benefits at institutions of higher education include access to computer and library facilities; eligibility for university-subsidized housing; leaves of absence for parenting; discounts on tickets to athletic events; and life and disability insurance. Recently, many universities have increased the spectrum of available benefits to include legal insurance, dental and optometric care, car or home insurance, long-term medical care insurance, and many other optional services.

Foremost among these employee benefits is health insurance. While it is easy to overlook other employee benefits in the quest for health insurance for domestic partners, it is important that same-sex domestic partners are afforded *all* of the benefits and opportunities of heterosexual spouses. Not only is this desirable from equality and economic perspectives; it provides the basis for a much more coherent and consistent argument when working toward the extension of benefits to domestic partners.

NO-COST OR LOW-COST BENEFITS

The extension of some benefits to employees' same-sex partners and their dependents can be accomplished at no additional cost to the institution. The specific benefits of this type vary from university to university but generally include the use of existing facilities. Examples of such opportunities that are typically extended to married partners and their dependents include the use of recreational, computer, and library facilities, the opportunity to purchase athletic tickets, and access to university housing. For most employees, the provision of short-term dependent care leave to care for domestic partners and inclusion of domestic partners in bereavement leave policies can be accomplished at no additional cost to the institution. Even for those employees whose absence requires the use of temporary help (nurses, for example), the expense incurred by the university will be negligible.

Depending on the political landscape of an individual college or university, a piecemeal approach to extending benefits may be appropriate The recognition of domestic partners in a few no-cost and non-threatening personnel policies may seem trivial, but it can form an extremely important precedent for more significant changes.

An excellent approach to ensuring domestic partners' inclusion in these policies is through the institution's definition of "family" for personnel purposes. This obviates the need for gradual policy-by-policy revisions. It may, however, be an incomplete remedy—health insurance and family housing may continue to be excluded, for example.

Family Housing

An emotionally charged issue in the equalization of benefits is the opening of family housing to committed same-sex partners. As in politics, discussion of family housing challenges people at a core level. Ironically, it is in discussing this fundamental civil right—housing—that the most uncivil discussions are likely to occur. Opponents may describe fears of child molestation, "recruitment" of vulnerable spouses, and children witnessing unnatural acts in public places. (When this issue was brought before the board of regents at the University of Michigan, a resident of family housing, flanked by his loving wife and children, described all of the above and concluded with the dire forecast that if those perverts were allowed into family housing, they would have to organize separate square dances.) Advocates must be prepared to ignore such spurious drivel and remain focused on the relevant issues of equal opportunity and nondiscrimination.

In discussing this potentially volatile topic, it is helpful to frame the issue more broadly. Many universities provide a variety of housing services in addition to a large residence hall system; these may include assistance in locating off-campus rental housing as well as the more familiar subsidized housing for newly hired faculty members, for married students, or for students with children ("faculty housing," "married student housing," and "family housing," respectively). In discussing equal access to housing opportunities for lesbians and gay men, it is helpful to consider all forms of "university-subsidized" housing, rather than "family" housing. Not only does this avoid some of the irrational family values arguments, but it is clearly a more accurate depiction of the distribution of university resources and services.

The provision of subsidized housing for married couples is a remnant of efforts several decades ago to encourage returning war veterans to attend universities. Today, as those same veterans' grandchildren are attending college, this historical form of financial aid puts universities in the curious position of providing housing for married students and their non-student spouses rather than for financially threatened pairs of students irrespective of their relationship. Unmarried students with children may also find themselves displaced by non-student spouses. Obviously, some of the most basic tenets underlying universities' allocation of housing resources are called into question and should be thoroughly reexamined. A coherent and consistent approach is simply that committed same-sex couples be provided that same access to university-subsidized housing as their married heterosexual counterparts.

It is also useful to gather data about who is actually living in university-subsidized housing. In contrast to widespread assumptions, closer inspection often reveals that the reality in university-subsidized housing reflects the diversity of family structures in overall society: single fathers with children, single mothers with children, married couples in which one spouse is actually living and working elsewhere, faculty, students, and even university staff members. It can also be useful to learn about any informal arrangements that have been made to accommodate a same-sex couple—the precedent can be quite valuable, although care must be taken to avoid identifying individuals who made these quasi-legal options possible.

It is possible to structure other housing programs to prevent discrimination against gay and lesbian students and their partners. Many colleges and universities assist students, faculty, and staff who are seeking off-campus rental housing. Some universities, including the University of Michigan, require landlords not affiliated with the university to sign an agreement to abide by the university's non-discrimination policies, which include sexual orientation. When landlords refuse to agree to these principles or have deleted sexual orientation from the clause, the university refuses to allow their participation in the placement program. (It is interesting to note that the University of Michigan was enforcing this policy at the same time it was excluding same-sex couples from its own housing.)

While restricting access to housing on the basis of marital status is clearly in violation of many states' civil rights laws, the remedy is not so clear-cut. For example, the Michigan Elliott-Larsen Civil Rights Act includes a specific exemption for university housing. Same-sex couples are eligible for university housing at an increasing number of universities, including the University of Michigan, the University of Iowa, the University of Wisconsin, the University of Minnesota, Stanford, Columbia, and MIT.

Financial Aid and Tuition Waivers

There are surprisingly few instances in which gay or lesbian partners' incomes (or lack thereof) affect students' financial aid. This is due to the clearly defined federal specifications to determine students' financial need, which do not include expenses associated with spouses, and the application of these specifications to other non-federal sources of aid. Nevertheless, it is important for two reasons to examine this issue at each institution: first, because policies vary among colleges and universities; and second, because it provides the best opportunity to address the "they want all of the rights and none of the responsibilities" argument. It is vital to leave no doubt that same-sex couples accept the attendant responsibilities of being recognized by the university. The issue of financial aid presents the opportunity to state this clearly: If students' financial aid is increased or, more important, decreased because of spouses' incomes, then gay and lesbian students' financial aid will be adjusted accordingly because of partners' incomes.

Unlike formal financial aid programs, tuition waivers or reductions are likely to affect a number of individuals if extended to gay and lesbian families. Many colleges and universities provide reduced tuition rates for spouses and dependents of employees, and these, too, should be made available to the partners and dependents of gay and lesbian employees.

Residency Status

At some state-supported colleges and universities, marriage to a state resident may qualify a student to classification as an in-state student for tuition purposes. Similarly, marriage to a state resident can be used as one of several factors in determining residency status. Committed same-sex relationships should be treated in the same manner as marriages in making residency determinations.

Other Low Cost Benefits

Many colleges and universities permit students' and employees' spouses and dependents to utilize numerous university facilities and resources. These may include the opportunity to obtain health care through the Student Health Service, to purchase tickets for athletic or cultural events at reduced rates, to use the university library, computer, or recreational facilities, as well as numerous others.

When seeking inclusion of same-sex partners in university policies, these should not be overlooked.

HEALTH INSURANCE

One of the most expensive benefits that universities provide to their employees is health insurance. Cost is one of the major arguments used to preclude providing health insurance to employees' same-sex partners and their dependents. The experience of the many institutions that have extended health insurance to same-sex partners has been that the costs are far less substantial than initially believed. The cost of extending health insurance to same-sex partners depends on the number of employees who enroll their partners and the cost for each enrolled partner. The experience of universities and corporations that have extended eligibility for insurance is that although many partners are eligible, only a small proportion of those eligible actually enroll. This is due, in part, to the fact that many partners already have health insurance through their own employers.

Calculating the Costs

When considering the extension of health insurance to same-sex couples, it is important to realistically estimate the likely cost to the institution and to consider that cost from the perspective of the total expenditure for employee benefits. To calculate the anticipated cost, comparative data from other colleges and universities are needed, especially from other institutions of similar size and composition or those that are considered "peer" schools. For example, in 1994, when considering extending health insurance to partners of gay and lesbian employees at the University of Michigan, we examined the experience of other universities that had already extended benefits. Table 10 depicts our findings.

Using the data in Table 10, we calculated the number of employees likely to enroll for same-sex partner health insurance at the University of Michigan. The number of benefits-eligible employees was multiplied by the average enrollment rate of 2.9 employees per thousand (.0029) to estimate that 73 people were likely to enroll if Michigan's experience were average. In fact, this estimate and the actual number who enrolled corresponded almost exactly. It is interesting to note that as increasing numbers of universities and corporations have extended benefits to same-sex partners, the average enrollment rate has remained unchanged from this early study. Nevertheless, it is advisable to collect current data from other institutions that are most similar to your own.

The overall financial implications of extending health insurance to same-sex partners can then be estimated by multiplying the number of benefits-eligible employees by the predicted enrollment rate, then multiplying the result by the average cost of spousal coverage for health insurance. We calculated that at the University of Michigan since the average spousal cost of dental and medical

Table 10
Health Benefit Enrollment Rates of LGBT Employees at Selected Institutions

Institution	# Enrolled	Total Eligible Employees*	Enrollment Rate of Same-Sex Couples
Stanford	37	11,000	.0049
Chicago	27	6,200	.0044
*Harvard	45	12,000	.0038
*Columbia	20	6,000	.0033
*Dartmouth	8	2,700	.0029
Iowa St.	6	4,000	.0015
MIT	12	8,700	.0014
*Iowa	16	14,000	.0011
Average (weighted or arithmetic)			.0029

* Indicates that Teaching Assistants and Resident Assistants are eligible to enroll partners.

insurance was approximately $2,000 annually, the cost associated with 73 additional enrollments would be around $150,000. While $150,000 is not trivial, it must be considered from the perspective of an annual total benefits expenditure of $260 million, of which $110 million was spent on health benefits. Indeed, would we even notice if 73 more of our 25,000 employees got married?

A major concern about extending health insurance to same-sex partners is the belief that health care costs are simply higher for lesbians and gay men. Yet institutions that have extended benefits to same-sex partners have found that the costs are the same as the expenses associated with married spouses. Before including same-sex partners and their dependents in its health benefits program, Stanford University examined financial data from universities and municipalities that had already extended benefits to same-sex partners. They found no discernible differences in costs per enrollee for same-sex and opposite-sex spouses and subsequently reported no discernible differences in its own per capita costs. The Stanford study also noted that in some instances insurance carriers raised their premiums, but in all of these cases, the increases were rescinded as a result of the claims experience. The other institutions we surveyed in Table 10 reported that costs per enrollee had not increased. Thus, the health insurance costs associated with same-sex partners are the same as those associated with married spouses.

DOCUMENTING PARTNERSHIPS

All institutions extending benefits to same-sex partners and their dependents have established policies for documenting the existence of committed same-sex relationships, or rather relationships that involve a significant commitment comparable to that of legal marriage. When establishing such a mechanism, it is important that employees in same-sex relationships be treated similarly to married couples and that they not face additional unnecessary scrutiny. When applying for spousal or partner benefits, the scope of evidence of commitment and the burden of proof within same-sex relationships should not be greater than that required of married couples.

Among universities that have extended benefits to same-sex partners, the required documentation of same-sex domestic partnerships varies from institution to institution. Many institutions, including Harvard and Michigan, require that the relationship be registered using the procedures of a public entity, such as a city that allows domestic partner registration. In the Harvard and Michigan cases, both the cities of Cambridge and Ann Arbor, respectively, have ordinances that allow same-sex couples to register their relationships, although both universities recognize registrations from other public entities. In cities without such ordinances, universities may require similar declarations of domestic partnership. Clearly, these requirements, and those demonstrating financial interdependence, pose a burden of proof on same-sex couples that is not demanded of married couples and contradict attempts to treat same-sex and married couples equally.

Some institutions require documentation of financial interdependence as proof of a domestic partnership. Specific requirements vary but generally focus on joint property. They may include evidence of financial interdependence such as joint ownership of a home; a joint lease; joint automobile ownership; designation of a domestic partner as prime beneficiary in an insurance policy, will, or retirement contract; durable powers of attorney; joint credit cards; or a joint bank account. (In must be noted that such property based requirements are biased against low-income employees and students.) Other institutions require couples to have shared a residence for a specified length of time.

Among institutions extending benefits to same-sex partners, there exists a common basic core of requirements for domestic partnership registrations. These core requirements are that both partners be over the age of 18; in a continuing and committed relationship with each other; each other's sole domestic partner and intend to remain so indefinitely; the same sex; unmarried; and not related to each other by blood in a manner that would bar marriage.

In designing Michigan's policy to determine domestic partnership, we examined eligibility requirements at all of the other institutions that had extended benefits and concluded, in true academic form, that we would create our own. We opted for the core requirements outlined above, in conjunction with official registration in Ann Arbor or another municipality. It is important that at each college or university eligibility criteria be closely examined and selected according to the individual needs of that institution.

Penalties for misrepresentation of same-sex partnerships should be as equally severe as those for fraudulent claims of marriage. Some universities include an acknowledgment of this in their registration forms. Likewise, the inception and termination restrictions of same-sex domestic partnerships should be equal to those required of married couples. Most universities require a newly married employee to apply for spousal benefits within an established period of time following the marriage and require notification within a specified period of time if the marriage is terminated in divorce. Similarly, employees' spouses may be eligible for coverage within a fixed period of time after termination of their own employment. The same eligibility limitations and notification periods should be applied to same-sex domestic partnerships. Since many states require a waiting period between filing for and being granted divorce, some universities impose a similar time restriction on same-sex couples before employees can designate another domestic partner.

Upon termination of eligibility for health benefits, the Consolidated Omnibus Budget Reconciliation Act (COBRA) of 1985 provides an extension of benefits to formerly-eligible employee's married spouses. Same-sex partners and their dependents should be granted extensions for a similar period.

SEPARATE BUT NOT EQUAL

Although many provisions can be made to include employees' same-sex partners in the university community in the same ways that married spouses are included, federal and state governments' lack of recognition of same-sex unions prevents true equality: Same-sex partners do not meet the strict Internal Revenue Service definitions of spouses or dependents. Consequently, partners' health insurance premiums are treated as taxable income paid to employees. In contrast, health insurance premiums for married spouses are not taxed. Unfortunately, this distinction is not within any college's or university's purview to change. Most commonly, an amount equal to partners' university-paid premiums is added to the employees' pay, taxed, and then deducted. It is important to ensure that the university's gay and lesbian community is well informed about these tax laws prior to benefit implementation.

UNMARRIED HETEROSEXUAL COUPLES?

When considering the extension of employee benefits to same-sex partners, the question logically arises of whether to include unmarried heterosexual partners. The inclusion of heterosexual couples requires a very different fundamental premise: It requires that the discrimination being corrected is the denial of benefits to unmarried partners, that is, to individuals who could be eligible for benefits but who have elected not to marry.

A much stronger and more solid argument can be made for the extension of benefit eligibility only to same-sex partners. In this case, benefits are being extended to individuals who could not, under current law, become eligible by choosing to marry. In this case, the fundamental discrimination is that of being unable to have a partnership officially recognized through marriage. This perspective is consistent with the existence of deeply committed partnerships in which the individuals elect, for any number of reasons, not to recognize their relationship formally through marriage or domestic partner registration. Eligibility for benefits, therefore, is not being precluded to any individual based on his or her sexual orientation but on the formally recognized status of the relationship.

CONCLUSION

The quest for extension of employee benefits to the partners of gay and lesbian faculty, staff, and students is not an easy undertaking. It guarantees frustration, illogical and seemingly indefensible contradictions, and hurtful—even hateful—moments. It will also reveal new allies and unexpected acts of tremendous courage. This struggle for basic rights carries no guarantee of success or achievement of equality. Yet, by its very existence, this process is one of education: education about the everyday reality of gay and lesbian lives, about how our complex institutions work, and about how a group of individuals dedicated to improving their institutions can make a difference. Change happens through education, and education, after all, is the reason we're here.

PART VIII

Lesbian, Gay, Bisexual, and Transgender Student Leadership and Organizations

CHAPTER 33

Leadership Development for Lesbian, Gay, Bisexual and Transgender College Students

J. Davidson "Dusty" Porter

Leadership development of all students is an essential component of the mission of most colleges and universities. Lesbian, gay, bisexual, and transgender (LGBT) students are a campus population that should be targeted for intentionally designed leadership development programs. Although leadership development efforts by institutions of higher education have historically focused on highly visible student leaders of campus organizations, fraternities and sororities, and student government associations (Denson & Sellers, 1981), leadership educators (Roberts & Ullom, 1989) recommend a student leadership program model that is "designed and directed to meet the needs of the various special populations that exist in a specific institution" (69). Arminio (1993) encourages leadership development practitioners to "take important differences into account when designing courses and creating educational interventions" (41).

THE IMPORTANCE OF LGBT STUDENT LEADERSHIP DEVELOPMENT

It is important to provide a leadership development experience for the campus LGBT community. Offering a specialized leadership program sends a message to the LGBT student population that they matter to the institution. By providing professional staff support and financial resources, the institution affirms the experiences of LGBT students and implicitly communicates a message of care about LGBT student leadership development and success.

There are other important justifications for leadership programming as well. LGBT students in college are often progressing in their individual identity development and their subsequent identification with the larger LGBT community. Numerous studies have pointed to the relationship between coming out and a positive sense of gay identity (Cass, 1979; Miranda & Storms, 1989). A leadership program can assist students who are in the coming out process by the visibility of prominent national or local LGBT leaders; opportunities to share in collective work with their peers; and by exposure to the history of the LGBT civil rights movement. Through leadership programs, campus faculty and staff can support the important struggle for identity and community of LGBT students (Rhoads, 1994b).

In addition, leadership development programming also provides the chance for LGBT students to engage in the processes of becoming visible as a campus community. Through coming together for a leadership development program, students are able to engage in activities of challenging institutional or societal stereotypes and of organizing for subsequent events or campus work following the program.

A well-designed leadership development program may also help LGBT students see the connections of their own experience to other types of oppression and make the connections between homophobia and racism and sexism. For example, the leadership strategies of collaborating and coalition building have been critical to the LGBT civil rights movement. How can these same leadership skills be taught to LGBT students as they seek to understand, support, and work with campus student groups, especially those representing students of color?

Finally, leadership development for LGBT students will prepare them for the ongoing challenges of fighting oppression and violence and for achieving equality and justice. The current realities clearly indicate the need for strong future leaders of the LGBT community: lack of a federal statute protecting LGBT people from employment or housing discrimination (Fassinger, 1991); continued high rates of harassment and assaults (D'Augelli, 1989a); and the recent failure to stop congressional passage of the Defense of Marriage Act (DOMA) all point to the need for training tomorrow's LGBT leaders. For faculty and staff, the important work in fostering future national leaders of the LGBT community must take place now, while students are in the laboratory of the academy and have the opportunities to risk, to grow, and to develop positive, healthy LGBT identities.

This chapter will begin by highlighting several leadership theories that will be useful as a foundation for designing LGBT leadership development programs. Next, a review of sexual identity development will be given, with a focus on understanding how identity development can inform the framework of an LGBT leadership development program. Finally, a step-by-step model of planning a leadership program for a specific college or university will be discussed.

As a caveat in these introductory remarks, it is important to acknowledge the complexity of leadership development for LGBT students. A myriad of factors can have an effect on the design of a successful leadership experience: the current campus environment for people of differing sexual orientations (faculty, staff, and students); the nature and support of student leadership development at the college or university; the amount of staff time and programming funds available for leadership programming; the quality of student officers of the LGBT campus organization; and the inherent diversity of the LGBT campus population. Each of these variables will need to be taken into account to prepare for the process of designing leadership development training.

LEADERSHIP DEVELOPMENT: THEORY AND PRACTICE

When thinking about leadership development for LGBT college students, what theoretical frameworks are most helpful in serving as a foundation for design? The leadership research field is rich with approaches from the business, psychology, and political science disciplines. One can find in any bookstore hundreds of leadership texts, each giving a different perspective on the nature of leadership and how best to put leadership ideas into practice. For the purpose of this chapter, three leadership theories or approaches will be discussed: James MacGregor Burns's (1978) idea of *transforming leadership;* the *social change model of leadership development* created by a team led by Alexander and Helen Astin (1996); and perhaps one of the newest frameworks for understanding leadership, the idea of *citizen-leaders* (Cronin, 1995; Mabey, 1995). These three approaches have been chosen because each includes the idea that leadership is about affecting change in a positive way; other existing leadership theories may not concentrate as much on this important theoretical aspect, if at all.

In his seminal work *Leadership* (1978), Burns discusses the difference between transactional and transforming leadership. While transactional leadership involves the exchange or bartering of wants and needs between leaders and followers, transforming leadership is about promoting change. Burns explains that "transforming leadership occurs when one or more persons engage with others in such a way that leaders and followers raise one another to higher levels of motivation and morality" (20). The overall purpose of transforming leadership is to bring about real change. Burns also notes that transforming leaders appeal to followers' higher ideals and moral values such as liberty, justice, equality, peace, and humanitarianism and not to the lesser emotions of fear, greed, jealousy, or hatred. Clearly, LGBT leaders of today are interested and invested in achieving the values of liberty and justice in American society.

The social change model of leadership development was created by an ensemble of leadership educators, led by Alexander and Helen Astin at the University of California at Los Angeles (UCLA), and was designed specifically for use with college students. The model uses seven values of leadership processes, known as the "7 Cs," to help students understand a framework for creating positive social change. The seven values outlined in the model, each within a domain of the individual, the group, or the community, are: citizenship, collaboration, commitment, common purpose, congruence, consciousness of self, and controversy with civility. The model is founded on the premises that values demand a conscious focus, that leadership ought to bring about desirable social change, and that leadership is a process instead of a position (H. Astin, 1996).

Finally, recent publications by authors in the leadership field have begun to concentrate on the idea of citizen-leaders (A. Astin, 1995; Center for Political Leadership & Participation, 1996; Mabey, 1995). In these publications, scholars and practitioners challenge faculty and staff to begin looking at the responsibility of the academy to prepare students to be more knowledgeable about the intersections of citizenship and leadership. For example, the authors of *Democracy at Risk* (Center for Political Leadership & Participation, 1996), a report of the federally-funded Eisenhower Leadership Project, point out that "the new model of leadership confirms that to collaborate is to prepare for civic engagement. The act of creating change—of making something better than it was before—proves to students that participation matters" (7).

Each of these leadership theories was chosen as a focus because it looks at the idea of change. As LGBT students come together in a leadership development experience, they will undoubtedly begin to focus on change: change in the institution, change in their student organizations, and/or change in their local community or in the larger society. Equipping these student leaders with the skills necessary to promote positive social change involves helping them understand existing leadership theories that focus on the change process. These three theories have been included because they inform our understanding of working with student leaders interested in change, in particular social change. One of the theories, or a combination, should be utilized in designing a campus leadership development experience for the LGBT population at the institution.

LGBT STUDENTS AND BELIEFS ABOUT LEADERSHIP

It is important to remember that LGBT students may not self-identify with the term *leader* or the concept of *leadership*. For many LGBT students, leadership may connote the idea of power, such as the power in society that has been used to keep LGBT individuals marginalized. For example, Lord, Foti, and Devader (1984), were able to show that college students shared consensual schemas, or prototypes, about 11 different types of leaders and what characteristics were associated with each one. These prototypes may also be shared by LGBT students; internalized ideas about what leaders *look like* or *act like* could cause an LGBT student to think, "I am not a leader, nor do I wish to become one."

Another important facet of leadership development and LGBT college students is understanding how culture influences leadership practices. Unfortunately, there has been little research in this area. Cheatham (1993) points to the existing irony of cultural influences of leadership by noting that "the reviewed literature makes no apparent nor specific accommodations to either general or cultural influences on leader values or behavior" even though "an abundant and growing literature exists that suggests conventional paradigms overlook partici-pants' world views and how these affect their behavior and interactions" (3). In other words, the identity development of LGBT students may result in divergent world views that have a subsequent influence on their leadership styles and ap-proaches. As students progress through the stages or fluid statuses of sexual identity development, their beliefs about leaders and the nature of leadership may also be changing; thus, the challenge is to help a student understand how being a gay, lesbian, bisexual, or transgendered individual influences her or his perception of leadership and her or his own leadership practices. Thus, the next section of this chapter focuses on identity development for students of differing sexual orientation.

IDENTITY DEVELOPMENT: WHY CONSIDER THEORY?

Why consider identity development theory when putting together a leader-ship development program? Identity development theory seeks to explain how the nature of personal identity, in such dimensions of race, gender, abil-ity/disability, sexual orientation and socioeconomic class, influences overall development of the student. Certainly, as McEwen (1996b) writes, the major use of identity theory is not to predict behavior but instead to help understand stu-dents in more complex and integrated ways. When planning a leadership experi-ence that will be pertinent for the LGBT student community, identity theory helps us to understand what types of leadership training and topics will likely be most salient for students.

First, significant themes weave through the experiences of all students of differing sexual orientation, such as the challenges of coming out (Coleman, 1982a, 1982b, 1982c) and the feeling of living in two worlds (L. Brown, 1989); either or both of these issues might emerge in a discussion of leadership for LGBT individuals. Second, identity development perspectives that are specific for gay men, lesbians, and bisexual or transgendered individuals will be re-viewed due to their importance in understanding each of these subcultures within the LGBT community. Finally, the importance of understanding how LGBT students may be experiencing multiple oppressions will be highlighted.

What are the common themes for LGBT students? By far, the most obvious experience all of these students face is coming out. Cain (1991), in summarizing several models of gay identity development, notes that the one important mile-stone event in all of the models is "the revelation of one's sexuality to others" (68). In general, sexual identity theorists such as Cass (1979) agree that the pro-cess of developing a healthy gay identity includes disclosing one's sexual ori-entation to significant others.

The coming out process is especially salient for traditional-aged college students. Troiden (1993), in summarizing retrospective studies of gay men, notes that they arrive at a "homosexual self-definition" on average between the ages of 19 and 21. Lesbians, also in retrospective studies, recall reaching these same identities slightly later, between the ages of 21 and 23. Many of the studies Troiden references in his synopsis were completed in the late 1970s and early 1980s; with the changes in society regarding visibility of LGBT individuals, these psychosocial developmental tasks might be changing to earlier in the adult life span (D'Augelli, 1991a; Swartwout, 1995).

The importance of coming out in adult development is summarized by Pope (1995b) using three domains of mental health. First, the coming out process allows LGBT persons to integrate their sexuality into every aspect of their lives and live their lives honestly around those individuals with whom they interact on a daily basis. Second, the coming out process has societal and professional consequences, as *out* LGBT individuals are often role models for other LGBT persons who may not be as far along in their identity development. Finally, the process of coming out often allows the individuals eventually to obtain health benefits for their partners, to bring their partners to business or social events, and to live their lives honestly and in a fully integrated capacity.

How do Pope's ideas connect to student leadership development? Serving in a leadership role in an organization often equates with increased visibility. Undoubtedly, students who are aspiring to leadership roles within organizations will be confronted with the lifelong challenge of when and how to be out (J. Woods, 1993). Also, LGBT persons may be in positions to affect change in their organization around the professional climate for LGBT employees, including domestic-partnership policies and a hassle-free workplace.

An important aspect for many LGBT students who are coming out is the culture of the LGBT community on their individual campus. Erickson (1968) discusses identity development as the sense of self that is produced from the connection between the individual and his or her social environment. Depending on the campus location (urban versus rural), the diversity of the student body (racial backgrounds, median age, commuter or residential), and types of student attitudes (progressive vs. conservative), the LGBT culture will vary widely from campus to campus.

As a student progresses through her or his sexual identity development, she or he may or may not feel a connection or identification with the campus LGBT community. Rhoads (1994a) describes a campus he names "Clement University" as one where many students in the LGBT community identify as *queer* instead of gay, lesbian, bisexual, or transgendered. On some campuses, the term *queer* may be alienating for LGBT students; for others, it may be an appropriate community descriptor.

Another salient aspect of identity for LGBT students appears to be the sense of feeling bicultural. In this case, *bicultural* describes the phenomenon of living in both the traditional heterosexual culture of America as well as a culture of differing sexual orientation. For example, Rhoads (1994b) profiles a student in an ethnographic study of gay college men who has "learned to modify his language based on whether he is amongst gays or straights" (19).

In addition to these common threads for LGBT individuals, there are also specific themes for the individual subcultures that need to be touched upon in the context of designing a leadership development program.

Lesbians

For lesbians, important themes in identity development may revolve around both gender and sexual orientation issues. Browning, Reynolds, and Dworkin (1991) emphasize that "growing up in a sexist culture creates a double bind for women, and therefore, lesbians" (178). As women-identified women, the process of coming out and self-identifying as lesbian may be very different than for men. For example, many lesbians have felt safer coming out in the women's movement as opposed to the traditionally male-dominated gay movement (Clinton, 1989). L. Brown (1995) also differentiates awareness of same-sex attraction for women from men. In her work, she summarizes the ideas of several researchers who have pointed to the idea that "awareness of same-sex attraction for women begins as a primarily affectional rather than sexual phenomenon" (18).

D'Emilio (1992), in writing about capitalism and gay identity, points to the historical visibility of gay men as opposed to lesbians who did not have as many opportunities to live their lives independently of traditional society due to economic implications. Although the "professional playing field" has been opened dramatically in the past 50 years, lesbians may still feel at risk for discrimination in non-traditional occupations (Browning, Reynolds, & Dworkin, 1991).

Gay Men

For gay male college students who are in the process of coming out, several issues may be important. Writers have pointed to the 1990s "gay male eros" that has entered into mainstream society, evidenced by magazine covers and Calvin Klein advertising models (Sadownick, 1995; Signorile, 1993). Gay male college students may be comparing themselves to these images of masculinity that often are unattainable and unrealistic. At the same time, the prevalence of HIV infection is entwined with a gay male identity (D'Emilio, 1992). The mental repercussions of sexual activity with other men at early levels of identity development are more than just shame and guilt; there is worry about infection and health risks.

Bisexual and Transgendered Students

Very little has been written about bisexual identity development, with little or no research on transgendered identity development. For bisexual students, a feeling of possible rejection from both heterosexuals and/or lesbian and gay student peers often results in yet another closet with which to contend (Hayes, 1993). Fox (1996) believes that bisexual identity development may be nonlinear and that bisexuality may be constructed as a predominantly fluid process. Coming out as bisexual can be both similar and different compared to the process for lesbian women and gay men (Fox, 1995; Weinberg, Williams, & Pryor, 1994).

Multiple Identities

Many writers have focused on the idea of multiple identities and oppressions (Loiacano, 1989; Reynolds & Pope, 1991; Wall & Washington, 1991) as they have explored the connections and interfaces between sexual orientation and gender, ethnic or racial background, spirituality, ability/disability, and social class. For LGBT students who represent all of the other differences we find in our student populations, the feeling of belonging to many different communities can be especially intense. As Luis Alfaro writes, "[B]elonging to multiple communities can sometimes leave you feeling schizophrenic" (cited in Sadownick, 1996, 16). The Reynolds and Pope (1991) multidimensional model of identity development challenges the leadership educator to be aware of how a LGBT student may be identifying with one or more aspects of self in segmented or combined ways. For example, Browning, Reynolds, and Dworkin (1991) note, "Lesbian women who are members of certain racial and ethnic groups need to balance their identities within the lesbian/gay culture and within their racial/ethnic communities" (181).

DESIGNING THE LEADERSHIP DEVELOPMENT PROGRAM

Leadership development programs come in all shapes and sizes, utilizing a breadth of formats and techniques. Examples of leadership programs include a series of workshops spread out over a semester, a weekend retreat at an off-campus location, a "Power Breakfast" series for nontraditional students over a morning meal, or an all-day conference in the student union. The process of choosing a programmatic design can be complex; the amount of time spent intentionally preparing for the leadership event, however, will result in a higher-quality program. There are several steps to consider in ensuring a successful program.

Identify Working Ensemble

In the LGBT community, the importance of having diverse voices around the table is especially significant. Prior to choosing a specific theme or format, select a team of students, faculty, and staff who are interested in working to plan the program. Each of these three campus groups can bring different perspectives about the leadership needs on the campus as well as ideas on how to design and promote the leadership development event. Students on the ensemble need to reflect the diversity of the LGBT community at the institution; think intentionally about how to involve students of color, nontraditional students, and the bisexual and transgendered populations in the planning process. Of course, depending on the campus environment, there may be only a few students who are out or who are interested in leadership roles; however, the process of planning this type of program is one way of getting new students involved in LGBT issues on the campus. Faculty ensemble members could represent either professors who publicly identify as LGBT or allies; it may be helpful to appoint a professor with high visibility who can help garner support in the institution for the program. In many ways, the act of putting together a leadership program for LGBT students can be considered political work; plan accordingly by pulling together a strategic team in regard to composition and know-how.

Assess the Campus Environment

The type of leadership development experience chosen for the campus will be driven by the campus environment for LGBT students, faculty, and staff. Environmental theory provides the leadership educator a basis from which to understand the relationship between students and their campus (Banning, 1989). If a campus is just beginning to recognize the existence of LGBT students, a short workshop for several hours on "Strategies for Becoming Visible" may be most appropriate. On the other end of the spectrum, institutions with a strong LGBT Campus Resource Center and a history of LGBT programming and visibility might challenge student leaders through an all-day conference on "Techniques for Coalition Building with Campus Constituencies." Take time with the working ensemble to discuss the campus environment for LGBT students, faculty, and staff. Conyne and Clack (1981) provide a helpful environmental model that includes the elements of a physical component (campus facilities, for example), a social component (students, their relationships), and an institutional component (college policies and procedures) that is helpful in analyzing an institution's climate for LGBT students. Based on the campus environment, what type of leadership event is most appropriate?

Identify Goals and Design the Curriculum

A leadership program for LGBT students on the campus will need to be carefully tailored to meet the specific needs of the institution's student population. What are the goals of the leadership programming—to empower or transform the campus LGBT community to a new level of activism, to attract more students into leadership roles of the campus LGBT student organization, or to help students learn leadership skills they can use in a job or internship? One approach is to think about the often cited "challenge and support" themes of Nevitt Sanford (1966). How will the LGBT leadership experience on the campus both support the student community as well as challenge them to grow and develop in more complex ways?

Now the exciting work begins. With the working ensemble, begin brainstorming workshop and seminar ideas. The ensemble might want to choose an overarching theme to help stimulate ideas, especially if the event is a day long program. How does LGBT student identity help inform the practice of putting together the leadership event? What issues are most salient for the LGBT population? How can the leadership development program meet the needs of gay men who are in the early stages of the coming out process, lesbians who are interested in discussing sexism within the LGBT leadership on campus, and/or bisexual students who feel the need to have their own programming? Should there be a special "program track" for LGBT student organization advisers or campus allies?

What leadership themes are most salient for LGBT students? Of course, students may be very interested in standard leadership workshop topics: Effective Communication, Conflict Resolution, Meeting Management. However, many of these workshops are accessible throughout the year at other leadership events. Examples of workshop themes from past LGBT leadership conferences have focused on such topics as Communicating LGBT Lesbian Issues, Organizing Campus groups, and Building Coalitions on Campus (Porter & Miller, 1994). Based on the short identity development section in this chapter, one can brainstorm many other ideas: Living in Two Worlds as an LGBT Student, Coming Out in the Classroom Environment, Multiple Oppressions and Their Effects in the LGBT Community, Connecting Homophobia to Other Oppressions, LGBT Cultural Influences on Leadership Styles, and Creating Change at the Institution: Leading the Way are just a few examples.

There are many guest speakers on the topic of leadership for LGBT students whom the planning ensemble might want to invite to campus. If a one- or two-day leadership conference format is being considered, the ensemble might want to make a "wish list" of keynote possibilities. If the ensemble is considering a format of one-hour workshops stretched out over the semester, contact the nearest LGBT community center to find out if any national leaders of note in the gay rights movement will be visiting the area who would consider speaking with college students. Once again, think carefully about balancing invited speakers in regard to gender, race, ability, and other aspects of difference.

Coming together as a community of LGBT students, faculty, and staff, participants and presenters may also warrant a social reception. Consider wrapping up the event with a time and place for conversation and networking. The ensemble may want to invite campus leaders to congratulate the participants for their participation. Guests might include student government officers, campus allies, and the president, the provost, or selected deans.

In choosing workshop themes, the ensemble may also explore two strategies utilized in other LGBT leadership development programs. The first is a technique of having "caucuses" where specific populations (gay men, lesbians, students of color, bisexual students, transgender students) are given time and space to meet to either identify themes salient for their group, hear a speaker in a safe space environment, or discuss specific items they would like to see addressed at the institution. Once again, depending on the campus environment, and the current status of the student organization or LGBT Campus Resource Center, this could be seen as either needed or somewhat divisive. Another programmatic strategy is setting aside time for a resource fair during session breaks or over lunch for organizations offering products or services to LGBT students; for example, the campus bookstore might want to offer a sale on LGBT-themed books, or the local Parents and Friends of Lesbians and Gays (PFLAG) chapter may consider providing information on their activities and recruiting volunteers for speakers.

Target Population and Promotion

Often, LGBT student leadership conferences will open their event to LGBT students from institutions in their same city, region, or state. There are reasons to consider inviting students (and faculty/staff) from other colleges and universities. First, depending on the size of the institution, inviting guests from other campuses can help increase attendance and offset program costs through additional registration fees. Second, college students often appreciate the opportunity to meet other LGBT students in their geographic area for both networking and socializing reasons. If students from out of town are invited, consider ways to assist them with their housing needs.

Once the working ensemble decides who will be invited to the leadership event, a successful promotional plan can be developed. As with any program, getting the word out is essential to success. How will the ensemble make sure students hear about the program? Since the LGBT student population is often invisible, the promotional piece can be especially critical. Consider advertising the event in LGBT community newspapers; students may be more likely to read these than school publications. Perhaps use the technology of the Internet and the World Wide Web to promote the event; LGBT students are often "plugged in" to the latest technology and will learn about the event while "browsing the net." If the leadership development program is open to students from other institutions, be sure to identify individuals on those campuses who can help spread the word about the event. Do not assume that another institution's Director of Student Activities will know to whom to give the registration information or where to put the event poster. Instead, find out which faculty or staff member has their finger on the pulse of LGBT life at the institution and ask them to help in promotional plans.

Budget and Evaluation

These two components are together because they are often the areas no one wants to talk about! The amount of money the planning ensemble is able to tap into certainly drives the chosen format for the event. If the LGBT leadership experience is a new event for the campus, there is probably no existing budget. Therefore, the members of the working ensemble will need to begin identifying resources within the institution who will want to support the leadership development program.

If the event will be cosponsored with the campus LGBT student organization or other clubs, there is a strong possibility that student organization leaders can ask the Student Government Association or another umbrella organization for event funding. Is the ensemble planning on bringing a keynote speaker? The Campus Speakers Bureau might be willing to serve as a cosponsor for that portion of the program. Are there other campus entities that might have funds to lend support to the leadership development efforts? Examples might include the Campus Leadership Program Office, Human Relations, Student Activities/Campus Programs, vice president of Student Affairs, or academic departments such as Human Development, Women's Studies, Psychology, Sociology, or Counseling. Every campus is different. Another reason to diversify the working ensemble for the event is to have many different ideas about whom to approach for funding.

Evaluation is an integral piece to the event. Through the evaluation component, the ensemble can help justify future budgets for LGBT leadership programs to the campus committees or individuals who disseminate the funds. If there are specific goals and objectives for the program participants, be sure and include those sentence stems in the assessment instrument. Other evaluation techniques to consider are focus groups with students after the event (one month, three months, six months), an independent evaluator who can speak with students during the program about how and what they are learning as well as their ideas for future directions, and asking for feedback from any program presenters or group facilitators regarding their perceptions of the event.

CONCLUSION

Leadership development programs are exciting and important components for institutions of higher education as they prepare students for the challenges of the twenty-first century. By offering leadership programs to the LGBT student population, institutions send messages of recognition and success to the students. The benefits of planning a well-designed leadership program for LGBT students, are numerous, and include aspects of promoting identity development, creating community visibility, and affecting institutional change. Leadership programs need to be designed carefully with a variety of voices from the diverse LGBT faculty, staff, and student population on the campus. The process of planning the leadership development program will be vital to the success of the actual event. By utilizing leadership theory, identity development literature, and an intentionally inclusive process, a successful leadership development program can be created for an institution's LGBT student population.

CHAPTER 34

Lesbian, Gay, Bisexual, and Transgender Student Organizations: An Overview

Sherry L. Mallory

On May 1, 1967—two years before the Stonewall Riots of 1969—Columbia University made front-page news in the *New York Times*. The headline, which read "Columbia Charters Homosexual Group," represented the culmination of a year long struggle between students and administration and marked an important moment in history (Johansson, 1990). Founded by Columbia sophomore Robert A. Martin to "create a movement presence," the Student Homophile League was the first recognized lesbian, gay, bisexual, and transgender (LGBT) student organization on an American college campus.

The following year Student Homophile League chapters were formed at New York University and Cornell. Nevertheless, it was not until after Stonewall that LGBT student groups began to flourish on campuses. According to Johansson (1990), by the end of the 1970s "virtually every major campus in the country had one" (1256). Although the groups tended to be concentrated in the Northeast and on the West Coast, by the end of the next decade, groups were well represented in the South and the Midwest. By 1989, there were over 300 student organizations registered with the National Gay and Lesbian Task Force's Campus Project (Berrill, 1989b), and the number continues to rise.

The road traveled by LGBT student organizations, however, has not been an easy one. As suggested by Stanley (1984), "[G]ay student organizations are often the most visible groups on college campuses today [and] perhaps in no other area in recent years have the asserted First Amendment rights of students clashed so with the will of college administrators" (398). Not unlike their counterparts at Columbia University who were faced with a barrage of angry letters when they made front-page news in the *New York Times* in 1967, administrators today continue to be faced with external pressure not to support LGBT student organizations.

This chapter offers an overview of LGBT student organizations on American college campuses. The types of organizations that exist are examined, as are the multiple roles of LGBT student groups. The legal issues faced by LGBT organizations are also presented, with public and private institutions addressed separately. The chapter concludes with suggested guidelines for faculty and administrators in recognizing or funding LGBT student organizations.

TYPES OF ORGANIZATIONS

Diversity exists among LGBT student organizations. Although most colleges and universities have only one LGBT group, it is not uncommon for multiple organizations to exist on a given campus (Berrill, 1989b). Twenty years after the founding of the Student Homophile League, for instance, Columbia University boasted 15 separate LGBT student organizations (Johansson, 1990). When more than one group emerges on a campus, the difference between groups may be based on ethnicity, gender, political ideology, religious affiliation, or function (Scott, 1991).

Membership in LGBT organizations varies from campus to campus and from group to group; organizations may have as few as 5 or as many as 500 members. Although fractionalization of the LGBT community is sometimes a concern on campuses with multiple LGBT groups—some believe that having more than one organization is "counterproductive to the furtherance of gay and lesbian issues"—it is generally acknowledged that having multiple groups is beneficial (Scott, 1991, 124). As Scott suggests, "[M]ultiple organizations allow more students to become involved both because of the existence of more leadership positions and because of the better chance for an individual to identify with a more specific purpose than the broad, general purposes that a sole organization tends to have" (125).

THE ROLE OF ORGANIZATIONS

LGBT student organizations fulfill a variety of roles on college campuses. These roles range from providing networking opportunities and resource libraries to offering social and educational programming and assistance for students who are dealing with issues related to their sexual orientation. Scott (1991) identifies six roles that are fulfilled by LGBT student organizations: social roles; political roles; support roles; service roles; educational roles; and developmental roles. Each will be discussed briefly.

LGBT student organizations, as suggested by Scott (1991), "can provide activities (and, consequently, places) at which students can meet, interact, and develop friendships while being open about their sexual orientation" (p. 119). It is not uncommon for LGBT college students to experience feelings of loneliness and isolation on campus. Organized activities such as dances, trips, and mixers allow these students the opportunity to meet others like themselves in a safe environment. For students who are just coming out, who are new to the community, or who are under 21, "organizational social activities may be the only way in which they [can] establish contact with other gay, lesbian [and bisexual] students" (Scott, 1991, 119).

LGBT student organizations can also serve as political action groups. In recent years, students have mobilized to protest the presence of ROTC programs on campus, have worked toward achieving equity in access to benefits and services, have advocated for the creation of LGBT studies programs, and have pushed for the inclusion of sexual orientation in university non-discrimination statements. LGBT student organizations can also provide a means for students to "become involved with and influence political candidate election campaigns, ballot initiatives, and legislative actions by providing informed comment on how potential legislation or candidates' platforms may affect gay men and lesbians" (119).

LGBT student organizations, as suggested by Scott, can "serve as a support mechanism for students who are coming out or who are having problems with family, friends, faculty and staff, or other students because of their sexual orientation" (119). Students who are dealing with issues related to their sexual orientation may feel hesitant to talk with family, friends, or staff members about what they are going through. Student-led support groups and one-on-one peer counseling give these individuals the opportunity to "talk about their feelings and problems, hear from others who have had similar problems, and explore potential solutions" in a safe, supportive, and informal environment (120).

LGBT student organizations can also fulfill a service role on campus, extending assistance to LGBT students in ways that are not provided by the institution or the community. Services offered can include hotlines or infolines, testing for sexually transmitted diseases, legal advice, referral services, library and resource centers, speakers panels, housing and job boards, newsletter and pamphlet distribution, and information on activities and organizations available in the community (Scott, 1991).

A somewhat related role of LGBT student organizations can be that of educating the campus community with regard to LGBT topics. Speakers, film series, panel discussions, art exhibits, workshops, conferences, safe zone programs, and awareness weeks "all can be part of a program designed to inform the campus community about sexual orientation, homophobia, the problems gay, lesbian [and bisexual] students encounter as the result of discrimination, and other such issues" (120).

Finally, LGBT organizations can play an important role in the development of students. Students who participate in campus organizations may be given the opportunity to learn both leadership skills, such as how to work with and organize groups of people, and practical skills, such as public speaking, financial management, and publicity techniques (Scott, 1991). Students may also have the opportunity to become more familiar with the campus community, to form connections with faculty and staff members, and to gain self-confidence. As asserted by Scott (1991), "[A]lthough these opportunities are available in most student organizations, gay, lesbian, [and bisexual] students may choose not to be involved in them for fear of rejection or harassment or may find the opportunity blocked by homophobia and discrimination" (120).

LEGAL ISSUES

Although the number of LGBT student organizations on college campuses has steadily increased, the requests of these organizations for official recognition have been met with opposition, have been subject to limitations not applied to other groups, and have been denied. As a result, a growing body of case law that deals with LGBT organizations and their rights to recognition, funding, and equity exists. At issue in all of the cases are two basic constitutional rights: the freedoms of association and speech as guaranteed by the First Amendment, and the rights of due process and equal protection as guaranteed by the Fourteenth Amendment (Mallory, forthcoming). In this section, the legal issues faced by LGBT student organizations at public and private institutions will be considered. Because private institutions are not faced with the same legal constraints as public state-supported institutions, they will be addressed separately.

LGBT Student Organizations at Public Institutions

The relevant body of case law has firmly established that a state-supported institution, when petitioned to register a LGBT student organization, is bound by the First and Fourteenth Amendments of the US Constitution to register that organization and to accord it the same rights and privileges extended to all other student organizations on campus (*Gay Activists Alliance* v. *Board of Regents*, 1981; *Gay Alliance of Students* v. *Matthews*, 1976; *Gay and Lesbian Student Association* v. *Gohn*, 1988; *Healy* v. *James*, 1972; *Student Coalition for Gay Rights* v. *Austin Peay University*, 1979). A refusal of recognition cannot be justified by the illegality of certain homosexual acts; public policy concerns; or a concern that the number of LGBT students on campus will increase (Mallory, 1997). Furthermore, campus organizations have no right to funding, but when funds are made available, they must be distributed in a viewpoint-neutral manner with all other factors being considered equal (*Gay and Lesbian Student Association* v. *Gohn*, 1988).

In spite of this legal precedent, LGBT student organizations continue to have difficulty finding acceptance, or even tolerance, at many institutions. A trend that has emerged in recent years is that of using the legislative forum to sidestep what has been established in the courts (Liddell & Douvanis, 1994). As Pedersen (1995) suggests, "[T]he problems associated with [the] nonrecognition of gay groups are not new, but are taking new twists . . . as members of state legislatures voice their opposition" (479). Illustrative examples of this trend have recently occurred at Auburn University, the University of South Alabama, the University of Indiana at Bloomington, and the University of Texas at Austin.

At Auburn University, the Auburn Gay and Lesbian Student Organization threatened litigation after being denied a permanent charter by the Student Government Association. When campus administrators overruled the decision and recognized the Auburn Gay and Lesbian Student Organization as a chartered organization, members of the student government approached the Alabama legislature and asked them to intervene. In response, the legislature proposed a bill that stated, in part, that "no public funds or public facilities shall be used by any college or university to, directly or indirectly, sanction, recognize, or support the activities or existence of any organization or group that fosters or promotes a lifestyle or actions prohibited by the sodomy and sexual misconduct laws." The bill, Section 16-1-28, subsequently passed (*Gay, Lesbian and Bisexual Alliance* v. *The Attorney General of the State of Alabama et al.,* 1996).

Shortly thereafter, the Gay, Lesbian, Bisexual Alliance at the University of South Alabama was denied an on-campus bank account and disqualified from receiving funding under the university's interpretation of Section 16-1-28. The student group brought suit against the attorney general of the state of Alabama, the president of the university, and the dean of students of the university, challenging the constitutionality of the statute and seeking the benefits they had been denied. In a recent decision, the US District Court for the Middle District of Alabama ruled in favor of the Gay, Lesbian, Bisexual Alliance, holding that Section 16-1-28, both facially and as applied to the organization, was in violation of the First and Fourteenth Amendments (*Gay, Lesbian and Bisexual Alliance* v. *The Attorney General of the State of Alabama et al.,* 1996). It is anticipated that the court's decision will be appealed.

Similar cases have occurred at the University of Indiana at Bloomington when State Representative Woody Burton threatened to slash the university's budget by half a million dollars if they financed an LGBT student organization. At the University of Texas at Austin, State Representative Warren Chisum threatened to push for cuts in the state appropriation for the university if public money was used to support events sponsored by the campus LGBT student organization (Mangan, 1995). In both cases, university administrators were able to head off legal action by financing the organizations with private money received from anonymous donors.

LGBT Student Organizations at Private Institutions

Private institutions, unlike public institutions, are technically free from federal constitutional constraints—including those of the First and Fourteenth Amendments—unless a clear relationship can be demonstrated between the action in question and the action of the state. Thus, private institutions may legally "prevent, limit, or refuse to authorize the peaceful assembly of any student group, including student organizations" (Barr, 1996, 133). As a result, private institutions are not bound by law to register LGBT student organizations or to accord them the same rights and privileges extended to other student organizations on campus.

Only one court case involving an LGBT student organization at a private institution has been recorded to date—that of the *Gay Rights Coalition* v. *Georgetown University* (1987). Georgetown University, which is affiliated with the Roman Catholic Church, denied the Gay Rights Coalition university recognition based on specific prohibitions that the Church has against homosexuality. Citing local anti-discrimination laws, the Gay Rights Coalition sued for university recognition and the privileges that accompanied that recognition.

In a complex ruling, the court asserted that although Georgetown had to provide the group the tangible services and facilities that it provided to other student groups, it did not have to recognize the group officially. It is important to note, however, that this case was based on a specific law in the District of Columbia. As a result, it is not applicable to any jurisdiction outside of the District of Columbia and does not establish legal precedent for the recognition of LGBT organizations at other private institutions.

SUGGESTED GUIDELINES FOR RECOGNIZING
AND FUNDING ORGANIZATIONS

The following guidelines are geared toward public institutions that as agencies of the state are bound by the First and Fourteenth Amendments of the Constitution in recognizing and funding LGBT student organizations. Although private institutions are not necessarily bound by these guidelines, it is suggested that faculty and administrators keep them in mind when faced with issues surrounding the recognition or funding of a student group. The guidelines include:

1. Rules must be applied evenly to all organizations on campus, even organizations with beliefs that differ strongly from those held by the institution.

2. Decision makers must act on facts and proven evidence. They must not be governed by fears, concerns, suppositions, or predictions.

3. Due process (i.e., the right to appeal any decision that is made) must be built into the recognition process for all campus organizations.

4. Legitimate reasons for denying recognition are if the group intends to restrict its membership, refuses to cooperate with university regulations, or indicates the intent to use violence or incite other criminal action (Leppo & Lustgraaf, 1989b).

Guidelines for dealing with the funding of an LGBT student organization include:

1. All established procedures and guidelines for funding student organizations must be followed carefully; it is essential that all groups that apply for funding are treated equally.

2. Funding may not be denied based on the views espoused by a group applying for funding. Although student organizations have no right to funding, when funding is made available, it must be distributed in a viewpoint-neutral manner.

3. Funding may be legitimately denied to an organization if the funding proposal is unrealistic, if the proposed activities or services will not reach a wide range of students on campus or will discriminate, or if the group has not met the criteria set forth in the institution's established procedures and guidelines for funding (Leppo & Lustgraaf, 1989a).

In addition to referring to these guidelines, it is important to keep ethical principles in mind if faced with the issue of recognizing or funding an LGBT student organization. As Liddell and Douvanis (1994) suggest, "[I]n the case of gay, [lesbian, and bisexual] student rights, legal and ethical principles can be viewed as complimentary, not dichotomous" (128). Institutions must stand firm in the face of pressure; when dealing with the recognition or funding of an LGBT student organization, it is likely that they will come up against the opposition of parents, alumni, politicians, and student constituencies. Applying King and Kitchener's (1985) five ethical principles—respect autonomy, do no harm, benefit others, be just, and be faithful—helps institutions to do the "right thing [and] the caring thing and affirm the presence and contributions of all students" (Liddell & Douvanis, 1994, 129).

CONCLUSION

In the three decades since the founding of the Student Homophile League at Columbia University, LGBT student organizations have had a great impact on campuses across the country. These organizations, which are quite diverse, fulfill a variety of social, political, support, service, educational, and developmental roles. The road traveled by these student groups, however, has not been an easy one. The requests of LGBT organizations for recognition and funding have repeatedly been met with opposition, subject to limitations not applied to other groups, and denied.

When making decisions that will affect LGBT student organizations, it is essential that faculty and administrators familiarize themselves with legal precedent and case law; when in doubt, legal counsel should be consulted. More important, faculty and administrators must understand and stand firm in the face of pressure and do not only what is legally right but also what is ethically correct.

CHAPTER 35

The Life Cycle of Campus LGBT Organizations: Finding Ways to Sustain Involvement and Effectiveness

Charles Outcalt

The cycle is all too common: Men and women, full of enthusiasm, organize a lesbian, gay, bisexual, and transgender (LGBT) group on campus. The group flourishes for a year or two, attracting new members and racking up accomplishments. However, the group eventually withers as burnout and infighting set in. Finally, the group disbands, often leaving behind an impressive record but disaffected and unhappy former members. Indeed, this phenomenon is often a typical scenario with non-LGBT groups as well.

How can this familiar cycle be broken? How can faculty and Student Affairs staff help students to sustain energy, initiative, enthusiasm, and innovation in the LGBT groups on their campuses? While there are no easy answers to these questions, I will offer some practical, proven techniques for keeping LGBT groups on campuses vital and effective. My comments are based on my experience as director of the University of California at Los Angeles (UCLA) LGBT Resources Office. However, recognizing that no two groups are exactly alike—that each campus presents unique challenges, rooted in local history, personalities, resources and goals—I have interviewed campus LGBT leaders from public and private schools across the country and will draw on their invaluable comments and experience as well.

I will conclude this chapter by outlining research undertaken by Drs. Alexander and Helena Astin at UCLA's Higher Education Research Institute (HERI, 1996). The Astins and their team have undertaken groundbreaking work on the means by which groups, particularly those composed of students, can maintain cooperative internal relationships while achieving their goals. The concepts and conclusions of this model of student leadership development can be helpful in understanding the principles behind a successful LGBT campus group.

UCLA: THE CAMPUS CLIMATE

I will contextualize the following discussion of the life cycles and effectiveness of UCLA's LGBT groups by outlining the conclusions of a recent UCLA campus climate study (Jacobi & Shepard, 1990). The study found that in facing most of the challenges and problems of building a successful academic career and creating a supportive social environment at UCLA, heterosexual and LGBT students were indistinguishable from one another. However, the study did find some significant patterns of difference between heterosexual and LGBT students. LGBT students were much less likely to be satisfied with "the degree to which students at UCLA are treated fairly regardless of race, religion, gender, disability, or sexual orientation" (10). Further, the study found that "LGB students are significantly more likely than their heterosexual counterparts to have experienced problems associated with harassment, discrimination and loneliness" (i). In addition, the study found that despite (or perhaps because of) the discrimination they encounter on campus, LGBT students were more, rather than less, concerned with community-building values, including pluralism, affirmative action, and the inclusion of a full range of voices, including those of ethnic minorities and women, in the classroom (Jacobi & Shepard, 1990).

However, as interested in creating community as UCLA students were shown to be by the Jacobi and Shepard study, their efforts to build and sustain groups have not always been successful. While each unhappy group is unhappy in its own way (with apologies to Tolstoi), they tend to share a few self-destructive traits, including a lack of shared vision, underdeveloped skills on the part of their leaders, and burnout. In addition to this formidable list of hurdles, LGBT groups often face further challenges, including those that result from homophobia and concerns regarding confidentiality.

Obstacle One: Lack of Common Purpose

Many of UCLA's unsuccessful groups suffered from a lack of shared goals or purpose. This, perhaps more than any other factor, can undermine the groups' vitality and longevity. As a UCLA student commented on her group's problems, "Mostly the group suffers from lack of direction" (Anonymous personal communication, November 1996). The comments of Bob Mack—co-chair of Harvard's LGBT faculty, staff, student, and alumni/ae group, the Caucus—echo those of the anonymous UCLA leader: "Harvard faculty are notoriously individualistic, and have no issue at present which compels them to collaborate. They did pull together around the ROTC issue, but subsequent efforts to involve them have not succeeded" (R. Mack, personal communication, November 1996).

Obstacle Two: Underdeveloped Leadership Skills

While a group's leader can have a positive effect on the success of the group, it would be useful to outline briefly some leadership traits and practices that do not work. One particularly destructive type of leadership fails to differentiate between a leader's personal goals and energies and those of the group. Some dedicated leaders equate effective leadership with their own activity on behalf of the group, and so the group's success is overly dependent on their personal attentions to it. Not only do these individuals fail to draw other members into the decision-making process of the group, but they almost inevitably eventually become disillusioned with their own and, consequently, the group's effectiveness. The anonymous UCLA student leader previously fell victim to this phenomenon. She expressed her concerns by stating, "I have not been able to delegate effectively so if no one volunteers, I just try to do it myself or it doesn't get done." As this student reports, her group is on the edge of dissolution, while her feelings toward the group and her role within it vary between engagement and disappointment. "I used to have a strong need to keep this group going. That personal need is waning and therefore my frustration is rising" (Anonymous personal communication, November 1996). Ironically, it is often the most committed leaders who over-identify with their group.

Obstacle Three: Burnout

Burnout, the tendency to work harder while accomplishing less and feeling worse, can affect everyone in a group, but it might be most damaging to those who put the greatest amount of their energy into the group and its goals. As Alicia Lucksted, a graduate student at the University of Maryland, comments: "The good people throw themselves into it then they start dropping the ball after others have come to rely on them to handle important things" (Personal communication, November 1996). Her concerns are seconded by Bob Mack, who summarizes the problem: "The chief problem for us, and I think for most groups, is leadership burnout. There is a natural tendency for people to throw themselves into a project with great energy at the outset. [S]ooner or later, the leader 'burns out' [and] loses interest in the project" (R. Mack, personal communication, November 1996).

Sara Sperling, a staff member at Stanford and former student leader from the University of California, Irvine, notes the relationship between burnout and LGBT groups by calling attention to the fact that most campuses do not have faculty or staff charged with the responsibility to serve the campus LGBT community. Sperling states that this lack of university support can translate into student burnout at Stanford, in part because Stanford's LGBT Center is run by students rather than professional staff. She comments, "[Students] run the entire operation of the Center. Without surprise, the students become very burned out by the end of fall quarter. [E]very year it is time to begin new again instead of being able to begin where the Center left off last year" (S. Sperling, personal communication, November 1996).

Obstacle Four: Lack of Continuity

Sperling's comment points to one of the consequences of burnout for LGBT groups: Not only do energetic people leave, but the progress they have made can be lost with them. When leaders and group members have burned out and groups are forced to begin anew, the group finds itself reinventing the wheel and repeating the efforts of those its predecessors. Student groups, with the turnover inherent in their membership, are particularly prone to this danger. Institutions that are not interested in making changes demanded by students (such as the creation of a professionally staffed LGBT Campus Resource Center) can often rest secure in the knowledge that today's activist students will leave campus relatively soon, often taking their agendas with them. However, faculty, staff, and alumni/ae groups are vulnerable to these periodic fluctuations and purges of leadership as well. As Phil Hoskins states: "[M]embership tends to be episodic, depending upon who is in the leadership ranks. It is difficult to sustain participation from the 'old' leaders after their stint because they get 'burned out' and 'want a break'" (P. Hoskins, personal communication, November 1996).

Obstacle Five: Communication and Confidentiality

Two related factors—communication and confidentiality—can impede a group's progress toward reaching its goals, and can, in the end, threaten the very well-being of the group. Some groups, particularly those based on large, non-centralized campuses, never reach the "critical mass" necessary for all potential members to be aware that the group exists, even though their leaders might try a variety of techniques, from flyers to word of mouth to paid advertisements (for those groups fortunate enough to have a budget). These groups might sputter along for years on the verge of dissolution, never reaching the membership levels or effectiveness they would achieve if enough people became aware of the group at the same time.

Homophobia and concern for the confidentiality of current and potential members can exacerbate the challenges of outreach and communication for LGBT groups. Signs and flyers for LGBT-related meetings at UCLA—and, by report, on many other campuses—are often defaced or removed immediately after being posted. Some faculty and staff can be reluctant to having LGBT groups publicized in their classes and offices. Once members do become aware of the existence of the group, common communication techniques, such as e-mail lists and phone trees, might not provide sufficient confidentiality to guard against inadvertent outing of members. As the above-quoted anonymous student leader at UCLA expressed it: "I'm reticent to send out names and phone numbers of people anonymously over e-mail after a couple of people on the list wrote to me that confidentiality was important to them. I have not been able to strike the balance between privacy and facilitating contacts effectively" (Anonymous personal communication, November 1996).

UCLA'S NATIONAL COMING OUT WEEK 1995:
AN UNEXPECTED SUCCESS

Some LGBT groups exceed all expectations: Their leaders are committed but not overextended, their members contribute, and perhaps most important, their goals are both valued by all members and reached. I will recount one such success story at UCLA while drawing on the experiences of others who have known similar successes on their campuses.

In 1994, UCLA celebrated National Coming Out Day by renaming it National Coming Out Week (NCOW) and staging a series of events that could only be described as spectacular. (For a discussion of UCLA's NCOW 1994 and the planning process that led to it (see Shepard, Yeskel, & Outcalt, 1995) which contains a full program of activities and examples of media coverage of the week.) As visible and celebratory as the 1994 events were, the planning group that produced them was severely burned out by the week's events, with many of them withdrawing from LGBT activism at UCLA after NCOW 1994. The success of the week was achieved at great personal and institutional cost.

The self-selected group that planned NCOW 1995 realized they needed to follow a different planning process. The planning model they developed resulted in a highly successful, yet relatively stress-free and complication-free week-long series of events. The key elements of this model were forming a common purpose and plan for the week by actively soliciting (and respecting) input from a wide range of campus "constituencies"; building diversity into the planning process; assigning planning group members individual and collective responsibilities for discrete segments of that common plan; and expressing appreciation for all who participated in the week.

Sharing a Vision

The group began its planning by forming a shared commitment to the success of the week. The group reached out to all interested constituencies within the university, solicited their input, and formed goals only after securing the cooperation of all interested parties. The NCOW that emerged from this process was less event filled, and perhaps less photogenic, than NCOW 1994, but its support was both broad and deep: Not only were students, faculty, staff, alumni/ae, and interested members of the non-UCLA community integral to the planning process, but each had opportunities to shape its overall form, and each was invested in its success.

Group members shared a commitment to incorporating UCLA's diversity into both the planning process and the week's activities. Men and women representing the campus's wide range of ethnic and racial groups participated in the planning process. In addition, students, faculty, staff, alumni/ae and interested community representatives had an active role, thus ensuring a wide range of ages, experience levels, and university affiliations. It is important to note that this diversity was central to the planning process from the very beginning. Rather than planning the week and then "inviting" other groups and constituencies to be a part of their plans, the NCOW planners took care to build diversity into their planning. It would be impossible to overestimate the importance of this commitment to diversity for the success of the week.

Once the broad outlines of NCOW 1995 had been determined, individuals had another opportunity to invest themselves personally: Each event had one or two "point people" who were responsible not only for the details but also for ensuring that the entire group's wishes were respected. For example, once the planning group had decided that there would be a rally, and that it would feature a diverse lineup of speakers and entertainers, the rally's point people took responsibility for investigating potential speakers and venues, soliciting the planning group's input on these possibilities, then securing the planning group's choices. In this way, individuals were personally responsible for and invested in the success of "their" segment of the week, yet they were responsible to the planning group as a whole as well.

Appreciating All Participants

The planning group used another simple, although often overlooked, technique: They made sure all participants knew they were heard, appreciated, and valued. Not only did the planning group formally thank all those who participated in the week's panels, rallies, discussions, and so on, at the conclusion of the week, but leaders also made a point of expressing their appreciation for the energy and ideas contributed by members during the planning process. Realizing that the first contact with a new or potential member is often the most important time to extend recognition of that person's potential value to the group, one NCOW planner stated: "[You must] make people feel valued (newcomers and old hands), make newcomers feel as welcome as possible so they'll be inclined to come again" (M. Pearson, personal communication, November 1996).

Creating Community

Perhaps the most important factor in the success of the NCOW 1995 planning team was not a technique at all but an understanding of the nature of the group itself. For all its success, the group was not solely issue oriented, according to some of its leaders. Rather, it functioned as an LGBT community, in which members could find a safe space on campus to be themselves and act in concert with their convictions. As one group leader put it, describing not only the NCOW group but LGBT organizations in general, "I feel that the most important groups are those which can help us create a feeling of 'gay' family on campus" (J. Robbins, personal communication, November 1996). Alicia Luck-sted comments that she has found that a great deal of the effectiveness of LGBT groups originates in their ability to make their members feel comfortable: "Much of the energy in the group, I think, comes from that which the members get from having a place (the group) where they can be openly GLB, comfort-able, among friends, out, and get support for all these things by working to-gether on GLB issues on campus" (A. Lucksted, personal communication, No-vember 1996).

From these comments, it appears that the comfort many LGBT men and women experienced in the NCOW planning group, as well as other LGBT groups on the UCLA campus, comes as much from finding a community as from finding a group of individuals with a nonheterosexual sexual orientation. As an NCOW 1995 leader explains of one of the groups whose members be-came instrumental in planning NCOW 1995, "The fact that it's a gay group is almost secondary; it gives us a common ground for interacting with each other." He continues, "[The group] gave me the networking opportunities to build up a group of friends, find out about other groups on campus, and get some tips on how to 'find my niche' socially" (M. Pearson, personal communication, No-vember 1996).

In the successful group on which I have focused—the team of students, fac-ulty, staff, alumni/ae, and community members who created UCLA's NCOW 1995—and in the other successful groups from which I have drawn examples, several characteristics surfaced repeatedly: Groups that retained members while meeting their goals had a common sense of purpose and had leaders who were committed to actively soliciting and respecting the opinions of all members. Successful groups were committed to reflecting the diversity of their campuses. In addition, these groups appreciated the contributions of current members, as well as the potential contributions of prospective members. Most important, some of these groups functioned as extended social and perhaps even kinship networks, providing perhaps the only space on campus in which their LGBT members felt comfortable and safe.

THE ASTIN/HERI MODEL

Although the model of leadership development created by Professors Alex-ander and Helena Astin, working with UCLA's Higher Education Research In-stitute (HERI, 1996), was not developed specifically for LGBT groups, its prin-ciples are highly relevant to the challenges and successes discussed previously. An exploration of the model will provide a theoretical framework to explain the principles underlying many successful groups. While not all effective campus LGBT groups share the structure of the Astin/HERI work, an examination of this model will highlight the characteristics that made the NCOW 1995 planning group, as well as some of the other groups mentioned in this chapter, successful.

Before discussing the Astin/HERI model, it would be helpful to examine an assumption held by the model's authors. The Astins and their colleagues posit that leadership is collaborative rather than dependent upon any one individual; therefore, they contend that leadership is a process rather than a position. In other words, the Astins and colleagues assert that leadership is dependent on productive group dynamics and interpersonal relationships rather than on the characteristics of that person chosen as "leader" (HERI, 1996, 10).

This assumption was borne out in the case of the NCOW 1995 planning committee, which never bothered to elect or even discuss a chair or other officers. Of course, neither the Astin/HERI model nor the NCOW 1995 experience preclude officers and titles; indeed, such hierarchical structures can be highly useful for defining responsibility within the group and for guiding outsiders who need to interact with it. Nevertheless, the Astin/HERI supposition that leadership is processual, rather than positional, contains much food for thought for those LGBT groups that become mired in debate over who will be titled what rather than who will enable the group to reach its goals.

Individual Values

The Astin/HERI team developed a listing of seven values critical to successful leadership, then organized these values into three sets: those that concern the individual, those that relate to the characteristics of the group, and those that apply to society as a whole. The individual goals describe the relationship of the individual man or woman to his or her personal values and beliefs. To be an effective leader or member of a group, one must first be aware "of the beliefs, values, attitudes, and emotions that motivate one to take action," an awareness the Astins describe as "consciousness of self" (HERI, 1996, 22). Once one has achieved this awareness, one can be fueled by the "passion, intensity and duration" that stem from commitment (22). If one has reconciled these passions with self-consciousness, then one can behave with congruence, that is to say, with "consistency, genuineness, authenticity, and honesty toward others." (22).

While LGBT groups often have an abundance of that passion that leads to commitment, the complex process of finding and acting on one's sexual identity inherent in coming out can create complications for group members struggling with their other values. To reach a state of congruence, or honesty and authenticity with oneself, one must first achieve awareness of one's own convictions, an awareness that can be challenging for those students attempting to form their identities as LGBT men and women in an often homophobic society.

Group Values

The group values defined in the Astin/HERI model describe relationships between group members and one another, and between members and the goals of the group. The first of these values is collaboration, or the ability to work together toward the second group value, common purpose. Common purpose, which the model describes as "work[ing] with shared aims and values" (23), is clearly evident in, and is clearly essential to, the effectiveness of those successful campus groups described above. This value was particularly important to achievements of the NCOW 1995 planning group, which made the achievement of a shared vision and commitment its first priority. The final group value described in the model is controversy with civility, or the agreeing to disagree without rancor or ill will. This quality is indispensable for LGBT groups on large campuses with energetically diverse populations, but the ability to reconcile opposing points of view is equally valuable on smaller campuses, on which one's circle of potential allies (not to mention enemies) is relatively limited.

Social Values

The one social value defined by the model is citizenship—"the process whereby the individual and the collaborative group become responsibly connected to the community and the society" (23). Citizenship is, in some ways, the ultimate product of the first six values. It allows groups to return value to their members, as these members understand that their activities have value, and return value to the wider community of which the group is a part. As citizens of their groups, LGBT men and women create valuable (and too uncommon) opportunities to act from within their LGBT identities as valued contributors to their campuses.

CONCLUSION

Perhaps the most appropriate conclusion for this chapter comes from a comment by Sara Sperling who admonishes faculty and staff charged with advising and supporting LGBT groups on their campuses. She said, "Really listen to your students. Find out what their needs are and how you can work with them to achieve them. Say 'yes' to their ideas as often as you can" (S. Sperling, personal communication, November 1996). All the case studies, techniques. and advice presented in this chapter can be summarized in Sperling's simple message: Listen actively, ask what can be done to lend support, and give this support as well as you can.

CHAPTER 36

Advising Student Organizations: Opportunities for Student Development

Allen Ward

University student organization advisers can have a significant influence on shaping campus climate. Students will be exposed to new thoughts and ideas about diversity in our classrooms, but they will freely speak their minds in the comfort of peers. The student organization adviser, considered a team player and student advocate, has a tremendous opportunity to help students understand and appreciate unique human experiences.

This chapter will offer suggestions on how student organization advisers can be better helpers at working with gay, lesbian, bisexual, and transgender (GLBT) and non-GLBT students. The ideas offered reflect lessons from personal advising experiences that include achievements and failures, as well as from knowledge gained by observing skillful colleagues. The intention is to assist the interested advisor with gaining professional comfort in helping all students with a fundamental development and identity issue.

Why should student organization advisers be concerned about GLBT issues? After all, some might argue, openly GLBT students represent a minority of the student body, and in terms of club/organizational participation, they appear to have the same rights to belong and participate as non-GLBT students. To understand the answer, it is useful to consider the role of heterosexuality on campus. For many non-GLBT students, their heterosexuality is a position of privilege and advantage never before examined. Students who are GLBT see how much heterosexuality is celebrated in both campus life and institutional traditions. All dimensions of student life on college campuses in some way endorse public affirmations of heterosexuality. On many campuses, cultural affirmations of homosexuality are rare, if they exist at all.

On the exterior, most would agree that a general understanding and appreciation of human diversity is at the heart of a liberal arts education. In our advisory capacities to student groups, we can do a great deal to advance the liberal arts experience by nurturing student organizations that are friendly to differences such as sexual orientation, race, gender, and ethnicity.

On a more substantial level, however, many of us who advise student organizations would also agree that our abilities to deal with sexual minority issues are limited. Curricular infusion of sexual orientation research and understanding is in its infancy. Our graduate preparations, although philosophically committed to diversity, probably did not emphasize an understanding of sexual identity development or provide practical ideas for assisting GLBT students. Additionally, our professional time to research and understand diversity issues, whatever the topic, may seem inadequate.

Students entering college today have grown up more broadly exposed to GLBT identities, equality debates, and homosexual icons than previous generations. Some students are comfortable with their sexuality, whereas others struggle to find themselves. Those searching for their sexual identity are sometimes dealing with abusive feelings of self-condemnation. Many students have not begun to resolve the conflict between what they have been taught about homosexuality and what they observe in actual homosexual or bisexual people. Some fear that if they associate with GLBT people or advocate for GLBT equality, they are turning their backs on so-called traditional values or threatening what they perceive to be masculinity and femininity.

Many GLBT students are invisible to us in the groups we advise, but they are vitally aware of our knowledge of and comfort with GLBT issues. Some are not open about their sexual orientation because they see the term *GLBT* as a stereotype to which they cannot relate. Openly GLBT students are becoming more interested in changing campus climates and university norms that they perceive to be heterosexist. As with other marginalized groups, they form networks of support across the campus and quickly form opinions on who is and who is not "GLBT-friendly."

The culture of campus organizations reflects this mix of student thought and development regarding homosexuality. A few groups, generally those that have traditionally valued diversity, promote acceptance of GLBT people and advocacy for GLBT equality. For some organizations, standard practices and behavior seem to be absorbed by homophobia. These groups are hostile environments where anyone perceived to be GLBT will be ostracized and, at times, harassed.

Most student organizations, however, operate on a wide continuum between intolerance and acceptance of GLBT students. These groups want to be seen as diverse and inclusive, but they have not come to terms with issues of sexual identity and have inherited traditions that are exclusively heterosexual. The experience of Bill, a student who pledged a fraternity, illustrates the inconsistent practices of some student groups.

Bill, an active student with a competitive grade point average, was approached by a fraternity about membership. After Bill joined the group, he informed his new brothers that he was GLBT. The organizational response to this information was fairly uneventful. There was no move to oust him for being a sexual minority and no grand celebration about a more diversified membership. Bill read this response from his new student organization as acceptance, and he felt free to enjoy the same group rights as every other member. When Bill proposed to bring a date to a social, however, he discovered his fraternity's inconsistency. The membership refused to allow Bill to bring a date to socials. Bill resigned in disgust over their decision. As Bill discovered, the organization welcomed GLBTs as members and wanted their talents and contributions; GLBTs were not, however, given equal rights and privileges.

We recognize that our educational role as student organization advisers is to promote the development of all students. Advisers want student involvement in campus organizations to be a meaningful experience: to bring together collective talents for the good of the individual student, the university, and the larger community. Our challenge in working with student groups, whether fraternities and sororities, academic organizations, student government, or other associations, is to recognize inequalities and inconsistencies and seek to raise the standards of civility and respect for all students. Our role is to engage students in safe dialogue that can bring hidden contradictions into rational light. Our influence on these issues can be significant and powerful.

In order to begin being a helper, there are a few professional considerations that must be examined. The considerations are addressed first to the non-GLBT advisor and secondly to the advisor who is GLB or T.

PROFESSIONAL CONSIDERATIONS FOR
THE NON-GLBT ADVISER

For the reasons mentioned previously, non-GLBT and GLBT student organization advisers see understanding and appreciating diversity as fundamental professional qualities. Graduate preparations strongly emphasize that in order to be effective helpers with diverse student populations, professionals need to learn about people who are different from themselves. In helping GLBT students, some of the most effective advisers are heterosexual women and men who have educated themselves about the coming out process and other fundamental GLBT concerns and who have the courage and self-confidence to risk their position of privilege for these students.

Heterosexual professionals who have achieved this level of proficiency understanding GLBT concerns and working with GLBT students appear to have as much of a personal commitment to the effort as a professional one. They demonstrate genuine empathy toward GLBTs who may be dealing with feelings of family rejection, isolation from peers, or other struggles that can be part of the coming out experience. They have read literature about research on sexual orientation and appreciate that coming to understand and accept one's sexual identity is as fundamentally significant as any development issue students face. They understand that GLBT students who do not develop emotional and psychological stability regarding their sexual orientation put their academic careers and, in some cases, their lives in jeopardy.

There are a number of reasons heterosexual advisers give for their hesitancy to address GLBT concerns in their professional capacities. Many of the reasons involve misunderstandings. At a recent professional workshop, one student organization advisor confessed that she was reluctant to talk about anything GLBT with her students because she was uncomfortable dealing with sex. In her thoughts, the terms *GLBT* and *sex* were almost synonymous. She had never considered the many ways heterosexuals publicly demonstrate their sexual orientation on campus without the risks that homosexuals must take.

Historically, this misunderstanding has caused contention between GLBT students and their institutions. Early efforts of GLBT students to form groups were met with hostile resistance by administrators who had extreme misconceptions about their purposes. In the late 1960s and early 1970s, several universities including Penn State, the University of New Hampshire, and Virginia Commonwealth University went to court trying to prevent GLBT student organizations from forming. In each of these cases, the universities' fears about what GLBT students sought were proven false.

PROFESSIONAL CONSIDERATIONS
FOR THE GLBT ADVISER

Student organization advisers who are GLBT have a unique professional opportunity and dilemma. GLBT advisers bring to their profession personal experience in understanding how institutions need to change in order to assist their GLBT students. As other minority advisers, GLBT advisers can provide professional leadership in reaching out to a marginalized student population and in educating all students about sexual identity. In their daily interaction with student organization leaders, GLBT advisers can work with them to confront organizational homophobia and create more embracing student organizations.

The dilemma for the GLBT advisor is, of course, whether to identify professionally as GLBT. Just as GLBT advisers must understand the risks for GLBT students to be open and out on campus, they must equally understand their own risks. What are the professional costs in being out? How will colleagues and supervisors react? How will students with whom the advisor works react? How will being out affect key professional relationships? These are just a few of the questions GLBT advisers must consider.

For many GLBT advisers, an additional pressure to this conundrum is a personal commitment toward education and helping students—the reason for being educators. Professional careers are devoted toward helping others develop, learn, and effect positive change in society. How can we reconcile these professional pursuits from within a closet? How can we challenge students to be honest about themselves if we are not honest about ourselves? Are the possible professional risks from being out more significant than the professional integrity one might enjoy from being open?

ADVISING PREDOMINANTLY HETEROSEXUAL STUDENT ORGANIZATIONS

Student organization advisers know that finding creative ways to help the majority understand and appreciate minority views can be an exciting challenge. Fortunately, advisers who want to learn how to make their organizations more friendly to GLBT students can look to other diversity models such as race and gender for ideas. Finding successful methods may vary depending on the type of organization and campus norms.

Student Government

There are a number of ways student government associations can make their organizations more friendly to the GLBT students they serve. Student government leaders may want to consider designating a cabinet or other position to be the liaison for GLBT concerns. This person could work with GLBT student organizations to develop student government assistance on issues important to GLBTs. Student government efforts on behalf of GLBT students can help modify institutional policies or practices that are unfriendly or develop new programs to assist students who are GLBT.

If the campus does not have an LGBT Campus Resource Center, the student government may want to develop one. While sending a strong message that student government is concerned about its GLBT student population, this office can provide various services and resource referrals. The student government advisor can help student leaders develop such an agency by researching models on other campuses and working with GLBT students to identify specific campus needs.

Relationships between GLBT students and student government can be strained if the elected officers (i.e., executive board, senators, student court officers, etc.) are unfamiliar with GLBT concerns or unknowledgeable about sexual minority issues. This can be particularly evident during annual club allocations for student activity fees. GLBT students may feel overly examined during this process—that their proposals are held to a higher level of justification because predominantly heterosexual student government leaders do not understand their issues. Advisers can help with this problem.

Advisers can work with student government officers to develop internal leadership programs that address diversity concerns. The advisor can facilitate workshops during annual senate or other student government retreats to raise awareness about various diversity concerns including sexual orientation. Case studies, educational videos, or role-playing can be effective techniques for this objective. Helping student government leaders understand GLBT concerns early in the leaders' time of office may improve the overall relationship between GLBT students and student government and may strengthen student governments' ability to serve GLBT students.

Fraternities and Sororities

Fraternities and sororities have been among the most reluctant dimensions of student life to embrace diversity. The selective nature of these organizations has created a system that is often segregated and at times hostile to outsiders. To GLBT students, fraternities, in particular, are seen as groups that have been responsible for harassment and violent acts against them.

Ironically, GLBT Greeks comprise a significant minority of fraternity and sorority memberships. Although these individuals may feel unable to be open about their sexual orientation, GLBT Greeks are present throughout the system, often holding positions of leadership in the chapter or governing councils. The array of volunteers and professionals who work to support fraternities on local or national levels also includes sizable numbers of GLBT people.

There are many ways, however, that advisers can work with fraternity and sorority leaders to make the Greek system a place for all students regardless of sexual orientation. An excellent place to start is leadership development programming. Fraternities and sororities have exceptional structures for helping members develop leadership skills. National fraternities offer leadership conferences on national and regional levels. There are regional and national leadership conferences/institutes for student officers of the Interfraternity, Panhellenic, and other Greek councils. Additionally, individual campuses may offer fraternity/sorority-specific leadership programming (such as Greek Life 101) as part of its Greek Affairs services.

Advisers can ensure that each of these leadership development opportunities includes programs designed to raise awareness about sexual orientation and identity. Advisers can help groups that have not pledged or accepted an openly GLBT student by inviting a GLBT alum to talk about his or her experience as a GLBT Greek.

Greeks can also reach out to GLBT students by participating in campus celebrations of GLBT history/awareness months. The timing of these celebrations may vary depending upon the campus; however, frequently activities are planned during October around National Coming Out Day or during June commemorating the 1969 Stonewall Riots.

Religious and Political Student Organizations

It is important to keep in mind that GLBT students, like heterosexual students, are politically and religiously diverse. The religious or political organization on campus that might appear to be the most intolerant of GLBTs includes members who are struggling with their own sexual identity. As these individuals accept their own homosexuality and become comfortable as GLBT persons, they will learn that one need not relinquish religious or political beliefs. Their internalized homophobia will then lessen with consequent positive effect on the group.

Advisers who work with religious and political student organizations can help members understand that there are broad ideological positions on the issue of homosexuality even within groups that have been critical of homosexuality. Advisers can help students who are struggling with how to accept their sexual orientation within a particular political or religious tradition understand these facts and find appropriate resources. Almost all religious and political organizations have national groups for GLBT members.

Academic, Honor Societies, and Other Student Organizations

Student organizations promoting a specific discipline or, more broadly, scholastic achievement in all areas may have untapped valuable resources at their disposal to help improve the campus climate for GLBT students. Generally, faculty are willing to assist these groups with programs or activities. Academic organizations or honor societies (including leadership honor societies) can invite faculty who are teaching GLBT or queer studies courses or who are researching sexual orientation topics to routinely present lectures. If other faculty members in related departments are aware of these programs, they may encourage their students to attend the presentations as well.

ADVISING PREDOMINANTLY LGBT
STUDENT ORGANIZATIONS

To the GLBT student, the existence of a visible campus student organization specifically for GLBTs is critically important. Even if the student is not open or does not choose to participate in the group, the knowledge that student life includes groups for GLBT students reduces her or his anxiety about being GLBT at the university. The presence of these groups also sends an appropriate message to heterosexual students—the university accepts and embraces all of its students regardless of sexual orientation.

Similarly, the value of service that GLBT student organizations can provide to students who participate is also important. On some campuses, the GLBT student organization may be the only real source of support and acceptance for GLBTs to be found. Some students may feel that the organization is the only place on campus where they can relax their guard and feel free to be themselves. Frequently, bonds develop among group members that last throughout the college experience and beyond.

If the campus does not provide an LGBT Campus Resource Center, the GLBT student organization may be approached to provide these services. For example, a student who has been the target of a homophobic incident may not feel comfortable discussing the problem with the judicial affairs office, the counseling center, or the minority student services office. That student may turn to the GLBT student organization, or GLBT student organization advisor, for help. The organization may also be approached for referrals about community services for GLBT people or asked to provide group counseling services if these are not being provided by the university's counseling center.

For advisers, there are a number of considerations that may be unique to GLBT student groups. One of these is determining group purpose. The beliefs and interests of GLBT students are varied; not all students come to the group with similar expectations. Developmentally, the group may include graduate students who are involved with gender/GLBT studies research as well as the first-semester first-year student who wants to make friends. Regardless of age, the members may also be at different places in their coming out process. Some students may not be ready to give up the comfort of presumed heterosexuality among their straight friends. They may fear that by participating in the group, other group members may out them.

This complicated group composition may mean that developing a group purpose becomes a challenge. Will the organization be a low-profile group satisfied with sponsoring occasional social outings for GLBT students? Will the group involve itself with political activism on campus? Is there a "critical mass" within the group willing to openly represent the organization during orientation, homecoming, and other campus club opportunities? Over time, the answers to these questions may change.

Understanding these considerations can assist the GLBT student organization advisor with determining her or his role. Annually, the advisor can work with group leaders to review the group's history and progression and to establish goals for the year. The advisor can challenge the group leaders to establish time lines and criteria for measuring success. The advisor can help group leaders identify resources that can assist the group in various areas of operation such as membership recruitment, finances, and scholarship.

At times, GLBT student organization advisers may find their roles shifting, depending on circumstances. For example, a particular campus event may heighten homophobic rhetoric and place the advisor in a guardian position. The advisor may feel the need, on the one hand, to shield and protect the students from campus intolerance while, feeling the need on the other hand, to suppress tendencies within the group toward overreaction. Successful advisers seem to balance their genuine concern and devotion to the organization and its mission with the realization that students deserve autonomy to make decisions and learn from the consequences of those decisions.

Programming within GLBT student organizations varies depending upon group purpose. Most GLBT student organizations offer social and recreational activities that may include movie nights, theme parties/dances, weekend camp-outs, or trips to area attractions.

Formats for group meetings also vary. Meeting agendas for some highly organized GLBT student organizations may include reports from various committees on special projects, fund-raisers, community service activities, or ally programs. The meetings of other groups consist of informal discussions on various topics of interest such as dating and relationships, gender roles, the coming out process, same-sex marriage, GLBT careers, political events, or health issues. Some groups sponsor annual banquets or programs to recognize individuals (students, faculty, administrators, or community leaders) who have contributed toward making the campus a more comfortable place for GLBT students.

Everyone wins when a campus celebrates the diversity and strength of its people. Student organization advisers who work with student leaders to develop these celebrations help create small community climates that may have monumental influences on society's climate.

PART IX

Programs and Possibilities

CHAPTER 37

Sexual Orientation Speakers Bureaus

Alicia Lucksted

Sexual orientation speakers bureaus are campus-based service groups that provide panels of openly lesbian, gay, bisexual, and transgender (LGBT) speakers to lead discussions about LGBT issues in classes, residence halls, and student or staff gatherings. Usually the speakers are volunteer undergraduate and graduate students; they sometimes include faculty, staff, and/or alumni.

These groups work to raise consciousness about LGBT issues on campus, dispel stereotypes and misinformation, and "encourage a supportive attitude toward human diversity" (K. O'Brien, personal communication, October 1996). Many also focus on leadership development among their speakers. While their methods and emphases vary, all share the goal of reaching individual audience members through relating personal stories, information, and opinions in an egalitarian discussion format (i.e., instead of a lecture). By all accounts, such bureaus are quite successful in these aims (Croteau & Kusek, 1992; Geasler, Croteau, Heineman, & Edlund, 1995; McClintock, 1992) and are valuable campus resources.

This chapter is written for the person thinking about starting, advocating for, or actively supporting an LGBT speakers bureau on campus. It briefly describes three common models, some respective pros and cons, the structure and operation of a speakers bureau, a prototype for basic presentations, and information about effectiveness and possible pitfalls. The material presented is drawn from published research, from my own nine years' experience with such groups, and information provided by 12 different bureaus at US colleges and universities. At different schools they are called *speakers panels, outreaches*, or *panel teams*. This chapter uses *speakers bureau* and *presentation* as umbrella terms for all of these.

MODELS

Each speakers bureau has a unique history and design. Three general models that cover most bureaus will be described. They vary by group structure and coordination, location vis-à-vis the campus (organizational) infrastructure, and sources of support.

Model I: Informal Network

Many campuses have no formal sexual orientation diversity speakers bureau. At some of these schools (e.g., Pacific Lutheran University), a few faculty, staff, and/or students have deliberately or reluctantly become "known" not only as openly LGBT but also as willing to speak publicly on LGBT issues in classes and other forums. Usually they compose a loose network with the one or two out faculty filling the role of defacto coordinator and with no official support or recognition from campus systems. Many times the people involved engage in informal networking and consciousness raising among colleagues to increase acceptance and support without overstepping the campus's tolerance level.

Such informal networks provide important services on these campuses: They foster constructive public discussion of LGBT issues in places where there may be few other such resources; they are flexible; and they are low cost (at least officially). Faculty involvement lends stability and credibility. The organizers are often pioneers regarding LGBT issues on their campus, and their contributions are often underacknowledged. Further, the responsibilities of coordinating a loose network and its activities—and often of being one of few openly LGBT people on campus—can be a tremendous emotional drain. Therefore, the unofficial nature and lack of resources limit what such networks are able to do.

Model II: Within Student LGBT Groups

The most common model seems to be the speakers bureau as a committee or project of the campus LGBT student group. Members of the student group fill coordinator and speaker roles (although speakers may also be non-members), and some portion of the student group's resources (space, energy, budget) supports the bureau's publicity and training. Thus, this model has some minor support within the campus administration through its recognition of the general student group, but it is operated completely by volunteer students.

Most student-operated speakers bureaus do an excellent job of covering the tasks involved, as we will discuss later. Coordination is somewhat centralized, and the peer-to-peers ethos is effective with other students. The student volunteers who coordinate and speak often put in many hours, motivated, as are those in all models, by a desire to improve people's knowledge and respect regarding LGBT people and issues. Often, they also seek to maintain their bureau's good reputation that has developed over the years among professors and residential staff (the main requesters of presentations).

There are also considerable drawbacks. The addition of speakers bureau responsibilities to academic, work, family, and priorities can become burdensome for coordinators and speakers. When this happens, burnout often complicates enthusiasm, with some coordinators/speakers eventually neglecting classes, the speakers bureau, or both. The naturally high turnover of students as they move through college also creates problems for continuity and group stability. Moreover, many bureaus express frustration that the campus has come to rely on their services and has high expectations, yet gives the bureau little recognition for its contributions nor resources with which to meet the campus need. Finally, some members of the campus community may denigrate these bureaus, especially for faculty/staff presentations, because they are student operated.

Model III: Within Campus Administrative Structure

A handful of campuses have an LGBT speakers bureau located within a formal campus unit—student services, an LGBT Campus Resources Center, human relations, and so on (e.g., Emery University, University of Michigan, UCLA). These programs have at least one part-time paid staff position that serves as bureau coordinator, carrying out the tasks covered by volunteers in the two other models. This ameliorates some of the continuity difficulties, lack of resources, and burnout previously discussed, although many such offices are rather spartan.

This model conveys a level of active institution that the other two models do not, as the institution openly devotes some resources to widely discussing LGBT issues on campus. This imparts additional legitimacy to the speakers bureau. The speakers are still volunteers—students and other members of the campus community—although sometimes the paid staff person(s) may also speak. Therefore, it usually works closely with the LGBT student group to recruit speakers, conduct training, and so on.

Organizers may encounter reluctance and resistance to instituting this type of bureau due to campus financial constraints and/or ignorance or insensitivity. Once established, the staff positions require knowledge of LGBT issues and the political realities of addressing them on campus, as well as the workings of an LGBT speakers bureau. Additionally, this type of bureau runs the risk of losing its collaborative connection with the LGBT students that comprise most of its speakers. That is, if speakers feel as if they are "working for" the speakers bureau instead of being invested in it themselves, certain vibrancy could be lost.

Model Variations

There are variations of each model, with some bureaus combining elements of several and a few falling outside all three. For example, in several places, campus presentations are done by an off-campus community-based speakers bureau (Indiana University, Harvard). Numerous bureaus have developed from Model I through Model III in that an informal network became an unofficial or student-operated bureau until a supported university unit was approved and created (Emery, Tufts, UCLA). However, most have not reached Model III, and many do not even have a Model I bureau.

SPEAKERS BUREAU ORGANIZATION

Despite variations, the different bureaus share common purposes and involve common tasks. This section summarizes some of these in order to outline their organization and functioning.

Speakers

The heart of any speakers bureau is its speakers. Therefore, recruiting, training, retaining, and scheduling speakers are fundamental tasks for any coordinator.

Attracting and Engaging Speakers. A speakers bureau asks its speakers to be out on campus and to tell specific personal details to an audience of mostly strangers who remain relatively anonymous. Thus, many longtime speakers have been hailed on campus by people they don't even recognize who nonetheless know a great deal about them (because they spoke to a class or group the person attended). For this and other reasons, most bureaus make it clear at the outset that although rewarding, being a speaker is not for everyone since it can be difficult, taxing, and even unpleasant at times. Nonetheless, bureaus generally need a roster of 20 to 30 speakers for successful scheduling. Therefore, most use periodic mass publicity (flyers, notices, mailing lists) together with informal networking, especially among members of campus LGBT student, faculty, and/or staff groups.

Training. Speaker training is essential for quality presentations and speaker preparation. Across different bureaus, training ranges from a one- to two-hour basic orientation to a multiple-day self-exploration and practice retreat, depending on group resources and needs. Training usually: introduces new speakers to how the bureau and its presentations are organized; highlights important do's and don'ts; and includes role-playing, observing experienced speakers, and/or other experiential practice. In addition to factual information, it is essential that training cover the *process* of being part of an LGBT speakers presentation. This includes discussion of the speaker's role and attitude during a presentation, managing the interactions, and responding to silent, obnoxious, or overtly hostile people in the audience. Thus, most trainings help new speakers respond calmly to difficult or baiting questions by monitoring their own and the audience's body language and emotional reactions, maintaining control of the presentation, staying respectful and confident, and addressing underlying issues.

Other process tasks include balancing "air time" among speakers and encouraging quiet audience members to talk. In addition to these training sessions conducted by seasoned speakers, most bureaus also hand out a training/orientation packet to new speakers.

Self-Management. An important, highly personal aspect of speaker training is learning how to monitor and manage one's self-presentation while speaking. Shy people may need to push themselves to talk, while gregarious ones may have to remind themselves not to answer every question. Bureaus do not usually regulate how speakers dress or talk, but rather ask them to be mindful of their purposes and the impact they will have on an audience. Reliability, mature behavior and attitude, confidence, comfort with oneself, and an ability to handle complexity are all important hallmarks of effective speakers. Also, speakers find it useful to be aware of questions that make them feel angry, defensive, or intruded on so they can practice measured responses or be ready to say they don't want to answer.

Expectations and Retention. Part of any training is conveying the bureau's expectations of new speakers. Some require that speakers attend periodic workshops or debriefing groups after initial training and/or be available for a certain number of presentations per semester. Others have a provisional period in which speakers try out the role and then determine with the coordinator if it is right for them. Feedback and evaluation during this and any period ranges from formal to nonexistent, although most agree that it is important.

Retention also depends on what the speaker gets from participating. For most, being a speaker is a way to help improve the campus community. Many also find it personally empowering because it requires them to clarify their own thinking on issues that come up during presentations, to improve their public speaking skills, and to meet certain challenges, as well as giving an opportunity to tell their story. Thus, speaker retention can be strengthened to the extent that a coordinator and the speakers themselves can enhance the feelings of making a contribution (e.g., by recognizing and acknowledging it) and the intrinsic rewards of participation (e.g., by making participation enjoyable and personally useful to the speakers). At the same time, even excellent speakers do turn over, burn out, and/or have conflicting responsibilities.

Publicity. Publicizing the availability of the bureau's services is crucial and usually done by the coordinator and speakers. Sending a descriptive letter to faculty and others who may be interested or have used the bureau in the past, and placing notices in campus publications, seem to be the most common methods. Publicity often includes education as coordinators and speakers help the campus community understand how they might want to use the speakers bureau, why there is a need for such presentations, and what typically happens at a presentation. This may involve work such as dispelling the myth that speakers will browbeat audience members, or reassuring someone who hesitates to so openly support the discussion of LGBT issues. The other substantial means of publicity is word of mouth from faculty, staff, and students who have used or attended a presentation, as well as from the coordinator and speakers.

When a presentation is scheduled for an open venue like a residence hall, student group, or public gathering (as opposed to a class), there is sometimes the additional task of publicizing it in order to attract an audience. This is usually taken care of by the staff or head of the hosting organization or campus unit. In contrast, some classroom instructors do not "advertise" that the LGBT speakers bureau is coming to class on a particular day but rather just say there will be "a guest speaker" because they find that too many students (harboring their own fears, prejudices, and discomfort) deliberately skip class when they know LGBT speakers will be talking.

Administration. In addition to recruiting and training speakers, and publicity, the coordinator(s)'s main focus is filling the requests for presentations by scheduling available and suitable speakers (including specific requests, such as all women for a sorority or women's studies course). This usually entails calling or e-mailing speakers until a given engagement is filled, usually by two to five speakers (depending on the school and the specific engagement). Most bureaus strive for gender, sexual orientation, ethnic, and other diversity on their panels, so as to better represent the breadth of LGBT people in the population. However, the reality of scheduling means that sometimes panels cannot be as balanced as one would like. Rarely, experienced speakers may even do a presentation alone (e.g., if others don't come), although this is problematic. Once a speaker has agreed to a given presentation, the coordinator makes sure they have all the basic information (time, date, place, contact person, etc.), as well as any special requests that have been made.

WHAT HAPPENS AT A SPEAKERS BUREAU PRESENTATION?

Basic Prototype

The sections below briefly outline the content and flow of a basic speakers bureau presentation. There are, of course, many variations from group to group and sometimes from presentation to presentation.

Audience. As with any public speaking, it is important for the speakers to know their audience. For example, talking in an advanced health education class can be very different than in an introductory psychology course. Usually, the speakers bureau coordinator will ask the requester for this information and then pass it on to the speakers beforehand.

Introductions. Most bureaus open their presentations by having one speaker introduce the organization and explain the presentation's format, purpose, and intent not to "change anyone's mind" but rather to offer personal experiences and observations for the audience to consider. This creates a set for interaction and participation, lets the audience know what to expect, and, one hopes, dispels some inaccurate presuppositions. Most bureaus then have each speaker introduce himself or herself by name, campus role, and brief information about being LGBT. The content and length of these introductions varies tremendously, from simply "My name is Shirell, I'm a junior biology major, and I've been involved in the speakers bureau for two years" to a practiced two- to three-minute summary of one's coming out story. Regardless, the speakers are introduced as unique individuals, share their stories, and spark questions from the audience. Some bureaus' introductions also include factual, didactic information such as certain definitions (e.g., coming out), research summaries, or answers to common questions.

Breaking the Ice. Following introductions, most bureaus do something to break the taboo against openly discussing LGBT issues. For example, the University of Maryland speakers simply reiterate their willingness to answer anything that is sincerely asked and their intention to let the audience set the agenda by their questions, and then say something like, "So, it only takes one person to start—who has a question?" In contrast, other schools (University of Michigan, Emery, UCLA) include a structured exercise at the beginning of most presentations. Usually, these are nonthreatening, interactive values-clarification activities. For example, volunteers from the audience might be asked to position themselves physically along a continuum that runs across the front of the room from "very comfortable" to "very uncomfortable" as a list of LGBT-related terms are read ("lesbians as parents," "LGBT equal rights," "Defense of Marriage Act [DOMA]. After a term is read the volunteers are each given the opportunity to say why she or he located her/himself at that spot on the continuum for that term.

Q&A and Discussion. The main part of most presentations is answering audience (verbal or written) questions. One or more experienced speakers take the role of facilitator. All speakers, but especially the facilitator, take responsibility for moving discussion along, making sure the tone and behavior of both audience and panel remains constructive, watching the time, and so on. The facilitator also takes the lead in monitoring the panel to ensure that no one speaker monopolizes or is left out of the discussion. One or more (perhaps even all) speakers will respond to a given question. Often they build off of each other's answers to create a cohesive overall response and to demonstrate the breadth of experience and views among LGBT people. The speakers and audience frequently discuss a topic briefly before moving to the next question. Although there can be wide variation, there are certain commonly asked questions (see Table 11), which are usually discussed in training. With experience, many speakers develop concise, highly articulate answers to common and complex questions.

Concluding. When the allotted time is up or discussion lags (usually the former) speakers close by thanking the audience, reiterating any campus LGBT resources, and offering to stay a few minutes afterward for individual comments or questions. Mentioning resources makes availability known to interested

Table 11
Commonly Asked Questions to Speakers

When did you come out to yourself? What was it like? How did you know?

What do you think causes homosexuality? Is it biological/genetic or is it a choice? Or how you were raised?

What do your parents think, if they know? Other family members?

Do you want to have kids, and how will you raise them? Won't they get harassed?

What can a person of the same gender give you sexually that a person of the other gender cannot?

The Bible condemns homosexuality. How do you deal with that? Are you religious?

Have you ever dated/slept with people of the other gender? If not, how do you know you are really gay? If so, doesn't that make you bisexual?

Is bisexuality a real sexual orientation?

Do you think the situation is getting better or worse for [LGBT people] in current society?

In your relationships, who plays the man and who plays the woman?

What is the climate like on campus?

What do you think of various current events such as the DOMA, "gays in the military"?

How do you tell that other people are gay, lesbian, or bisexual?

Have you ever experienced discrimination?

LGBT and non-LGBT audience members and reinforces the image of the campus LGBT community as part of the larger whole.

Staying for a few minutes after the presentation is often very important. "Tears have been shed, hugs, handshakes, and more happen in the ten minutes after a panel" (E. Linn, personal communication, September 1996). Many times people who did not speak in the larger group come forward with questions or to continue discussions. Occasionally an LGBT member of the audience comes forward to meet people, ask questions, and/or express interest in the speakers bureau. People questioning their own or someone else's sexual orientation ask for reassurance or advice. Some of these conversations are very powerful. At times audience members will make comments on their way out that show the impact the presentation has had on them. In addition, some bureaus have the speakers gather for a few minutes after a presentation to review how it went and how the speakers are feeling.

Presentation Variations

As mentioned previously, most speakers bureaus are flexible and tailor their presentation to a requester's needs. This may include expanding the introduction to include certain didactic material or concentrating on certain topics that are particularly relevant to the audience. Such requests are worked out ahead of time, and speakers are prepared. Second, in some instances (very large classes, audience silence) many bureaus ask audience members to write down questions anonymously and pass them forward, or have the speakers ask the audience for their views on various LGBT issues to get things started. Third, some schools include heterosexual allies on their panels. Fourth, some bureaus have developed different presentation formats for different audiences. For example, the University of Michigan has the prototype presentation described above for general audiences and then a more "advanced" presentation that assumes basic knowledge for certain other ones. Fifth, some bureaus do speak off campus at high schools, other colleges, and community groups. This usually involves tailoring their presentation to these settings.

Tips and Pitfalls

It is impossible to cover every detail of starting and operating a sexual orientation diversity speakers bureau in one short chapter. The sections above gave an abstract summary of the typical content and process of a bureau and its work. Tables 12 and 13 list common, specific suggestions and cautions from experienced speakers and coordinators to add concrete guidance and detail to the previous discussion.

Table 12
Speakers Bureau Organizational Suggestions

Make it easy for requesters and speakers to contact the coordinator; reassure them with confirmation calls.

People who are unsure of themselves, uncomfortable with their sexual orientation, or very angry or judgmental may not make good speakers.

Speakers must be dependable as well as skilled. Not showing up wastes others' time and damages the bureau's reputation.

Involvement from a mix of undergraduate and graduate students, staff, and faculty is optimal.

Organizational consistency and continuity are enhanced by administrative support and written procedures and policies.

Constructive screening and feedback of speakers aren't easy, but they are essential.

Be vigilant for signs of burn out among speakers and coordinators.

For safety reasons, avoid disclosing the exact locations of LGBT community spots, groups, or speakers' residences.

Effectiveness

Only a few researchers have empirically evaluated LGBT speakers bureaus' effectiveness, although coordinators, requesters, speakers, and audience members have extensive experience seeing their impact. Some speakers bureaus distribute evaluation forms to requesters, the audience, and/or speakers for their own information, but very few are able to conduct formal program evaluations. Both academic and experiential information conclude that the bureaus have positive effects on a number of levels: the immediate audience members, the overall campus climate, and the speakers themselves (Croteau & Kusek, 1992).

Table 13
Suggestions for a Successful Speakers Bureau Presentation

Presentation format should be "designed and facilitate in a manner that attends to the emotional safety of both panelists and the participants" (McClintock, 1992, 52).

Discuss coming out and being LGBT as an ongoing processes in one's life, not as a one-time thing.
Panels should be as diverse as possible.
Although respectful disagreement can be constructive in demonstrating the variety of views among LGBT people and giving the audience more in-depth information, speakers should not bicker with each other.
Personal stories are more effective than abstractions.
Speakers need not have absolute self-clarity and should not shy away from presenting themselves in some depth and complexity.
Everyone should not answer every question; concise responses are essential.
Relaxed, confident, poised demeanor and a sense of humor are important to an optimal presentation.
Disagreeing constructively with audience members and knowing when to stop disagreeing and move on to another question are important speaker skills.
Speakers should be prepared to deal gracefully with the rare expressions of overt hostility (e.g., someone walking out, heckling).
Speakers should be prepared for the possibility of coming out to people they know who happen to be in the audience (high school friends, one's students, coworkers, faculty).
Arriving a few minutes early allows speakers to check in with each other and confirm any special instructions.

Individual Audience

Faculty often remark that their classes discuss speakers bureau presentations long after they are over. They note that students seem to better appreciate LGBT people as people and are often struck by the invalidity of stereotypes and the variety among LGBT people (L. Goodman, personal communication, August 1996; K. O'Brien, personal communication, October 1996). Others note that students seem more able to talk openly about LGBT issues after a presentation. Many faculty include presentation material on their exams and find that students do retain the information. In addition, coordinators and speakers relate many instances of people coming up afterward to thank them and talk about their positive reactions and new perspectives. One coordinator (E. Linn, personal communication, September 1996) related the story of a 1995 presentation in which a man asked about having a gay sibling. After the presentation he said that he hadn't spoken to his own gay brother in over a year because his family had rejected him but that the presentation made him reconsider and decide to call his brother. She concluded, "We were in awe at the effect we had in that situation."

In keeping with these prevailing anecdotal reports, Geasler, Croteau, Heineman, and Edlund's qualitative study (1995) of heterosexual students who attended an LGBT speakers bureau found that almost all became more "affirming of lesbian, gay, and bisexual people and issues" (485). Sometimes frankly and sometimes subtly, students revealed that the presentation had changed their thinking by dispelling myths and stereotypes, demonstrating the commonalties between the audience and panelists, promoting empathy with the struggles involved in being LGBT, and sparking self-reflection. Croteau and Kusek (1992) hold that the peer speakers have these positive effects because the audience comes to include the speakers in their own (peer) reference group. McClintock (1992) adds that personally meeting LGBT people puts "a human face to an 'issue' that for many [heterosexual audience members] has been clouded in secrecy" and abstraction (54).

For LGBT people in the audience, similar effects are evident. Breaking down stereotypes and seeing positive examples of other LGBT people can be very supportive, especially for people newly out or in the process of questioning their sexual orientation. Some current speakers said that attending a presentation was instrumental in their own coming out. For all LGBT people (faculty, staff, students, etc.), attending a presentation and meeting speakers can increase feelings of community, solidarity, and belonging on campus and may bring them new information.

Overall Campus Climate

Even less formal research has been done concerning bureaus' effects on campus climate. Logically one would expect that the individual effects outlined in the previous section have "a cascade effect on the population" that makes up the campus community (E. Linn, personal communication, September 1996). This is also the impression of residence hall staff and faculty. The follow-up discussions that occur after presentations and the individual-level research both suggest that the speakers bureau's effects last well past the immediate presentation. These experiential conclusions are supported by the fact that speakers bureaus report high demand for their presentations, and some note that requests increase each year (S. Chesnut, personal communication, October 1996).

Effects on LGBT Speakers

The effects of *being* a speaker is of key interest to all speakers bureaus, for whom leadership development and support are goals. A few report that their "primary target group is the peers [speakers] themselves. We are looking to develop leadership skills, increase the number of gay, lesbian, bisexual and transgendered leaders on campus and give them more support so they last longer. Our secondary target is the groups that we actually talk to" (C. Waldron, personal communication, October 1996). Through participation, speakers develop skills, often feel more confident and proud to be LGBT, and therefore better able to deal with the struggles involved. In her 1992 article, Mary McClintock wrote, "Speaking up is a self-empowering act in a world that continually tells me I should hide and be ashamed of who I am. I speak about my experience of being a lesbian in a homophobic world because it is one way that I can break the silence about our lives" (53). Speakers say they also find it rewarding when requesters and audience members express respect for their ability and courage to speak publicly and skillfully on such personal and controversial issues.

Nonetheless, speaking can be stressful and demanding. Speakers reveal personal information to many strangers in the course of a semester, some of whom react with hostility. The intensity and unpredictability of presentations (and audiences) can be draining as well as rewarding. Speakers are also among the most out people on campus because of their participation, which entails risks and stresses as well as benefits. Therefore, speakers often find it personally helpful to debrief informally with each other after a presentation and to meet occasionally in larger groups to discuss their experiences (Croteau & Kusek, 1992).

CONCLUSION

Although more formal program evaluation research would be useful, it is clear that sexual orientation diversity speakers bureaus are valuable campus resources for discussing LGBT issues in open, constructive ways that educate and benefit audience members (and hence campus climate), increase respect for LGBT people, and develop leadership skills among the speakers themselves. The various organizational models and presentation designs are effective responses to each bureau's particular setting and situation. Thus, attention to local issues is essential in creating a successful speakers bureau, although campus support, both informal and institutional, certainly helps in all cases.

CHAPTER 38

Creating a Safe Zone Project at a Small Private College: How Hate Galvanized a Community

Kathleen (KC) Burns Hothem and Christopher D. Keene

The United States possesses the finest higher education system in the world. For learning at the advanced level, we are the envy of our international competitors. Although students from around the world travel to the United States to attend the research universities, small liberal arts colleges also contribute to our reputation for excellence in higher education. Living in a residential setting, attending classes with fewer students, and having ample opportunity for leadership are a few of the hallmarks of the small college education.

The intimacy of the smaller institutions allows for a learning experience vastly different from that of the major research universities. The campus environment can take on a feeling more akin to a large extended family than a college community. However, small liberal arts colleges are not perfect. The intimacy of the small campus can also mean difficulty in maintaining personal privacy. In addition, student populations are often less diverse, especially at private colleges. The student body may become very "clonelike" in attitudes, values, and appearance. Students not fitting the campus "norm" can often find themselves socially isolated or victims of discrimination. On a smaller campus, it is more difficult for these students to find support among their peers. Students who are exploring feelings of sexual identity are especially at risk at a small college. Therefore, it is crucial that administrators and faculty reach out to support these students.

Randolph-Macon College in Ashland, Virginia, is typical of a private, small liberal arts institution. Founded in 1830 by Methodists, it continues a fine tradition of teaching excellence. Its students are from predominantly white, middle-to upper-class conservative suburban households. Randolph-Macon students usually have traditional tastes in clothing, music, art, and food. Their social views are equally traditional. Students walking around in the sunshine greet anyone who crosses their path; it is a place of green grass, year-round flowers, beautiful old buildings, and a scenic fountain in the center of campus: It looks like the perfect place to go to college. However, a closer look behind the residence hall doors will reveal Confederate flags and fraternity members who still celebrate the glory of the Old South. It is a campus with a minority population of only 8 percent. Certainly one will not see lesbian, gay, bisexual, or transgender (LGBT) students ever meeting in the Campus Center. Randolph-Macon is more than a college with a "conservative" atmosphere; it has witnessed several recent incidents of intentional discrimination against students, faculty, and staff. For example, during a "Take Back the Night" march, participants were verbally assaulted when passing fraternity row; a residential adviser (RA) was called a "nigger faggot" while on routine rounds; and, a student's life was threatened via a graphic telephone message. Students who are different from the majority feel isolated and frightened. LGBT students often find minimal, if any, support at smaller colleges like Randolph-Macon.

Discrimination against LGBT students is not uncommon; however, these students may not feel capable of addressing an incident of harassment if there is no established support system on campus. Aside from a college's harassment policy protocol, LGBT students may need additional support and counsel because of the emotionality when dealing with sexual orientation issues. Students may be very closeted on their campuses; reporting a hate crime to anyone would effectively "out" the person to the campus community and make them more vulnerable to further harassment. Because being the target of violence is a real possibility when one discloses his or her sexual orientation, the pressure to remain closeted is not irrational. Remaining in the closet may make life on campus safer, but there are tremendous emotional and social costs. Over time, these costs can take the toll of depression, substance abuse, social isolation, academic failure, and—for some—suicide. The students attending smaller campuses are especially vulnerable because of the absence of LGBT student groups, LGBT Campus Resource Centers, and out LGBT faculty. One way in which smaller institutions can address the lack of resources and support is to create a network of "safe zones" on their campuses.

SAFE ZONE DEVELOPMENT

The safe zone concept is simple; the college community identifies, educates, and supports campus members who are concerned about the well-being of LGBT students. When a person volunteers to be a safe zone contact, he or she is pronouncing nothing about personal sexuality but is instead underscoring an interest in the college's LGBT population. Although the safe zone model was originally designed for faculty and staff participation, students may wish to develop a parallel program or become involved in the core network.

How the Safe Zone Program Began at Randolph-Macon

In the Fall of 1995, the Virginia Association of College and University Housing Officers Task Force on LGBT Issues proposed a statewide safe zone program. This seemed to be a great opportunity for Randolph-Macon College to support its LGBT students visibly. This would be a chance to begin a sanctioned support network for LGBT students and a terrific tool in which to educate the entire college community. Because this is a statewide program endorsed by a well-regarded professional organization, introduction of the program would be less threatening for a conservative college like Randolph-Macon.

The Student Affairs staff met and after many discussions was successful in having the dean of students schedule a meeting with the president's cabinet. The purpose of this meeting was to discuss the negative image the college had regarding LGBT issues. Several incidents of harassment on campus and the description of Randolph-Macon College as a homophobic school in the 1995 *Princeton Review* caused concern with upper-level administrators. Student Affairs staff members attended the meeting to solicit support for a safe zone program and to express the need for protection for project volunteers (a non-discrimination clause to include sexual orientation). While this was being done, the Safe zone resource guide and training manual was under development. The concept of safe zone encouraged the college to look at itself critically and to acknowledge its homophobic climate. For some, the safe zone program was a tangible way to begin addressing these concerns.

Then it happened. Martin, in his final semester of his senior year, received a phone message early one Sunday morning. The call was a graphic message of hatred and violence; Martin saved the message. He then contacted a member of the residence life staff to whom he forwarded the message. The staff member reviewed several options with him both within and outside of the college system. At that time, a person who was experiencing discrimination had the opportunity to invoke the Harassment Policy. The policy prescribed that the college ombuds act as a good-faith mediator between the parties involved. The mediation process can culminate in a formal complaint to the dean of students if the complainant is not satisfied with the outcome. Another option for Martin was to bring the complaint to the College Judicial Board, which was a student-run board upholding the College Code of Student Conduct. Finally, charges could be pressed outside of the college with the commonwealth's attorney.

While Martin had conversations with Campus Safety and the Dean of Students Office, an investigation was conducted. It identified the two male students who made the phone call from a college-sanctioned fraternity house. Martin decided to use the College Judicial Board, which would enforce a minimum punishment of suspension if the two men where found guilty. (Their voices were on tape, and both had made a statement to Campus Safety claiming responsibility for the offense.)

The time delay from the incident to the Judicial Board hearing was frustrating for Martin. After two weeks, he assumed that little was being done to address his complaint. To draw campus-wide support, Martin sent the recorded message of harassment to all faculty members, some staff, some members of the administration, and key student leaders. Those who heard the message were outraged: Its level of baseness even appalled some of the most homophobic people on the campus. They wanted to know why nothing had been done on Martin's behalf.

At this point, the administration "officially" endorsed the safe zone proposal. While the safe zone wasn't triggered by this incident, it was adopted, accepted, and embraced by the community out of a sense of urgency. Staff members who first proposed the program jumped at the chance to implement it even though the training materials were still in development. Though the situation was not ideal, starting the network when campus energy was high proved to be an outstanding opportunity.

In what often happens when taking advantage of a critical incident, reality began to ring true. People lost sight of the original intent of the safe zone concept. In the well-intentioned spirit to be supportive of LGBT students, many interested faculty and staff members were demanding safe zone stickers at Randolph-Macon: The sticker was in danger of becoming a banner of political support for LGBT students instead of identifying trained volunteers. Safe zone leaders had the difficult task of reemphasizing the true intent of the program and the meaning behind the sticker. These discussions were often emotionally charged; some perceived the resistance to casually distribute stickers as another example of administration inaction. As the faculty met, a safe zone leader was present to explain the purpose of the sticker on one's door. When students met to organize their efforts in response to Martin's harassment, safe zone was shared with them. The students discussed developing their own "Students for Safe Zone" program. In addition, the safe zone project was fully explained at the annual spring meeting of the trustees. The governing members were told that the safe zone was not a reaction to the Martin incident but had been in development prior to the harassment. To the surprise of many, the entire college community became supportive and interested in responding to Martin's situation, and the safe zone program found advocates throughout the campus.

Martin's incident began to transform from an issue of intolerance and hatred into something very different. It became symbolic of a conflict between the faculty and the administration. Martin, unfortunately, got caught in this struggle. When this happened, it was easy to forget the needs of the victim in exchange for political advantage.

Recruiting Participants

To differentiate the safe zone program from other political efforts addressing intolerance on campus, it is important to educate the whole community about the safe zone concept. Once clarification is made about the project, the next concern is about recruiting and training volunteers. The critical incident on the Randolph-Macon campus made recruitment easy; however, other campuses will have to solicit support from the very top of the college administration. It must be clear that volunteering to be a safe zone does not put one in jeopardy of termination or tenure consideration. On campuses with comprehensive non-discrimination policies that include sexual orientation, safe zone participants should feel less threatened. If a college does not protect members of its community with such a policy, parties interested in establishing a safe zone on their campus should investigate the possibility of revising their current policy to include sexual orientation. Gathering support from campus leaders—students, department heads, alumni, senior administrators, and key trustee board members—is crucial. Such backing will facilitate both policy change and the viability of the safe zone. Once interest and support of establishing a safe zone network are present, then training, resources, and financial backing are the next steps to address.

Creating Safe Zone Manuals

There are no prepackaged safe zone kits for purchase; there is no "Center for Safe Zone Training" a staff person can attend; training models will be unique to each campus depending on the expertise and resources available to those creating the network. Training guides or manuals should contain sections addressing LGBT identity, homophobia, issues in the classroom, campus/community resources, and a glossary of the language and symbols of the LGBT community. In addition, an up-to-date bibliography is useful for safe zone participants who wish to do further reading. Modified training materials may be developed for student volunteers. These materials should be adaptable to the methodology used when training today's student leaders; for example, the use of group interaction and role-playing exercises may be necessary to maintain student enthusiasm. Trainers must be aware that student participants may be working through personal sexual identity issues; they should be prepared to address emotional reactions to the training process. It is advisable to consult with the college's counseling staff prior to any training.

Once safe zone volunteers have been recruited and trained, a method of follow-up and communication should be established. Possible methods may include a coordinating office or individual, a campus listserv, or regular meeting times for volunteers. Assessment should be a part of any safe zone program. An effort must be made to ascertain whether LGBT student and safe zone volunteer needs are being met. Revisions may be necessary to materials, training, or resources based upon yearly evaluation.

The campus impact of a safe zone can be greatly increased by the creation of a program web site. Because sexual orientation issues are so emotionally charged, students may find it more comfortable to do their first information exploration from the anonymity of a computer that is often in the privacy of their own room. There is a wealth of information on the Internet that can be linked to a safe zone homepage. For example, the national organization, Parent and Friends of Lesbians and Gays (PFLAG) has a site with information relevant for students and their parents. Furthermore, Internet information is often updated more frequently than printed materials. The Internet also allows LGBT students on smaller campuses to reach out to peers around the world for discussion, ideas, and support. Even on the most homophobic campuses, a student with an Internet connection can find pockets of acceptance, tolerance, and understanding.

Safe zone leaders should also investigate established resources in their area. Such organizations can provide a source of guest speakers, materials, and programming options. Training may also be available in some communities. In addition, other institutions of higher education may have resources addressing LGBT issues. These outside organizations may have support groups or social activities that are unavailable on the smaller campus. However, sending the LGBT student across town is not a replacement for an on-campus network like safe zone.

The success of any safe zone program relies on the support and commitment from all facets of the college community. First, the college must make a statement that intolerance and hatred in any form will not be tolerated—that all students, faculty, and staff are considered valuable members of the community. Therefore, everyone must be protected by a non-discrimination policy that includes sexual orientation. It is important that the policy be consistent throughout all college documents from residence housing agreements to employee rights. The policy can provide a focal point in educating the campus about discrimination, civil rights, and personal responsibility. Everyone must know his or her rights and what actions to take when they are violated. The policy sets a tone of respect and concern for everyone that is crucial for creating positive change. For instance, Randolph-Macon College is currently taking this step by rewriting its harassment policy into an all-inclusive non-discrimination policy for all members of the campus community. The challenge for Randolph-Macon is to make the written policy an integral part of college life. This can be done first by education and second by active enforcement. The commitment to the policy must come from all levels of the college, from the president's office to the classroom and into the student's residence hall room.

As issues of retention concern a growing number of college administrators, the loss of one student due to a hate crime is distressing. If the campus climate is so intolerant that many LGBT students do not return, then the issue becomes one of financial concern. The few dollars a safe zone program may cost could prove to be a wise investment in keeping bright students enrolled at your college. In fact, the presence of a safe zone network may make the campus more attractive to incoming students. While a safe zone project will not solve an institution's financial worries, the program can have a positive effect on both retention and recruitment. A safe zone project will not end homophobia and intolerance, but it is a good place to start in supporting LGBT students on your campus.

PART X

Unique Institutions

CHAPTER 39

An Oasis: The LGBT Student Group on a Commuter Campus

Glorianne M. Leck

This chapter is written as a first-person narrative about one faculty adviser's perception of concerns and issues relevant to providing student services to lesbian, gay, bisexual, and transgender (LGBT) students on a primarily commuter campus. The descriptive narrative is followed by specific suggestions and analysis.

FIRST CONTACTS

"Hello?" (silence)

"Hi. My name is Brian and I was calling to ask about GALA."

"Hi, Brian, my name is Glorianne. I am one of the faculty advisers to State University's Gay and Lesbian Alliance. I would be glad to answer any questions you have. Do you feel comfortable talking with me right now on the phone?"

"Uh, yeah, I'm okay."

"Good. I'll do my best to try to answer your questions."

"Uh, like, what do you guys do at GALA?"

And so it begins, a first call or contact, that a frightening step into a different reality, perhaps for the first time saying out loud to someone else, "I think I'm gay." The phone allows the anonymity and thus that first step. A call made from a phone to an unknown person allows a young gay man, in this instance, to connect with others who may understand him. That first phone call is usually a peek out of a big secret, a tentative step out of a closet. For a young adult living at home and attending college as a commuter student, managing an opening— finding a way out of the day-to-day world where it is assumed that everyone is heterosexual—can be very difficult.

For closeted LGBT people, every moment is usually wrapped in secrecy, in fear, and too often, in guilt and shame. Finding a way out of secrecy and alienation is an overpowering challenge in dealing with one's own sexual feelings. Drugs, alcohol, promiscuity (often while trying to be heterosexual), and suicide frequently are options as the young person seeks relief from the sexual and related emotional confusion of heterosexual expectations.

SEEKING COMMUNITY

"Hi! My name is Pam. I saw you on TV and decided I wanted to make contact with you. I've been having sex with this girl and we really don't know any other lesbians, so I thought maybe you could tell us what's going on and if there are any groups or activities we could get involved in."

"Glad to meet you, Pam, and I am pleased to know that my being on TV helped us make this contact. I do understand that it is a lonely world out there when you don't know many other people with your lifestyle and sexual orientation."

Having access to an "out" individual can be a first step in validating one's relationship with another person and joining up with a community and/or an identity group. LGBT folks have many common characteristics as we interactively struggle for identity and place in a society that assumes that all people are or should be heterosexual. For many LGBT people, as with many non-LGBT young people, there comes a time when we feel we must move away from our families of origin. This may be a move to college, to a larger city, or simply making the financial break and taking an apartment across town. For college students who wish to get a university degree, but who cannot afford to move away from their parents' home the "escape to freedom" is not as easily managed.

SPECIAL NEEDS

"I'm returning your call after receiving your number from the social service hotline. My name is Glorianne. I am an adviser to YSU (Youngstown State University) GALA. How might I help you?"

"My name is John, and I am a cross-dresser. I know what I am doing is bad, but I can't stop it."

"John, what is it you think I might be able to do for you?"

"I was wondering if you could tell me someone I could talk with, someone else who is a cross-dresser or who has worked through it."

"John, have you thought about talking to a counselor?"

"No, I really don't think I want to talk to a counselor."

"John, is cross-dressing part of what you do to get dates, or are you primarily into the dressing-up part?"

"I just like getting dressed up and going out. It doesn't have anything to do with sex; in fact I don't want that."

"John, if I could find someone to talk with you, would you prefer someone who is gay or someone who is straight?"

"I'm straight, and I think I would prefer to talk to someone who is straight, but I wouldn't mind talking with a gay guy."

The Gay and Lesbian Alliance on campus in this midsize city—regional area of about 120,000 people—is an oasis, a discernible location that holds promise of some relief from frustration and confusion. For those who are questioning their sexuality, their gender experiences, their erotic triggers, and their associations, the campus GALA organization appears to be one of very few places to discuss such matters; for many it may be their only source of hope. Sometimes the college campus group is a flashing neon light on an otherwise dark and unfamiliar country road. And lest campus groups become a mirage, we have to respond to many inquiries and many questions as they come to us, whether by phone, visits, or drop-in folks to our weekly GALA meetings.

GALA has an office in and among the student government offices, but it doesn't have members available all the time to answer phones. Through the use of an answering machine, contact with the local social services hotline number, and publication of the phone numbers of the two organizational advisers, we handle calls as best we can.

CAMPUS CIRCUMSTANCES

My voice, and the point of view from which this narrative is written, is that of a faculty member, a student organization adviser, and lesbian activist who has been on a small state university (13,000 students) campus for 20 years. I have been an out lesbian for the entire time I have been here. I came out officially—as an open advocate and lesbian-identified person on television, in local politics, and so on—in the last 10 years.

In 1975, I was asked to serve as an adviser to a feminist group on campus which had a large lesbian contingent. Since 1980, I have served as an adviser to one of the serial campus LGBT groups. Each of these groups has had its origins with a couple of political and self-assured individuals who felt they were able to handle "the home front," meaning parents and family (if they found out). Each of these groups lasted two to four years, usually until the founding members graduated and left the campus and the city.

My assumption was that as politics at the national, state, and local levels became more public about gay issues, the group would stabilize and a more consistent membership pattern would evolve; that doesn't seem to be the case. In fact, if anything, students have expressed to me that there appears to be less of a "need" on a commuter campus for a thriving group to exist. They express that they are receiving more support in the popular media and that, along with an increased collegiate acceptance of bisexuality and sexual experimentation, they don't need to commit themselves publicly to a gay or lesbian identity. They tell me this has allowed them as individuals to have the lifestyle without claiming an identity in sexual orientation and civil rights struggles. Pop culture provides a place, it seems, for more diverse sexual activities and group identities that don't require one to identify as LGBT or as straight.

Because some religious groups have also been working to offer solace to their LGBT members, new places of acceptance are appearing in the broader community. Most recently an LGBT and gay-friendly group started its own ecumenical church in the area. Some churches and Parents, Family and Friends of Lesbians and Gays (PFLAG) provide a less "outlaw" appearing option for people who have some family support or very deep ties to their spiritual roots in organized religion. These organizations also represent a broader base of the community since they are not made up entirely of students.

Youngstown has a city ordinance that provides equal protection in housing, employment, and social services to groups including consenting adults of the same sex. That ordinance and the presence of gay-friendly political figures seem to serve as a sense of validation and increasing legitimization for residents of the city where the university is located.

DETERRENTS

Student government, in keeping with state regulations on funding, has taken the position of discouraging groups that might organize simply for social purposes; it insists instead on "educational purposes" as a common theme for student organizations. Therefore, groups are unable to get and keep funds and office space if they do not do a certain amount of social service outreach and educational programming. Along with an abundance of paper work, requirements about officers and qualifications, and a bureaucratic nightmare of forms for each and every purchase with student government money, the officers, whose original intentions were to deal with LGBT issues and community, are soon overwhelmed with "keeping the organization going." Inevitably, as the leadership is drawn into prescribed kinds of programming, the student members get tired of meeting to talk about organizational matters, and the exodus begins. Before long, the well-intentioned groups of students who start these organizations are burdened, distracted, and find their own identity development put on hold for the sake of being legitimized by the university student organizational structure.

Students at this and most commuter campuses work at least 20 hours a week and carry a full load of college classes. Add to that the risk of public association in their own community and the fact that the number of people willing to stay the course as out-front members of an LGBT organization remains very small. Each group that I have been asked to advise has had fewer than 15 "signed-on" student members. Each year the officers have had conflicts with the university administration who insist on publishing the home phone numbers of all student organizations' officers.[1]

The current GALA group is bolstered by an alumni contingent that consists of some staff and community people who graduated from this university and who come to the meetings to provide support for the current undergraduate students. Even that has not worked well since much of the alumni work has also become support work for required activities, and they have not had much time to just socialize with or mentor the undergraduate students. This alumni involvement has also had the effect of not allowing undergraduates to feel that they have the ultimate responsibility for keeping the organization going, that the officers, faculty advisers, and the alumni will keep the group going if something needs to be done.

Another confounding factor has been the tendency of a single strong leader to emerge and, because of the demands of organizational matters, to neglect the development of new leadership. Delegation of responsibility to other members, so the leaders say, is seen as taking more time than "just doing it myself."

POLITICS AND GENDER IDENTITY

Another problem that has occurred in this commuter setting is that fewer women students come to this group in that they can belong to another group called Humans against Gender Stereotyping—that's right, HAGS! HAGS is a much more politically active and maverick organization which is bolstered by what is now an established feminist politic. GALA must still deal with identity and social access to companionship before it ignites its members to political action.

There is the problem of male dominance in GALA. Ever-present sexism continues to alienate many of the women who come to GALA meetings. Women who are new to these cultural exchanges attend for a few times, seem to become alienated, then disappear. It continues to be a problem to get a female co-chair of GALA, as the lesbian-identified students seem not quite comfortable with the ways and programs of the GALA group.

ISSUES OF RESIDENCE HALLS

The commuter campus does not permit the same kind of experimentation and exaggerated risks that a sheltered residential campus can provide.

> I just stopped by to tell you that I have been accepted at Ohio State and am going there next semester. There just is not a social life here, and everything is geared to heterosexual folks living at home with their parents. I want you to know GALA was the best thing about this campus. Thank God for you guys, or I would have gone crazy here. You were my family, and I'm sorry to have to leave you.

Later, the same student sent a letter:

> Just wanted you to know how happy I am at this larger campus. There is so much going on. I have a guy friend, we haven't done anything sexual, we are just dating. He is really great. I am getting involved with the LGBT group and running for a seat on student government. People seem so nice. I don't feel like a freak in this setting.

It is obvious that the larger residential campuses appear to allow for greater tolerance and advocacy for those valued activist LGBT students. The anonymity a large campus may provide will offer some cover for identity struggles and experimentation that can't be cultivated on the commuter campus. Programming for LGBT events at larger residential campuses offers the prospect of larger student audiences, thus affording an entirely different level of programming that can include appearances by and interaction with nationally known LGBT activists and speakers. Residential and larger campuses can also usually draw students from other campuses to events and programming. The commuter campus lacks audience, support, and funding for such "big" programs.

Our most successful programming was a Friday-Saturday workshop in antibigotry training. It was for our own university students and for other leaders who were invited to our community for a meeting of a statewide LGBT (OUT-Voice). We were able to bring Pat Griffin and Matt Oulette—both from the University of Massachusetts—to the campus for this event. The honorarium was raised by OUTVoice; the hospitality was handled through student government and local donors. To make that program a success we scheduled it nearly a year in advance. We solicited registrations from our GALA members so they could make arrangements to be off work on that particular weekend. For many, it was a high cost in lost wages needed to pay their tuition and book payments. In addition to the problems for LGBT students living at home with their heterosexual families' expectations, commuter campuses tend to bring an additional set of problems related to socioeconomic class and financial resources.

POLITICS OF CLASS

Students attending this state university tend to be from families that are less able to afford college education for their children. As indicated earlier, many of these students work at least 20 hours a week while going to school full-time, or they work full-time and attend school part-time. There is also a significantly large number of so-called nontraditional students, those returning to or starting the university after age 25. These students are more than likely to be managing a family in addition to working and going to college. Tuition is kept lower than that at most other state universities in the region, thus permitting some who would otherwise never be able to afford college to try such a venture.

Under these conditions, students tend to be vocationally oriented. They see little value in or have little time for extracurricular activities and are not likely to attend college events. Therefore, when a student seeks out the GALA organization, it is a good indication that they have a high need for the social group.

Socioeconomic class plays out in yet another way on this commuter campus in that people live at home, and their place of residence is likely to reveal the general status of the families' income. Youngstown is a city in considerable poverty and is surrounded by suburbs that can be identified with class and a range of privilege. Within the commuter campus framework, one's high school also indicates some class standing. These class differences and the social status they carry do appear to have influence in the social interactions among students. Most of the students we see at the GALA meetings are from working-class suburbs, rural communities, and inner-city neighborhoods; we see few students who come to the campus from the more well-to-do suburbs. This often reveals the availability or nonavailability of a car, but more important it seems to have to do with one's access to the larger cities of Pittsburgh and Cleveland or access to residential campuses where friends may be able to introduce students to a more robust LGBT life.

To "play" out of town is an issue of privilege. Those with access to other communities and LGBT enclaves can afford to avoid the risk and the effort on working with a local LGBT group under the eyes of one's family and family acquaintances.

WHAT WE CAN DO

The following are specific as well as general suggestions for university and college student personnel services at commuter schools: First, provide opportunities for faculty and student personnel workers to be advocates and role models for LGBT students. These individuals must be encouraged to be available to the media and available to students for consultation on LGBT issues. The social comfort level of these staff members can help to create a healthy atmosphere for the presence and emotional well-being of LGBT students. Second, each institution must have a non-discrimination policy that includes sexual orientation. Administrative spokespeople for institutions must refer all listed groups in the policy with ease and conviction about their rights to all services and to full inclusion without harassment. Third, student government and its member organizations need to provide different guidelines so that groups are not buried in paperwork. If such paperwork is unavoidable, there should be a provision for clerical resource people. A distinction between service and social groups may need to be made. This is not to say that LGBT groups ought not have to provide some educational services and to share in support of campus-wide programming, but such demands need to be balanced by the needs and purposes of the organization. Fourth, much of student government and student organizational development is about creating leadership and civic involvement for students during their college experience. That may not be the appropriate agenda for LGBT, feminist, and racially oppressed groups. It is specifically the need of LGBT, women's, and students from racially, religiously, or ethnically oppressed groups to have a place where they can work on identity and safety issues for themselves; this is not the same as the generic prescription for students as a whole. Fifth, relationships with local social service agencies and religious services are of utmost importance, because they provide connections for intergroup support among LGBT people. It would be particularly helpful to have a counselor employed at the health services center who was able to provide support for persons struggling with LGBT identity and, as such, provide opportunity for personal crisis or developmental counseling for LGBT persons. And sixth, institutions of higher education need to display leadership that does not continue to rely on linear absolutes in policy and rule-based organizational behavior. Prescriptions for "all" student organizations is a lazy and insensitive policy base, but more important it confuses equality with justice. A young lesbian or gay man in the coming out process is not in the same place or needing the same services as a young heterosexual person who is looking to enhance a resume or join a group to get to know some new or like-minded people. The university bears a certain social and intellectual responsibility to use its knowledge base with a clear understanding of the differing concepts of "equal access to facility" and "equal access to opportunity for success."

NOTE

1. LGBT students are particularly vulnerable to phone harassment by young people who are homophobic. Gay bashing, the physical and verbal abuse of people suspected of being LGBT, continues to be a serious problem in our social climate.

CHAPTER 40

Exploring Sexual Orientation Issues at Colleges and Universities with Religious Affiliations
Beth Kraig

Rationales used to condemn sexual minority people have varied historically, but seldom has the so-called biblical argument been as prominent as it is today. There are obvious historical reasons for the contemporary tendency of anti-gay spokespeople to base their criticisms on religion; other sources of condemnation—the criminalization of sexual minority people or references to their psychopathology—have gradually lost ground as growing bodies of evidence have demonstrated that lesbian, gay, bisexual, and transgender (LGBT) people are as safe, and as sane, as their heterosexual counterparts. Thus, references to religion seem increasingly to be the only "legitimate" way to condemn and belittle LGBT people.

Yet historians of social movements like abolitionism and the women's rights struggle know that religion has often been a final, significant ally in a group's effort to garner acceptance and equality. In the Jewish and Christian traditions that represent much of the United States' (US) religious heritage, calls for social justice, peacemaking, and neighborly love have clearly motivated significant changes in dehumanizing institutions like racism and sexism. While it would be ridiculous to suggest that the path toward reducing or eliminating anti-gay prejudice and discrimination has been blazed by religious leaders, it may be less foolish to predict that more religious voices will have to join the chorus of affirmation before LGBT people can receive respect and equality in this country.

Religion has played a significant role in shaping the values and political goals of many people in the US in the late twentieth century, and certainly it will continue to influence social beliefs and practices in the next century. Thus, whether for reasons of personal spiritual belief or pragmatic political policy,

LGBT people and their heterosexual allies need to understand the language and nature of faith organizations. LGBT people need to engage in, rather than spurn, opportunities to situate their identities and human rights within the larger frameworks of religion and theology in the US. That said, what role in this process can colleges and universities with religious affiliation play?

It is important to note that such institutions cannot be characterized easily. Some major private universities like the University of Chicago or the University of Southern California have historical connections to particular denominations but do not have institutional affiliations to religion that involve or affect the administration of the university. Other major private universities, like Notre Dame or Duke, do preserve more direct affiliations that create opportunities for possible or probable administrative influence from religious leaders in the case of controversial university policies. Many smaller private universities and colleges also have wide-ranging forms of governance and affiliation that link them to a variety of religions and religious denominations. In some cases, institutions are owned by particular religions or denominations and thus may find that church policies directly preclude obvious support—or discrimination toward—LGBT people.

The particular religion or denomination with which an institution is affiliated will greatly shape the direction that a college or university may follow in serving its LGBT members. The United Church of Christ, for example, is LGBT-affirmative at the level of national policy; in contrast, Southern Baptists are aggressively condemnatory of LGBT people at the level of church teachings and policies. Within a religion or denomination, too, regional and institutional factors may shape a particular college's response to sexual minority issues; thus, one may find Catholic colleges or universities in which levels of affirmation are high, and included in policy statements, but may also find Catholic colleges or universities that provide little or no institutional support for sexual minority members of their campuses.

Given the enormous range of institutional structures and the wide variety between and among religious denominations, what should the individual administrator, faculty member, or staff member do to assess the climate or culture at his or her place of employment? Conversations with colleagues are certainly a starting point, although it is important to note that such sources of information are notoriously subjective and may reflect elements of pessimism that speak to past circumstances more than to future possibilities. Individual denominations are experiencing fairly rapid change on issues pertinent to sexual orientation (consider, for example, the 1996 decision of an Episcopal Church tribunal not to bring heresy charges against a bishop who had ordained an openly gay man). Beyond personal conversations, then, one should examine available policy statements about homosexuality from the denomination in question and should determine if there are organized gay-affirmative groups active within the denomination (see Table 14).

Some institutions may already have an active student or community group

Table 14

Guidelines and Suggestions for Designing and Guiding Dialogues: Religious-Spiritual Identities and Sexual-Affectional Identities

- What is your religious-spiritual identity? (need not be disclosed to others)
- What is your sexual-affectional identity? (need not be disclosed to others)
- What are the many spiritual and religious identities?
  - US religious-spiritual minorities? US religious-spiritual majorities?
  - What is your particular religious identity? What is your particular sexual-affectional identity?
- What will we consider?
  - Texts, theologies, socio-religious phenomena, sexual-affectional phenomena
- What tools and methods will we use?
  - Exegeses, hermeneutics, historical research, contemporary research, personal experiences
- Should we discuss one topic at a time or allow topics to roam freely?
- How will we listen, record others' ideas (while maintaining anonymity), think about ideas?

1. Do we focus primarily on denominations that are considered part of Christianity or Judaism or just our own?
2. Should we use biblical texts in shaping our discussion? Why/why not?
3. What roles do religious-spiritual leaders and scholars play in shaping your beliefs and identity?
4. How do your beliefs and identity guide your social and interpersonal actions and policies?
5. Which moral principles guide your moral behavior and judgments? Do you give priority to some? Why/why not?
6. Do spiritual-religious beliefs affect laws and government? Should they? Why/why not?
7. What is sexuality? What is a sexual-affectional identity? Who defines these things?
8. How do you link your moral principles to your sexual-affectional identity?
9. What factors compel us to take someone seriously? When do we consider a speaker to be an "authority"?
10. How does it feel when someone questions our beliefs? How does it feel when someone says that we are not good people, or are not human?
11. Do we have a responsibility not to hurt other people? How do we evaluate "degrees" of pain in others?

dedicated to affirmation of LGBT people. Obviously, the members of such a group should be involved in any efforts to engage the larger institution in discussions about affirmation, campus policies, and church policies. However, often such groups exist in relative isolation and may be understandably detached from the religious elements of the college's identity or administration. A first step toward engaging the larger campus in dialogue about religion and affirmation of LGBT people could involve meeting frequently with the LGBT members of the campus to learn about experiences with religion and self-identified religious people.

These preliminary discussions will serve a variety of purposes. LGBT people can begin to express their dissatisfaction with the condemnations and attacks directed against them with religious "justification." What are these stories of pain, anger, and hurt? Astonishingly, many heterosexual members of a denomination may lack awareness of the damage done to LGBT people by statements like "Love the sinner, hate the sin" or, similarly, "tolerant" slogans. Also, as sexual minority people share their stories, they can begin to analyze their own views regarding religion and may assess their willingness to participate in more extended dialogues. Effective discussions with heterosexual members of a campus ministry, campus congregation, or church leadership will depend on the skill and commitment to dialogue of LGBT people in the campus community.

In guiding members of a campus organization for LGBT people in these preliminary discussions, it may be useful to provide copies of the kinds of "conversation starters" and "conversational guidelines" that would be used in larger discussions with other members of the campus and church communities (see Tables 14 and 15). Of particular use for opening discussions with the LGBT people on campus is the second set of questions in Table 15. Discussion may branch out to include readings on the use of religion and spirituality to motivate protests against slavery, Jim Crow segregation, and African apartheid. Texts on or about liberation theology may also be useful, particularly ones relevant to sexual minority people and their struggles (see Table 16).

As these initial dialogues are developing, others who wish to participate in the organization of larger discussions with the campus community and church may begin to locate appropriate speakers and discussion leaders. One source of such participants may be the college's or university's own faculty in a department of religion or religious studies. Ideally, some faculty will be both willing to take up some of the organizational tasks and able to address particular issues involved in sexual minority affirmation. For example, issues of church history related to other social struggles may be usefully taught (and it is possible that some faculty might have been directly involved in relatively recent denominational dialogues about the ordination of women, divorce and remarriage, or racial integration). Scholars of the Old and New Testaments may be willing to lead discussions of those texts if the college's affiliation is Christian; Torah scholars may be willing to lead discussions if the college's affiliation is Jewish, and so on.

Table 15

Religious Groups by Denomination who Affirm LGBT People*

1. American Baptist Churches in the USA: American Baptists Concerned for Lesbian, Gay, & Bisexual People
2. Church of Christ, Scientist: Emergence (gay/lesbian Christian Scientists and their supporters)
3. Episcopal Church: Integrity (gay and lesbian Episcopalians and their families and friends)
4. Evangelical Lutheran Church of America: Lutherans Concerned
5. Mennonite Church: Brethren/Mennonite Council for Lesbian & Gay Concerns
6. Metropolitan Community Church: Christ-centered ecumenical church committed to ministry for all people regardless of sexual orientation
7. Pentecostals: National Gay Pentecostal Alliance
8. Presbyterian Church (USA): Presbyterians for Lesbian & Gay Concerns
9. Religious Society of Friends (Quakers): Friends for Lesbian and Gay Concerns
10. Roman Catholics: Dignity (a faith community of lesbian, gay, bisexual Catholics and their families and friends
11. Union of American Hebrew Congregations (Reform): World Congress of Gay and Lesbian Jewish Organizations
12. Unitarian Universalist Association: Unitarian Universalists for Lesbian, Gay, and Bisexual Concerns
13. United Church of Christ: United Church Coalition for Lesbian/Gay Concerns
14. United Methodist Church: Affirmation: United Methodists for Lesbian & Gay Concerns

* Select list.

Table 16
Engaging in Dialogue about Religious-Spiritual Identities and Sexual-Affectional Identities

1. How does it feel to be hated, degraded, rejected, and attacked? What forms of faith enable the "despised" person to remain dignified, self-affirming, and willing to engage in dialogue with others?

2. What does it mean to love one's neighbors? How do we love others as we would wish to be loved?

3. It is never easy to reconsider traditional practices and positions. Traditions often create comfort for those they benefit, and therefore it is usually uncomfortable to evaluate traditions in a new light. For example, for thousands of years the tradition of slavery offered much comfort and privilege to those who owned slaves, and others who did not own slaves found it more comfortable to "accept" slavery than to stand up against it.

4. But slavery caused much pain in those who were enslaved. And for some people—not enslaved themselves, but sickened by the pain that enslaved people experienced—strong belief in the principle of loving one's neighbors led them to reject slavery.

5. An important first step in reconsidering a tradition involves realizing that it diminishes human dignity and worth. How does this apply to sexual minorities today? Traditions of heterosexism hurt; they make us all angry, afraid, confused, sorrowful, and impatient. Acceptance of the traditions of heterosexism means the ongoing degradation of some of your neighbors. Reconsideration of those traditions is a difficult and detailed process. People may be attacked or dismissed by their friends.

As the efforts at outreach begin, it is possible and even likely that voices of opposition will sound off. The desirability of "controlling" the point at which this occurs is debatable (and therefore should be discussed early in the process opening these dialogues by those who are initiating the process). Clandestine efforts to bring some individuals quietly into dialogue can backfire. Almost certainly, such efforts to "manage" the process of discussion will cause some hurt feelings and may imply that the discussion has a "shameful" quality to it and that those who are organizing it fear criticism. At the same time, if the institution in question is especially conservative on issues of gay affirmation, timing may be critical; those who are organizing a dialogue may wish to build a list of allies before "going public."

When the opposition does arise, its nature and its noisiness will be important clues to the climate of the institution. Who is in opposition—key administrators, important faculty members, religious leaders, clergy serving on the college or university's board of directors or board of regents? Key alumni or donors to the institution may also speak up.

On the other hand, the opposition may be more subtle and less obviously linked to the college or university's circles of influence. Retired faculty or administrators, perhaps less involved in contemporary issues and college environments, may be factors. Parents of students may also be involved, but individually and in small numbers. Since colleges and universities with religious affiliations are all private and tend to rely heavily on tuition and donations as resources, less direct damaging criticism may come from less direct or visible sources. Few college administrators enjoy controversy, given the possibility that it might dissuade some parents from enrolling their students at an institution.

But whether it be significant and powerful, or subtle and indirect, discouraging donations or opposition to the religious affirmation of LGBT people can actually be seen as an opportunity. Its emergence "proves" the need for dialogue; opposed voices within a community with a spiritual or religious foundation represent a problem that most religious communities prefer to address in a conciliatory fashion. How can such tensions be reconciled? This question is paramount to the process, since it speaks to the overarching issue of reconciling traditional, religious condemnations of LGBT people (and the great dehumanizing damage those condemnations have caused) with the actual lives and gifts of LGBT people.

The materials offered in Tables 14 and 16, or similar documents, should be kept on hand to guide the dialogues that can (and should) emerge at colleges with religious affiliations. Ideally, these dialogues will unfold smoothly, in an atmosphere characterized primarily by goodwill; if the dialogues begin under less pleasant circumstances, in the face of hostility, it may be even more important to shape them with reference to written outlines. For example, if an opening conversation occurs through a panel presentation by LGBT members of the campus to an "all-comers" audience, copies of such outlines should be handed out to audience members and may shape some of the panel's comments. If smaller convocations precede such an event, such outlines may be useful and instructive to administrators, faculty, staff, and clergy and might suggest the kinds of topics that larger forums might address.

Regardless of how the opposition surfaces, and when, and under what circumstances the dialogues begin to occur, more successful outcomes will rest on considerable planning. Take a good look at your own institution as you plan the kinds of discussions, events, and goals that you wish to create. No single plan could ever work for all colleges and universities. For example, if your institution is isolated geographically, much of your plan may center on "in-house" discussions, unless you have financial resources available for guest speakers; likewise, colleges and universities in urban areas may readily call upon a wide range of outsiders to participate in, and guide, campus conversations. Such "outsiders" could include heterosexual religious leaders from local congregations that are gay-affirmative (such lists are usually obtained from local LGBT organizations; many large urban areas have "gay phone books" that include listings of such local congregations). LGBT people with backgrounds or education in religious fields may also be located readily in many urban areas. And although the isolated campus may not be blessed with such local "talent," colleges and universities that are willing to commit some financial resources to a dialogue about gay affirmation can bring speakers from urban areas. Video presentations may also be useful for more isolated campuses.

Numerous small discussions on campus in a variety of settings may also be important in a plan to bring sustained dialogue to a college. If the college is primarily residential, intimate discussions in dormitories can be organized and may bring comfortability to some students who would be nervous raising questions in an open forum. Institutions with large numbers of commuter students may find it more difficult to arrange such discussion opportunities, but "brown-bag" talks at mealtimes can be a viable option in these cases.

All right, people are talking—what's the point? Plan a list of outcomes, then be prepared to amend it as circumstances dictate. Direct goals might include amending a campus non-discrimination policy to include *sexual orientation*, developing an ongoing series of workshops or classes on issues of LGBT people in religious settings, or working to create a resolution or statement of LGBT affirmation for a campus congregation. Less measurable but vitally important goals include bringing consistent and well-informed advocacy of LGBT people into local congregations and local church administrations. For example, if the religion or denomination in question has leadership programs and opportunities for young people, can students who are well versed in the reasons for affirming LGBT people be nominated for such programs? Are individual local clergy be prepared to commit their energies to policies of affirmation? What about seminary students? If one affiliated with the college or university is nearby, is it possible to involve such students in the activities of affirmation and thus prepare them for roles of advocacy for sexual minority people in their future ministries?

Be prepared to notice and celebrate the achievements that come serendipitously, too. By opening up and maintaining a process of dialogue at a religiously affiliated college or university, you will almost certainly accomplish many things targeted to your original plan. A heterosexual student who becomes active in discussions may take his or her insights home and educate a father or mother who serves as a clergy person or religious administrator. An outspoken and service-oriented LGBT student may decide to switch majors from social work to religion, in order to pursue the religious affirmation of LGBT people more directly. Alumni with LGBT family members may recognize and applaud the commitment to dialogue and affirmation and might provide welcome financial support for future programs.

Finally, regardless of the outcomes that an individual set of faculty, staff, and administrators seek for their campus, one valuable accomplishment should be recognized. It is an inevitable part of all religion-centered dialogues that invite college students to engage in the process of making their faiths more inclusive of sexual minority people. Too often, social communities crack into separate parts as a result of civil and human rights issues; "sides" are taken, and opponents fail to understand one another's language and visions. Ironically, and perhaps even tragically, those who have been outcast may begin (in self-defense) to describe their oppressors as subhuman. Separatism, even when necessary for survival, may create new versions of "us versus them" that presage a future filled with discord, not mutual understanding. Colleges and universities with religious affiliations can contribute something special to social discourse regarding sexuality and LGBT people. Dialogue and engagement are preferable to silence and detachment. On such small changes, through the efforts of people committed to such beliefs, historical change is established.

PART XI

Technology and the Lavender Web

CHAPTER 41

Technology: A Potential Ally for Lesbian, Gay, Bisexual, and Transgender Students

Aaron F. Lucier

The Internet has changed the way many of us in the United States live today. Information and opinions on every topic imaginable are only a computer and an Internet connection away. The Internet has also changed the lives of lesbian, gay, bisexual, and transgender (LGBT) students as well. It is now easier for them to find information about their sexuality, to find other LGBT people, to share their experiences with others, and sometimes even to form their first relationships. It is now possible for LGBT student organizations to have a soapbox for their issues and concerns and to promote their existence and events on campus and to the world. In some cases the Internet has provided an excellent way to communicate with other LGBT people without either party coming out via the Internet.

The growth of the Internet continues to increase, as does the number of users. In 1995 the estimated number of consistent Internet users in the United States was about 27 million (Kantor & Neubarth, 1996), up from 1 million in 1994. Since early in the Internet's history, there has been a visible gay presence. The higher number of men on the net (Kantor & Neubarth, 1996) accounts for a higher level of gay male presence. The types of resources vary, but even in its simplest form the amount of information is staggering. The Queer Resources Directory (QRD), one of the largest and oldest LGBT sites on the Internet, has over 10,000 pages of information (Buckmire, 1996) on a very broad range of topics. The QRD is accessible from anywhere in the world. This allows students at a small college in the Midwest to have access to much of the same information on LGBT issues as someone living in an area with a large LGBT population.

This chapter is divided into three sections, each dealing with one aspect of the Internet in relation to LGBT students. The first section defines the Internet in relation to the development of the individual student. The next section shows how the Internet can be used by LGBT student organizations. The last section defines some of the possible pit falls on the Internet and basic legal issues in relation to the LGBT community. Use of the term *organization* or *student organization* refers to a group that has part of its purpose to serve LGBT students in some way on a college or university campus.

DEVELOPMENT OF THE LGBT INDIVIDUAL

The Internet as an Information Source

During the second stage (identity comparison) of sexual identity development (Cass, 1979), gathering information and making contacts with other LGBT people become very important. At this stage, resources for information can be critical to students questioning their sexuality: At this same time these students often will not have easy access to it. In particular, rural or smaller schools often do not have many resources on LGBT issues readily accessible on campus. Students at this stage want to find information, but at the same time typically they will want to keep their questioning secretive. The Internet is very useful for this quest for information. Searching on the Internet and the World Wide Web (WWW) is often anonymous, and worldwide searches for information are performed in the corner of a campus computer lab or in the privacy of one's room.

Most of the Internet's many resources are accessible with some level of anonymity. Even if people on the Internet gain access to one's real name and location, they would not know where one works and what one looks like, unless that information is made available. In addition, there are millions of people using the Internet from all over the world, so in some ways the Internet provides the same level of anonymity as a large city. People might have access to your name and area, but they are not your neighbors and they often do not really take a note of you or what you are doing. E-mail, research, on-line live chats, and even live Internet video conferencing can all be done without anyone knowing your real name or address. This level of anonymity can provide a safe haven to students just exploring their sexual identity. E-mail can be used in a safe way for students to contact other people, and it allows other people to get back in touch with them. On-line chat areas are places where students can have their first contacts with people that self-identify as LGBT in a very safe and nonthreatening way.

Internet Chat Systems

Most chat systems on the Internet allow people to use a "handle" or nickname system that protects privacy as well as allows the user to identify in a unique way. The users of chat systems are often identified by a name of their own selection alongside their Internet address. Also, chat systems come in a number of forms on the Internet, but most have the common element of two types of communication: open typed conversations in "rooms," and private messages between two users. On many chat systems, rooms can be set up by anyone, whereas on others the rooms are preset. Either way, most larger chat systems have LGBT spaces.

New contacts can be anywhere in the world, but sometimes LGBT students find other people who attend the same school or who live in the area. These contacts can be difficult for people who are just coming out: They can meet and connect with people from around the world, but they might still be alone on their own campus. Articles in such periodicals as *The Advocate* have debated if coming out on-line or in chat areas slows or helps one's coming out process (Friess, 1996). Some argue that coming out on-line may make it easier for one to come out to family and friends. It remains to be seen if coming out in the virtual safety of the Internet will provide an outlet that might discourage a student from the potential risks of coming out in the campus environment.

As a person comes out, the role of on-line contacts serves to find connections when the local community is small or if the person finds it difficult to meet people in person. In a local LGBT community, a bar might be the main social gathering point. The on-line world offers an alternative for those who do not want to go to a bar or are unable to enter due to age restrictions. People who have already begun to come out can use the Internet to find people who have common interests or needs such as LGBT people with disabilities, science fiction fans, or nursing students.

Use of the Internet by LGBT Organizations

LGBT student groups often are faced with the same issues that all newly forming groups face: lack of office space, no phone or other contact medium, poor internal communications, and limited resources for outreach and marketing. The Internet can prove a valuable resource to new groups as well as to student groups with a long history.

Electronic Mail (E-mail). E-mail is a very important two-way communication tool. Students wanting to get in contact with the group in an indirect or discrete way can use e-mail to contact a student group that does not have a phone. In addition, e-mail is often a free resource for students and most student groups. Therefore, e-mail can be a good alternative or an addition to the use of a phone line and some type of voice answering system.

An e-mail account can often be set up for a student group simply by contacting the office in charge of campus computer systems. The organization can designate one or two people charged with the responsibility of checking the account on a regular basis. An official organization e-mail account allows for some consistency of the e-mail address, so it does not change as the officer in charge of the account changes. An organization having its own e-mail also allows officers to maintain a level of privacy in terms of their own accounts. An official e-mail account for the group adds to the group's credibility and recognizes that the group is sanctioned. If the student organization is not recognized by the college or university, or there are no student organization e-mail accounts, using either a student, staff, or faculty member's account is always an option. Another option can be using an off-campus Internet Service Provider for e-mail and other Internet services, usually at a monthly charge.

In terms of internal communications for an organization, e-mail can be an easy way to get the word out to group members without organizing phone trees and the expense of mailings. If e-mail is a readily available resource for students, it might be useful to ask members if they want to be kept on an e-mail list. One organization officer can send out e-mail to people on the list to remind them of upcoming events, meetings, or organization emergencies. The effectiveness of such lists depends on how often students read their mail and how many of the organization's members use e-mail. E-mail reaching students' computer accounts in seconds is not going to help get the word out if the e-mail is not read until two weeks after the event. E-mail can get the word out faster than other methods, but timeliness in communications is still important.

World Wide Web. Pages on the WWW can serve as a marketing and communication tool for the group. WWW pages are computer documents, complete with text and sometimes graphics, that can be accessed by other computers around the world via the Internet. A WWW page is accessible 24 hours a day from around the world to anyone with an Internet connection and software program called a WWW browser. Like e-mail, many campuses provide opportunities to create WWW pages to students, staff, faculty, and recognized student organizations. Organizations might have the talent to set up WWW pages on the Internet within their own ranks. In addition, there are numerous software packages on the market to assist in creating and editing WWW pages. Other options for developing WWW pages might be the professional staff in a computer-related department; someone in a computer-related or marketing major looking for an internship; or someone who would be paid to set up the pages for the organization.

Organizations that have received campus recognition often have a WWW link from the official college or university WWW pages. This means that a potential student looking into the institution who is curious about a LGBT group on campus will be able to find out information on the organization. Student organizations are usually listed somewhere on college and university WWW pages for access by people interested in the institution. If the student organization is officially recognized, it is often wise to make sure the representation of the organization is the same that other officially recognized groups receive on the college's or university's WWW pages. A link from the official university WWW pages to an organization's WWW pages adds credibility to the organization and creates traffic for more people to see the information.

Organizations will want to discuss the presentation and content of information on the WWW pages. Questions that should be considered are: Should a phone number be posted? Should full names of officers be posted? Should locations of meetings be shown? Generally, the organization should consider the information, just as it would for a flyer posted throughout campus. Pictures of group activities need to be checked carefully to make sure that they show those who are ready to be out to whoever views the pages.

WWW pages can link to other pages, which allows groups to connect people visiting their site to other sites on the Internet. This makes it easier for a group just beginning WWW pages to offer access to a large amount of information without having to replicate it. As pages are designed and links to other pages added, the links need to be clearly identified, noting that the link leaves the organization's site and goes to pages owned and maintained by others. It is generally a good idea to check with the owner of a page before you link to it. Such sites should be checked to make sure they have useful information that agrees with the perspectives of the organization.

The organization can place information such as its e-mail address and WWW site on print flyers and brochures they have printed up over the academic year. This would allow someone who might have picked up a flyer earlier in the semester to have a way of getting up-to-date information on the group's activities and a way to contact the group if desired. WWW pages should be updated regularly. Outdated WWW pages or pages that have no useful information on them are generally visited only once or twice by a person and then forgotten. Up-to-date and useful information will make a WWW page visited more often, and it will be a more effective marketing tool for the organization. Checking e-mail and responding to inquiries on a regular basis are important for the same reasons. A poorly maintained and outdated WWW pages along with a slow response to e-mail will cause a bad impression for the group. Indeed, someone might question if the group is even still active.

Anonymous Contacts. Just as e-mail allows students to contact an LGBT organization with some level of anonymity, WWW pages allow a student to read information about the group at any time of the day and in almost any location. This can help a student just coming out deal with the anxiety of approaching organization officers in public or walking up to an information table at a campus activities fair. A student can read about the organization on the WWW and ask questions via e-mail. E-mail should then be used to respond back to students who are concerned with their privacy.

Activism. The WWW can provide a platform for students or student organizations to express concerns about campus and social issues, especially when campus issues addressed to the institution have not received attention. Sometimes campus media can be helpful, but the WWW makes it easy for groups or individuals to spread their own message. Developing WWW pages and finding a computer site to host the pages on the Internet are not difficult. There are many sites on the Internet that offer free web pages to nonprofit groups and individuals, and most Internet Service Providers host pages as part of their standard services. The WWW allows anyone with a message to make it available to anyone with a computer and an Internet connection. Student groups having trouble gaining recognition might be able to attract attention to their cause via the WWW. Alumni, parents, and potential students performing a WWW search will often take time to view pages that mention an institution to which they feel connected.

It might not be wise to use officially sanctioned WWW pages or pages linked to the main college or university page to be overly critical of the institution. In a situation where the administration feels the message is inappropriate, the link to the college or university WWW page might be removed. Students may voice their concerns about university policies on their own private pages, perhaps keeping the issue separated from any particular organization. When it is not clear who is delivering a message, it is common practice to list the owner of the WWW page on the bottom of the page.

Pitfalls and Basic Legal Issues

The freedom created from the high level of anonymity on the Internet also creates a space for hate speech as well. Internet chat rooms are a prime area for such attacks against rooms set up specifically for LGBT topics. Operators of such chat areas react in different ways, some using freedom of speech as a defense for nonaction, others attempting to punish offenders by banning them from the chat site. Sometimes chat areas do not have the ability to ban certain users, or offending users have access to more than one account. Response to hate speech on web pages can happen in several ways: e-mail to the system administrator who operates the site; an educational letter to the creator of an offensive page; or a message on the same open forum on which a hate message appears.

The problem of tracking hate speech can also apply to e-mail as well; but usually there is a return address for e-mail responses to the sender. It is also a good idea to send a copy of hate mail and responses to it to the staff that operates the system from which the offender originated. The best reaction to mail using hate speech is to send a copy of the offending e-mail to the system administrator of the host site. To do this, send the letter to the postmaster or administrator at the same site as the offender's address (the site is the part of the e-mail address after the @ sign). Reactions vary from site to site, but system administrators do not like to get complaints. Responses can range from a stern letter to closing the offender's e-mail account. There must be an understanding that e-mail messages can be faked with some work. The system administrators have to take your word that you did receive the e-mail and that it was sent from the person on the address.

Care needs to be taken that people responding to hate speech do not do the same to the offender. If a student responds with offensive language in his or her reply, he or she may face the same responses from the system administrators that the offending person might receive. Someone who offends out of ignorance can often be educated by a calm e-mailed response. An angry response may simply support the offending behavior. An organization does not need to spend a great deal of time responding to hate speech; a polite response with an address for an informative LGBT WWW site is usually all that is needed.

Legal Issues. The legal issues around technology and the Internet are changing almost as fast as the technology itself. During 1996 there were a number of new laws and court cases concerning the freedom of speech on the Internet, and more are expected over the next few years. These could impact information available on the WWW and how one would respond to hate speech. Unfortunately, information on safer sex, sexuality, and LGBT issues have been cited as potentially being forced to be restricted from minors on the WWW.

In particular, the Communications Decency Act (CDA), which was passed in 1996 and later struck down in federal court, is currently awaiting review by the Supreme Court. The CDA and similar laws passed in a number of states use language that could make just posting general information about LGBT issues a criminal act. Concerns have been raised on how laws similar to the CDA might affect information on reproductive rights and safer sex as well. The text of the law makes it a criminal act if someone

uses any interactive computer service to display in a manner available to a person under 18 years of age: any comment, request suggestion, proposal, image, or other communication that, in context, depicts or describes, in terms patently offensive as measured by contemporary community standards, sexual or excretory activities or organs, regardless of whether the user of such service placed the call or initiated the communication. (Communications Decency Act, 1996)

If the CDA does not survive the review by the Supreme Court, another law similar to it may be passed in its place. Whatever the future for the CDA and laws like it, clearly the issue of freedom of speech on the Internet will continue as a major issue for the future. It would be wise to have a good idea of the current environment on the Internet before publicly posting information that might be considered controversial or dealing with frank discussions of sex or sexuality.

CONCLUSION

The Internet can be an ally for LGBT students and student organizations. It can help individual students take the first steps in coming out and provide information that might not otherwise be available on campus. For the LGBT student organization, the Internet can provide a base for outreach as well as internal communication.

The Internet can also be a soapbox for issues that otherwise might not be raised on campus. However, the Internet as an ally is like any other tool—it can have its drawbacks. It is not yet clear if the anonymous environment of the Internet is the best place to come out. The same free speech that student organizations or student activists may enjoy might also harbor hate speech and intolerance. It is important to be educated and informed about the Internet to make the best use of it.

CHAPTER 42

The Lavender Web: LGBT Resources on the Internet

David C. Barnett and Ronni L. Sanlo

There has been an explosion in the amount of information about lesbian, gay, bisexual, and transgender (LGBT) concerns on the Internet. There is a wealth of data about LGBT studies programs, college and university organizations for LGBT students, LGBT Campus Resource Centers that serve campus LGBT populations, and general information. Indeed, there are far too many resources available on the Internet to list here: It would require the entire book. We compiled this list of World Wide Web (WWW) sites, LGBT newsgroups, and ten mailing lists to that one may subscribe via e-mail to begin connection with information and services relating to our campuses. You may also want to refer to the resources compiled by Robert Ridinger (1996) as well. His article is available on the web at http://www.ala.org/acrl/resnov.html for your convenience.

E-MAIL LISTS

Electronic mail lists, also known as listservs—named after one of the software programs that operates these lists—are lists onto that one may subscribe at no cost simply by e-mailing a request. Each list is described with brief instructions on how to subscribe. Most lists send a welcome message to new subscribers that offers detailed information about the list. To request subscription, use the following instructions:

1. The request to subscribe goes in the message field of your e-mail message.
2. Leave the subject line blank.
3. The request itself should be the only text in your message field.

4. Send this request without a signature or other information in your message.

These messages are handled by computers that will be confused by text such as a phone number or even a "thanks for letting me subscribe" note. If you have multiple accounts, be sure to send these subscription requests from the e-mail account to that you want messages sent and from that you will post messages. The computer programs that manage these lists pull your address from headers on your e-mail request and send all messages to that address.

The selection of mailing lists that follows is not complete; there are dozens more for you to discover and explore. We think these ten are good starting places as you begin to discover the vast amount of information, ideas, and support you can receive by e-mail. The Queer Resources Directory (QRD) keeps a list available on the web of LGBT mailing lists. The web address for the QRD is http://qrd.tcp.com/qrd/electronic/e-mail/

Be aware that some information will be "cross-posted" to multiple lists. Thus, you may find the most useful and unique information for your needs from one particular list and decide not to subscribe to others. Be careful when subscribing to many new lists at once. The amount of mail you may receive is hard to predict and can be overwhelming. We suggest the following lists:

GLBT-WORKPLACE is devoted to discussions of topics related to gay/lesbian/bisexual/transgender issues in the workplace. These include being closeted, outed, and coming out; interactions with coworkers and managers; activism to attain equitable treatment; or workplace activities in the community. News stories, action alerts, and questions are often posted here. While not strictly limited to academic settings, many subscribers are based on campuses and can provide support, offer an exchange of ideas and resources, and facilitate activism.
Access: To join the list, send a request to majordomo@queernet.org with a one-line message: subscribe glbt-workplace

NGLTFCAMPUS, sponsored by the National Gay and Lesbian Task Force (NGLTF), coordinates communication among individuals across the country on college and university campuses. This forum offers more detailed information on activities of NGLTF with youth and college populations as well as information on NGLTF conferences.
Access: To join the NGLTFCAMPUS mailing list, send a request to ngltfcampus-request@nenet.org with a one-line message: subscribe ngltfcampus

GLB-NEWS, a repository for news of interest to LGBT folk, offers readers information about news and events, action alerts, conference information, and more. This list is unlike other lists described here in that it is not intended to facilitate conversation between readers. Rather, it is edited—one or more people approve all articles for publication. When an article is submitted, it is reviewed to determine whether or not it will be distributed to the list. The volume of messages tends to be low but of high quality.
Access: To subscribe to this list, send a request to listserv@brownvm.brown.edu with a one-line message: subscribe glb-news YourFirstName YourLastName

GAYNET addresses gay, lesbian, and bisexual concerns with a focus on college campuses, including but not limited to: outreach programs, political issues, HIV/AIDS education, dealing with school administrations, social programs, and just finding out what other support groups are doing. It also has a lot of gossip, idle speculations, and "flaming" (attacks on other subscribers). It was one of the first Internet sites to emerge for LGBT topics and is a highly active site for debates. Items of general LGBT interest are welcomed. The list is not moderated. Warning: The high volume of messages on this list can fill your mailbox very quickly. In our opinion, the amount of useful information versus "noise" on this list sometimes seems minimal. Most of the really useful messages are cross-posted to other lists. This list appears here because it is a "classic." It is also available through UseNet (bit.listserv.gaynet)—please see the next section.
Access: To subscribe to this list, send a request to majordomo@queernet.org with a one-line message: subscribe gaynet

GLB-concerns targets members of the National Association of Student Personnel Administrators (NASPA) who are part of their Network on Gay, Lesbian, Bisexual Concerns. You can look to this list for notices or information such as LGBT job postings, requests for program information, campus activist alerts, conference roommate requests, and LGBT campus news.
Access: To join the list, send your request to networks@listserv.naspa.org with a one-line message: join glb-concerns

ACPA-SCLGBTA is for the Standing Committee for Lesbian, Gay, Bisexual, and Transgender Awareness of the American College Personnel Association (ACPA). While both it and the NASPA list address internal dealings of their committees, a lot of useful information is shared on the list. It is a good resource for submitting requests for information, campus news, job postings, conference announcements, and so on. Subscriptions are moderated; membership with ACPA is encouraged. Many cross-postings occur with this and the NASPA list.
Access: To join the list, send your request to listproc@ucdavis.edu with a one-line message: subscribe acpa-sclgba

ACUI_GLBCC is a list for Association of College Unions International's Gay/Lesbian/ Bisexual Concerns Committee members. It was established as a means to link professionals and students with interests in college unions and LGB concerns. They request no job listings or candidate postings be sent to this list.
Access: To join the list, send your request to majordomo@indiana.edu with a one-line message: subscribe acui_glbcc

DOMESTIC is a list for people interested in learning/sharing information about domestic partner benefits. Many colleges and universities are exploring if and how to offer benefits such as health insurance to same-sex couples. The list covers corporate, nonprofit, and governmental workplaces but often has information specific to higher education.
Access: To join the list, send your request to majordomo-domestic@cs.cmu.edu with a one-line message: subscribe domestic

QUEERLAW is devoted to discussion, analysis, and promulgation of queer legal theory and other aspects of sexual orientation and the law. The list facilitates discussion between diverse groups ranging from law students and professors to individuals interested in how the law affects, and is affected by, sexual minorities. We recommend the digest version. This compiles all messages for the day into one longer e-mail message. The volume on this list can be high, and some postings are a bit specialized for non-attorneys. The digest version makes this list more manageable. The discussion tends to be of high quality. As more cases of significance to LGBT people are argued in courts, this list is useful for following and comprehending ramifications of a specific tactic, argument or decision. If you would like to explore past postings, an archive of queerlaw digests exists at http://abacus.oxy.edu/pub/queerlaw/

Access: To join the list, send a request to majordomo@abacus.oxy.edu with a one-line message: subscribe queerlaw-digest.

QSTUDY-L is a forum for academic discussions pertaining to Queer Theory, an umbrella term encompassing lesbian, gay, bisexual, and transsexual/transgender studies. QSTUDY-L promotes networking and information sharing between teachers, researchers, librarians, and students—anyone involved or interested in queer studies. Posting announcements about relevant conferences or publications, calls for papers, job opportunities, and so on, is encouraged.

Access: To join the list, send a request to listserv@listserv.acsu.buffalo.edu with a one-line message: subscribe qstudy-l FirstName LastName

NEWSGROUPS

Usenet is a global bulletin board where millions of people offer information on every imaginable topic. Although similar to mailing lists, Usenet is much more far-reaching and functional. To read or post to a mailing list, you have to subscribe to the list. In contrast, Usenet is available to almost every user of the Internet and can be a good starting point to explore resources on-line. Access to specific Usenet groups varies by campus computer systems and by Internet Service Providers.

Usenet is divided into regions known as "newsgroups," each covering different subject areas. Instead of receiving messages by e-mail, messages are stored on your host computer and accessed via programs called "newsreaders" (or via the newsreader functions of a web browser). The Usenet Calculator estimates that over 500 megabytes (equivalent to 200,000 pages of text) are posted to Usenet newsgroups every day. LGBT information makes up a good chunk of this. You can use the search engine at http://www.dejanews.com to find newsgroups. Using Netscape Navigator, one can access a relatively complete listing of groups. The newsgroups that follow are a sample of those with LGBT content:

alt.activism	alt.discrimination	alt.homosexual
alt.feminism	alt.lesbian	alt.politics.equality
alt.politics.homosexuality	alt.politics.sex	alt.religion.sexuality
alt.society.civil-liberty	alt.support.aids.partners	bit.listserv.gaynet
misc.health.aids	soc.bi	soc.gender-issues
soc.men	soc.motss	soc.rights.human
soc.support.transgendered	soc.women.lesbian-and-bi	

WWW SITES

An entire book just listing World Wide Web sites that address LGBT issues was written by J. Dawson (1996) entitled *Gay & Lesbian Online*. Instead of duplicating Dawson's work, we selected sites we think provide a good introduction to LGBT topics, offer an index of other resources, or provide specialized information useful to those working in academic settings. We provided the name of the WWW site, a brief description of each site, and the URL (Uniform Resource Locator)—the address you type into your web browser. We recommend using Netscape Navigator or Internet Explorer as your browser when exploring the web. Many LGBT sites use technology that may not always be understood by other browsers. Please note that unlike e-mail addresses, web site addresses are case sensitive; make sure you match upper- and lower-case characters. Do not include extra spaces or punctuation, and type the address exactly. Keep in mind this still may not work. Web addresses are not permanent. You may find one of these addresses points you to a new one, or you might discover that the site has been discontinued.

Gateways

When one considers the diversity and complexity of LGBT communities, a beginning WWW searcher may wish to begin by visiting sites that attempt to provide gateways through a large number of links. Attempts to use standard search engines such as Alta Vista, Excite, or Lycos may be frustrating. Keywords such as *gay, lesbian, queer, bisexual* , or *transgender* will yield hundreds, if not thousands, of links. These gateways have categorized the myriad links available to help you refine your search.

QRD (Queer Resources Directory). This site is one of the most established LGBT directory sites. It has minimal graphics and loads quickly. At last count, it had 18,249 files on every aspect of LGBT culture. Major subcategories include events, families, health, international information, legal, media, organizations, politics, religion, workplace, youth on campus.
Access: http://www.qrd.org/qrd/

Planet Out's NetQueery. NetQueery offers links to more than 3,000 LGBT web sites, mailing lists, and people worldwide. About 1,700 individuals' personal home pages are featured. The directory can be searched by name or geography. You can browse by geography, word or phrase, or general subject headings. The site will soon offer a means to add new links. NetQueery is based on the InfoQueer server at Berkeley (that has not been updated since 1995).
Access: http://www.planetout.com/netqueery/

Yahoo's Gay, Lesbian and Bisexual Resources Pages. This listing of over 2,200 web sites in categories encompasses antiviolence resources, bisexuality, community centers, computers, cultures, education, entertainment, events, government, health, history, legal resources, libraries, marriage and domestic partnership, media, organizations, parenting,

relationships, religion, sexuality, sports, transgendered, and youth. These entries are not annotated but rather just lists of names of sites hyperlinked to the web address. Yahoo tries to be as comprehensive as possible and this set of links is reasonably thorough and current.
Access: http://www.yahoo.com/yahoo/society_and_culture/sex/gay_lesbian_ and_bisexual_resources/index.html

Queer America Resource Database. This database of over 3,700 entries is published by !OutProud!, the National Coalition for Gay, Lesbian & Bisexual Youth. It includes information on community centers, support organizations, PFLAG (Parents and Friends of Lesbians and Gays) chapters, LGBT youth groups, and more. To get a referral list for a specific area, one completes a form requesting organizations within a certain zip code or area code. The site generates a customized list of organizations near you. You cannot limit the search to just college or youth groups. Rather, it generates all groups in its database in or near that zip or area code.
Access: http://youth.org/outproud/

Gay and Lesbian Studies

E-Directory of Lesbigay Scholars compiled by Louie Crew. This site offers a selection of listings from Louie Crew's directory of scholars of lesbian, gay, and bisexual topics. The site is updated monthly and includes archives of his regular e-mailings to Lesbigay Scholars. In addition, he offers links to WWW home pages of lesbigay scholars.
Access: http://newark.rutgers.edu/%7Elcrew/lbg_edir.html

Harvard Gay and Lesbian Review. This is the site for one of the leading new journals in lesbian and gay studies. It provides indexes for earlier volumes, a list of recent articles, and the full text of several significant recent articles.
Access: http://www.hglc.org/hglc/review.htm

Programs in Gender and Lesbian, Gay, & Bisexual Studies at Universities in the USA & Canada. John Younger has prepared a relatively complete list of colleges and universities in the United States offering gay/lesbian studies courses.
Access: http://www.duke.edu/web/jyounger/lgbprogs.html

College and University Sites

LGBT Campus Resource Directors. This site is the endeavor of an informally organized group of professionals staffing offices at colleges and universities that serve LGBT populations. It offers links to pages or sites about most of these offices, information on their meetings, lists of institutions with inclusive non-discrimination statements, and an annotated bibliography of campus climate surveys. We believe it is one of the best LGBT sites for campus concerns.
Access: http://www.uic.edu/orgs/lgbt/

Stanford Queer Resources. This site, sponsored by Stanford's Lesbian, Gay and Bisexual Community Center, is both beautiful and comprehensive. It offers detailed information on the center including a photo tour and campus office resources; listings of queer events this week in or near Stanford (as well as upcoming and recent events); home pages of out Stanford students, staff, faculty; and a detailed list of queer organizations and resources.

This site is very easy to navigate (especially with its use of color) and provides a wealth of information about what is available both on and off campus.
Access: http://www-leland.stanford.edu/group/QR/

The University of Illinois at Chicago (QUIC). This very large site provides links to pages on current happenings on campus, to the Office of Gay, Lesbian and Bisexual Concerns (including the office library and video catalogs), to LGBT student organizations, and to the Chancellor's Committee on the Status of Lesbian, Gay and Bisexual Issues. The latter sponsors a mentor's program and allows people to sign up on-line. In addition to listing home pages of people who are out on campus, the site offers a comprehensive listing of LGBT Internet sites with a particular focus on the Midwest United States. The site is well organized and graphically interesting.
Access: http://www.uic.edu/depts/quic/

The University of Massachusetts' Stonewall Center. This is a good example of a university office page. It gives information on LGBT events at the University of Massachusetts, links to student groups, information on the "Two in Twenty" floor in the residence halls, information on their speakers bureau, and LGBT academic information. In addition, it provides information on campus and community resources and health information. The site is well organized and attractive but would benefit from some additional navigation pointers.
Access: http://www.umass.edu/stonewall/

The University of Michigan Office of Lesbian Gay Bisexual Transgender Affairs. This site posts issues of a twice weekly newsletter, a monthly listing local events and meetings, as well as the history of this office (now 25 years old!) and contact information. In addition, one can find queer-specific campus policies, student groups, and Ann Arbor businesses and an excellent selection of links to other Internet resources for LGBT publications, local and nonlocal (including a University of Michigan LGBT Library Research Guide). They also highlight current projects such as the Family Connections Mentoring Program. This site tends to update its look more often than most college sites and is always visually appealing and informative.
Access: http://www.umich.edu/~inqueery/

The University of Minnesota's GLBT Programs Office. This site sports one of the best logos for LGBT offices and offers a wealth of information as well. One can get information about the office, descriptions of its programs (that include speakers, training, and consultation), and its weekly newsletters. The best feature, however, is the GLBT Information & Referral Database. This is updated regularly and includes action alerts, a bulletin board and a set of truly excellent library research guides. The site also offers information on support resources on the campus and the GLBT Alumni Group.
Access: http://www.umn.edu/glbt/

Organizations

American Civil Liberties Union. This link (part of the ACLU's large web site) focuses on gay and lesbian civil rights. The content varies but has included information as on topics such as: Hawaii gay and lesbian marriage law; ACLU Lesbian & Gay Rights Project Docket; challenges to the "Don't Ask, Don't Tell" military policy; and the Employment Non-Discrimination Act.

Access: http://www.aclu.org/issues/gay/hmgl.html

American Library Association Gay, Lesbian, and Bisexual Task Force. Founded in 1970 as the Task Force on Gay Liberation, this is the oldest professional homosexual caucus in the United States. Complete listings of all recipients of the Gay and Lesbian Book Awards and conference programs are included.
Access: www.outline.com/ala/ala.hp.html

Digital Queers. The Digital Queers offer a professional forum for lesbians and gays employed in the high-tech industries. Some of their activities include lobbying for domestic partner benefits and providing computer training for LGB groups. They try to help these groups acquire donated software and sometimes hardware to get them "wired" into the net.
Access: http://www.dq.org/

Gay and Lesbian Alliance Against Defamation (GLAAD). This is the only national gay and lesbian multimedia watchdog organization dedicated to "promoting fair, accurate and inclusive representation as a means of challenging discrimination based on sexual orientation or identity." They offer information on Lesbian and Gay History Month, Freedom to Marry Project, and the GLAAD archives.
Access: http://www.glaad.org/

GLSEN (Gay, Lesbian, and Straight Educators Network). GLSEN is the largest national organization of parents, educators, students, and other concerned citizens working to end homophobia in K through 12 schools and to ensure all students are valued and respected, regardless of sexual orientation. Their site details their conference calendar, provides a regional chapter locator, and offers a "tool kit" of resources to use in schools. Many of these can be readily adapted for use with undergraduates or incorporated into teacher education programs.
Access: http://www.glstn.org/respect/

Human Rights Campaign (HRC). The United States' largest gay and lesbian national lobbying organization centers on comprehensive lesbian and gay rights and HIV/AIDS issues. The HRC is primarily Washington, DC focused. At its action center, one can send messages to senators and representatives on current, critical issues as well as check out their voting records.
Access: http://www.hrcusa.org/

Lambda Legal Defense and Education Fund (LLDEF). Founded in 1973, this is the largest legal organization in the US. Its staff works to secure civil rights for gays, lesbians, and persons with HIV via education, public policy work, and litigation. With nearly 50 cases across the country, Lambda's work addresses discrimination in employment, housing, and the military; AIDS-related and HIV-related policy and health care reform; parenting and relationship issues; challenging anti-gay ballot initiatives and sodomy laws; and immigration.
Access: http://www.gaysource.com/gs/ht/oct95/lambda.html

National Directory of Gay and Lesbian Community Centers. Arranged by state and budget, this site is helpful if you need to identify a local or regional agency to make re-

ferrals from your campus. It is provided as a service of the Lesbian & Gay Community Center of New York.
Access: http://www.gaycenter.org/natctr/

NASPA Gay, Lesbian, Bisexual, Transgender Issues Network. This site offers information on the Network, its newsletter, leaders, mailing list, domestic partner information, safe space program information, and career services information. It also offers a list of links related to NASPA and to LGBT sites.
Access: http://ecuvax.cis.ecu.edu/~rllucier/naspaglb.html

National Gay and Lesbian Task Force (NGLTF). Self-described as the "frontline activist organization and national resource center for grassroots lesbian, gay, bisexual and transgender organizations," the task force's web site also offers press releases, full text of selected publications, and data on upcoming NGLTF conferences.
Access: http://www.ngltf.org/main.html

PFLAG (Parents and Friends of Lesbians and Gays). This is a national nonprofit grassroots organization that promotes the well-being of lesbian and gay people, their families, and friends through education and advocacy. On-line information on Project Open Mind offers hate crime and teen suicide statistics. The site also offers a directory of chapters across the country. PFLAG is a particularly useful resource for parents of students who are coming out in college or for faculty and staff when one of their students comes out to them.
Access: http://www.pflag.org/

Domestic Partner Benefits

Domestic Partner Information. Scott Safier assembled this collection of links to definitions of a family, domestic partner policies (especially at universities), same-sex marriage sites, adoption, legal information, and other domestic partner sites.
Access: http://www.cs.cmu.edu/afs/cs.cmu.edu/user/scotts/domestic-partners/ mainpage.html

Partners Task Force for Gay & Lesbian Couples. Partners presents information and resources under the premise same-sex couples deserve the same treatment as other couples. Their material is categorized in such categories as marriage, domestic partnership, safeguarding your relationship, surveys, information lists and resources, and outside links.
Access: http://www.buddybuddy.com/toc.html

Safer Sex and HIV Information

The Body: A Multimedia AIDS and HIV Resource. This site provide basic information on AIDS (what is it, who gets it, safer sex, HIV testing), treatment (overview, medications, infections), explores quality-of-life issues (diet, mental health, financial issues, legal issues), and government resources (including information from the Centers for Disease Control and Prevention (CDC).
Access: http://www.thebody.com/

Hot Sex, Safely: A Guide to Safer Sex Techniques. Produced by the Society for Human Sexuality, this site offers a wealth of information for people of all genders and sexual

orientations. The goal of this guide is to give people of all genders, orientations, and preferences the information they need to perform a wide variety of sexual acts safely, pleasurably, and comfortably.
Access: http://weber.u.washington.edu/~sfpse/safesex.html

The Safer Sex Page. A well-known site on the web, the Safe Sex Page is certainly the most comprehensive source of information on safer sex, condoms, and HIV prevention on the Internet. It covers the basics on safer sex, condoms, and assorted health issues. It also offers excellent information for counselors and provides a forum for people to express their reactions to the site, to make suggestions, or to pose requests.
Access: http://www.safersex.org/

ACCESSING UPDATED INFORMATION
http://www.uic.edu/orgs/lgbt/internet_chapter.html

New web sites are added to the Internet every day and some web sites discontinue. To facilitate the need for current information and to ease the ability to access web sites by our readers, David Barnett placed this chapter in the LGBT Campus Resource Center Directors web site and added links directly to each of the sites listed in this chapter. The web address is the bold set of letters above.

By coordinating this chapter with an active web site, we are able to assure the most up-to-date information related to LGBT campus issues, events, and opportunities for information. For your convenience, you may also access the Greenwood Publishing Group web site. It is linked to the bold address above to order copies of this book. We invite you to visit our web site frequently.

Glossary

The terms in this glossary are found throughout the book. Most definitions of these terms are from Blumenfeld (1992), Lorde (1984) and Zuckerman and Simons (1994) and are used consistently by each contributor.

ALLY. Someone who is willing to stand up and support another, reaching across differences to achieve mutual goals.

BISEXUAL. *See* **SEXUAL ORIENTATION**.

CLOSET. A figure of speech used to describe the hiding of a personal secret such as one's sexual orientation—e.g., in the closet, out of the closet, closeted, out.

COMING OUT. *Also* **OUT**. Telling self and others about one's sexual orientation.

DOMESTIC PARTNER. One who lives with her or his beloved and/or is at least emotionally and financially connected in a supportive manner with another.

E-MAIL ADDRESS. Very similar to a postal address. It tells a computer where a person is on the Internet. An e-mail address looks like someone@someplace with no punctuation at the end of it. The first part is the person's account name, the second part is the actual location of the person's computer or computer service on the Internet.

GAY. An umbrella term for homosexual people, although it most specifically refers to men who are attracted to and love other men. It is equally acceptable and more accurate to refer to gay women as lesbians.

HETEROSEXISM. The assumption that everyone is heterosexual, and the belief that those who are heterosexual are inherently better than those of other orientations.

HETEROSEXUAL. *See* **SEXUAL ORIENTATION**.

HOMOPHOBIA. Fear of homosexuality; the fear of feelings of love for members of one's own sex and therefore the hatred of those feelings in others.

HOMOSEXUAL. *See* **SEXUAL ORIENTATION.**

LESBIAN. A woman who is attracted to and loves women.

LESBIGAY. An abbreviated term for lesbian, bisexual, and gay.

LGB, *also* **GLB**. An abbreviated term for lesbian, gay, and bisexual, or gay, lesbian, and bisexual.

LGBT, *also* **GLBT**. An abbreviated term for lesbian, gay, bisexual, and transgender, or gay, lesbian, bisexual, and transgender.

LINK. Information on a World Wide Web document used to connect to another Internet resource such as another WWW page.

OUT. Making your sexual orientation known to self and others.

OUTING. Making someone else's sexual orientation known without his or her permission.

PARTNER. *See* **DOMESTIC PARTNER.**

QUEER. A term used most often by young lesbian, gay, bisexual, and transgender people that is inclusive of all parts of their identity and behavior. Many older LGBT people feel the word has been hatefully used against them for too long and are reluctant to embrace it.

RACISM. The belief in the inherent superiority of one race over all others and thereby the right to dominance.

RAINBOW FLAG. The LGBT Rainbow Freedom Flag was designed in the 1970s to designate the great diversity of the LGBT community. It has been recognized by the International Flagmakers Association as the official flag of the lesbian, gay, bisexual, and transgender civil rights movement.

SEXISM. The belief in the inherent superiority of one sex and thereby the right to dominance.

SEXUAL ORIENTATION. Used to describe everything that goes into why people are attracted to each other.

> **BISEXUAL.** A person who is attracted to and loves members of either sex, though not necessarily simultaneously.

> **HETEROSEXUAL.** A person who are attracted to and loves members of the opposite sex.

HOMOSEXUAL. A person who is attracted to and loves members of the same sex.

STRAIGHT. A heterosexual person.

TRANSGENDER. The umbrella term used to include all people who cross gender lines, including transsexuals, cross-dressers, and drag queens.

TRANSITIONING. The process of changing gender and could include hormone therapy, mental health counseling, cross-living, and sex reassignment surgery.

TRANSSEXUAL. One who wants to have, has had, or should have sex reassigned surgery. This also includes non-surgical transsexuals.

TRANSVESTITE/CROSS DRESSER. One who from time to time wears the clothes of another gender.

TRIANGLE. A symbol of remembrance. Gay men in the Nazi concentration camps were forced to wear the pink triangle as a designation of being homosexual. Lesbians had to wear the black triangle which symbolized political prisons. The triangles are worn today as symbols of freedom, reminding us to never forget.

WORLD WIDE WEB (WWW). A vast collection of interconnected documents spanning the world via the Internet. It allows easy "point and click" access to large amounts of information from any computer with an Internet connection and browser software.

References

Abelove, H., Barale, M. A., & Halperin, D. M. (1993). Introduction. In H. Abelove, M. A. Barale, & D. M. Halperin (Eds.), *The lesbian and gay studies reader* (xvx-vii). New York: Routledge.

Altman, D. (1993). *The homosexualization of America, the Americanization of the homosexual.* New York: St.Martin's Press.

Alyson, S. (1986). What librarians should know about gay and lesbian publishing. In *Alternative library literature 1984/85* (114–115). Jefferson, NC: McFarland.

American College Personnel Association. (1995, September). *Domestic partners project research.* Richmond, VA: ACPA Standing Committee for Lesbian, Gay, Bisexual Awareness.

American Library Association. (1990). American Library Association policies on sexual orientation. In C. Gough and E. Greenblatt (Eds.), *Gay and lesbian library service*, (337–339). Jefferson, N. C.:McFarland.

American Library Association. (1995). *ALA handbook of organization 1995/1996.* Chicago: Author.

American Psychiatric Association. (1980). *Diagnostic and Statistical Manual of Mental Disorders* (3rd ed.). Washington, DC: Author.

Americans with Disabilities Act of 1990, 42 U.S.C.A. S 12101 *et seq.* (Thompson 1995).

Angelo, T. A. (1993). A "teacher's dozen": Fourteen general, research-based principles for improving higher learning in our classrooms. In T. J. Marchese (Ed.), *AAHE Bulletin, 45* (8), 3–7. Washington, DC: American Association for Higher Education.

Anonymous. (1996). *Super LCCS: Gale's Library of Congress classification schedules: Class R, medicine* (p. 126). Detroit: Gale Research.

Arminio, J. (1993). Racial identity as development theory: Considerations for designing leadership programs. *Campus Activities Programming, 25* (8), 40–46.

Association of American Colleges and Universities. (1995). *The drama of diversity and democracy: Higher education and American commitments.* Washington, DC: Author.

Association of Fraternity Advisors. (1990). *Resolution on heterosexism within the Greek community.* (Minutes of the December 1, 1990, AFA Annual Meeting).

Astin, A. (1990). Faculty cultures, faculty values. In W. G. Tierney (Ed.), *Assessing academic climates and cultures*. San Francisco: Jossey-Bass.

Astin, A. (1993). *What matters in college: Four critical years revisited.* San Francisco: Jossey-Bass.

Astin, A. (1995). Promoting the cause of citizenship. *Chronicle of Higher Education, 42* (6), B1.

Astin, H. (1996). Leadership for social change. *About Campus, 1* (3), 4–10.

Atkinsons, D. R., Morten, G., & Sue, D. W. (1993). *Counseling American minorities: A cross-cultural perspective.* Madison, WI: W.C. Brown & Benchmark.

Aubrey, S. (1973, Winter). Queer reading. *Librarians for Social Change, 14,* 17.

Banning, J. H. (1989). Impact of college environments on freshmen students. In M. L. Upcraft, J. N. Gardner, & Associates (Eds.), *The freshman year experience: Helping students survive and succeed in college* (53–62). San Francisco: Jossey-Bass.

Barr, M. (1996). Legal foundations of student affairs practice. In S. R. Komives, D. B. Woodard, & Associates (Eds.), *Student services: A handbook for the profession* (3rd ed., 126–144). San Francisco: Jossey-Bass.

Baxter Magolda, M. B. (Ed.). (1992). *Knowing and reasoning in college: Gender-related patterns in students' intellectual development.* San Francisco: Jossey-Bass.

Beam, J. (1986). Brother to brother: Words from the heart. In J. Beam (Ed.), *In the life,* (230–242). Boston: Alyson.

Beane, J. (1981). I'd rather be dead than gay: Counseling gay men who are coming out. *Personnel and Guidance Journal, 60,* 222–226.

Bell, A., & Weinberg, M. S. (1978). *Homosexualities: A study of diversity among men and women.* New York: Simon and Schuster.

Bennett, R., Whitaker, G., Smith, N., & Sablove, A. (1987). Changing the rules of the game: Reflections toward a feminist analysis of sport. *Women's Studies International Forum, 10* (4), 369–380.

Bensimon, E. M. (1992). Lesbian existence and the challenge to normative constructions of the academy. *Journal of Education, 174,* 3, 98–113.

Bergman, D. (1991). *Gaiety transfigured: Gay self-representation in American literature.* Madison, WI: University of Wisconsin Press.

Berman, S. (1979, Spring). Gay access: New approaches in cataloging. *Gay Insurgent,* 14–15.

Berrill, K. (1989a). *Anti-gay violence, victimization, and defamation in 1988.* Washington, DC: National Gay and Lesbian Task Force.

Berrill, K. (1989b). *Report of the campus project of the National Gay and Lesbian Task Force.* Unpublished report. Washington, DC: National Gay and Lesbian Task Force.

Berrill, K. (1990). Anti-gay violence and victimization in the United States: An overview. *Journal of Interpersonal Violence, 5,* 274–294.

Berrill, K. (1992). Organizing against hate on campus: Strategies for activists. In G. M. Herek & K. T. Berrill (Eds.), *Hate crimes: Confronting violence against lesbians and gay men* (259–269). Newberry Park, CA: Sage Publications.

Bethell, T. (1993). The sad story of Zoe Rastus–Canard. *National Review, 45,* 40.

Birrell, S. (1988). Discourses on the gender/sport relationship: From women in sport to gender relations. In K. B. Pandols (Ed.), *Exercise and sport science reviews* (Vol. 16, 459–502). New York: Macmillan.

Blasingame, B. M. (1992). The roots of biphobia: Racism and internalized heterosexism. In E. R. Weise (Ed.), *Closer to home: Bisexuality and feminism.* Seattle, WA: Seal

Press.

Blasius, M. & Phelan, S. (Eds.). (1997). *We are everywhere: a historical sourcebook in gay and lesbian politics.* New York: Routledge.

Blimling, G. S. & Miltenberger, L. (Eds.). (1990). *The resident assistant: Working with college students in residence halls.* Dubuque, IA: Kendall/Hunt.

Blinde, E., & Taub, D. (1992a). Homophobia and women's sports: The disempowerment of athletes. *Sociological Focus, 25,* (2), 151–154.

Blinde, E., & Taub, D. (1992b). Women athletes falsely accused deviants: Managing the lesbian stigma. *Sociological Quarterly, 33,* 521–533.

Blumenfeld, W. (1992). *Homophobia: How we all pay the price.* Boston: Beacon Press.

Bourassa, D., & Cullen, M. (1988). Programming: Bringing gay, lesbian, and bisexual issues to the forefront. In *Profile.* Columbia, SC: National Association for Campus Activities.

Bourdieu, P. (1991). *Language and symbolic power* (G. Raymond & M. Adamson, Trans.). Cambridge, MA: Harvard University Press.

Bowser, B. P., Fullilove, M. T., & Fullilove, R. E. (1990). African-American youth and AIDS high–risk behavior: The social context and barriers to prevention. *Youth & Society, 22* (1), 54–66.

Boyer, E. L. (1990). *Campus life: In search of community.* Princeton, NJ: Carnegie Foundation for the Advancement of Teaching.

Boykin, K. (1996). *One more river to cross: Black and gay in America.* New York: Anchor Books.

Bradford, J. B., & Ryan, C. (1994). National lesbian health care survey: Implications for U mental health care. *Journal of Consulting and Clinical Psychology, 62* (2), 228–242.

Branson, R. P. (1995). Know your rights. In R. A. Rasi and L. Rodriguez-Nogues (Eds.) *Out in the workplace: The pleasures and perils of coming out on the job.* Los Angeles: Alyson Publications.

Brogan, J. E. (1978). Teaching gay literature in San Francisco. In L. Crew (Ed.), *The gay academic* (152–163). Palm Springs, CA: ETC Publications.

Brookfield, S. D. (1990). *The skillful teacher.* San Francisco, CA: Jossey-Bass.

Brown, D. & Brooks, L. (Eds.). (1996). *Career choice and development* (3rd ed.). San Francisco: Jossey-Bass.

Brown, K. (1991). Homophobia in women's sports. *Deneuve, 1* (2), 4–6, 29.

Brown, K. (1992). Homophobia in women's sports. *Fever, 1,* 26–27, 57.

Brown, L. S. (1989). New voices, new visions: Toward a lesbian/gay paradigm for psychology. *Psychology of Women Quarterly, 13,* 445–458.

Brown, L. S. (1995). Lesbian identities: Concepts and issues. In A. R. D'Augelli & C. J. Patterson (Eds.). *Lesbian, gay, and bisexual identities over the lifespan* (3–23). New York: Oxford University Press.

Browning, C., Reynolds, A. L., & Dworkin, S. H. (1991). Affirmative psychotherapy for lesbian women. *The Counseling Psychologist, 19* (2), 177–196.

Brownworth, V. (1994a, March/April). Benched by bigotry: Lesbians in sport. *Deneuve,* 16.

Brownworth, V. (1994b). The competitive closet. In S. Rogers (Ed.), *Sportsdykes: Stories from on and off the field.* (75–86). New York: St. Martin's Press.

Bryant, E. (1995, June 15). Pride & prejudice. *Library Journal, 120,* 37–39.

Bryson, L. (1987). Sport and the maintenance of masculine hegemony. *Women's International Forum, 10,* 349–360.

Buckmire, R. (1996, February 27). QRD: frequently asked questions (faq) [WWW Document]. URL: http://www.qrd.org/qrd/www/faq.html

Burns, J. M. (1978). *Leadership.* New York: Harper & Row.

Burrell, G., & Hearn, J. (1989). The sexuality of organization. In J. Hearn, D. L. Sheppard, P. Tancred-Sheriff, & G. Burrell (Eds.), *The sexuality of organization.* London: Sage Publications.

Burton-Nelson, M. (1991). *Are we winning yet?: How women are changing sports and sports are changing women.* New York: Random House.

Burton-Nelson, M. (1994). *The stronger women get, the more men love football: Sexism and the American culture of sports.* New York: Harcourt Brace & Company.

Cady, J. (1992). Teaching homosexual literature as a "subversive" act. In H. L. Minton (Ed.). *Gay and lesbian studies* (89–109). New York: Harrington Park Press.

Caetano, R. (1987). Acculturation and drinking patterns among US Hispanics. *British Journal of Addictions, 82,* 789–799.

Cage, M.C. (1994, December 14). A course on homosexuality. *Chronicle of Higher Education, 41* (16), A19–20.

Cahn, S. (1995). *Coming on strong: Gender and sexuality in women's sport.* New York: Free Press.

Cain, R. (1991). Stigma management and gay identity development. *Social work, 36* (1), 67–73.

Carmichael, J. V., & Shontz, M. L. (1996). The last socially acceptable prejudice: Gay and lesbian issues, social responsibilities, and coverage of these topics in M.L.I.S./M.L.S. programs. *Library Quarterly, 66,* 21–58.

Carmody, D. (1992, March 2). New gay press is emerging, claiming place in mainstream. *New York Times,* A1+.

Carmona, J. (1994, March 30). Anti-gay initiatives cause anxiety on state campuses. *Chronicle of Higher Education,* A32.

Cart, J. (1992, April 6). Lesbian issue stirs discussion. *Los Angeles Times,* C1, C12.

Caserio, R. L. (1989). Supreme court discourse v. homosexual fiction. *South Atlantic Quarterly,* 88 (1), 267–299.

Cass, V. C. (1979). Homosexual identity formation: A theoretical model. *Journal of Homosexuality, 4,* 219–235.

Cass, V. C. (1984). Homosexual identity formation: Testing a theoretical model. *Journal of Sex Research, 20,* 143–167

Cassignham, B., & O'Neil, S. (1993). *And then I met this woman: Previously married women's journeys into lesbianism.* Racine, WI: Mother Courage.

Catania, J. A., Dolcini, M. M., Coates, T. J., Kegeles, S. M., Greenblatt, R. M., Puckett, S., Corman, M., & Miller, J. (1989). Predictors of condom use and multiple partnered sex among sexually active adolescent women: Implications for AIDS-related health interventions. *Journal of Sex Research, 26* (4), 514–524.

Cayleff, S. E. (1995). *Babe: The life and legend of Babe Didrikson Zaharias.* Urbana: University of Illinois Press.

Center for Political Leadership & Participation. (1996, May). *Democracy at risk: How schools can lead. A report of the Eisenhower Leadership Group.* Unpublished report. College Park, MD: University of Maryland.

Chan, C. S. (1989). Issues of identity development among Asian-American lesbians and gay men. *Journal of Counseling and Development, 68,* 16–20.

Chapman, B. E., & Brannock, J. C. (1987). Proposed model of lesbian identity development: An empirical examination. *Journal of Homosexuality, 14,* 69–80.

Cheatham, H. E. (1993). Cultural influences on leadership. *Concepts and Connections: A Newsletter of the National Clearinghouse for Leadership Programs, 2,* 2–4.

Chesler, M. A., & Zuniga, X. (1991). Dealing with prejudice and conflict in the classroom: The pink triangle exercise. *Teaching Sociology, 19* (2). 173–181.

Chickering, A. W. (1969). *Education and identity.* San Francisco: Jossey-Bass.

Chickering, A. W., & Reisser, L. (1993). *Education and identity* (2nd ed.). San Francisco: Jossey-Bass.

Chojnacki, J. T., & Gelberg, S. (1994). Toward a conceptualization of career counseling with gay/lesbian/bisexual persons. *Journal of Career Development, 21*(1), 3–10.

Clinton, K. (1989, June 25). Kate Clinton: The gay '90s. *San Francisco Examiner,* 63.

Coleman, E. (1982). Developmental stages in the coming out process. In J. C. Gonsiorek (Ed.), *A guide to psychotherapy with gay and lesbian clients.* New York: Harrington Park Press.

Coleman, E., & Remafedi, G. (1989). Gay, lesbian, and bisexual adolescents: A critical challenge to counselors. *Journal of Counseling and Development, 68,* 36–40.

Comstock, G. D. (1991). *Violence against lesbians and gay men.* New York: Columbia University Press.

Conyne, R. K., & Clack, R. J. (1981). *Environmental assessment and design: A new tool for the applied behavioral scientist.* New York: Praeger (Out of print).

Cox, S. & Gallois, C. (1996, August). Gay and lesbian identity development: A social identity perspective. *Journal of Homosexuality, 30* (4), 1.

Cronin, T. E. (1995). Leadership and democracy. In J. T. Wren (Ed.), *The leader's companion* (303–309). New York: Free Press.

Croteau, J. M., & Hedstron, S. M. (1993). Integrating commonality and difference: The key to career counseling with lesbian women and gay men. *Career Development Quarterly, 41* (3), 201–209.

Croteau, J. M. & Kusek, M. T. (1992). Gay and lesbian speaker panels: Implementation and research. *Journal of Counseling and Development, 70,* 396–401.

Croteau, J. M. & Lark, J. S. (1995). A qualitative investigation of how biased and exemplary student affairs practice concerning lesbian, gay, and bisexual issues. *Journal of College Student Development, 36,* 5, 472–482.

Croteau, J. M. & Thiel, M. J. (1993). Integrating sexual orientation in career counseling: Acting to end a form of the personal–career dichotomy. *Career Development Quarterly, 42* (2), 174–179.

Crumpacker, L., & Vander Haegen, E. M. (1984). *Integrating the curriculum: Teaching about lesbians and homophobia.* (Working Paper No. 138). Wellesley, MA: Wellesley College, Center for Research on Women. (ERIC Document Reproduction Service No. ED 337 379)

Crumpacker, L., & Vander Haegen, E. M. (1987). Pedagogy and prejudice: Strategies for confronting homophobia in the classroom. *Women's Studies Quarterly, 15* (3&4), 65–73.

Cullen, M., & Smart, J. (1991). Issues of gay, lesbian, and bisexual student affairs professionals. In N. J. Evans & V. A. Wall (Eds.), *Beyond tolerance: Gays, lesbians, and bisexuals on campus* (179–194). Alexandria, VA: American College Personnel

Association.

D'Augelli, A. R. (1989a, November). Homophobia in a university community: Views of prospective resident assistants. *Journal of College Student Development, 30,* 546–552.

D'Augelli, A. R. (1989b). Lesbians and gay men on campus: Visibility, empowerment, and educational leadership. *Peabody Journal of Education, 66* (3), 124–142.

D'Augelli, A. R. (1989c). Lesbians' and gay men's experiences of discrimination and harassment in a university community. *Journal of Community Psychology, 17,*317–321.

D'Augelli, A. R. (1991). Gay men in college: Identity processes and adaptations. *Journal of College Student Development, 32,* 140–146.

D'Augelli, A. R. (1992a). Lesbian and gay male undergraduates' experiences of harassment and fear on campus. *Journal of Interpersonal Violence, 7* (3), 383–95.

D'Augelli, A. R. (1992b). Sexual behavior patterns of gay university men: Implications for preventing HIV infection. *Journal of American College Health, 41,* 25–29.

D'Augelli, A. R. (1992c). Teaching lesbian/gay development: From oppression to exceptionality. *Journal of Homosexuality, 22,* 213–227.

D'Augelli, A. R. (1993). Preventing mental health problems among lesbian and gay college students. *Journal of Primary Prevention, 13* (4), 245–261.

D'Augelli, A. R. (1995, August, 28). *Statement to the Judiciary Committee: House of Representatives, Commonwealth of Pennsylvania.* Hearings to amend the Ethnic Intimidation Act to include sexual orientation. Harrisburg, PA.

D'Augelli, A. R., & Rose, M. (1990). Homophobia in a university community: Attitudes and experiences of heterosexual freshman. *Journal of College Student Development, 31,* 484–491.

Dawson, J. (1996). *Gay & Lesbian Online.* Berkeley, CA: Peachpit Press.

Delta Lambda Phi National Social Fraternity (1995). *Delta Lambda Phi mission statement and strategic plan.* (Minutes of the July 23, 1995 annual business meeting).

D'Emilio, J. (1990). The campus environment for gay and lesbian life. *Academe, 76* (1), 16–19.

D'Emilio, J. (1992). *Making trouble: Essays on gay history, politics, and the university.* New York: Routledge.

de Monteflores, C. (1986). Notes on the management of differences. In T. S. Stein & C. J. Cohen (Eds.), *Contemporary perspectives on psychotherapy with lesbians and gay men* (73–101). New York: Plenum.

de Monteflores, C., & Schultz, S. J. (1978). Coming out: Similarities and differences for lesbians and gays. *Journal of Social Issues, 34,* 59–72.

Denson, R. J., & Sellers, J. E. (1981). Promoting leadership potentials of minority students. In D. Roberts' (Ed.) *Student leadership programs in higher education* (126–129). Carbondale: American College Personnel Association.

DeSantis, J. (1994). *Gay and lesbian materials in the Amherst College Library: A bibliography.* Amherst, MA: The Library.

DeSurra, C. J. & Church, K. A. (1994). *Unlocking the classroom closet: Privileging the marginalized voices of gay/lesbian college students.* Paper presented at the annual meeting of the Speech Communication Association, New Orleans, LA (ERIC Document Reproduction Service No. ED 379 697).

DeVito, J. A. (1979, November 10–13). *Educational responsibilities to the gay and lesbian student.* Paper presented at the 65th annual meeting of the Speech Communication Association, San Antonio, TX.

Dewar, A. (1993). Would all the generic women in sport please stand up?: Challenges facing feminist sport sociology. *Quest, 45,* 211–229.

DiErasmo, S. (1991, October 3). The gay nineties. *Rolling Stone,* 83+.

Dillon, C. (1986). Preparing college health professionals to deliver gay-affirmative services. *Journal of American College Health, 35* (1), 36–40.

Duggan, L. (1995). Making it perfectly queer. In L. Duggan & N. D. Hunter (Eds.), *Sex wars: Sexual dissent and political culture* (155–173). New York: Routledge.

Duke University Coordinating Committee for Lesbian, Gay, and Bisexual Studies. (1995, May 10). *Proposal for a certificate-granting program or minor in the study of gender and sexualities.* Unpublished manuscript, Duke University.

Eliason, M. J. (1995). Accounts of sexual identity formation in heterosexual students. *Sex Roles: A Journal of Research, 32* (11–12), 821–34.

Elliott, J. E. (1993). Career development with lesbian and gay clients. *Career Development Quarterly, 41*(3), 210–216.

Erikson, E. H. (1968). *Identity: Youth and crisis.* New York: Norton.

Erting, C. J. (Ed.). (1994). *The deaf way: Perspectives from the international conference on deaf culture.* Gallaudet University Press, Washington, DC.

Escoffier, J. (1992). Generations and paradigms: Mainstreams in lesbian and gay studies. In H. L. Minton (Ed.), *Gay and lesbian studies* (7–27). New York: Harrington Park Press.

Etringer, B. D., Hillerbrand, E., & Hetherington, C. (1990). The influence of sexual orientation on career decision-making: A research note. *Journal of Homosexuality, 19,*(4). 103–111.

Evans, N., & Levine, H. (1990). Perspectives on sexual orientation. In L. V. Moore (Ed.), *Evolving theoretical perspectives on students.* San Francisco: Jossey-Bass.

Evans, N., & Wall, V.A. (Eds.). (1991). *Beyond tolerance: Gays, lesbians and bisexuals on campus.* Alexandria, VA: American College Personnel Association.

Faderman, L. (1984). The "new gay" lesbian. *Journal of Homosexuality, 10,* 85–95.

Faderman, L. (1991) *Odd girls and twilight lovers.* New York: Columbia University Press.

Fahy, U. (1995). *How to make the world a better place for gays and lesbians.* New York: Warner Books.

Fairchild, B., & Hayward, N. (1989). *Now that you know* (2nd ed.). New York: Harcourt Brace.

Fassinger, R. E. (1991). The hidden minority: Issues and challenges in working with lesbian women and gay men. *Counseling Psychologist, 19* (2), 157–176.

Fassinger, R. E. (1994, February). *Sexual orientation and identity development: Human dignity for all?* Invited address at the 20th annual Maryland Student Affairs Conference, University of Maryland, College Park, MD.

Fassinger, R. E. (1995). From invisibility to integration: Lesbian identity in the workplace. *Career Development Quarterly, 44,* 148–67.

Fassinger, R. E. (1996a). Adolescence: Options and optimization. *Counseling Psychologist, 24,* 482–490.

Fassinger, R. E. (1996b). Notes from the margins: Integrating lesbian experience into the vocational psychology of women. *Journal of Vocational Behavior, 48,* 160–175.

Fassinger, R. E., & Miller, B. A. (1997). Validation of an inclusive model of homosexual identity formation in a sample of gay men. *Journal of Homosexuality, 32*(2), 53–78.

Fein, E. B. (1992, July 6). Big publishers profit as gay literature thrives. *New York Times*, D1+.

Feinberg, L. (1996). *Transgender warriors*. Boston: Beacon Press.

Ficarrotto, T. J. (1990) Racism, sexism, and erotophobia: Attitudes of heterosexuals towards homosexuals. *Journal of Homosexuality, 19*, 111–116.

Fichten, C. S., Goodrick, G., Tagalakis, V., Amsel, R., & Libman, E. (1990). Getting along in college: Recommendations for college students with disabilities and their professors. *Rehabilitation Counseling Bulletin, 34* (2) 103–125.

Finkenberg, M. E., & Moode, F. M. (1996). College students' perceptions of the purposes of sports. *Perceptual and Motor Skills, 82* (1), 19–22.

Fischer, D. (1995, November). Young, gay, and ignored? *Orana, 31*, 220–232.

Fisher, J. D. (1988). Possible effects of reference group-based social influence on AIDS-risk behavior and AIDS prevention. *American Psychologist, 43*(11), 914–920.

Flora, J. A., & Thoresen, C. E. (1988, November). Reducing the risk of AIDS in adolescents. *American Psychologist, 43*(11), 965–970.

Flores-Ortiz, Y. G. (1994). The role of cultural and gender values in alcohol use patterns among Chicana/Latina high school and university students: Implications for AIDS prevention. *International Journal of the Addictions, 29* (2), 1149–1171.

Fontaine, S. I., & Hunter, S. (Eds.). (1993). *Writing ourselves into the story: Unheard composition studies*. Carbondale, IL: Southern Illinois University Press.

Forrest, K. (1995). *Curious Wine* (2nd ed.). Tallahassee, FL: Naiad.

Fowler, J. W. (1981). *Stages of faith: The psychology of human development and the quest for meaning*. San Francisco: Harper & Row.

Fox, R. C. (1995). Bisexual identities. In A. R. D'Augelli & C. J. Patterson (Eds.), *Lesbian, gay, and bisexual identities over the lifespan* (48–86). New York: Oxford University Press.

Fox, R. C. (1996). Bisexuality in perspective: A review of theory and research. In B. A. Firestein (Ed.), *Bisexuality: The psychology and politics of an invisible minority* (3–50). Thousand Oaks, CA: Sage.

Freire, P. (1970). *Pedagogy of the oppressed*. New York: Continuum.

Freudenberg, N. (1994). Towards a new agenda for HIV prevention and services for young people: Seven dilemmas that divide AIDS workers serving adolescents. *Networker, 5*, 5–9.

Friess, S. (1996, December). Virtual animosity. *The Advocate*, 40–44.

Friskopp, A., & Silverstein, S. (1995). *Straight jobs, gay lives: Gay and lesbian professionals, the Harvard Business School, and the American workplace*. New York: Scribner.

Fritz, A. (1995). *Gay and lesbian holdings: University of Washington libraries, as of October 1995*. Seattle: The Library.

Gamache, D. E. (1991). *DRGs: Their design and development*. Ann Arbor, MI: Health Administration Press.

Garber, L. (Ed.). (1994). *Tilting the tower: Lesbians teaching queer subjects*. New York: Routledge.

Garnets, L., Hancock, K. A., Cochran, S. D., Goodchilds, J., & Peplau, L. A. (1991). Issues in psychotherapy with lesbians and gay men. *American Psychologist, 46*, 964–972.

Garnets, L., Herek, G., & Levy, B. (1992). Violence and victimization of lesbians and gay men: Mental health consequences. In G. Herek and K. Berrill (Eds.), *Hate crimes: Confronting violence against lesbians and gay men* (207–226). Newbury Park: Sage Publications.

Geasler, J. J., Croteau, J. M., Heineman, C. J., & Edlund, C. J. (1995). A qualitative study of students' expression of change after attending panel presentations by lesbian, gay, and bisexual speakers. *Journal of Counseling and Student Development, 36* (5), 483–492.

Gelberg, S., & Chojnacki, J. T. (1996). *Career and life planning with gay, lesbian, and bisexual persons.* Alexandria, VA: American Counseling Association.

Gever, M. (1990). The names we give ourselves. In R. Ferguson, M. Gever, Trinh T. Minh-ha, & C. West (Eds.), *Out there: Marginalization and contemporary cultures* (191–202). New York: New Museum of Contemporary Art.

Ghaill, M. (1991). Schooling, sexuality, and male power: Towards an emancipatory curriculum. *Gender and Education, 3* (3), 291–309.

Gilligan, C. (1982). *In a different voice: Psychological theory and women's development.* Cambridge, Mass: Harvard University Press.

Gittings, B. (1978). Combating the lies in the libraries. In L. Crew (Ed.), *The gay academic* (107–118). Palm Springs, CA: ETC Publications.

Gittings, B. (1990). *Gays in library land: The Gay and Lesbian Task Force of the American Library Association. The first sixteen years.* Philadelphia: Barbara Gittings.

Gordon, L. R. (1997). Introduction. In L. R. Gordon (Ed.), *Existence in black* (1–9). New York: Routledge

Gough, C. (1990a). Gay and lesbian history and culture: A library pathfinder. In C. Gough & E. Greenblatt (Eds.), *Gay and lesbian library service* (317–322). Jefferson, NC: McFarland.

Gough, C. (1990b). Library exhibits of gay and lesbian materials. In C. Gough & E. Greenblatt (Eds.), *Gay and Lesbian Library Service* (125–140). Jefferson, NC: McFarland.

Gough, C. (1990c). Making the library more user–friendly for gay and lesbian patrons. In C. Gough & E. Greenblatt (Eds.), *Gay and lesbian library service* (109–124). Jefferson, NC: McFarland.

Gough, C., & Greenblatt, E. (1990). A core collection of nonfiction books by, for, and about lesbians and gay men. In C. Gough & E. Greenblatt (Eds.), *Gay and lesbian library service* (203–210). Jefferson, NC: McFarland.

Gough, C., & Greenblatt, E. (1992). Services to gay and lesbian patrons: Examining the myths. *Library Journal,* 59–63.

Gove, P. B., (Ed). (1986). *Webster's third new international dictionary of the English language unabridged.* Springfield, MA: Merriam-Webster.

Greenblatt, E. (1990). Homosexuality: The evolution of a concept in the Library of Congress subject headings. In C. Gough & E. Greenblatt (Eds.), *Gay and lesbian library service* (75–101). Jefferson, NC: McFarland.

Griffin, P. (1991). Identity management strategies among lesbian and gay educators. *International Journal of Qualitative Studies in Education, 4,* 189–202.

Griffin, P. (1992). Changing the game: Homophobia, sexism, and lesbians in sport. *Quest, 44,* 251–265.

Griffin, P. (1993). Homophobia in women's sports. In G. Cohen (Ed). *Women in sport: Issues and controversies.* Newbury Park, CA: Sage Publications.

Griffin, P. (1994). Homophobia in sport: Addressing the needs of lesbian and gay high school athletes. *High School Journal, 77* (1,2), 80–87.

Griffin, P., & Genasci, J. (1990). Addressing homophobia in physical education: Responsibilities for teachers. In Messner, M. & Sabo, D. (Eds.) *Sport, men, and the gender order: Critical feminist perspectives*. Champaign, IL: Human Kinetics.

Groff, D. (1993, May–June). Queer publishing: Between the covers. *Poets & Writers Magazine*, 48–55.

Grossman, A. H. (1993). Ten percent of those we teach and they serve: A case study of incorporating gay and lesbian studies into the curriculum. *Schole: A Journal of Leisure Studies and Recreation Education, 8,* 51–60.

Hall, A. (Ed.). (1987). The gendering of sport, leisure, and physical education. [Special Issue] *Women's Studies International Forum, 10* (4).

Handbook of Accreditation Standards Procedures. (1994). Commission on Accredidation of the Council on Social Work Education: Author.

Hansen, W. B., Hahn, G. L., & Wolkenstein, B. H. (1990). Perceived personal immunity: Beliefs about susceptibility to AIDS. *Journal of Sex Research, 27,* 622–628.

Hardiman, R., & Jackson, B. W. (1992). Racial identity development: Understanding racial dynamics in college classrooms and on campus. *New Directions for Teaching and Learning, 53,* 21–37.

Hargreaves, J. (1994). *Sporting females: Critical issues in the history and sociology of women's sports.* New York: Routledge.

Harper, P. B. (1992). Racism and homophobia as reflections on their perpetrators. In W. J. Blumenfeld (Ed.), *Homophobia: How we all pay the price* (57–66). Boston: Beacon Press.

Harry, J. (1995). Sports ideology, attitudes towards women and anti–homosexual attitudes. *Sex Roles: A Journal of Research, 32* (1–2), 109–116.

Harshbarger, L. (1970). The search for church-university relational models. In C. E. Minneman (Ed.), *Students, Religion, and the Contemporary University* (129–159). Ypsilanti, MI: Eastern Michigan University Press.

Hart, G., Boulton, M., Fitzpatrick, R., McLean, J., & Dawson, J. (1992). "Relapse" to unsafe sexual behavior among gay men: A critique of recent behavioral HIV/AIDS research. *Sociology of Health and Illness, 14* (2), 216–232.

Hayes, J., & Gelso, C. (1993). Male counselors' discomfort with gay and HIV-infected clients. *Journal of Counseling Psychology, 40,* 86–93.

Hayes, R. B., Kegeles, S. M., & Coates, T. J. (1990). High HIV risk-taking among young gay men. *AIDS, 4,* 901–907.

Hayes, S. F. (1993, August). *Empowering multiple cultural identities of bisexual women and men.* Paper presented at the annual meeting of the American Psychological Association (ERIC Document Reproduction Service No. ED 373 287).

Hein, K. (1993). "Getting real" about HIV in adolescents. *American Journal of Public Health, 83* (4), 492–494.

Heller, S. (1990, October 24). Gay- and lesbian-studies movement gains acceptance in many areas of scholarship and teaching. *Chronicle of Higher Education*, A4+.

Helms, J. E. (1990). *Black and white racial identity: Theory, research, and practice.* Westport, CT: Greenwood Press.

Hemphill, E. (Ed.). (1991). *Brother to brother: New writings by black gay men.* Boston: Alyson Publications, Inc.

Herek, G. M. (1986). *Sexual orientation and prejudice at Yale: A report on the experiences of lesbian, gay, and bisexual members of the Yale community.* Unpublished manuscript.

Herek, G. M. (1989). Hate crimes against lesbians and gay men: Issues for research and social policy. *American Psychologist, 44*, 948–955.

Herek, G. M. (1990). The context of anti-gay violence. *Journal of Interpersonal Violence, 5,* 316–333.

Herek, G. M. (1995). Psychological heterosexism in the United States. In A. R. D'Augelli & C. J. Patterson (Eds.), *Lesbian, gay, and bisexual identities over the lifespan: Psychological perspectives* (321–346). New York: Oxford University

Herek, G. M., & Berrill, K. (1990). Documenting the victimization of lesbians and gay men. *Journal of Interpersonal Violence, 5,* 301–315.

Hetherington, C., Hillebrand, E., & Etringer, B. D. (1989). Career counseling with gay men: Issues and recommendations for research. *Journal of Counseling and Development, 67,* 452.

Hetherington, C., & Orzek, A. (1989). Career counseling and life planning with lesbian women. *Journal of Counseling and Development, 68,* 52–57.

Hetrick, E., & Martin, A. D. (1987). Developmental issues and their resolution for gay and lesbian adolescents. *Journal of Homosexuality, 14* (1–2), 25–43.

Higher Education Research Institute. (1996). *A social change model of leadership development* (3rd ed.). Los Angeles: University of California.

Hingson, R. W., Strunin, L., Berlin, B. M., & Heeren, T. (1990). Beliefs about AIDS, use of alcohol and drugs, and unprotected sex among Massachusetts adolescents. *American Journal of Public Health, 80* (3), 295–299.

hooks, b. (1992). *Black looks: Race and representation.* Boston, MA: South End Press.

hooks, b. (1994). *Teaching to transgress: Education as the practice of freedom.* New York: Routledge.

Hopper, C. E., (1980). *Sex education for physically handicapped youth.* Springfield, IL: Thomas Books.

Humphries, A. C. (1986, April 15). Lesbians and gays in librarianship: On a clear day you can see the second class. *Bibliophile, 10,* 3.

Hunter, J., & Schaecher, R. (1994). AIDS prevention for lesbian, gay, and bisexual adolescents. *Families in Society: Journal of Contemporary Human Services, 75*(6), 346–354.

Huntington, P. (1997). Fragmentation, race, and gender: Building solidarity in the postmodern era. In L. R. Gordon (Ed.), *Existence in black* (185–202). New York: Routledge.

Hutchins, L., & Kaahumanu, L. (Eds.). (1991). *Bi any other name: Bisexual people speak out.* Boston: Alyson Publications.

Icard, L. (1986). Black gay men and conflicting social identities: Sexual orientation versus racial identity. In J. Gripton & M. Valentich (Eds.), *Social work practice in sexual problems* [special issue] *Journal of Social Work and Human Sexuality, 4*(1–2), 83–93.

Isay, R. A. (1989). *Being homosexual: Gay men and their development.* New York: Farrar, Straus, Giroux.

Jackson, D., & Sullivan, R. (1994). Developmental implications of homophobia for lesbian and gay adolescents: Issues in policy and practice. In T. DeCrescenzo (Ed.), *Helping gay and lesbian youth: New policies, new programs, new practice* (93–110). New York: Haworth Park Press.

Jacobi, M., & Shepard, C. F. (1990). *Report on the quality of campus life for lesbian, gay, and bisexual students.* Los Angeles: University of California Student Affairs Information and Research Office.

Jemmott, J. B., Jemmott, L. S., & Fong, G. T. (1992). Reductions in HIV risk-associated sexual behaviors among black male adolescents: Effects on an AIDS prevention intervention. *American Journal of Public Health, 82* (3), 372–377.

Jennings, K. (1994). *Becoming visible: A reader in gay and lesbian history for high school and college students.* Boston: Alyson Publications.

Johansson, W. (1990). Students, gay. In W. R. Dynes, W. Johansson, S. Donaldson, & W. A. Percy (Eds.), *Encyclopedia of Homosexuality* (1254–1257). New York: Garland Publishing.

Johnson, J. L. (1990–1991). Preventive interventions for children at risk: Introduction. *International Journal of the Addictions, 25* (4–A), 429–434.

Johnson, P. (1994). *Recruiting, educating, and training librarians for collection development.* Westport, CT: Greenwood Press.

Julien, I., & Mercer, K. (1991). True confessions: A discourse on images in black male sexuality. In E. Hemphill (Ed.), *Brother to brother* (167–173). Boston: Alyson.

Jung, P. B., & Smith, R. F. (1993). *Heterosexism: An ethical challenge.* Albany: State University of New York Press.

Kane, T., (1994). Deaf gay men's culture. In C. J. Erting (Ed.), *The deaf way: Perspectives from the international conference on deaf culture.* Washington, DC: Gallaudet University Press.

Kantor, A., & Neubarth, M. (December, 1996) The state of the net. *ZD Internet World,* 44.

Katz, B., & Katz, L. S. (1992). *Magazines for libraries.* New Providence, NJ: R. R. Bowker.

Keaton, D. (1992, September). Out of the closet. *Women's Sports & Fitness, 14,* 60–63, 86.

Kegeles, S. M., Adler, N. E., & Irwin, C. E. (1988). Sexually active adolescents and condoms: Changes over one year in knowledge, attitudes, and use. *Journal of Public Health, 78,* 460–461.

Kelly, J. A., St. Lawrence, J. S., Diaz, Y. E., Stevenson, L. Y., Hauth, A. C., Brasfield, T. L., Kalichman, S. C., Smith, J. E., & Andrew, M. E. (1991). HIV risk behavior reduction following intervention with key opinion leaders of population: An experimental analysis. *American Journal of Public Health, 81* (2), 168–171.

Killion, A. (1994). Fighting the whispers. In R. Rapoport, (Ed.) *A kind of grace: A treasury of sportswriting by women.* Berkeley, CA: Zenobia Press.

Kimmel, D. C. & Sang, B. E. (1995). Lesbians and gay men in midlife. In A. R. D'Augelli & C. J. Patterson (Eds.), *Lesbian, gay, and bisexual identities over the lifespan: Psychological perspectives.* New York: Oxford University Press.

Kinsey, A. C., Pomeroy, W. B., & Martin, C. E. (1948). *Sexual behavior in the human male.* Philadelphia: W.B. Saunders.

Klein, F. (1993). *The Bisexual option* (2nd. ed.). Binghamton, NY: Haworth Press.

Klein, G. (1992). Helping students find sensitive material: A guide to the literature of homosexuality for librarians and faculty. In Linda Shirato (Ed.). *What is good instruction now? Library instruction for the 90s* (57–62). Ann Arbor, MI: Pierian Press.

Kohlberg, L. (1981). *The philosophy of moral development: Moral stages and the idea of justice.* San Francisco: Harper & Row.

Koopman, C. Rosario, M.; & Rotheram-Borus, M. J. (1994, Jan-Feb.). Alcohol and drug use and sexual behaviors placing runaways at risk for HIV infection. *Addictive Behaviors, 19* (1), 95–103

Koss, M. P. (1988). *I never called it rape: The MS. report on recognizing fighting and surviving date and acquaintance rape.* New York: Harper & Row.

Krane, V. (1996). *Performance related outcomes experienced by lesbian athletes.* Paper presented at the annual meeting of the Association for the Advancement of Applied Sports Psychology.

Ku, L., Sonenstein, F. L., & Pleck, J. H. (1992). Patterns of HIV risk and preventive behaviors among teenage men. *Public Health Reports, 107*(2), 131–138.

Kuh, G., & Whitt, E. (1988). *The invisible tapestry: Culture in American colleges and universities.* ASHE–ERIC Higher Education Report No. 1. Washington, DC: Association for the Study of Higher Education.

Kurdek, L. A. (1988). Correlates of negative attitudes toward homosexuals in heterosexual college students. *Sex Roles, 18,* 727–738.

Lambert, B. (1990, June 22). Relapses into risky sex found in AIDS study. *New York Times,* A18.

LaSalle, L., & DeVries, D. (1993, April). *Research informing practice: Addressing the campus climate foe lesbian, gay, and bisexual people.* Unpublished paper. Presented at the American Educational Research Association annual meeting.

Lederman, D. (June 5, 1991). Penn State's coaches comments about lesbian athletes may be used to test university's new policy on bias. *Chronicle of Higher Education,* A27–A28.

Lenskyj, H. (1986). *Out of bounds: Women, sport, and sexuality.* Toronto: Women's Press.

Lenskyj, H. (1990). Power and play: Gender and sexuality issues in sport and physical activity. *International Review for Sociology of Sport, 25,* 235–245.

Leppo, J., & Lustgraaf, M. (1989a). *Funding of gay/lesbian student organizations.* Washington, DC. ACPA: Standing Committee on Gay, Lesbian and Bisexual Affairs.

Leppo, J., & Lustgraaf, M. (1989b). *Recognition/registration of gay/lesbian student organizations.* Washington, DC: ACPA: Standing Committee on Gay, Lesbian and Bisexual Affairs.

Levine, H., & Evans, N. J. (1991). The development of gay, lesbian and bisexual identities. In N. J. Evans & V. A. Wall (Eds.), *Beyond tolerance: Gays, lesbians, and bisexuals on campus* (1–24). Alexandria, VA: American College Personnel Association.

Lewis, L. A. (1984). The coming-out process for lesbians: Integrating a stable identity. *Social Work, 29* (5), 464–9.

Liddell, D., & Douvanis, C. J. (1994). The social and legal status of gay and lesbian students: An update for colleges and universities. *NASPA Journal, 31,* 121–129.

Lipsyte, R. (1991, May 24). Gay bias moves off the sidelines. *New York Times,* B11

Loiacano, D. K. (1989). Gay identity issues among Black Americans: Racism, homophobia, and the need for validation. *Journal of Counseling and Development, 68,* 21–25.

Lord, R. G., Foti, R. J., & Devader, C. L. (1984). A test of leadership categorization theory: Internal structure, information processing, and leadership perceptions. *organizational Behavior and Human Performance, 34*, 343–378.

Lorde, A. (1984). *Sister outsider*. Freedom, CA: The Crossing Press.

Louganis, G. (1995). *Breaking the surface*. New York: Random House, Inc.

Luckenbill, D. (1993). With equal pride: (Re)presenting UCLA sources for Gay and Lesbian Studies. *UCLA Librarian, 46*, 24–31.

Mabey, C. (1995). The making of a citizen-leader. In J. T. Wren (Ed.), *The leader's companion* (310–317). New York: Free Press.

Malinowsky, H. R. (1988). Reference materials for or about gays and lesbians. *Booklist*, 1647–52.

Malinowsky, H. R. (1990). Gay and lesbian periodicals. In C. Gough & E. Greenblatt (Eds.), *Gay and lesbian library service* (155–165). Jefferson, NC: McFarland.

Mallory, S. L. (1997). The rights of gay student organizations at public state-supported institutions. *NASPA Journal. 34*(2), 82–90.

Malyon, A. K. (1981). The homosexual adolescent: Developmental issues and social bias. *Child Welfare, 60*, 321–330.

Mangan, K. (1995). Conservative students challenge support for campus gay organizations. *Chronicle of Higher Education*, A38.

Mann, W. J. (1995, Spring). The gay and lesbian publishing boom. *Harvard Gay & Lesbian Review, 2*, 24–27.

Marin, B. V., & Marin, G. (1990). Effects of acculturation on knowledge of AIDS and HIV among Hispanics. *Hispanic Journal of Behavioral Sciences, 12* (2), 110–21.

Marsiglio, W. (1993). Attitudes toward homosexual activity and gays as friends: A national survey of heterosexual 15- to 19-year-old males. *Journal of Sex Research, 30*, 12–17.

Marso, J. L. (1991). *Addressing the developmental issues of lesbian and gay college students*. Position paper (ERIC Document Reproduction Service No. ED 328 861).

Massachusetts Governor's Commission on Gay and Lesbian Youth. (1993, July). *Making colleges and universities safe for gay and lesbian students: Report and recommendations of the Governor's Commission on Gay and Lesbian Youth*. Boston: Higher Education Committee of the Governor's Commission on Gay and Lesbian Youth.

Masters, K., & Ogles, B. (1995). An investigation of the different motivation of marathon runners with varying degrees of experience. *Journal of Sports Behavior, 18* (1), 69–79.

Mays, V. M., Cochran, S. D., Bellinger, G., & Smith, R. G. (1992). The language of black gay men's sexual behavior: Implications for AIDS risk reduction. *The Journal of Sex Research, 29* (3), 425–434.

McAllan, L. C. & Ditillo, D. (1994). Addressing the needs of lesbian and gay clients with disabilities. In Sexuality and disability: Dimensions of human intimacy and rehabilitation counseling practice [Special issue]. *Journal of Applied Rehabilitation Counseling, 25* (1), 26–35.

McCarn, S. R. (1991). *Validation of a model of sexual minority (lesbian) identity development*. Unpublished master's thesis, University of Maryland, College Park.

McCarn, S. R., & Fassinger, R. E. (1996). Revisioning sexual minority identity formation: A new model of lesbian identity and its implications for counseling and research. *The Counseling Psychologist, 24* (3), 508-534.

McClintock, M. (1992). Sharing lesbian, gay, and bisexual life experiences face to face. *Journal of Experiential Education, 15* (3), 51–55.

McDonald, A. (1994, June 27). Of genders and genres. *Publishers Weekly, 241*, 25–28.

McDonald, G. J. (1982). Individual differences in the coming out process for gay men: Implications for theoretical models. *Journal of Homosexuality, 8* (1), 47–60.

McDonald, H. B., & Steinhorn, A. I. (1990). *Homosexuality: A practical guide to counseling lesbians, gay men, and their families.* New York: Continuum.

McEwen, M. K. (1996). New perspectives on identity development. In S. R. Komives & D. B. Woodard, Jr. (Eds.), *Student services: A handbook for the profession* (3rd ed.). San Francisco: Jossey-Bass.

McLaughlin, D. & Tierney, W. G. (1993). *Naming silenced lives: Personal narratives and the process of educational change.* New York: Routledge.

McLean, D. A. (1994). A model for HIV risk reduction and prevention among African-American college students. *Journal of American College Health, 42* (5), 220–223.

McMillan, J. H., & Forsyth, D. R. (1991). What theories of motivation say about why learners learn. In R. J. Menges (Series Editor in Chief) & M. D. Svinicki (Eds.), *New directions in teaching and learning: No. 45. College teaching: From theory to practice* (39–52). San Francisco, CA: Jossey-Bass.

McMillen, L. (1992, July 22). From margins to mainstream: Books in Gay and Lesbian Studies. *Chronicle of Higher Education,* A8+.

McNaron, T. (1991). Making life more livable for gays and lesbians on campus: Sightings from the field. *Educational Record, 72* (1), 19–22.

McNeill, J. J. (1994). Tapping deeper roots: Integrating the spiritual dimension into professional practice with lesbian and gay clients. *The Journal of Pastoral Care, 48*(4), 313–324.

McWhirter, D. P., & Mattison, A. M. (1984). The male couple: How relationships develop. Englewood Cliffs, NJ: Prentice-Hall.

Messner, M. (1988). Sports and male domination: The female athlete as contested ideological terrain. *Sociology of Sport Journal, 5*, 197–211.

Messner, M., & Sabo, D. (Eds.). (1990). *Sport, men, and the gender order: Critical feminist perspectives.* Champaign, IL: Human Kinetics

Meyer, I. H. (1995). Minority stress and the mental health of gay men. *Journal of Health and Behavior, 36* (1): 38–56.

Miller, M. A., & Porter, J .D. (1994). Designing effective leadership development programs for selected campus populations. *Journal of College Student Development, 35*, 386–387.

Miller, R. E. (1994). Fault lines in the contact zone. *College English, 56*, 389–408.

Miranda, J., & Storms, M. (1989). Psychological adjustment of lesbians and gay men. *Journal of Counseling and Development, 68*, 41–45.

Mohr, R. D. (1984). Gay 101: On teaching Gay Studies. *Christopher Street, 8* (5), 49–57.

Monette, P. (1992). *Becoming a man: Half a life story.* New York: Harper.

Monteiro, K. P., & Fuqua, V. (1995). African-American gay youth: One form of manhood. In G. Unks (Ed.), *The gay teen* (159–187). New York: Routledge.

Montgomery, M. S. (1996). *Resources in gay/lesbian/bisexual/transgender studies in the Princeton University Library.* Princeton, NJ: Princeton University Press.

Mooney, C. J. (1994, November 16). Religion vs. gay rights. *Chronicle of Higher Education,* A39.

Moore, L. V., & Upcraft, M. L. (1990). Theory in student affairs: Evolving perspectives. In L. V. Moore (Ed.), *Evolving theoretical perspectives on students*. San Francisco: Jossey-Bass.

Moore, W. S. (1991). Issues facing student affairs professionals. In T. K. Miller & R. B. Winston (Eds.), *Administration and Leadership in Student Affairs* (765–787). Muncie, IN: Accelerated Development.

Morales, E. S. (1990). HIV infection and Hispanic gay and bisexual men. *Hispanic Journal of Behavioral Sciences, 12* (2), 212–222.

Morgan, K. S., & Brown, L. S. (1991). Lesbian career development, work behavior, and vocational counseling. *Counseling Psychologist, 19*, 273–291

Mott, R. (1996, May 6). Homophobia now out in the open as an issue for discussion. *NCAA News*, 1, 18.

Munroe, J. W. (1988). Breaking the silence barrier: Libraries and gay and lesbian students. *Collection Building, 9*, 43–46.

Murray, M., & Matheson, H. (1993). Competition: Perceived barriers to success. In G. Cohen (Ed), *Women in sport: Issues and controversies*. Newbury Park, CA: Sage.

Murstein, B. I., & Mercy, T. (1994). Sex, drugs, relationships, contraception, and fears of disease on a college campus over 17 years. *Adolescence, 29* (114), 303–322.

Myers, P. (1993). Lesbian studies and multicultural teaching: A challenge in diversity. In D. Schoem, L. Frankel, X. Zuniga, & E. Lewis (Eds.), *Multicultural teaching in the university* (133–146). Westport, CT: Greenwood Publishing Group.

National Association of Student Personnel Administrators. (1989). *Points of view.* Washington, DC: Author.

National Association of Student Personnel Administrators (1993, March). *A status report on the awareness and presence of sexual orientation issues on campus.* Washington, DC: National Association of Student Personnel Administrators, Network on Gay, Lesbian and Bisexual Concerns.

National Association of Student Personnel Administrators & National University Teleconference Network. (1992). *Understanding and meeting the needs of gay, lesbian, and bisexual students: Participant's guide.* (ERIC Document Reproduction Service No. ED 344 142).

National Collegiate Athletic Association. (1991). *NCAA study on women's intercollegiate athletics: Perceived barriers of women in intercollegiate athletic careers.* Overland Park, KS: Author.

National Gay and Lesbian Task Force (NGLTF) Policy Institute. (1993). *Anti-gay/lesbian violence, victimization and defamation in 1992.* Washington, DC: Author.

Neisen, J. H. (1993). Healing from cultural victimization: Recovery from shame due to heterosexism. *Journal of Gay & Lesbian Psychotherapy, 2* (1), 49–63.

Noel, L. & Levitz, R. (Eds.). (1982). How to succeed with academically underprepared students: A catalog of successful practices. *ACT National Center for the Advancement of Educational Practices, 132*, 28.

Norris, W. P. (1992). Liberal attitudes and homophobic acts: The paradoxes of homosexual experience in a liberal institution. *Journal of Homosexuality, 22*, 81–120.

Obear, K. (1991). Homophobia. In N. J. Evans & V. A. Wall (Eds.), *Beyond tolerance: Gays, lesbians, and bisexuals on campus* (39–66). Alexandria, VA: American College Personnel Association.

Ocamb, K. (1990, Oct. 9). Gay Studies makes the grade: How and where to find the lavender curriculum. *The Advocate, 561*, 40.

Odets, W. (1994). AIDS education and harm reduction for gay men: Psychological approaches for the 21st century. *AIDS & Public Policy Journal, 9* (1), 3–19.

Opffer, E. (1994). Coming out to students: Notes from the college classroom. In R. J. Ringer (Ed.), *Queer words, queer images: Communication and the construction of homosexuality*. New York: New York University Press.

Owens, M. O. (1993, August–September). Pump up the volumes. *Out*, 84–87.

Palmer, P. J. (1993). *To know as we are known: Education as a spiritual journey*. San Francisco: HarperCollins.

Palzkill, B. (1990). Between gym shoes and high heels—the development of a lesbian identity and existence in top class sport. *International Review for the Sociology of Sport, 25*, 221–233.

Paradis, B. A. (1991). Seeking intimacy and integration: Gay men in the era of AIDS. In Men and men's issues in social work theory and practice [Special issue]. *Smith College Studies in Social Work, 61* (3), 260–274.

Parkinson, P. (1987, March). Greater expectations: Services to lesbians and gay men. *New Zealand Libraries, 45*, 92–97.

Parks, S. (1986). *The critical years: The young adult search for a faith to live by*. New York: HarperCollins.

Parsonage, R. R. (Ed.). (1978). *Church related higher education*. Valley Forge, PA: Judson Press.

Pascarella, E. (1980). Student–faculty informal contact and college outcomes. *Review of Educational Research, 50*, 545–595.

Pascarella, E. (1985). College environmental influences on learning and cognitive development: A critical review and synthesis. In J. S. Smart (Ed.), *Higher education: Handbook of theory and research* Vol. 1. New York: Agathon.

Pascarella, E., & Terenzini, P. (1991). *How college affects students*. San Francisco, CA: Jossey-Bass.

Paul, W., Weinrich, J. D., Gonsiorek, J. C., & Hotvedt, M. E. (1982). *Homosexuality: Social, psychological, and biological issues*. Beverly Hills, CA: Sage

Pedersen, R. (1995). Empty rhetoric? *Synthesis: Law and Policy in Higher Education, 6* (4), 478–482.

Pellegrini, A. (1992). S(h)ifting the terms of hetero/sexism: Gender, power, homophobias. In W. J. Blumenfeld (Ed.), *Homophobia: How we all pay the price* (39–56). Boston: Beacon Press.

Peper, K. (1994). Female athlete = lesbian: A myth constructed from gender role expectations and lesbiphobia. In J. Ringer (Ed.), *Queer words, queer images: Communication and construction of homosexuality* (193–208). New York: University Press.

Perry, C. L., & Sieving, R. (1991). *Peer involvement in global AIDS prevention among adolescents*. Unpublished report. Geneva, Switzerland: Global Program on AIDS, World Health Organization.

Peterson, M., & Spencer, M. (1990). Understanding academic culture and climate. In W. Tierney (Ed.), *Assessing academic climates and cultures*. San Francisco, CA: Jossey-Bass.

Pharr, S. (1988). *Homophobia: A weapon of sexism*. Iverness, CA: Chardon Press.

Piernik, T. E. (1992). Lesbian, gay, and bisexual students—radically or invisibly at risk. *Campus Activities Programming, 25* (6), 47–51.

Ponce de Leon, J. (1989, December 8). Gay & lesbian publishing. *Publishers Weekly, 236*, 14–28.

Pope, M. (1995a). Career interventions for gay and lesbian clients: A synopsis of practice, knowledge, and research needs. *The Career Development Quarterly, 45*, 191–203.

Pope, M. (1995b). The "salad bowl" is big enough for us all: An argument for the inclusion of lesbians and gay men in any definition of multiculturalism. *Journal of Counseling and Development, 73* (3), 301–304.

Pope, R. L, & Reynolds, A. L. (1991). The complexities of diversity: Exploring multiple oppressions. *Journal of Counseling and Development, 70*, 174–180.

Powers, B., & Ellis, A. (1995). *A manager's guide to sexual orientation in the workplace*. New York: Routledge.

Preston, J. (1991). *Hometowns: Gay men write about where they belong*. New York: New American Library/Dutton.

Prince, J. (1995). Influences on the career development of gay men. *Career Development Quarterly, 44* (2), 168–77.

Pronger, B. (1990). Gay jocks: A phenomenology of gay men in athletics. In M. Messner & D. Sabo, (Eds.), *Sport, men, and the gender order: Critical feminist perspectives*. Champaign, IL: Human Kinetics Press.

Racevskis, K. (1988). Michel Foucault, Rameau's nephew, and the question of identity. In J. Bernauer & D. Rasmussen, (Eds.), *Final Foucault* (21–33). Cambridge, MA: Harvard University Press.

Rankin, S. R. (1991). *Hidden voices in higher education*. Unpublished paper presented at the American Association for Higher Education Annual Conference. Chicago, IL.

Rankin, S. R. (1994). *The perceptions of heterosexual faculty and administrators toward gay men and lesbians*. Unpublished doctoral dissertation. Pennsylvania State University.

Reynolds, A. J. (1989). Social environmental conceptions of male homosexual behavior: A university climate analysis. *Journal of College Student Development, 30*, 62–69

Reynolds, A. L. & Pope, R. L. (1991, September–October). The complexities of diversity: exploring multiple oppressions (Special Issue: Multiculturalism as a Fourth Force in Counseling). *Journal of Counseling and Development, 70* (1), 174–181.

Rhoads, R. (1994a). *Coming out in college: The struggle for a queer identity*. Westport, CT: Bergin & Garvey.

Rhoads, R. A. (1994b, November). *Representation, voice, and student identity: An ethnographic study of gay college students*. Paper presented at the annual meeting of the Association for the Study of Higher Education (ERIC Document Reproduction Service No. ED 375 709).

Rich, A. (1980). *Invisibility in academe*. New York: W. W. Norton

Rickert, V. I., Jay, M. S., & Gottlieb, A. (1991). Effects of a peer-counseled AIDS education program on knowledge, attitudes, and satisfaction of adolescents. *Adolescent Health, 12*, 38–43.

Rickert, V. I., Jay, M. S., Gottlieb, A., & Bridges, C. (1989). Females' attitudes and behaviors toward condom purchase and use. *Journal of Adolescent Health Care, 10*, 313–316.

Riddell, G. (1988, February). Library services for lesbians and gays. *Library Association Record, 90*, 84+.

Riddle, D., & Morin, S. (1977). Removing the stigma: Data from individuals. *APA Monitor*, 26.

Rider, G. (1994, March–April). Schools of thought. *10 Percent, 2,* 40+.

Ridge, D. T., Plumer, D. C., & Minichiello, V. (1994). Young and gay men and HIV: Running the risk? *AIDS Care, 6* (4), 371–378.

Ridinger, R . B . (1996). Internet resources in gay and lesbian studies. College & Research Libraries News, 57 (10), 658–671.

Roberts, D., & Ullom, C. (1989). Student leadership program model. *NASPA Journal, 27* (1), 67–74.

Rockhurst College (1992). *Rockhurst College Student Handbook 92/92.* (8–9). Kansas City, MO.

Roesler, T., & Deisher, R. W. (1972). Youthful male homosexuality: Homosexual experience and the process of developing homosexual identity in males aged 16 to 22 years. *JAMA: Journal of the American Medical Association, 219* (8), 1018–1023.

Rogers, M., & Williams, W. (1987). AIDS in blacks and Hispanics: Implications for prevention. *Issues in Science and Technology, 3,* 89–94.

Rosario, M., Meyer-Bahlburg, H., Exner, T. M., & Gwadz, M. (1996, Spring). The psychosexual development of urban lesbian, gay, and bisexual youths. *Journal of Sex Research, 33*(2), 113–127.

Rotella, R., & Murray, M. (1991). Homophobia, the world of sport, and sport psychology counseling. *The Sports Psychologist, 5* (4), 355–364.

Rotheram-Borus, M. J. (1989, Spring). Evaluation of suicide risk among youths in community settings: Strategies for studying suicide and suicidal behavior. *Suicide and Life-Threatening Behavior, 19* (1), 108–120.

Rotheram-Borus, M. J., & Fernandez, M. I. (1995). Sexual orientation and developmental challenges experienced by gay and lesbian youths. *Suicide and Life–Threatening Behavior, 25,* 26–34.

Rotheram-Borus, M. J., Rosario, M., Reid, H., & Koopman, C. (1995). Predicting patterns of sexual acts among homosexual and bisexual youths. *American Journal of Psychiatry, 152* (4), 588–595.

Rubin, G. S. (1993). Thinking sex: Notes for a radical theory of the politics of sexuality. In H. Abelove, M. A. Barale, and D. M. Halperin (Eds.), *The lesbian and gay studies reader* (1–44). New York: Routledge.

Rudolph, J. (1988). Counselors' attitudes toward homosexuality: A selective review of the literature. *Journal of Counseling and Development, 65,* 165–168.

Rudolph, J. (1990). Counselors' attitudes toward homosexuality: Some tentative findings. *Psychologists Report, 66,* 1352–1354.

Rullman, L. J. (1991). A legal history: University recognition of homosexual organizations. *ACU–I Bulletin, 59* (2), 4–9.

Rutgers President's Select Committee for Lesbian and Gay Concerns. (1989). *In every classroom: The report of the President's select committee for lesbian and gay concerns.* New Brunswick, NJ: Rutgers.

Ryan, D., & McCarthy, M. (Eds.). (1994). *A student affairs guide to the ADA & disability issues* (National Association of Student Personnel Administrators Monograph No. 17). Washington, DC: NASPA.

Sadownick, D. (1995). *Sex between men.* San Francisco: HarperCollins.

Sailer, D., Korschgen, A., & Lokken, J. (1994). Responding to the career needs of gays, lesbians, and bisexuals. *Journal of Career Planning and Employment, 54* (3), 39–42.

St. Lawrence, J. S., Brasfield, T. L., Jefferson, K. W., & Allyene, E. (1994). Social support as a factor in African-American adolescents' sexual risk behavior. *Journal of Adolescent Research, 9* (3), 292–310.

Sanford, M., & McHugh, C. (1995). Attitudes toward gay and lesbian students: An investigation of resident advisors. *Journal of College and University Student Housing, 25* (2).

Sanford, N. (1966). *Self and society.* New York: Atheron Press.

Saslow, J. M. (1991, September 24). Lavender academia debates its role: Gay and Lesbian Studies programs experience growing pains. *The Advocate, 586,* 66–69.

Schinke, S. P., Botvin, G. J., Orlandi, M. A., & Schilling, R. F. (1990). African-American and Hispanic-American adolescents, HIV infection, and preventive intervention. *AIDS Education and Prevention, 2* (4), 305–312.

Schmitz, T. J. (1988). Career counseling implications with the gay and lesbian population. *Journal of Employment Counseling, 25,* 51–56.

Schoenberg, R. (1989). Lesbian/gay identity development during the college years (Doctoral dissertation University of Pennsylvania, 1989). *Dissertation Abstracts International, 50,* 27 52243.

Scott, D. (1991). Working with gay and lesbian student organizations. In N. J. Evans & V. A. Wall (Eds.) *Beyond tolerance: Gays, lesbians and bisexuals on campus* (117–130). Alexandria, VA: American College Personnel Association.

Sears, J. T. (1995). Black-gay or gay-black? In G. Unks (Ed.), *The gay teen* (135–157). New York: Routledge.

Sedlacek, W. E., & Brooks, G. C. (1976). *Racism in American education: A model for change.* Chicago: Nelson–Hall.

Seidman, S. (1993). Identity and politics in a "postmodern" gay culture: Some historical and conceptual notes. In M. Warner (Ed.), *Fear of a queer planet* (105–142). Minneapolis: University of Minnesota Press.

Shepard, C. F., Yeskel, F., Outcalt, C. (Eds.). (1995). *Lesbian, gay, bisexual and transgender campus organizing: A comprehensive manual.* Washington, DC: National Gay and Lesbian Task Force.

Sherrill, J. M., & Hardesty, C. A. (1994). *The gay, lesbian, and bisexual students' guide to colleges, universities, and graduate schools.* New York: New York University Press.

Signorile, M. (1993). *Queer in America.* New York: Random House.

Siker, J. J. (1994, July). How to decide? Homosexual Christians, the Bible, and Gentile inclusion. *Theology Today,* 219–234.

Singer, B. L., & Deschamps, D. (Eds.). (1994). Gay & lesbian stats: A pocket guide of facts and figures. New York: New Press.

Singer, M., Flores, C., Davison, L., Burke, G., Castillo, Z., Scanlon, K., & Rivera, M. (1990). SIDA: The economic, social, and cultural context of AIDS among Latinos. *Medical Anthropology Quarterly,* 72–113.

Slater, B. R. (1993). Violence against lesbian and gay male college students. In L. C. Whitaker & J. W. Pollard (Eds.), *Campus violence: Kinds, causes, cures.* New York: Haworth Press.

Sloane, S. (1993). Invisible diversity: Gay and lesbian students writing our way into the academy. In S. I. Fontaine & S. Hunter (Eds.), *Writing ourselves into the story: Unheard voices from the composition classroom* (29–39). Carbondale, IL: Southern Illinois University Press.

Smith, J. (1995). Concerns of gay, lesbian, bisexual, and transgender graduate students. *New Directions for Student Services, 72,* 111–119.

Sophie, J. (1986). A critical examination of stage theories of lesbian identity development. *Journal of Homosexuality, 12* (2), 39–51.

Stall, R., Burrett, D., Bye, L., Catania, J. A., Frutchey, C., Henne, J., Lemp, G., & Paul, J. (1992). A comparison of younger and older gay men's HIV risk-taking behaviors: The communication technologies 1989 cross-sectional survey. *Journal of Acquired Immune Deficiency Syndrome, 5,* 682–687.

Stall, R., Ekstrand, M., Pollack, L., McKusick, L., & Coates, T. J. (1990). Relapse from safer sex: The next challenge for AIDS prevention efforts. *Journal of Acquired Immune Deficiency Syndromes, 3,* 1181–1187.

Stall, R., McKusick, L., Wiley, J., & Coates, T. J. (1986). Alcohol and drug use during sexual activity and compliance with safe sex guidelines for AIDS: The AIDS behavioral research project. *Health Education Quarterly, 13* (4), 359–371.

Stanley, W. R. (1984). The rights of gay student organizations. *Journal of College and University Law, 10* (3), 387–418.

Stevenson, M. R. (1988). Promoting tolerance for homosexuality: An evaluation of intervention strategies. *Journal of Sex Research, 25,* 500–511.

Streitmatter, R. (1995, Summer). Creating a venue for the "love that dare not speak its name": origins of the gay and lesbian press (Minorities and the Media). *Journalism & Mass Communication Quarterly 72* (2), 436–448

Sullivan, A. (1995). *Virtually normal.* New York: Albert A. Knopf.

Summer, B. (1992, June 29). A niche market comes of age. *Publishers Weekly, 239,* 36–41.

Summer, B. (1993, June 7). Gay & lesbian publishing: The paradox of success. *Publishers Weekly, 240,* 36–40.

Summers, C. J. (Ed.). (1995). *The gay and lesbian literary heritage: A reader's companion to the writers and their works, from antiquity to the present.* New York: Henry Holt.

Sussman, T., & Duffy, M. (1996). Are we forgetting about gay male adolescents in AIDS–related research and prevention? *Youth and Society, 27* (3), 379–393.

Swartwout, D. L. (1995). *Increasing visibility: Developmental issues and characteristics of lesbian undergraduate students.* Unpublished doctoral dissertation, University of Maryland, College Park.

Sweetland, J. H., & Christensen, P. G. (1995). Gay, lesbian, and bisexual titles: Their treatment in the review media and their selection by libraries. *Collection Building, 14* (2), 32–41.

Taraba, S. (1990). Collecting gay and lesbian materials in an academic library. In C. Gough & E. Greenblatt (Eds.), *Gay and lesbian library service* (25–37). Jefferson, NC: McFarland.

Taylor, M. J. (1993). Queer things from old closets: Libraries—gay and lesbian studies—queer theory. *Rare Books & Manuscripts Librarianship, 8,* 19–34.

Thomas, S., & Quinn, S. C. (1991). Implications for HIV education and AIDS risk education programs in the black community. *American Journal of Public Health, 81* (11), 1498–1504.

Thorngren, C. (1990). *Pressure and stress in women's college sports: Views from coaches.* Paper presented at the annual convention of the American Alliance for Health, Physical Education, Recreation, and Dance, New Orleans.

Thorson, J., Bader, R., Chambers, R., Dolan-Greene, C., Gordan, V., Kahn, P., Ross, M., Summers, C. (1991). *From invisibility to inclusion: Opening the doors for lesbians and gay men at the University of Michigan.* Ann Arbor: University of Michigan.

Tiberius, R. G., & Billson, J. M. (1991). Effective social arrangements for teaching and learning. In R. J. Menges (Series Editor in Chief) & M. D. Svinicki (Eds.), *New directions in teaching and learning. No. 45. College teaching: From theory to practice* (87–110). San Francisco, CA: Jossey-Bass.

Tierney, W. G. (Ed.). (1990). *Assessing Academic Climates and Cultures.* San Francisco, CA: Jossey-Bass.

Tierney, W. G. (1992). Building academic communities of difference: Gays, lesbians, and bisexuals on campus. *Change, 24* (2), 40–46.

Tierney, W. G. (1993). Academic freedom and the parameters of knowledge. *Harvard Educational Review, 63* (2), 143–160.

Tierney, W. G, & Dilley, P. (1996). Constructing knowledge: Educational research and gay and lesbian studies. In W. Pinar (Ed.), *Queer theory in education.* New Jersey: Lawrence Erlbaum.

Troiden, R. (1989). The formation of homosexual identities. *Journal of Homosexuality, 17* (1–2), 43–73.

Troiden, R. (1993). The formation of homosexual identities. In L. D. Garnets & D. C. Kimmel (Eds.), *Psychological perspectives on lesbian and gay male experiences* (191–218). New York: Columbia University Press.

Tsang, D. C. (1990). Censorship of lesbian and gay materials by library workers. In C. Gough & E. Greenblatt (Eds.), *Gay and lesbian library service* (116–170). Jefferson, NC: McFarland.

University of Colorado at Boulder Task Force for Lesbian, Gay, and Bisexual Concerns. (1991). *Diversity or discrimination?: A report on the 1991 UCB sexual orientation survey.* Unpublished report. Boulder: University of Colorado.

University of Minnesota Select Committee on Lesbian, Gay, and Bisexual Concerns. (1993). *Breaking the silence.* Minneapolis/St. Paul, MN: Author.

Upcraft, M. L. (Ed.). (1984). Orienting students to college. San Francisco: Jossey-Bass.

Upcraft, M. L., & Gardner, J. N. (1989). The freshman year experience: Helping students survive and succeed in college. San Francisco, CA: Jossey-Bass

Uribe, V., & Harbeck, K. M. (1992). Addressing the needs of lesbian, gay, and bisexual youth: The origins of PROJECT 10 and school–based interventions. *Journal of Homosexuality, 22,* 9–28.

van Griensven, G., Koblin, B. A., & Osmond, D. (1994). Risk behavior and HIV infection among younger homosexual men. *AIDS, 8* (1), 125–130.

Vazquez, C. (1992). Appearances. In W. J. Blumenfeld (Ed.), *Homophobia: How we all pay the price* (157–166). Boston: Beacon Press.

Vincke, J., Bolton, R., Mak, R., & Blank, S. (1993). Coming out and AIDS-related high-risk sexual behavior. *Archives of Sexual Behavior, 22* (6), 559–586.

Walker, W. (1990). *Gay and Lesbian Studies: A research guide for the UCLA Libraries.* Los Angeles: The Library (ERIC Document Reproduction Service No. ED 328 271).

Wall, V. A., & Washington, J. (1987). *Gay, lesbian, bisexual support environment assessment.* Unpublished manuscript.

Wall, V. A., & Washington, J. (1991). Understanding gay and lesbian students of color. In N. J. Evans & V. A. Wall (Eds.), *Beyond tolerance: Gays, lesbians and bisexuals on campus* (67–78). Alexandria, VA: American College Personnel Association.

Washington, J., & Evans, N. J. (1991). Becoming an ally. In N. J. Evans & V. A. Wall (Eds.), *Beyond tolerance: Gays, lesbians, and bisexuals on campus* (195–204). Alexandria, VA: American College Personnel Association.

Wayle, E. M. (1991, July–August). A gay and lesbian core collection. *Choice, 28,* 1743–1751.

Weinberg, M. S., & Williams, C. J. (1974). *Male homosexuals: Their problems and adaptations.* New York: Oxford University Press.

Weinberg, M. S., Williams, C. J., & Pryor, D. W. (1994). *Dual attraction: Understanding bisexuality.* New York: Oxford University Press.

West, C. (1993). *Race matters.* New York: Vintage Books.

Whitt, E. J. (1993, Summer). The information needs of lesbians. *Library and Information Science Research, 15,* 275–88.

Willimon, W. H. & Naylor, T. H. (1995). *The abandoned generation: Rethinking higher education.* Grand Rapids, MI: Wm. B. Eerdmans.

Winthrop, J. (1985). *A model of Christian charity.* Norton Anthology of American Literature (2nd ed.). New York: W. W. Norton.

Woods, J. D. (1992). *The corporate closet: Managing gay identity on the job.* Unpublished Doctoral Dissertation. University of Pennsylvania.

Woods, J. D. (1993). *The corporate closet.* New York: Free Press.

Woods, S. (1992). Describing the experiences of lesbian physical educators: A phenomenological study. In A. Sparks (Ed.), *Research in physical education and sport.* London: Falmer.

Wyatt, M. (1978, October). Gays and libraries. *New Zealand Libraries, 41,* 88–93.

Yuh, M. (1987, Spring). Res Ed urges gays to be RAs. *The Stanford Daily.* Stanford University.

Zeller, W. J. & Mosier, R. (1993). Culture shock and the first–year experience. *Journal of College and University Student Housing, 23,* 2.

Zipter, Y. (1988). *Diamonds are a dyke's best friend.* Ithaca, New York: Firebrand Press.

Zirkle, K. & Hudson, G. (1975). The effects of residence hall staff members on maturity development of male students. *The Journal of College Student Personnel, 16,* 1.

Zuckerman, A., & Simons, G. F. (1996). Sexual orientation in the workplace: Gay men, lesbians, bisexuals, and heterosexuals working together. Thousand Oaks, CA: Sage Publications.

CAMPUS CLIMATE REPORTS

Ad Hoc Committee on Lesbian, Gay, and Bisexual Concerns. (1990). *Report to the general faculty of Oberlin College.* Unpublished report. Oberlin, OH: Oberlin College.

Anderson, J. (1989). *In every classroom: The report of the President's Select Committee for Lesbian and Gay Concerns.* Unpublished report. New Brunswick: Rutgers.

Bell, A., & Lion, E. (1993). *Final report: Indiana university educational task force on gay, lesbian, and bisexual concerns.* Unpublished report. Bloomington: Indiana University.

Brown University Faculty Committee on the Status of Sexual Minorities. (1989). *Lesbian, gay and bisexual students on the Brown University campus: A study in progress.* Providence, RI: Brown University.

Campbell, J., Winkle, C., & Johnson, J. (1995). *Diversity in the academic community: A campus climate survey of faculty and staff.* Unpublished report. Chicago: University of Illinois.

Cavin, S. (1989). *Rutgers Sexual Orientation Survey: A report of the experiences of lesbian, gay and bisexual members of the Rutgers community.* Unpublished manuscript excerpted in *In every classroom: The report of the President's Select Committee for Lesbian and Gay Concerns.* New Brunswick, NJ: Rutgers State University.

Chancellor's Ad Hoc Committee on Gay, Lesbian, and Bisexual Issues. (1991, 1992). *A preliminary report and second year report by the Chancellor's Ad Hoc Committee on Gay, Lesbian, and Bisexual Concerns.* Unpublished report. Davis: University of California at Davis.

Chancellor's Campus Wide Task Force on Sexual Orientation. (1987). *Final report of Chancellor's Campus Wide Task Force on Sexual Orientation.* Unpublished report. Champaign: University of Illinois.

Committee for Lesbian and Gay Concerns. (1994). *UNL Committee for Lesbian and Gay Concerns, annual report.* Unpublished report. Lincoln: University of Nebraska.

Committee on Gay, Lesbian, and Bisexual Needs and Concerns. (1990). *Report to the president of the committee on gay, lesbian and bisexual needs and concerns.* Unpublished report. Princeton: Princeton University.

Community Affairs Subcommittee. (1989). *Report of the Community Affairs Subcommittee on Sexual Orientation and Minority Harassment.* Unpublished report. Nashville: Vanderbilt University.

Cowmeadow, M. (1993). *Breaking the silence: Final report of the Select Committee on Lesbian, Gay, and Bisexual Concerns.* Unpublished report. Minneapolis: University of Minnesota.

Douglas, S. (1990). *Creating safety, valuing diversity: Lesbians and gay men in the university.* A report to the president of the University of Oregon by the Task Force on Lesbian and Gay Concerns. Unpublished report. Eugene: University of Oregon.

Lesbian-Gay Concerns Committee (1989). *Student council survey on sexuality.* Unpublished manuscript. Charlottesville: University of Virginia.

Machen, J. B., Thorson, J., Brewer, C., Chambers, R., Cockrell, C., Courant, P., Gordan, V., Ketefian, S., Luskin, E., Schuster, T., Thomas, L., Wixson, K. (1994). Report of the bylaw 14.06 task force. The University of Michigan. Unpublished report.

Massachusetts Governor's Commission on Gay and Lesbian Youth. (1993, July). *Making colleges and universities safe for gay and lesbian students: Report and recommendations of the Governor's Commission on Gay and Lesbian Youth.* Boston: Higher Education Committee of the Governor's Commission on Gay and Lesbian Youth.

Nelson, R., & Baker, H. (1990). *The educational climate for gay, lesbian, and bisexual students at the University of Santa Cruz.* Unpublished report. Santa Cruz Office of Analysis and Planning: University of California.

O'Shaughnessey, M. E. (1987). *Chancellor's campus-wide task force on sexual orientation: Final report.* Champaign: University of Illinois.

Rutgers President's Select Committee for Lesbian and Gay Concerns. (1989). *In every classroom: The report of the President's Select Committee for Lesbian and Gay Concerns.* New Brunswick, NJ: Rutgers.

Shapiro, B. (1987). *A report on the experiences of lesbian, gay, and bisexual members of the Emory community.* Unpublished report by the Office of Lesbian/Gay/Bisexual Life. Atlanta, GA: Emory University.

Task Force on Gay, Lesbian, and Bisexual Concerns. (1989). *Task Force on Gay, Lesbian, and Bisexual Concerns: Final report.* Unpublished report. Poughkeepsie, NY: Vassar College.

Task Force on Lesbian, Gay, and Bisexual Issues (1993). *Report of the Task Force on Lesbian, Gay, and Bisexual Issues.* Unpublished report. Medford, MA: Tufts University.

Task Force on Lesbian, Gay, and Bisexual Issues. (1994). *Report of the Task Force on Lesbian, Gay, and Bisexual Issues.* Unpublished report. Milwaukee: University of Wisconsin.

Task Force to Improve the Climate for Gay, Lesbian, and Bisexual Students, Faculty, and Staff. (1994). Unpublished report. River Falls: University of Wisconsin.

Thorpe, K. (1992). *President's Task Force on Gay, Lesbian, and Bisexual Concerns recommendations.* Unpublished report. Denver: Metropolitan State College.

Thorson, J., Bader, R., Chambers, R., Dolan-Greene, C., Gordan, V., Kahn, P., Ross, M., Summers, C. (1991). *From invisibility to inclusion: Opening the doors for lesbians and gay men at the University of Michigan.* Ann Arbor: University of Michigan.

Tierney, W. G., Bensimon, E., Rankin, S.,& Upcraft, M. L. (1990). *Enhancing diversity: Toward a better campus climate.* Unpublished report of the Committee on Lesbian and Gay Concerns. University Park: Pennsylvania State University.

University of Colorado at Boulder Task Force for Lesbian, Gay, and Bisexual Concerns. (1991). *Diversity or discrimination?: A report on the 1991 UCB sexual orientation survey.* Unpublished report. Boulder: University of Colorado.

University of Maryland System Gay and Lesbian Faculty Association, (1996, July) press release. Baltimore: Author.

University of Minnesota Select Committee on Lesbian, Gay, and Bisexual Concerns. (1993). *Breaking the silence.* Minneapolis/St. Paul, MN: Author.

University-Wide Task Force on Lesbian and Gay Issues. (1992). *Moving forward: Lesbians and gay men at Michigan State University.* Unpublished report. East Lansing: Michigan State University.

Welton, D. (1993). *Faculty and staff perceptions of homophobia at California State University, Chico: Implications for policy.* Unpublished report. Chico: California State University.

Yeskel, F. (1985). *The consequences of being gay: A report of the quality of life for lesbian, gay, and bisexual students at the University of Massachusetts.* Unpublished report. Amherst: University of Massachusetts.

SELECTED NATIONAL ORGANIZATIONS

Able-Together, P.O. Box 460053, San Francisco, CA 94146. Phone: (416) 522–9091. A newsletter for gay and bisexual men who experience themselves as different from what is usually perceived as "normal."

The Academy of Leadership, 1126 Taliaferro Hall, University of Maryland, College Park, MD 20742. Phone: (301) 405–5751. Web site: http://asdg–99.umd.edu/CPLP

American Educational Gender Information Service (AEGIS), P.O. Box 33724, Decatur, GA 30033–0724. Phone: (770) 939–2128. E-mail: AEGIS@mindspring.com Web site: http://www.ren.org/rafil/AEGIS.html. Publishes the journal *Chrysalis* and the newsletter *AEGISNews*.

Bisexual Resource Center (BRC) P.O. Box 639, Cambridge, MA. 02140 Phone: (617) 424–9595. E-mail: brc@panix.com

The Center for Creative Leadership, One Leadership Place, P.O. Box 26300, Greensboro, NC 27438–6300. Phone: (910) 288–7210. Web site: http://www.ccl.org/

Coming Together News (CTN), Box 14431, San Francisco, CA 94114. FAX: (415) 626–9033; E-mail: CTNMag@aol.com. A magazine for, by and about Deaf Lesbians, Gays, and Bisexuals.

FTM–International, 5337 College Avenue, #142 Oakland, CA 94618, E-mail: info@ftm–intl.org. Website: http://www.ftm–intl.org. A peer support group for FTM transvestites and transsexuals.

International Conference on Transgender Law and Employment Policy (ICTLEP), P.O. Drawer 35477 Houston, TX 77235–5477, Phone (713) 777–8452 FAX: (713) 777–0909 E-mail: ICTLEP@aol.com. Holds a yearly conference and publishes the conference proceedings.

International Foundation for Gender Education (IFGE), P.O. Box 229, Waltham MA 02154–0229, Phone: (617) 899–2212, E-mail: IFGE@world.std.com. Web site: http://www.transgender.org/tg/ifge. Publishes Transgender Tapestry magazine.

Multiple Sclerosis Society of Canada, 250 Bloor Street East, Suite 1000, Toronto, Ontario, Canada M4W 3P9 Phone: (416) 922–6065. Sexuality and Multiple Sclerosis, Third Edition by Michael Barrett. This book provides information resources, research findings, and positive approaches to sexual adjustment with MS. Included are sections for gay men, lesbians, and married couples.

National AIDS Hotline for Deaf and Hearing–Impaired People. TDD and TTY Phone: (800) /243–7889

National Clearinghouse for Leadership Programs, University of Maryland, College Park, MD 20742. Phone: (301) 405–0799.

National Gay & Lesbian Task Force, 2320 Seventeenth Street N. W., Washington, DC 20009–2702. Phone: (202) 332–6483. Website: http://www.ngltf.org/

New Mobility, P. O. Box 8987, Malibu, CA 90265–8987. Phone: (800) 543–4116, ext. 480. Website: http://www.newmobility.com.

Sexuality Information and Education Council of the United States (SIECUS). 130 West 42nd Street, Suite 350, New York, NY 10036. Phone: (212) 819–9770.

Signs of Sexual Behavior, T.J. Publishers, 817 Silver Spring Avenue, Silver Spring, MD 20910 Phone (301) 585–4440. An Introduction to Same-Sex-Related Vocabulary in American Sign Language by James Woodward. Illustrations, comprehensive explanations and notes introduce sexuality-related ASL vocabulary. A video is also available.

LEGAL CASE REFERENCES

College Republicans of Colorado, Colorado State University, and Metropolitan State College of Denver v. *Kaplan, Dadabhoy, Pacheco, Bliss, Garcia, Hock, Isgar, Mabry, Scully, & Warren*, No. 95 N 2712 (US District Court for the State of Colorado, filed August 29, 1996).

Gay Activists Alliance v. *Board of Regents*, 638 P.2d 1116 (1981).

Gay Alliance of Students v. *Matthews*, 544 F.2d 162 (4th Cir 1976).

Gay and Lesbian Students Association v. *Gohn*, 850 F.2d 361 (8th Cir 1988).
Gay, Lesbian and Bisexual Alliance v. *the Attorney General of the State of Alabama, et al.*, Civil Action No. 93–T–1178–N (1996).

Gay Rights Coalition v. *Georgetown University*, 536 A.2d 1 (D.C. App 1987).

Healy v. *James*, 408 US 169, 92 S.Ct 2338, 33 L.Ed 2d 789 (1972).

Meyer v. *Nebraska*, 262 US 390 (1923).

Student Coalition for Gay Rights v. *Austin Peay University*, 477 F.Supp 1267 (1979).

Victoria L/ Davidson v. *Aetna Life & Casualty Insurance Co.*, 101 Misc. 2D 1, 420 N.Y.S.2d 450 S.Ct. (1979).

Index

About the Editor and Contributors

DAVID C. BARNETT is director of the Office of Gay, Lesbian and Bisexual Concerns at the University of Illinois at Chicago. He pursued his graduate training in counseling psychology at Iowa State University and has worked at university counseling centers in Colorado, Iowa, Texas, Connecticut and Illinois. He is a founding convenor of the National Consortium of LGBT Campus Resource Center Directors.

DOUG BAUDER is the coordinator of Indiana University's Gay, Lesbian and Bisexual Office. An ordained minister, he is a member of the campus anti-harassment team and the city's Human Rights Commission. Doug is the proud father of a daughter and a son, both students at the University of Wisconsin.

DAN BAUER is an assistant professor of English at Keuka College, New York, where he teaches professional writing, literature, composition, journalism, and language history. His doctorate is in Rhetoric and Professional Communication from New Mexico State University in Las Cruces. Though no longer a competitive athlete, he still enjoys a brisk run from time to time.

KERIN McQUAID BORLAND has worked in career services at the University of Michigan for over 12 years. She offers assistance to students through a variety of direct service and administrative roles. She holds a Master's and a Bachelor's degree from Michigan State University.

DOUGLAS N. CASE is the coordinator of Fraternity and Sorority Life at San Diego State University. Doug served as national president of the Association of Fraternity Advisers in 1991. He is an alumnus of Kappa Sigma Fraternity and an honorary member of Delta Lambda Phi Fraternity.

SARALYN CHESNUT is director of the Office of Lesbian/Gay/Bisexual Life and adjunct assistant professor in the Graduate Institute of the Liberal Arts at Emory University. She also teachers Women's Studies and les/bi/gay studies courses. She is currently working on an oral history of Atlanta's lesbian-feminist community during the 1970s.

JOHN R. COWLES is an academic adviser and doctoral student at Southern Illinois University at Carbondale. He was the assistant director of Disability Services at Wayne State University in Detroit, Michigan.

MICHAEL J. DUMAS is an educator and cultural activist. A graduate of Fairhaven College and the University of Maryland, he is currently a doctoral student in the University of Michigan School of Education.

LAURA C. ENGELKEN received her Masters in Higher Education and Student Affairs Administration from the University of Vermont in 1996. She currently serves as the director of A People United, a multicultural consulting firm providing education and training to individuals and organizations in Eastern Oregon.

RUTH E. FASSINGER is an associate professor in the Counseling Psychology Program at the University of Maryland-College Park. She is an affiliate faculty in Women's Studies and is director of the College of Education Honors Program. Her primary scholarly work is in the psychology of women and gender, particularly women's career development, and in the development of sexuality and sexual orientation.

RAELYNN J. HILLHOUSE is a novelist who earned an M.A. in Russian and East European Studies and a Ph.D. in political science from the University of Michigan. She has published numerous academic articles in the United States and Europe, and was a professor at the University of Hawaii.

KATHLEEN (KC) BURNS HOTHEM is assistant director of Residence Life and the sexual assault coordinator at Randolph-Macon College in Ashland, Virginia. She is a member of the National Association of Student Personnel Administrators (NASPA), the American College Personnel Association (ACPA), the Virginia Association of Student Personnel Administrators and the Virginia Association of College and University Housing Officers.

KIMBERLY A. HOWARD received her M.A. from Boston College in 1996. She is a doctoral student in the Counseling Psychology Program at Boston College.

RICHARD P. KEELING is director of University Health Services and Professor of Medicine at the University of Wisconsin-Madison. He is editor of the Journal of American College Health. He has served as president of the Society for the Scientific Study of Sexuality, the American College Health Association, the International Society for AIDS Education, and the Foundation for Health in Higher Education. He has written, presented, and consulted widely about campus services for lesbian, gay, and bisexual students.

CHRISTOPHER D. KEENE is assistant director of the Center for Counseling and Career Planning at Randolph-Macon College in Ashland, Virginia. He is a member of the Virginia Association of Student Personnel Administrators and is a licensed professional counselor in South Carolina. He is also an adjunct instructor at the College of William and Mary.

BETH KRAIG is an associate professor of US history at Pacific Lutheran University, in Tacoma, Washington, and is chair of the honors program. She has served as faculty advisor to a variety of student organizations, including several that support and advocate equality for sexual minority students. She has also given presentations and delivered papers on issues related to sexual minority people in contemporary and historical contexts.

GLORIANNE M. LECK is a professor of education at Youngstown State University. She has served as chair of Ohio's OUTVoice organization as well as the Chair of the Youngstown Human Relations Commission. Dr. Leck's related publications can be found in several anthologies including *Beyond the Lavender Lexicon*, *The Gay Teen*, and *Power and Method*.

LISA J. LEES is a systems analyst in the Department of Computer Science at Michigan State University. She is a professional member of the American Educational Gender Information Service (AEGIS). She is in a legal same-sex marriage, has two young children who she helps educate at home, facilitates a transgender support group, and writes and speaks on many topics.

AARON F. LUCIER is the coordinator for technology at East Carolina University Housing Services. He received his Masters from Florida State University and his B.A. from University of Pittsburgh at Johnstown. He is the web site manager for the National Association of Student Personnnel Administrators (NASPA) GLBT Issues Network.

ALICIA LUCKSTED is a Ph.D. candidate in clinical and community psychology at the University of Maryland, College Park. She is a former coordinator and long-time speakers bureau participant.

ELISA A. LUCOZZI graduated from and is a staff member of Lesley College in Cambridge, Massachusetts. Elisa has spent the past eight years working in student services. She currently serves as co-chair of the Board of Directors for the Gay, Lesbian and Bisexual Speakers' Bureau of Boston.

MICHAEL A. LUTES is a Government Documents and Reference Librarian at the Hesburgh Library, University of Notre Dame. He has contributed to *Gay and Lesbian Literature* and the *Gay and Lesbian Literary Companion.* He is a book reviewer for library professional and gay/lesbian publications and is a collector of early gay literature.

SHERRY L. MALLORY is a doctoral student in higher education at the University of Arizona and is a graduate associate in the Dean of Students Office. She received her Bachelor's Degree in psychology from the University of California at Santa Cruz in 1992.

TIMOTHY M. MATHENEY is pursuing a Ph.D. in educational administration at the University of Michigan. A former high school teacher, he includes education policy, social studies, and lesbian and gay issues in schools among his research interests.

SABA INEZ McCRARY received her M.A. from Boston College in 1996. She is a mental health counselor at a youth services organization in Boston.

MICHAEL S. MONTGOMERY is a humanities reference librarian at the Princeton University Library where he selects books and serials in LGBT studies and philosophy. His bibliography, *American Puritan Studies,* was published by Greenwood in 1984, and his articles on bisexuality have appeared in various periodicals and anthologies.

BONNIE J. MORRIS received her doctorate from Binghamton University and teaches women's studies at George Washington University. When not in the classroom, she works as a host and coordinator at women's music festivals. She tours with her one-woman play, *Revenge of the Women's Studies Professor.* She is the author of two books on Jewish women's history in America.

KAREN NAKAMURA is a doctoral candidate in socio-cultural anthropology at Yale University. Her chapter is based on a larger, ongoing research project involving transsexual and transgender life narratives.

PETER A. NEWMAN is a doctoral candidate in the joint program in social work and social psychology at the University of Michigan. His research focus is on HIV prevention. He was a clinical social worker at the University of California San Francisco AIDS Program at San Francisco General Hospital. He is a founding member and vice president of the National Social Work AIDS Network and is an associate of the National Center for Research and Training in Social Work.

KIRSTEN M. O'BRIEN was the administrative director for the Lesbian, Gay, Bisexual, and Transgender Community Resource Center at California State University, Northridge. She is pursuing a degree in anthropology.

CHARLES OUTCALT was the director of University of California, Los Angeles LGBT Resources Office until 1997 when he became assistant dean of students and entered UCLA's Ph.D. program in education. His previous graduate work was at Harvard where he co-chaired the LGBT Leadership Council, and at the University of Chicago where he studied lesbian identity. He is a founding convenor of the National Consortium of LGBT Campus Resource Center Directors.

J. DAVIDSON "DUSTY" PORTER is a leadership educator interested in the intersections of identity development and leadership attitudes and behaviors. He is completing his Ph.D. in college student personnel administration at the University of Maryland. He thanks both Dr. Marylu McEwen for her help with this chapter and his partner, Tim Ring, for his unending support.

SUSAN R. RANKIN is a senior diversity planning analyst in the office of the Vice Provost for Educational Equity at Pennsylvania State University where she was the head softball coach for 16 years. She is a founding convenor of the National Consortium of LGBT Campus Resource Center Directors.

KRISTEN A. RENN is assistant dean of student life and liaison for LGBT Concerns at Brown University. She is a Ph.D. candidate in higher education at Boston College. Her research interests include LGBT issues, bi/multiracial college students, and the development of identity in postmodern society. She is a founding convenor of the National Consortium of LGBT Campus Resource Center Directors.

MATTHEW W. ROBISON is a law student at Stanford Law School. While an undergraduate at the University of Michigan he was a resident assistant and a resident director. He has presented workshops at numerous conferences addressing homophobia in residence halls.

KATYA SALKEVER is the director for programs and services for Lesbian and Bisexual students and the assistant field hockey and assistant lacrosse coach at Wellesley College.

RONNI L. SANLO is the director of the University of California, Los Angeles Lesbian Gay Bisexual Transgender Campus Resource Center and former director of the University of Michigan Office of Lesbian Gay Bisexual Transgender Affairs. She earned her M.Ed. in Counseling and her Ed.D. in Educational Leadership, both with an emphasis on sexual orientation issues, from the University of North Florida, in Jacksonville, FL. She is the national chair of the LGBT Issues Network for the National Association of Student Personnel Administrators (NASPA) and is a founding convenor of the National Consortium of LGBT Campus Resource Center Directors.

FERDINAND J. SCHLAPPER is an associate director of University Health Services at the University of Wisconsin-Madison. He led the development of the first university-sponsored student health insurance plan to propose offering domestic partner benefits in the State of Wisconsin.

PATRICIA SULLIVAN is assistant director of the Student Center for Community Involvement at Rice University in Houston, TX. She received a Bachelor of Science degree in Political Science from Santa Clara University in California and a Master of Science degree in Student Affairs in Higher Education from Colorado State University.

SIMONE HIMBEAULT TAYLOR has worked in career services for over 17 years, the past six as director of Career Planning and Placement at the University of Michigan-Ann Arbor. Educated at the University of Michigan, she holds a Ph.D. from the Center for the Study of Higher and Post-secondary Education where she currently serves as adjunct assistant professor.

JEAN H. THORESEN holds an M.A. in sociology, an M.S. in human relations, and a law degree. She has taught for over 30 years and publishes poetry and short stories on lesbian themes.

JAYNE THORSON is an assistant dean at the University of Michigan Medical School. She was the primary author of the landmark study, *From Invisibility to Inclusion: Opening the Doors for Lesbians and Gay Men at the University of Michigan*. She is a past president of the UM Gay and Lesbian Alumni Society. In recognition of her work on sexual orientation issues, she was the inaugural recipient of the Leadership for a New Century award from the National Association of Women in Education.

RIC UNDERHILE is a doctoral student in Counselor Education at Southern Illinois University at Carbondale.

SHARON D. VAUGHTERS is an associate director of Career Planning and Placement at the University of Michigan. She received her M.A. degree from Ohio State University in higher education. Her professional interests lie in student affairs administration, developing partnerships with academic departments, career counseling and in integrating diversity/multiculturalism into student affairs practice.

ALLEN WARD is assistant dean of student affairs at Florida Atlantic University in Boca Raton. He received his B.S. in business management and his

M.A. in educational psychology from Tennessee Technological University. He is currently a doctoral student in higher education administration at the University of Miami.

BRIAN L. WATKINS is the campus life coordinator at Beaver College. He holds a B.A. in psychology from Hope College and an M.Ed. in student affairs administration from the University of Vermont. His chapter contains excerpts from his Masters thesis, *A Dark Spot on the Ivory Tower: Heterosexism in Higher Education.*

ROGER L. WORTHINGTON graduated with his Ph.D. from the University of California, Santa Barbara in 1995. He is currently an assistant professor in the Department of Counseling, Developmental Psychology and Research Methods at Boston College.

JOYCE WRIGHT was the interim director of the Sexual Assault Prevention and Awareness Center (SAPAC) at the University of Michigan. She has been active in the domestic violence/sexual assault movement for nearly 20 years. She conducts presentations for medical staff, law enforcement personnel, clergy, the judicial system, and civic organizations.